AF743501

HOSPITALITY REVENUE MANAGEMENT

Concepts and Practices

HOSPITALITY REVENUE MANAGEMENT

Concepts and Practices

Edited by

Peter Szende

APPLE ACADEMIC PRESS

First edition published 2021

Apple Academic Press Inc.
1265 Goldenrod Circle, NE,
Palm Bay, FL 32905 USA
4164 Lakeshore Road, Burlington,
ON, L7L 1A4 Canada

CRC Press
6000 Broken Sound Parkway NW,
Suite 300, Boca Raton, FL 33487-2742 USA
2 Park Square, Milton Park,
Abingdon, Oxon, OX14 4RN UK

© 2021 Apple Academic Press, Inc.

Apple Academic Press exclusively co-publishes with CRC Press, an imprint of Taylor & Francis Group, LLC

Reasonable efforts have been made to publish reliable data and information, but the authors, editors, and publisher cannot assume responsibility for the validity of all materials or the consequences of their use. The authors, editors, and publishers have attempted to trace the copyright holders of all material reproduced in this publication and apologize to copyright holders if permission to publish in this form has not been obtained. If any copyright material has not been acknowledged, please write and let us know so we may rectify in any future reprint.

Except as permitted under U.S. Copyright Law, no part of this book may be reprinted, reproduced, transmitted, or utilized in any form by any electronic, mechanical, or other means, now known or hereafter invented, including photocopying, microfilming, and recording, or in any information storage or retrieval system, without written permission from the publishers.

For permission to photocopy or use material electronically from this work, access www.copyright.com or contact the Copyright Clearance Center, Inc. (CCC), 222 Rosewood Drive, Danvers, MA 01923, 978-750-8400. For works that are not available on CCC please contact mpkbookspermissions@tandf.co.uk

Trademark notice: Product or corporate names may be trademarks or registered trademarks and are used only for identification and explanation without intent to infringe.

Library and Archives Canada Cataloguing in Publication

Title: Hospitality revenue management : concepts and practices / edited by Peter Szende.

Names: Szende, Peter, editor.

Description: Includes bibliographical references and index.

Identifiers: Canadiana (print) 20200153501 | Canadiana (ebook) 20200153552 | ISBN 9781771888882 (hardcover) | ISBN 9781003019923 (ebook)

Subjects: LCSH: Revenue management. | LCSH: Hotel management. | LCSH: Hospitality industry—Management.

Classification: LCC HD60.7 .H67 2020 | DDC 647.940681—dc23 | 658.15/54—dc23

Library of Congress Cataloging-in-Publication Data

Names: Szende, Peter, editor.

Title: Hospitality revenue management : concepts and practices / edited by Pete Szende.

Description: Palm Bay, Florida : Apple Academic Press, [2020] | Includes bibliographical references and index. | Summary: "This new textbook, Hospitality Revenue Management: Concepts and Practices, provides a comprehensive, in-depth introduction to the basic concepts and best practices of hospitality revenue management. With a real-world, hands-on approach, the book places students in the role of a revenue manager striving to succeed in an ever-changing hospitality business environment. The book takes a unique multi-author, collaborative approach, with chapters from outstanding industry leaders who share their experience and provide the information necessary to arm students with the most up-to-date tools and methods they to be effective in the hospitality revenue management field. The chapters cover the important topics in hospitality revenue management, including hotel pricing, hotel segmentation, distribution channels, competitive analysis, hotel forecasting, performance analysis, market data, supply and demand management, and more. This comprehensive and contemporary textbook effectively meets the curricular requirements of undergraduate and graduate courses. The book can also be used as a reference for practitioners and as a text for executive education programs. Each chapter includes features to keep students interested and engaged. These include case studies, internet activities, team projects, spreadsheet assignments, brief histories, and more"-- Provided by publisher.

Identifiers: LCCN 2019057617 (print) | LCCN 2019057618 (ebook) | ISBN 9781771888882 (hardcover) | ISBN 9781003019923 (ebook)

Subjects: LCSH: Hospitality industry--Finance. | Hospitality industry--Management. | Revenue management.

Classification: LCC TX911.3.F5 H66 2020 (print) | LCC TX911.3.F5 (ebook) | DDC 910.68/1--dc23

LC record available at https://lccn.loc.gov/2019057617

LC ebook record available at https://lccn.loc.gov/2019057618

ISBN: 978-1-77188-888-2 (hbk)
ISBN: 978-1-00301-992-3 (ebk)

ABOUT THE EDITOR

Dr. Peter Szende has over 25 years of management experience in the hospitality industry in both Europe and North America. He joined the Boston University School of Hospitality Administration as Assistant Professor in 2003. He was promoted to Associate Professor of the Practice in 2010. He was promoted again in 2017 to Professor of the Practice. Between 2016 and 2019, he served as Associate Dean of Academic Affairs.

Dr. Szende received a Fulbright U.S. Scholar Grant in 2014. He was presented with the Chef Herman Breithaupt Award from International CHRIE in 2017.

Currently, Dr. Szende is Programme Lead in Hospitality Management at Oxford Brookes Business School, Oxford Brookes University, UK.

CONTENTS

MEET THE CONTRIBUTING AUTHORS

Marianna B. Accomando

As both Vice President of Sales & Marketing and Assistant General Manager for the Four Diamond Seaport Hotel and World Trade Center in Boston, Marianna holds multiple responsibilities. She is responsible for leading all sales and marketing efforts to all key customer-facing business segments. Her role includes leading several teams, such as group, exhibition, transient, revenue management, reservations, catering, and weddings for the property. In addition, she manages the guest service experience for one of Boston's leading and consistently in the top 5 Trip Advisor Boston rated hotels.

A graduate of the University of New Hampshire, Ms. Accomando brings over 35 years of hospitality experience to this position.

Calvin Anderson

Calvin serves as Chief Commercial Officer at Domio, a luxury apartment-hotels company that offers the amenities of a hotel, with the footprint and features of fully equipped apartments in every room. Prior to Domio, Anderson led all commercial verticals for OYO North America including data science, brand and revenue channels as the company scaled from zero to more than 300 hotels in its first year. Additionally, Calvin served as CRO of RLHC overseeing top line of a 1,400-hotel portfolio and carried senior revenue strategy rolls at Duetto, Hilton and Highgate before that. Anderson also taught grad school courses at the NYU Tisch Center for Hospitality and Tourism, serves on the HSMAI Americas Board, was named 20 Next-Gen Leaders by Hotel Magin 2018 and was also named one of 10 Technology Rock Stars by Hospitality Upgrade in 2020.

Nicholas Catalfamo

Nicholas is the Director of Revenue Management at the Courtyard by Marriott Boston Cambridge with Highgate. He previously served as the Revenue Analyst at the Boston Park Plaza, where he began his vocation in revenue management. A graduate of Boston University's School of Hospitality Administration, Nicholas co-authored a study published in the *Journal of Hospitality and Tourism Education* in 2018.

Bob Chamberlin

A graduate of Boston University with a BS in Hotel and Food Administration and an MBA with a concentration in Marketing from Bentley College, Bob has 25 years of hospitality experience with Sheraton, Westin, Starwood, Hilton, and Vista International. Bob is a Senior Business Analyst with Liberty Mutual, working with the Meeting and Event Strategy team, and Opening Revenue Manager for the Encore Boston Harbor, the first urban resort casino in the United States. As Manager of Strategic Analysis and Business Optimization at the Seaport Hotel & World Trade Center Boston, he developed the space optimization principles for the 200,000 sq. ft. of meeting space, boosting banquet revenue by 41% over a 10-year period.

Theresa Doherty

Theresa Doherty is a graduate of the Cornell University School of Hotel Administration. She has served as an Adjunct Professor at Boston University's School of Hospitality Administration, teaching several courses in revenue management. Theresa has spent the majority of her revenue management career with Marriott where she is currently an Area Director of Revenue Management.

Elyana Falk

Elyana Falk has a passion for hospitality and currently leads the Expedia lodging team in the Pacific Northwest as Area Manager. Elyana and her team work closely with more than 1,000 properties throughout the Pacific Northwest US, helping partners to build their visibility, increase guest interest, and drive bookings through the many brands of Expedia, Inc. Elyana has worked in three varying territories with Expedia, including Newport, Rhode Island; New York City; and currently Seattle, Washington. Prior to Expedia, Elyana worked at a variety of hotels with roles ranging from housekeeping to revenue, giving her a unique perspective of combining operations with the online travel market. Elyana is an active member of HSMAI and is a board member of the Cornell Hotel Society.

Gabor Fenyves

Gabor Fenyves is currently the Vice President of Revenue Management for Crescent Hotels and Resorts, based in Toronto, Canada. Prior to joining Crescent, he worked at the Westmont Hospitality Group as Corporate Director of Revenue Management. Gabor graduated from Cornell University with a Master's of Management in Hospitality. He holds a BA from École Hôtelière de Lausanne in Switzerland and has traveled the world extensively, working for multiple hotel brands, including IHG, Marriott, Fairmont, and Hilton. His expertise lies with independent properties and incorporating out-of-the-box revenue management strategies in the day-to-day hotel operations.

Carolyn Fredey

Carolyn Fredey is a hospitality revenue management professional and adjunct professor based in New York, New York. She holds a MMH degree from the School of Hotel Administration at Cornell University, as well a BA from Florida State University. She enjoys teaching her students and employees the importance of pricing and having a revenue management strategy that considers brand integrity and profitability.

Jonathan Jaeger

Jonathan Jaeger currently serves as a Senior Managing Director with LW Hospitality Advisors, based in New York City. During his tenure at LWHA, Mr. Jaeger has been responsible for the management and execution of over 1000 lodging/gaming consulting and valuation assignments throughout the United States, Canada, Mexico, and the Caribbean on an annual basis. From February of 2014 through August of 2019, Jonathan was a Managing Director with the firm. Prior to joining LWHA, Mr. Jaeger had been with Pinnacle Advisory Group from January of 2008 through January of 2014. He graduated with a Bachelor of Science from the Boston University School of Hospitality Administration in addition to earning a minor in Business Administration from the Boston University School of Management. Mr. Jaeger also serves as a member of the Adjunct Faculty at New York University and at Boston University.

Leslie Lew

Leslie Lew is an entrepreneur, hotel executive and Founder of Public Boardroom Inc. Lew has over 20 years of experience in the hospitality industry starting his career at a five-diamond resort gift shop to leading the revenue management, distribution and e-commerce organization as Vice President of Revenue at Provenance Hotels. He graduated with honors from Boston University School of Hospitality Administration, guest lectured at New York University Tisch Center for Hospitality and served on the board of National Society of Minorities in Hospitality. Lew creates economic opportunity and mobility through education.

Roy Madhok

Roy Madhok is the Vice President of Revenue Management for Real Hospitality Group, Roy Madhok, CRME, CHIA, where he oversees revenue management and distribution for the RHG portfolio of over 100 hotels. Prior to joining the Real Hospitality Group, Roy was a Regional Director of Revenue for Highgate and also served as an Adjunct Professor at Boston University's School of Hospitality Administration, teaching both introductory and advanced revenue management courses. Roy has been a speaker at various panels and conferences such as the HSMAI Revenue Optimization Conference, the Expedia Partner Conference, Cornell Hotel

Society's Lodging Pulse, and others. In addition to speaking at events, he sat on New York City's HSMAI Board and Revenue Management Committee.

Raul Moronta

Raul Moronta is a passionate hotel revenue management leader responsible for overseeing revenue strategy for Crescent Hotels & Resorts. Prior to this role, he was responsible for franchise revenue management operations for the full-service portfolio at Starwood Hotels & Resorts. He holds a BS from the Pontificia Universidad Catolica Madre & Maestra in the Dominican Republic and an MBA from the University of New Haven, Connecticut. He has a Certificate in Hotel Real Estate Investment and Asset Management from Cornell University and is a past board member of the HSMAI Boston Chapter.

Lambis Pahiyiannakis

Lambis Pahiyiannakis is responsible for underwriting acquisition opportunities and assisting Asset Management with quarterly and yearly reporting at Cornerstone Real Estate Advisers. He also plays a critical role in underwriting and reviewing lending opportunities for the core mortgage and alternative investments group. Prior to joining Cornerstone in 2013, Mr. Pahiyiannakis was a Business Development and Acquisitions Analyst for Pyramid Hotel Group in Boston for over two years. There, he was actively engaged with business development efforts and assisted with adding and retaining more than 20 management contracts to the existing portfolio of approximately 50 hotels. Mr. Pahiyiannakis earned a BS degree from Boston University with a double major in Economics and Hospitality Administration.

Kristin V. Rohlfs

Kristin V. Rohlfs is an independent consultant and researcher based in Rochester, New York. She holds a PhD in Revenue Management and an MMH degree from the School of Hotel Administration at Cornell University, as well as a BBA degree from The University of Texas at Austin. Her research interests focus on small-business application of operations management and revenue management and customer reactions to revenue management practices. Her authored works include a dissertation, "The Role of Space in Revenue Management" (2009), and an article, "Best Available Rate Pricing," published in the *Cornell Quarterly* (2005). A 2011 article co-authored with Breffni Noone and Kelly McGuire, *"Social Media Meets Hotel Revenue Management: Opportunities, Issues, and Unanswered Questions,"* can be found in the *Journal of Revenue and Pricing Management.*

Adam Snitzer

Adam Snitzer is President of Peak Revenue Performance, Inc., an international pricing and revenue strategy consulting firm with expertise in consumer products, financial services, and travel, particularly cruise lines, riverboat companies, and tour operators. For sixteen years, he occupied senior revenue management positions at cruise lines such as Royal Caribbean, NCL, Cunard, Costa, and Seabourn. He lectures on cruise line revenue management and writes frequently on pricing and revenue management topics.

FOREWORD

It is hard to believe that both Dr. Peter Szende and I got our starts in the hotel and restaurant business before revenue management was "invented" in the industry and certainly before the term was coined. As the notion of yield management has given way to the larger concept of revenue management and as terms such as "opaque rates," "rate parity," "dynamic pricing," "BAR," and "LRA" have entered the hospitality lexicon, it has become more and more important for students, professionals, and academics to become experts in this still-emerging field.

When I joined the Boston University faculty in 2011, Dr. Szende was working hard on developing a series of hospitality management learning modules centered around food and beverage management. He and I commuted to home from work together nearly every night; the one-mile walk and conversation was interrupted only by a stop at the grocery store for the daily samples, and we would remark on how and why they could price bananas at only 19 cents each (29 cents for organic)—an interesting revenue management question!

Our conversation on this walk usually focused on the progress of his module project and what major project he would pursue next. As a then 25-year industry, practitioner who had just made the transition to academia, I was keenly interested in identifying areas that were important to practitioners but had not yet been fully explored by scholars. I had a particular interest in those topics that were not necessarily taught (or taught well) to students in hospitality programs. Dr. Szende's mind was, as usual, working at a feverish pace, looking to apply his many years of direct operational experience to solving hospitality-related problems.

He described for me, many times, what ultimately became this textbook, which brilliantly combines, as the title indicates, both *concepts* and *practices*, making this a single-source resource for practitioners, faculty members, and students. He has identified, hounded, and, in some cases, harassed many leading experts in their respective subject areas to deliver their expertise in a manner that expands their reach far beyond their current roles. These experts include seasoned industry professionals as well as relative newcomers to the revenue management field, including many of whom were Dr. Szende's students, others who are adjunct faculty members at a number of leading institutions, and others who are bringing to light, for the first time formally, revenue management insight from additional allied hospitality segments.

Chapter 1 begins with a broad introduction to hotel revenue management. From this very first chapter, care is taken to include the numerous pedagogical elements outlined in the Editor's Preface and which should be of tremendous benefit to students learning from this textbook.

The various fundamentals of hotel revenue management are then presented in a logical sequence, although each chapter serves as a self-contained presentation of a given topic. This sequence begins with Chapter 2 on the most fundamental revenue management concept, pricing hotel guest rooms. As we have learned over time, the way hotels mix and stack business is critically important; hence, Chapter 3 introduces the concept of hotel segmentation.

Further investigation into hotel segmentation leads to distribution channels in Chapter 4 as optimal building of each segment and the overall hotel is dependent on reaching the right audience in the most effective manner. This then transitions into Chapter 5 with the evolution of competitive analysis and the creation and use of STR reports, which, coming from someone who recalls counting cars in the parking lots of roadside motels for feasibility studies in the mid-1980s, have been a most welcome addition to the industry.

With the current environment in mind, there is likely no chapter more useful than Chapter 6, which details how to translate the voluminous data produced by revenue management systems and its focus on revenue forecasting and budgeting. Chapter 7, which provides the tools for both *pre-hoc* and *post-hoc* performance analysis, contains novel material that can be readily applied to real-life scenarios. Chapter 8 then concludes the hotel revenue management portion of the text with practical ideas on how to benchmark performance.

Among the unique features of this textbook is the inclusion of a comprehensive series of chapters on restaurant revenue management. This section of the text begins with basic concepts in Chapter 9 and then walks through advanced concepts related to demand in Chapter 10 and supply in Chapter 11.These chapters provide the most comprehensive overview of restaurant revenue management to appear in print to date, and the chapters included provide this in a logical and thoughtful progression that can add a current view to any restaurant management curriculum.

The final chapters of the text expose the reader to additional areas of revenue management that have only recently been codified. The presentation in Chapter 12 of how best to optimize function space has become a critically important tool in an environment where group demand growth is often exceeding transient demand growth, and where properties are either functionally or economically limited in their ability to expand their meeting space.

Significant ancillary spend, fixed embarkation and debarkation dates, and the ability to physically move the product have resulted in revenue management in the cruise industry developing its own unique systems and vernacular as explained in Chapter 13. Chapter 14 moves on to present both a framework for applying revenue management concepts to new areas as well as identifying opportunities for applying these principles to golf and spa operations.

Finally, Chapter 15 brings everything full circle and provides the hotel owner's perspective on the revenue management process. After all, what use is maximizing revenue if it does not ultimately improve profit?

When I made the decision to return to the industry in 2013 after a six-year absence, one of the areas where I knew my skills had fallen behind was understanding the dramatic evolution that was occurring in the revenue management area. Quite frankly, it's been a challenge to keep up with it, and I had never identified quite the right resource to learn from and use to teach within my own organization. Fortunately, Dr. Szende has recruited outstanding industry leaders as authors and gathered the information necessary to prepare and produce this exemplary textbook on the topic that will undoubtedly be utilized by students of all varieties in universities and companies throughout our great industry.

—Barry A.N. Bloom, PhD
President and Chief Operating Officer
Xenia Hotels & Resorts, Inc.

EDITOR'S PREFACE

Hospitality Revenue Management: Concepts and Practices provides an in-depth review of basic concepts and best practices of hospitality revenue management. Unlike standard textbook construction, in which chapters build upon the knowledge gained from previous chapters, each chapter of this book is a self-contained view of a specific aspect within hospitality revenue management. Our aim is to offer a comprehensive and contemporary textbook to effectively meet the curricular requirement of undergraduate and graduate students. The book can also be used as a reference for practitioners and as a text for executive education programs.

Through its real-world approach, students are placed in the role of a revenue manager striving to succeed in an ever-changing business environment.

This book has been designed with distinctive features:

- ***A self-contained structure that allows for greater teaching flexibility***

Because each chapter is self-contained, the sequence of chapters can be altered to fit any class timeline, and the material can be used in a variety of formats to fit personal teaching preferences or time constraints of individual courses. Although chapters are standalone, our goal has been to develop a product that follows a logical flow of ideas both within each chapter and from one chapter to the next.

- ***Multi-author, collaborative approach***

Given the constant changes in the field of revenue management and to ensure that the book content would be relevant and include the most updated information, multiple authors contributed to this textbook. The purpose of this was to capture the collective expertise of contributors in the hospitality revenue management field yet remain cohesive in content and style. By engaging a number of topic experts, the expertise each contributor brings surpasses what any single author could have achieved.

Once we identified the contributors, we established the emphasis of each chapter and the overall organization of the book. The uniform orientation of the text reflects the ideas and styles of individual contributors, but we have also been able to integrate the chapters into a coherent whole.

- ***Pedagogical features that keep students engaged and challenged***

Distinguishing pedagogical features define the overall tone of any textbook. Although the chapters in this book are standalone, a uniform pattern of pedagogical aids across all chapters has been designed to create a consistent learning experience, while accommodating a variety of teaching styles.

Learning Objectives: Each chapter opens with a list of learning objectives that serve to focus the reader's attention on key concepts.

Key Terms: Key terms are emphasized in bold when first used in the text and listed at the end of each chapter in the glossary.

Boxed Features: Each chapter includes five standard, boxed pedagogical features. These boxes are intended to briefly depart from the flow of the chapter in order to expand upon the concepts presented and enliven the discussion.

- ***So What?***—An opener designed to draw the student into the chapter and stimulate them with a critical-thinking question

- ***Think Historically***—A reflection on historical events intended to promote a deeper understanding of the material and demonstrate ways in which past events relate to current management issues.

- ***Real People***—A presentation of difficult situations that real managers have faced, which helps students understand and relate chapter content to managerial practices.

- ***Pros/Cons***—Features that present opposing views on a relevant issue and prompt debate or discussion.

- ***Seeing Further***—A theme that reflect the latest hot topics or professional concerns related to the topics discussed.

Spreadsheet Exercises: Proficiency with spreadsheets is a great advantage to revenue managers. In order to develop students' computational skills, each chapter includes two practical problems that can be solved using Excel.

Discussion Questions: Questions challenge students to think critically about the material.

Applications: Short case studies allow students to analyze and dissect chapter concepts through real-life scenarios.

Team Activity: Each chapter includes an experiential activity that will assist learners in the practical application of the chapter's concepts.

Internet Activity: Designated internet activities link the chapter and the Internet to create a dynamic learning environment.

Glossary: The glossaries provide students with an accessible reference tool and a list of key concepts that they should master.

The password protected instructor area is available for qualified instructors only. It includes:

- ***Instructor's Manual:*** The comprehensive instructor's manual contains answers/solutions for all discussion questions, problems, spreadsheet exercises, and applications.

- ***Test Bank:*** The exam test bank contains 20 multiple choice questions for each chapter (10 easy and 10 advanced).

ACKNOWLEDGMENTS

We must first thank each of the contributing authors, who graciously agreed to share their knowledge.

I would also like to express my gratitude to the following undergraduate students at Boston University School of Hospitality Administration: Emily Stewart and Namrata Sridhar, who selflessly supported every step of the book's development. I would like to acknowledge Allyson Rung, also a Boston University student, for her valuable contribution to the cruise revenue management chapter.

We are especially grateful to Nicholas Catalfamo, Director of Revenue Management at Highgate, for serving as our editorial assistant throughout the publication process.

We owe special thanks to Timothy Kenney, Director of Revenue Management at Kimpton Hotels & Restaurants, who served as an early reviewer of the manuscript.

CHAPTER 1

Hotel Revenue Management: An Introduction

Carolyn Fredey and Roy Madhok

OVERVIEW

Revenue management is the art of selling the right inventory to the right customer at the right price at the right time to yield optimal profit. The practice of revenue management can be applied to a multitude of industries that share similar characteristics, including high fixed costs, fixed capacity, perishable inventory, variable demand, price sensitivity, and segmentation. In this chapter, we will specifically discuss the management of hotel room inventory, but the same principles can be applied to other hospitality sectors such as airlines, cruise lines, rental cars, catering, and restaurants.

LEARNING OBJECTIVES

After studying this module, you should be able to:

- Underline the fundamental concepts of revenue management in order to optimize hotel revenues and profit
- Identify the components of the revenue cycle in order to recall the economic relationships at play
- Define segmentation, channel mix, and the differences in buying behavior
- Calculate basic room statistics, market share, and profit measurements
- Demonstrate a clear understanding of organizational structure as it relates to revenue management
- Articulate revenue management strategy with various industry stakeholders

OUTLINE

INTRODUCTION

Hotel revenue management (HRM) focuses on how a hotel can produce the highest amount of "profitable" revenue given its fixed number of rooms to sell and varying levels of demand. Traditional **yield management** would suggest that HRM is only necessary when demand exceeds capacity and is limited to the practice of inventory allocation of already established price points and the "opening and closing" of qualified rates (rates that a guest must qualify for, such as corporate negotiated rates). However, in the last two decades, with escalating rate transparency and the tools available, the practice of HRM has evolved into a more comprehensive profession with more involvement beyond traditional yield management. HRM is now fully integrated with all sales and marketing disciplines to optimize pricing level, segmentation, and distribution **channel** mix in several organizations. Proper communication of the HRM strategy throughout the organization is paramount, with clear and concise reporting and regular strategy meetings.

Mastering the basic principles and components of HRM is critical in building a strong foundation to later apply to more advanced revenue management applications, such as demand forecasting, segment specific pricing, channel management, and strategic inventory management. Obtaining a clear picture of the hotel revenue management discipline and gaining the necessary tools to perform the basic and widely adopted performance metrics will be the focus of this chapter.

The goal of any business is to create a valuable product or service and to maximize profits through revenue generation and cost control. Revenue generation can be accelerated with the skillful combination of guest satisfaction, demand creation, and optimization commonly referred to as the **revenue cycle**. Revenue management is primarily tasked with generating the strategies and tactics that will optimize demand.

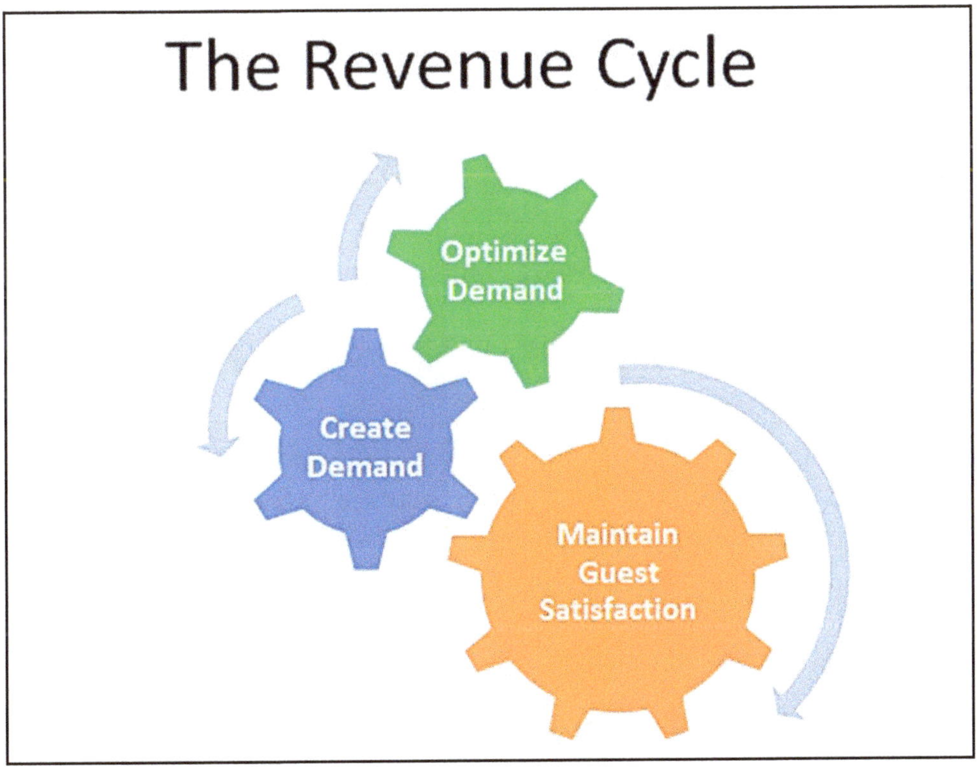

Figure 1.1: The Revenue Cycle

HRM optimizes demand by selling the right room to the right customer at the right price at the right time to yield optimal profit.

The **revenue manager** (RM) is not directly responsible for executing against guest satisfaction or creating demand but is reliant on these functions and therefore must be involved in business development and stay informed.

QUALIFICATIONS FOR APPLYING REVENUE MANAGEMENT

There are several characteristics that exist in hotels and other industries that make it necessary to apply revenue management in its operations:

Fixed Costs versus Variable Costs

- Hotels generally have high fixed costs in proportion to their variable costs (mainly labor). The hotel must absorb these fixed costs regardless of the occupancy level. **Fixed costs** may include mortgage, insurance, property taxes, management salaries, and benefits. In addition, fixed costs include any hourly wages, administrative expenses, and utilities expenses that must be maintained even if the hotel is empty. **Variable costs** for guestrooms include the expense of labor and supplies to service the room after use, the expense of the utilities associated with the guest's occupancy, and a designated cash reserve toward a capital budget for replacing furniture, generally every 3-7 years, as part of a regularly scheduled refurbishment (Lesure, 1983).

Fixed Capacity

- A hotel has a fixed number of rooms or "keys" that are sold on a nightly basis. Building new rooms may not be feasible, and construction takes considerable time, so for all intended purposes, the RM can only sell the limited amount of product available.

Perishable Inventory

- If a hotel room goes empty on any given night, the hotel has lost the sale. Given the relatively low variable cost, it is very compelling to sell a room rather than let it go empty, even at a price discount. Each unsold room is considered **spoilage**, and each room sold for less than what could have been gained is lost revenue.

Variable Demand

- In most cases, a hotel has fluctuating demand by day of week and season, resulting in the need of the revenue management application. In Chart 1, it is clear that this hotel has more demand on certain days of the weeks. The total demand including excess demand above capacity is often referred to as **unconstrained demand**. For example, Sunday and Monday lag the demand on Tuesday and Wednesday. To manage the variable demand, a revenue manager may apply revenue management tactics such as price differentials and length-of-stay restrictions. Without strategies in place, the hotel risks selling out the rooms on Tuesday and Wednesday too quickly and will not be able to accommodate all the reservations requests for arrivals on Sunday and Monday.

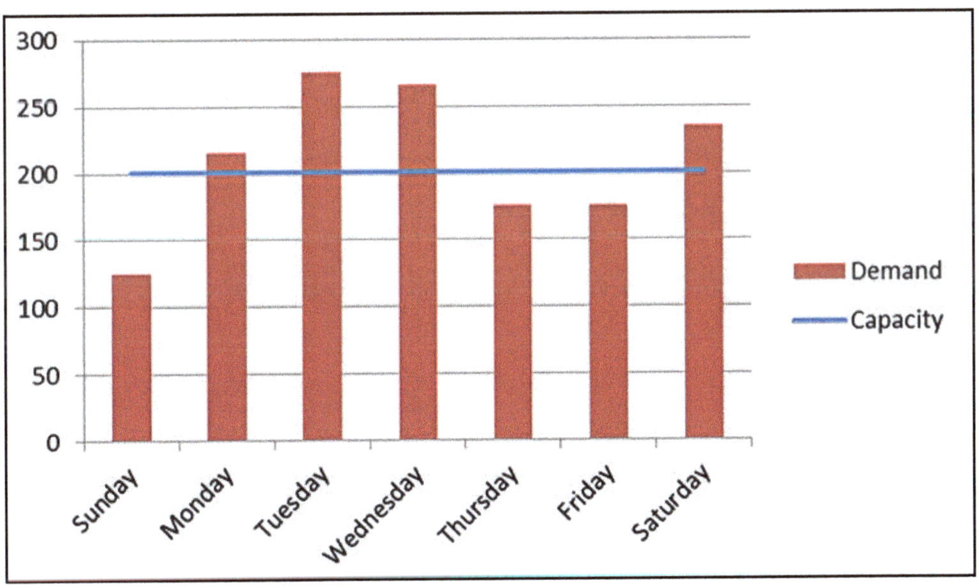

Chart 1

THINK HISTORICALLY

This ad for the Hotel Boswell appeared in the *Tulsa Daily World* newspaper in 1917.

Source: Tulsa Daily Dorld, June 17, 1917, p.8.

Questions to Consider:

What are your initial impressions of The Hotel Boswell's revenue management efforts?

How would you compare this listing to current hotel price listings?

SEGMENTATION

Since different guests are willing to pay a different price for the same product, hotels have to create ways to provide their rooms at different prices. This practice, known as **segmentation,** is where revenue managers classify and target customers in specific groups based upon their characteristics, behaviors, and preferences (Talluri & van Ryzin, 2004). Segments are in all industries: economy and luxury cars, student discounts at museums, wholesale discounts for food, corporate discounts for airlines, and others.

Segmenting customers allows a revenue manager to take advantage of variable demand by targeting multiple groups of people. Price segmentation ultimately allows a revenue manager to lower the entry price to buy a room while also offering the same room to other guests for a higher rate (Smith, 2012).

SO WHAT?

What are some other businesses that could use revenue management that currently do not?

What characteristics exist that would make revenue management fit those business models?

Hotels track and target three major segments in order to fully capture demand: Transient, Group, and Contract.

- Group: Rooms sold in minimum blocks of ten or more
- Contract: Rooms guaranteed as deemed by a signed contract such as airlines
- Transient guests however, are considered to be anything not a part of group or contract sale (Hayes & Miller, 2011) and are those guests that are traveling independently and their decision for which hotel to book are ultimately up to them.

Group and contracted rooms are, however, decided in bulk, for the most part not taking the unanimous decision of all people staying within the negotiated blocks.

Hotels as a whole are tasked with achieving the optimal amount of each segment at the right price, known as the optimal mix. For example, in an airport area, hotels will likely have significant airline contract volume; in a suburban area where there is little transient demand, there will likely be significant group volume; and in high-demand areas for individual travel, there is likely mostly transient occupancy.

Revenue managers work with sales and marketing to shape the segmentation of the hotel, where revenue management sets prices and guides the sales team on how much of each segment would be best for the hotel.

As hotel revenue management has become more sophisticated, so has price segmentation. Hotels have identified the need to break out Transient, Group, and Contract into sub-segments in order to have a targeted pricing strategy.

Table 1.1: Examples of Transient and Group Sub-Segments

Segment	**Sub-Segment**	**Description**
Transient	Retail	Standard rates being offered through the hotel directly to all guests
Transient	Online Travel Agent (OTA)	Standard rates being offered through online travel agents such as Expedia, Booking.com, Priceline.com, etc.
Transient	Government	Guests traveling for business but who work for the government and can show valid government identification
Transient	Opaque	Guests who book through websites such as Priceline and Hotwire, where hotels offer steeply discounted rates without disclosing the hotel prior to sale
Group	SMERF	Groups booked that fit into the following classifications: Social, Military, Education, Religious, Fraternal
Group	Preferred Corporate	Corporations book groups for meetings and events
Group	Government	Different governments will often travel to host meetings and events

BUYING BEHAVIOR WITHIN SEGMENTS

Every segment of customers behaves differently, and all have varying levels of price sensitivity. Therefore, revenue managers need to understand buying behavior within segments to make sure they are not discounting those guests willing to pay the most. The ability to charge different customers different rates comes through being able to create **rate fences** or **segmentation hedges**. Rate fences take five basic forms: physical, controlled availability, customer characteristics, transaction characteristics, and product line (Dolan & Simon, 1996).

Table 1.2: Rate Fence Basic Forms

Fence	Description
Physical	Offering varying room types: King Bedded Rooms, Suites, Two Beds, etc.
Controlled Availability	Setting an advance purchase window of 90+ days with a 20% discount to entice early bookers looking for a discount
Customer Characteristics	Offering discounts to leisure guests through AAA and senior discounts
Transaction Characteristics	Making a reservation fully non-refundable upon booking
Product Line	Offering different versions of the same product, i.e. King Room with butler service versus without

Source: The table is based on Dolan & Simon, 1997.

For example, hotels understand that corporate guests are not as price sensitive as other guests, given that their company often pays for their stay. Hotel teams are therefore tasked with finding a way to make corporate guests pay more than others for the same inventory. Revenue management and sales therefore work together to price corporate guests higher by offering business travelers free internet, turndown service, and breakfast.

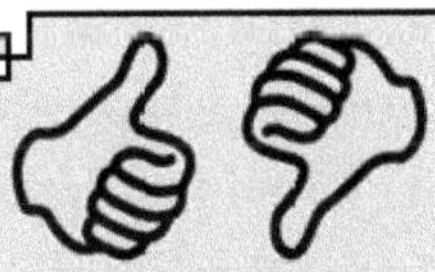

PROS & CONS

While applying rate fences helps revenue management drive RevPAR, there are challenges associated with implementing each type of rate fence. What are the pros and cons of each fence used within revenue management?

This process of including additional services within a rate is called **bundling** and is a key tool used to help revenue managers price particular guests higher than what would be charged to other, less profitable **market segments** (Kimes, 2010). Similarly, revenue managers take advantage of offering AAA and senior citizen discounts to target leisure customers, offering advance purchase discounts for those looking to secure their room very far out, or offering discounts for those traveling in large groups. Groups typically agree to book a certain number of rooms at an agreed-upon rate.

The contractual basis of group rooms allows hotel revenue management to build a base of rooms that they know will materialize. A group booked on any set of dates is referred to as a "group base" and is an integral segment within hotels, providing stability within the hotel and allowing revenue managers to cut back on other lower rated and more unreliable transient segments. Group business for full service hotels in companies such as Marriott International as a whole can represent over half of the hotel's revenue (Hormby et al., 2010).

OPTIMAL MIX OF SALES

The composition of the various segments staying in a hotel on any particular day, week, month, or year is called **mix of sales** or market segmentation. Two similar hotels can run the same occupancy percentage, but their mix of sales can determine which hotel had a higher ADR and therefore RevPAR. Revenue managers consistently look backward at their mix of sales and critique where they could have cut back on lower rated segments and conversely look and see if there was opportunity to sell more rooms via discount channels to gain RevPAR.

In order to achieve an optimal mix of segments to maximize both RevPAR and profit, hotels have to understand booking patterns, seasonality, customer preferences, and more. Hotel revenue managers know, for example, that corporate clientele are willing to pay the most and typically book closer to arrival because of last minute travel plans. The revenue manager has to understand how many high rated corporate rooms it will sell in the future and therefore has to understand how many low rated rooms to sell to leisure guests in advance. Limiting early leisure bookings and protecting too many rooms for high rated guests can result in discounting last minute high rated guests and leaving rooms empty (See Bodea & Ferguson, 2014, p. 84).

CHANNEL MANAGEMENT

Mix of business can only be considered optimal if *channel management plays a key role in shaping the segmentation*. Segments should not be treated equally given that each segment books through a different source and because each reservation has a different cost of booking, or **cost of acquisition**. For example, online travel agents charge a **commission** as a percentage of each room sold. Whereas if a hotel sells rooms through their own website, the cost of selling is significantly less (Table 1.3).

Table 1.3: Sample Channel Costs

Channel	Room Rate	Sample Cost/Commission	Net Rate
Brand.com	$249.00	3.00%	$241.53
Reservation Center	$249.00	6.00%	$234.06
GDS (Global Distribution System)	$249.00	11.00%	$221.61
OTA (Online Travel Agency)	$249.00	15.00%	$211.65

In Table 1.4, both Hotels A and B earn the same amount of revenue, but Hotel B produced more through the OTA channels. With higher costs compared to the retail segment, the OTA segment and channel makes an immediate impact on the profitability of Hotel B.

Table 1.4: Segment and Channel Relationship

Hotel A				Hotel B						
Segment	Rooms	ADR	Revenue	Segment	Rooms	ADR	Revenue	Segment Cost %	Hotel A	Hotel B
Retail	50	$210.00	$10,500.00	Retail	30	$210.00	$6,300.00	5.00%	$525.00	$315.00
OTA	30	$210.00	$6,300.00	OTA	50	$210.00	$10,500.00	20.00%	$1,260.00	$2,100.00
Total	80	$210.00	$16,800.00	Total	80	$210.00	$16,800.00		$1,785.00	$2,415.00

A hotel that optimizes both segmentation and channel mix will be a hotel that drives occupancy, ADR, RevPAR, and most importantly, profit. In recent years this segment and channel relationship has been a bone of contention to ownership groups as there has been a visible escalation of overall distribution costs for the hotel industry as the channel mix of OTAs has increased. The difficulty in managing channel mix is the existence of **rate parity** agreements, where hotels are forced to offer the same pricing and, in nearly all cases, the same availability. While the revenue manager would like to drive more mix into **brand.com** (the brand or hotel's own website), there is a compelling case that providing rate parity across channels increases good will and brand equity.

QUESTIONS TO CONSIDER

What are some strategies to increase production on brand.com?

Is rate parity a good thing across all channels?

What are some arguments for and against rate parity?

PERFORMANCE METRICS

Hotels as a business have metrics that are important to the overall business performance. Revenue managers must identify, track, and improve those metrics that matter most in terms of revenue management, including room statistics, house profit, market share, and forecast accuracy.

Room Statistics

In hotel revenue management there are a growing number of key performance indicators (KPIs) that help revenue managers measure their effectiveness. The core of hotel revenue management revolves around five indicators: occupancy, average daily rate (ADR), **revenue per available room (RevPAR)**, revenue, and of course, profit.

The hotel typically will **benchmark** against itself and its **competitive set** in terms of overall numbers and segment. Market share is best described by how the hotel's room statistics stack up against the competitive set.

Occupancy

As discussed earlier, perishability in the hospitality industry dissolves prospective revenue once an available room goes unsold. Hotels measure occupancy levels by using occupancy percentage, defined as the number of rooms occupied of the available inventory. For hotel and market reporting, typically only occupancy that is paid (which removes occupied rooms that do not have any revenue associated, otherwise known as compensatory or simply, "comps"). Therefore we can simplify paid occupied rooms as "sold rooms."

Occupancy Percentage = Sold Rooms / Available Rooms
Example:
200 sold rooms / 250 available rooms = 80 percent occupancy

Occupancy levels also dictate various room statistics that impact cost.

- **Arrivals**: The amount of rooms set to arrive
- **Departures**: The amount of rooms that will or have checked out
- **Stayovers**: Rooms that occupy the room overnight and for subsequent nights

Revenue managers not only control occupancy percentages by selling rooms but also control the **length of stay (LOS)** by restricting reservations to a minimum number of nights. For two hotels with the same overall occupancy percentage, the hotel with a significantly longer LOS can benefit from reduced costs associated with not having to clean the room each day, having to purchase fewer amenities, and the ability to control other variable expenses associated with occupancy.

Average Daily Rate (ADR)

Average daily rate (ADR) is the average price that rooms are sold for during any time period. The importance of ADR is the theoretical absence of a ceiling on how high this metric can climb. In some cases, it is the only way a hotel can improve revenue, especially after reaching stabilized occupancy levels. In simpler terms, if a hotel ran 100 percent occupancy on a full year basis, there would be only one way to increase its room revenue: by increasing ADR.

Average Daily Rate = Total Room Revenue / Total Rooms Sold
Example:
$45,000 Room Revenue / 200 Rooms Sold = $225 Average Daily Rate

Revenue per available room (RevPAR) is simply the combination of occupancy and ADR, or revenue generated by each available guest room over a period of time. Another way to consider the metric, RevPAR is the output of balancing the two inputs, occupancy and ADR, to maximize revenue.

Calculation 1 to calculate RevPAR:

RevPAR = Average Daily Rate × Occupancy Percentage

Example:

$220 ADR × 86% Occupancy Percentage = $189.20 RevPAR

Calculation 2 to calculate RevPAR:

RevPAR = Room Revenue / Available Rooms

Example:

$37,840 Revenue / 200 Available Rooms = $189.20 RevPAR

Profitability

The goal of any business is to accumulate as much profit as possible. In hotels, **room revenue** is what the hotel receives for the sale for all sales generated relative to rooms. Total revenue in a hotel would consist of room revenue plus any revenue coming from food and beverage, non-room fees, or other outlets.

At the expense of profit, companies or hotels can spend on marketing, advertising, and sales in order to increase revenue. Successful companies and hotels, however, are those that can keep costs low in order to see a profit while still maintaining high revenue levels.

Being an effective revenue manager requires understanding of cost as much as the understanding of revenue. A revenue manager's responsibility is to develop strategies to gather as much revenue as possible while limiting cost and therefore increasing profits.

House profit is defined as the difference in the amount earned and the amount spent, or revenue minus operating cost. The costs used to calculate house profit only consider the variable costs mentioned earlier and any other costs that are managed by the hotel operators.

House Profit = Revenue – Operating Costs

Example:

$100,000 revenue – $60,000 cost = $40,000 profit

Profit margin is defined as the percentage of house profit compared to the revenue source. It is often a key performance goal for a general manager and other key personnel at a hotel. Revenue managers are often incentivized by house profit or profit margin because it ensures that decisions are made to drive profitability.

Profit Margin = House Profit/Revenue

Example:

$40,000 profit/$100,000 revenue = 40% Profit Margin

Refer to Table 1.5 below, which revenue manager was more effective? Both Revenue Managers generated the same amount of revenue. However, a hotel that sells fewer rooms at a higher ADR likely can drive extra profit because there are more variable costs with selling additional rooms.

Table 1.5: Revenue Manager Comparison

Revenue Managers A & B with Identical Products and Identical Services

Room Statistic	**Revenue Manager A**	**Revenue Manager B**
Rooms Sold	150	120
Average Daily Rate	$285.00	$356.25
Revenue	$42,750	$42,750

Table 1.6: Examples of Room Statistics in a Profit & Loss Statement

	Year to Date	Budget	Last Year	Variance to Budget	Variance to Last Year
Available Rooms	54,750	54,750	54,750	0	0
Rooms Sold	46,720	45,990	45,260	730	1,460
Rooms Revenue	$ 6 ,572,500	$ 7,245,063	$ 6,545,910	($672,563)	$26,590
House Profit	$ 3 ,943,500	$ 4,419,488	$ 3,993,005	($475,988)	($49,505)
House Profit Margin	60%	61%	61%	-1.0%	-1.0%
Occupancy	85%	84%	83%	1.3%	2.7%
Average Daily Rate	$140.68	$157.54	$144.63	($16.86)	($3.95)
RevPAR	$120.05	$132.33	$119.56	($12.28)	$0.49

QUESTIONS TO CONSIDER *(Refer to Table 1.6)*

The Case of Being "Out of Balance"

Review the profit and loss statement for the hotel. Ask the questions:

1. Did the hotel meet or exceed budget in any categories?
2. Did the hotel meet or exceed prior year performance in any of the categories?
3. What would you contribute to the increase in rooms revenue?
4. Which metric did not improve over the prior year? What are the likely focus areas for the revenue manager?
5. What other data or market intelligence would you like in order to understand the performance?

MARKET SHARE

Market share is the performance metric used to measure how a hotel does compared to a defined competitive set. A **competitive set** is a list of competitors that the hotel ownership and management select in order to measure their results against based upon which hotels are believed to be direct competitors for sales and bookings. Reports are generated by a neutral party and distributed daily, weekly, and monthly. Market share reports go beyond explaining how external factors such as the economy, **citywide** activity, unusual weather, and more affect the hotel and competitors. External factors may increase or decrease revenue for both the hotel and the competitive set, but market share assists us in determining if the hotel's success or failure is better or worse than the competitive set and better illustrates whether the revenue strategies employed were successful.

Refer to the sample market share report for examples.

Table 1.7: Sample Market Share Report

Sample Market Share Report			% Change
Occupancy	Property	87.1%	0.0%
	Comp Set	91.8%	2.0%
	Index	94.9%	-2.0%
	Rank	3 out of 4	
Rate	Property	$306.87	2.0%
	Comp Set	$260.62	0.0%
	Index	117.7%	2.0%
	Rank	1 out of 4	
RevPAR	Property	$267.28	2.0%
	Comp Set	$239.25	2.0%
	Index	111.7%	0.0%
	Rank	3 out of 4	

In the sample market share report in Table 1.7, you will find the key statistics that most market share reports show. In the occupancy section, the property had an occupancy percentage of 87.1 percent this year compared to the competitive set occupancy of 91.8 percent.

Occupancy Index (Market Penetration Index or MPI) =
Hotel Occupancy Percentage / Competitive Set Occupancy Percentage

Example: .87 / .92 = 95.0 percent

The hotel had no change year over year (0.0 percent) while the competitive set gained 2 percent year over year. This then means that the hotel lost -2 percent in share, as they did 2 percent worse versus the competitive set in occupancy compared to last year.

Rate (ADR) and RevPAR read the same way. The property posted an ADR of $306.87 and the competitive set posted $260.62. The property was able to grow 2 percent while the competitive set was flat year over year.

Overall, this resulted in a gain in share of 2 percent, an ADR ranking this year of 1 out of 4, and an index of 117.7 percent.

- ADR Index (Average Rate Index or ARI) = Hotel ADR / Competitive Set ADR

Example: $306.87 / $260.62 = 117.7 percent

- RevPAR Index (Revenue Generation Index or RGI) = Hotel RevPAR / Competitive Set RevPAR

Example: $267.41 / $239.03 = 111.9 percent

- Percentage Change = (Current Value / Previous Value) – 1

The increase or decrease in year over year performance (YoY). The market share report will not include last year numbers but rather show the change YoY.

Example: 117.7 percent Hotel ARI in current year / 115.3 percent Hotel ARI prior year = 2.0 percent

SPREADSHEET EXERCISE 1-1

To Do: Calculate the blue cells in the market share report.

			% Change
Occupancy	Property	88.00%	-2.22%
	Comp Set	w%	0.00%
	Index	97.78%	-2.22%
Rate	Property	$x	4.58%
	Comp Set	$225.00	0.00%
	Index	y%	4.58%
RevPAR	Property	$220.88	2.26%
	Comp Set	$202.50	v%
	Index	%z	2.26%

A hotel's pricing, strategy, and marketing all dictate the occupancy, ADR, and RevPAR share they garner. Pricing too high will turn away guests, leading to low market penetration. Selling too few rooms instead forfeits market traction, potentially ruining investor expectations on financial return (Smith, 2012).

A hotel that artificially prices itself too low will likely gain market penetration and lose ADR index; this can result in a low RevPAR index and can also perpetuate the image of a low quality product and tarnish brand integrity.

The concept of gaining or losing share is key in hotels and measures the progress a revenue manager is making using strategies to shift demand. Gaining share is when a hotel's occupancy, ADR, or RevPAR percentage change over a period of time is greater than its competitor's percentage change over the same period of time. Conversely, a hotel has lost share in occupancy, ADR, or RevPAR when their percentage change is less than that of the competitive set's percentage change.

REAL PEOPLE

Michael Lopez*, revenue manager in a high occupancy market, shared instances where the market share report was deceiving and required either understanding of real success/failure and how market share data can be misleading.

My hotel has sometimes lost share in occupancy as my occupancy has no room for growth; how can I use the market share report to understand my successes and failures given my inability to grow occupancy share?

Sometimes, my competitive set shows significant gains in occupancy, therefore creating a large loss in my occupancy index over last year and ultimately a large loss in RevPAR index share. What could have happened in the competitive set that the occupancy could gain by so much year over year?

On occasion my competitive set will show an unusually low ADR, causing my RevPAR index to look significantly better than usual. What could have happened out of the norm amongst my competitors?

My results on particular days are often questioned despite strong weekly and monthly performance. Is there credence to the questioning I receive and what should my response be to these questions?

*Name has been concealed

FORECASTING AND BUDGETING

Forecasting and budgeting is a primary task of the revenue manager. Forecasting impacts both the revenue maximization process and the hotel operations team.

The first objective of forecasting is to predict unconstrained demand by segment and day level to enable a revenue optimization process. The revenue manager generally relies heavily on systems for the development of the unconstrained demand forecast. The system forecast uses a combination of historical data, user inputs, and statistical modeling to predict future demand.

Secondly, forecasting must communicate to the hotel operations team how many rooms will be sold on a daily basis and the projected revenue. Preparing the revenue forecast allows the finance department to complete the expense-and-profit forecast, generally done on a monthly basis for the next several months. On an annual basis, the projection process is done in a rigorous manner and includes detailed segmentation so that the hotel can set goals for the following year to present to key stakeholders. This is generally referred to as the rooms budget.

Forecasts and budgets are used as benchmarks for how well the hotel performed. Revenue managers are responsible for critiquing performance against the forecast and the budget. Declines in key metrics versus forecast and budget need to be explained, and strategies are put into place to rectify results going forward.

INVENTORY MANAGEMENT

Inventory management is generally considered the art of "selling the right product at the right time for the right price to the right customer." It is complex, with the reality of variable demand throughout the year and across a given week of time, as we learned earlier.

With a limited amount of inventory, hotels have no choice but to make the most of what they have. For this reason, it is imperative that each room, and each room type, be sold for the appropriate amount. Offering discounts for rooms with multiple beds when demand in high can be costly for any hotel. Times of the year such as summer weekends or holidays are popular

SEEING FURTHER

With the importance of forecasting, given the direct relationship of the unconstrained demand projection with the revenue strategy, accuracy is critical. Both the system forecast error and the revenue manager's forecast should be measured to track progress. If the forecast error increases, there may be a change in the trend, incorrect data, or human error. As the system forecast plays such an important role and relies on user inputs and overrides, it is recommended that goals be established and managers held accountable.

Mean absolute percentage error (MAPE) expresses accuracy as the average percentage of error across a number of instances. It can be easier to understand than other statistics. For example, if the MAPE is 7 percent, on average, the forecast is off by 7 percent.

The MAPE equation:

$$\left(\frac{1}{n}\sum\frac{|Actual - Forecast|}{|Actual|}\right)*100$$

Example:

DOW	Forecast Rooms Sold	Actual Rooms Sold	Absolute Difference	Absolute Error %
Sunday	100	110	10	9%
Monday	150	160	10	6%
Tuesday	165	165	-	0%
Wednesday	165	165	-	0%
Thursday	145	140	5	4%
Friday	115	100	15	15%
Saturday	145	165	20	12%
Total	985	1,005	20	2%
			MAPE	7%

It is important to note that in this example that the combined rooms forecast error is 2 percent but the MAPE calculation measures the average error for each instance (n), which is 7 percent.

for family travel and therefore make it important to maximize ADR opportunity for double bedded rooms or suites.

SPREADSHEET EXERCISE 1-2

To Do: Two hotels are listed below with same amount of total rooms and have the same rate for each of the room types. Using spreadsheet software, calculate the total revenue for each hotel.

Room Type	Hotel A			Hotel B	
	Rate	Rooms Sold	Revenue	Rooms Sold	Revenue
Queen @ $x Rate		20	$3,180.00	20	
King @ $169	$169.00	40		20	$3,380.00
King @ $179	$179.00		$7,160.00		$10,740.00
DBDB @ $199	$199.00	20		10	
DBDB @ $x Rate		40	$9,160.00		$11,450.00
Suite Tier 1	$349.00	20	$6,980.00	5	
Suite Tier 2	$399.00	20		35	
Total		200		200	

1. Which hotel had better inventory management?
2. What could Hotel A have done better? Hotel B?

Revenue managers are tasked with creating a strategy that will set the hotel up for success in the short and long term. Granular details such as room type availability and macro concepts like contractual inventory restraints can have a significant impact on the long-term success of a property. A hotel that allows each account the ability to book the **last room available** will suffer as last minute high rated demand will repeatedly be lost. In the short term, revenue management also has to understand when to **overbook** the hotel and by how many rooms. Cancellations, **no-shows,** and **early departures** all take away from what would have been an occupied room and therefore need to be tracked to determine the overbooking limit.

COMMUNICATION

It the responsibility of revenue management to articulate the hotel's strategies and results to all stakeholders, including the sales team, front office, ownership, and executive leadership. An effective revenue manager is as well versed in communication as strategy.

Sales Strategy Meeting

The sales strategy meeting, typically a weekly call or meeting, is a revenue management strategy discussion conducted by revenue leadership. A sales strategy meeting consists of critiquing past performance with a variety of reports, analyzing data and strategy for the upcoming 12 months, and coming up with both micro and macro level strategies that will be executed in the near and long term.

Ownership Meetings

Revenue management over time has become the function of the hotel responsible for communicating strategies to improve RevPAR and profit for the hotel. Industry professionals and educators collectively agree that communication skills are the most important skill a recent hotel school graduate can have followed by the ability to improve revenue (Mayo, 2013).

Ownership involvement in hotels can be daily, and therefore it is critical for the revenue manager to understand what the ownership group is looking for and to gauge the level of detail they are looking for. Ownership groups are typically most focused on their return on investment (ROI), revenue, procurement and development (Cullen & Helsel, 2010). Revenue managers have to identify ownership expectations and knowledge level. Some hotel owners may not understand segmentation or unconstrained demand, and it is the responsibility of revenue management to articulate key ideas to ownership.

While ownership understanding and involvement varies, ownership groups typically revolve around performance versus expectations (budget, forecast, and last year) as well as performance versus competitors and the market. Revenue management is also responsible for communicating short- and long-term forecasts that ultimately guide the owners' future business plans (Law, 2004).

Daily Interaction with Property Operations and Sales

As with ownership, the hotel operations and sales team have a varying level of revenue management understanding and have their incentives laid out in directions that may be contrary to the goals of revenue management. Since sales members are often measured on volume instead of profit, it is the job of the revenue management professionals to stress short-term and long-term strategy focused on profitability (Cullen & Helsel, 2010). This daily interaction ensures that group rates, group contracts, corporate rates, wholesale contracts, and other types of business are all in the best interest of the hotel. The revenue management team also has to convey need areas in terms of e-commerce and marketing, whereas the sales and marketing team needs to focus their efforts so that the channel management efforts can be fully realized.

The interaction with operations is arguably the most overseen portion of revenue management in hotels. Most revenue managers create an **operations forecast** that is used by operations leaders to appropriately staff the hotel. However, beyond the operations forecast, revenue management has little involvement with the operations team.

DISCUSSION QUESTIONS

Question 1: How does the reality of perishability impact pricing?

Question 2: Why is market share utilized in the hotel industry? Is it foolproof? What other metrics would you use to critique performance from an owner's perspective?

Question 3: What is unconstrained demand and why is it more meaningful than an occupancy forecast? If a forecast changes, what strategies must be reviewed?

Question 4: Brainstorm market segments that are targeted in various industries. What new market segments should the hotel industry start to target? Which, if any, market segments in any industry do you see as cannibalizing one another?

Question 5: What would be the process you would go through to forecast a hotel's revenue for the next month? What data would you need and what would you be looking to find out?

Question 6: Given various costs of distribution, would you as the leader of a company decide to eliminate any distribution channels? If not, how would you reduce cost using revenue management?

APPLICATIONS

Case #1:

Please generate room statistics and a market share report based on the following information showing full year results compared to prior year full year:

Property Size: 200 rooms

Comp Set Size – 800 rooms

This Year Data:

Property Rooms Sold – 64,240
Comp Set Rooms Sold – 262,800
Property Rooms Revenue This Year – $16,124,240
Comp Set Rooms Revenue Last Year – $59,130,000

Last Year Data:

Property Rooms Sold – 65,700
Comp Set Rooms Sold – 262,800
Property Rooms Revenue This Year – $15,768,000
Comp Set Rooms Revenue Last Year – $59,130,000

Please answer the following questions:

1. Is the hotel getting its fair share of occupancy?
2. Did the property gain or lose RevPAR index ?
3. What room statistic drove the results?
4. Would you expect the property to be more or less profitable than last year?
5. What strategies should be employed to grow RevPAR index the following year?

Case #2:

The revenue manager of Hotel Calhawk, a hotel in the downtown area of a major market, has noticed that each year the Sunday, Monday, and Tuesday prior to Thanksgiving have the following problems:

- Guests cancel last minute
- Rooms with multiple beds sell out ahead of time
- Prices for single beds erode as the day of arrival approaches

Please answer the following questions:

1. What 3 different segments would you target to achieve success in occupancy and ADR over these dates?
2. What rate fences would you put in place to avoid the 3 problems that the revenue manager has faced?

INTERNET ACTIVITY

You are getting married and you are planning your honeymoon. Please shop for rates for a 1-bedroom suite with an ocean view for one resort.

Select one week (Saturday arrival for 7 nights) and compare rates on at least 5 websites and/or search engines, including the resort's website and TripAdvisor.com.

Please answer the following questions:

1. Is the resort's pricing and content consistent across all sources?
2. Were the reviews at TripAdvisor.com and various other sites similar?
3. Which provided the most information for the honeymoon couple?
4. What site would you prefer to book?
5. As a revenue manager, what did you learn and what did you take away from this assignment?

TEAM ACTIVITY

As a team, identify the high and low seasons for a hotel in your area. Contact local hotels, research when conventions are, and do a general search to see when hotel rates are highest and when they are lowest.

1. Pick two seasons as a team.
2. Identify your pricing, inventory, and segmentation strategy for each season. Tie in what you forecast the occupancy to be for that season and what the ADR would be for that time period.
3. Present to another team or the class your strategy as though they are the ownership group.

Be prepared to answer questions regarding:

- How will you limit high cost channels?
- If you are forecasting low occupancy, what strategies can you put in place or what can the hotel do to garner more occupancy?
- If you are forecasting high occupancy, how can you drive more average rate or shift your mix of business to capture more profit?

- What are you doing to take advantage of the different room types in each season?
- Why did you not choose to target particular segments and choose to target other segments?

GLOSSARY

Arrivals – amount of rooms set to arrive.

Brand.com – main reservation booking website for the hotel or chain.

Bundling – inclusion of additional services to a room offering.

Channel/source – platform or engine responsible for delivering a booking transaction. This could range from the hotel/brand call center, the hotel website, an online travel agency (OTA), a global distribution service (GDS), or the internal hotel sales team.

Channel management – where the sources of reservations are controlled for purposes of revenue and profit enhancement.

Citywide – event in the market that results in lodging demand adequate to fill the vast majority of all hotels

Commission – cost associated with booking a room where a percentage of revenue is due to the OTA or travel agent

Competitive benchmarking – Conducting an analysis to understand the position of a hotel against that of its competitors.

Competitive set (comp set) – a group of similar and directly competing lodging properties to which an individual hotel's operating performance is comparable and compete for the same business.

Cost of acquisition – fees, commissions, and expenses attributed to each booking from third party distributors or internal payroll including GDS commissions, OTA commissions, direct marketing expenses and all customer acquisition payroll.

Departures – amount of rooms that will or have checked out.

Early departures – rooms that are scheduled to depart on a later date but have checked out earlier than expected.

Fixed costs – costs maintained even if the hotel was empty.

House profit – the difference in the amount earned and the amount spent, or revenue minus operating cost.

LRA (last room availability) – a condition granted to special corporate accounts where the negotiated rate is automatically available if the hotel is selling standard inventory.

LOS (length of stay) – duration of a guest's stay beginning with arrival date. Revenue managers must manage revenue by adjusting strategies by arrival pattern as this is the control point.

Market segment – a subset of a customer group that can be easily identifiable by one or more common characteristics such as demographics, purpose of travel, and buying behavior.

No-shows – rooms that are scheduled to arrive but do not before a new date arrives.

OTA (online travel agent) – travel website allowing customers to plan and book travel.

Operations forecast – forecast utilized by operations leaders to appropriately staff the hotel.

Overbook – selling hotel rooms beyond the hotel's capacity.

Profit – total revenue minus costs.

Profit margin – percentage of profit out of total revenue.

Rate fences or segmentation hedges – restrictions put in place to change the price point offered to a guest. Fences consist of 5 basic forms: physical form, controlled availability, customer characteristics, transactions characteristics, or product line.

Rate parity –identical retail rate is quoted across all channels.

Retail rate / best available rate (BAR) - the rate a customer pays "off the shelf", often referred to as "best available"

Revenue cycle –the ability of a hotel to drive and optimize demand while maintaining guest satisfaction.

Revenue manager (RM) – The individual or team responsible for maximizing revenue within the constraints of available capacity and unconstrained demand through effective yield management.

RevPAR (revenue per available room) – Total rooms-related revenue per the number of available rooms in the hotel over a period of time: [rooms revenue / (rooms available * number of days)].

Rooms revenue – what a hotel receives for the sale of its rooms

Sales strategy meeting – revenue management strategy meeting consisting of all members of the revenue management committee

Segmentation/mix of sales – how revenue managers and marketers classify and target customers in specific groups based upon their characteristics, behaviors, and preferences.

SMERF – groups booked that fit into the following classifications: social, military, education, religious, and fraternal

Spoilage – each unsold room at the end of a period.

Stayovers – rooms that occupy the room overnight and for subsequent nights.

Unconstrained demand – total demand in a segment or overall in the absence of any constraints

Variable costs – expenses from labor and supplies to service the room after use, the expense of the utilities associated with the guest's occupancy, and a designated cash reserve toward a capital budget for replacing furniture, generally every 3–7 years, as part of a regularly scheduled refurbishment

Yield management – a variable pricing strategy, based on understanding, anticipating and influencing consumer behavior in order to maximize revenue or profits from a fixed, perishable resource (such as airline seats or hotel room reservations).

REFERENCES

Bodea, T. & Ferguson, M. (2014). *Segmentation, Revenue Management, and Pricing Analytics.* New York, NY: Routledge.

Cullen, K & Helsel, C. (2010). *The Evolving Dynamics of Revenue Management: A Comprehensive Revenue Optimization Road Map for Hotel Owners, Operators and Practitioners.* Maclean, VA: HSMAI Foundation.

Dolan, R. J. & Simon, H. (1997). *Power Pricing: How Managing Price Transforms the Bottom Line.* New York, NY: The Free Press.

Hayes, D. K. & Miller, A. (2011). *Revenue Management for Hospitality Industry.* Hoboken, NJ: John Wiley & Sons, Inc.

Hormby, S., Morrison, J., Dave, P., Meyers, M. & Tenca, T. (2010, January-February). Marriott International Increases Revenue by Implementing a Group Pricing Optimizer. *Interfaces, 40*(1), 47-57.

Kimes, S. E. (2010). *Strategic Pricing through Revenue Management.* Retrieved from Cornell University, School of Hospitality Administration site: http://scholarship.sha.cornell.edu/articles/346.

Lesure, J. D. (1983). Break-even analysis — a useful management tool in the lodging industry. *International Journal of Hospitality Management, 2*(3), 115-120.

Smith, T. J. (2012). *Pricing Strategy: Setting Price Levels, Managing Price Discounts, & Establishing Price Structures.* Mason, OH: South-Western Cengage Learning.

Tallury, K.T. & van Ryzin, G.J. (2004). *The Theory and Practice of Revenue Management.* New York, NY: Springer Science + Business Media.

CHAPTER 2

The Fundamentals of Pricing Hotel Guest Rooms

Raul Moronta and Carolyn Fredey

OVERVIEW

Hotel room pricing is one of the most complex areas of revenue management. At its core, the role of a revenue manager is to maximize a hotel's performance by selling rooms, profitably, better than the competitive set. These factors may include available inventory, projected hotel occupancy, competitors' pricing, and much more. Total hotel revenue maximization includes other revenue streams such as meeting space, food and beverage outlets, golf, spa, and gaming in some locations. In most cases the room revenue is the most profitable segment for the hotel; hence it tends to be one of the main focuses when determining the price of a room.

LEARNING OBJECTIVES

After studying this module, you should be able to:

- Describe the fundamentals that make it imperative to practice strategic hotel revenue management (HRM) and dynamic hotel rooms pricing (HRP)
- Evaluate a hotel's segmentation, or mix of customers, and assess each segment's desired experience and willingness to pay for each room's product
- Practice strategies to elevate a customer's perceived value
- Interpret price positioning for a hotel against a competitive set with similar brand, location, service, and product offerings

- Discuss the differences in pricing amongst the various segments and tactics that allow a hotel to maximize revenue while maintaining brand equity
- Assess the effectiveness of the retail pricing strategy with both metrics and tools, including a comprehensive segmentation analysis

OUTLINE

Introduction

Rooms Pricing Fundamentals

Value Creation

Retail Pricing Evaluation

- Setting Your Benchmark Rate

Pricing Tactics

Discussion Questions and Applications

SO WHAT?

Hotel room pricing and positioning are some of the most complex areas of the hospitality industry, which involve numerous factors.

How is the pricing of hotel rooms different from other industries?

- Why do hotel room rates change (often daily) versus other products that have more price stability?
- From a customer perspective, when do you think pricing volatility is helpful or hurtful? Has this changed over time and why?

INTRODUCTION

Hotel rooms pricing (HRP) requires detailed rate analysis, and the "art of pricing" has become far more sophisticated in recent years with increased technology and higher expectations from all stakeholders to "get the pricing right." Furthermore, in today's digital marketplace, with the advent of smartphones, mobile apps, and social media, pricing is more transparent to both the customer and the competitor. A pricing adjustment to a hotel's retail rate is only a piece in the pricing puzzle. Often, there does not seem to be a definitive solution, only a better and easier fit. Let us get busy in putting this together!

THINK HISTORICALLY

The original principles of hotel pricing are often attributed to the deregulation of the airline industry in 1978. This meant that the Civil Aeronautics Authority was no longer setting fares, which allowed for new competition to enter into the market as well as an increase in passengers. More specifically American Airlines was one of the pioneers of what at the time they called yield management, as stated on the 1987 annual report.

Since then, however, the competitive and distribution landscape has significantly changed. The Internet, new technology, and the rise of big data analytics (large quantities of consumer-related information used in strategic decision-making) have further enhanced the hospitality industry's ability to find the optimal pricing for hotels. Other worldwide events have also shaped revenue management practices and increase in distribution channels.

- How you think the evolution of the Internet has affected hotel distribution?
- What about the mobile revolution?

Source: Smith et al, 1992.

PRICING FUNDAMENTALS

Perishable products and services, such as hotels that utilize revenue management, will most likely have more dynamic pricing strategies than consumer products that can be stored and be sold at a later time. The hotel aims to sell every room, every night, at the maximum price possible, based on market conditions and property demand. Revenue managers must use different tactics based on some core pricing concepts, outlined below, to manage the rooms inventory as each individual stay date approaches.

Segmentation

Hotels offer a variety of rates to a variety of different groups or segments to ensure that a hotel has every chance to sell out on any given night. Hotels organize into three major buckets: transient, group, and contract. The transient bucket is the most complex, and rates are offered to attract both the business traveler segment and the more price-sensitive leisure travel segment. The revenue manager must not only determine the price of the retail rate (sometimes referred to as the BAR—best available rate) but must also evaluate the additional transient rates that are offered to attract other segments. Some of the rates offered are heavily discounted and may be yielded out during busy times. In addition, some of the segments may flex in price or discount and must be carefully maintained. We will discuss this in more detail in a later part of the chapter.

Variable Demand and Seasonality

In most cases, a hotel has fluctuating demand by day of week, time of year, and dates of holidays and special events, resulting in the need for variable pricing throughout the year. This can be forecasted with the hotel's historical booking data, and daily pricing and mix strategies can be set one year out. Most hotels utilize a demand forecasting system and validation process managed by the revenue manager to accurately predict the remaining **unconstrained demand** and determine when there is a surplus of rooms that warrant a price increase or need to filter out discounts. The pricing power for a hotel escalates when there is more remaining demand than **remaining supply** (rooms). For example, pricing over Tuesdays and Wednesdays is typically set higher than weekends for a hotel near a corporate office park. A family ski resort will offer higher rates during peak school vacations.

Figure 2.1: Levers to Increase Price

Booking Pace

The demand forecasting system and revenue manager will utilize booking pace trends and competitive pricing to predict **remaining demand** and pricing power as a stay date approaches. While a more generic strategy may be set one year out, as booking data materializes, adjustments are made constantly until the day of arrival. Booking pace can be defined as how fast rooms are being sold compared to a prior time period (i.e., same time last year, rolling average of the last 6 weeks, etc.). For example, if a hotel in the prior year had 90 out of the 100 rooms sold 5 days prior to arrival and the hotel sold out, then the hotel picked up 10 rooms in the last 5 days of booking. If this year the hotel has 92 rooms sold 5 days prior to arrival on a comparable stay date, it can be predicted that the hotel is "ahead of pace" and will sell out. The hotel will likely employ a pricing technique to maximize the additional property demand. In the opposite scenario, when the hotel has not sold as many rooms as in the past for a comparable time period, the revenue manager might have to use additional tactics to speed up the sale of those rooms as the hotel is "behind pace." This might include revising the price, opening discounts for specific customers, or utilizing opaque product strategies in order to stimulate demand and maximize revenue.

QUESTIONS TO CONSIDER

Revenue managers rely on the system's forecasted unconstrained transient demand to be accurate as calculations that compare remaining demand with remaining capacity drive its pricing recommendations. The system does require user input to identify outliers such as unusual weather or special events.

- What other outliers do you think would be difficult for a system to detect?
- What strategies, outside of price, could be utilized in very high or very low demand?
- In unusually high demand, do you think it is fair to price a product more than twice the average price? Why or why not? When can a high rate be considered price gouging?

VALUE CREATION

Economic Value

The expected price of a hotel room will vary greatly based on the property and market demand of the specific time frame requested by the customer, combined with the perceived experience that will be delivered. The concept of economic value can useful to illustrate the customer's willingness to pay for a hotel room. The total economic value is the reference price (best alternative offer) plus the net differential value of the specific product or service as illustrated in Figure 2.2.

Simply put, economic value is the sum of all the benefits and features that a product or service offers a customer. If a product offers a benefit or feature that is unique, the economic value is higher. In the case of a hotel room, the rate a prospective guest is willing to pay is based on the price of similar hotels and the perceived experience premium (or deficit) offered at a specific hotel. For example, in the case of a family resort, a pool with slides and other water features is worth more to a customer than a resort that does not offer this feature. The prospective guest searches for the best option based on the desired benefits and features that are offered for each similar hotel option. Then she or he will compare prices. At times, the price may be less or more than the perceived economic value. The traveler will choose the hotel that offers him personally the most economic value or utility for the price paid. Value can also be described as the relationship between total price and total experience.

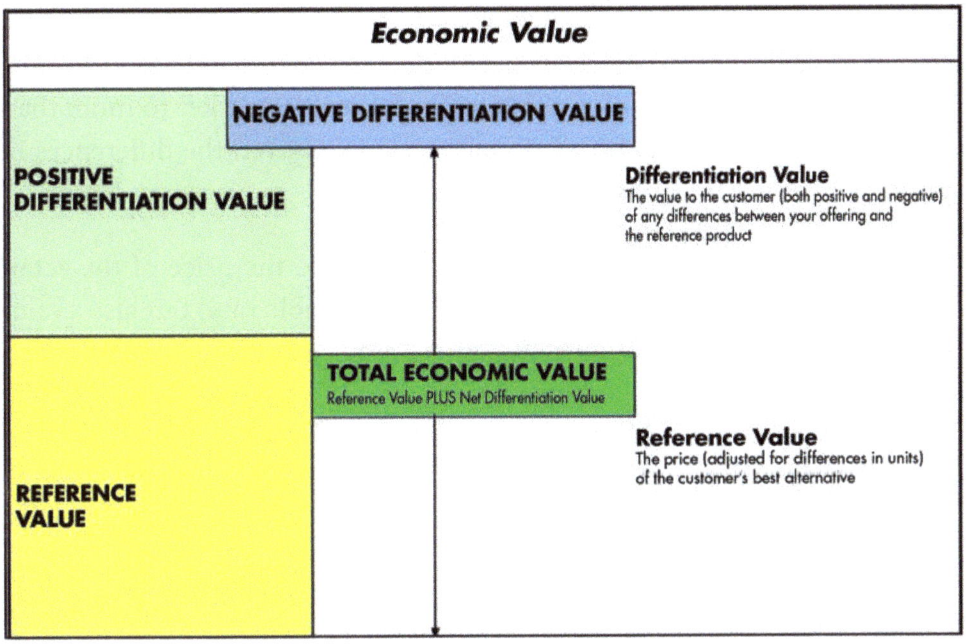

Figure 2.2: Economic Value.
Source: Nagel, et al., 2016, p20.

PROS & CONS

The role of a revenue manager is to maximize revenues for the hotel. This means that often times there will be conflicts with the sales team, who is very focused on meeting their selling goals and making sure their clients are happy. Also, the revenue managers can be in conflict with the front office team when they oversell the hotel or have very high rates that are not in line with the customer's experience or expectations.

- What do you think is the best way to balance these conflicting hotel priorities?
- Who is the most important customer—a repeat guest, the highest paying, or the most satisfied?
- How can regular sales strategy meetings involving Sales, Revenue Management, and Operations contribute to the process?

Segmentation

Segmentation is best described as the practice of dividing a market into smaller segments that share similar characteristics, such as buying behavior and the level of importance placed on attributes that make up a product and/or service. It is generally necessary for a hotel to market to more than one segment to fill all the hotel's rooms, especially given the differences in customers over weekday and weekend time frames.

The revenue manager must not only determine the price of the **retail rate** (sometimes referred to as the BAR (best available rate) but also evaluate the additional transient rates that are offered to attract other segments. Some of the rates offered are heavily discounted and may be yielded out during busy times. In addition, some of the segments may flex in price or discount and must be carefully maintained.

Segments

➤ Group

There are also negotiated rates for a group of rooms for a specific date and often non-repeating. These groups have different profiles, such as a corporate meeting, an association, family reunion, or a tour. Often these rooms also include meetings and events at the hotel with meals. Given that the client is spending additional dollars on other areas of the hotel and may require meeting rooms and audiovisual services, the price of the rooms tend to be negotiated based on the entire value of the event, day of the week, season, etc. Generally, pricing for group rooms is done through a combination of a set discount off the retail rate with consideration of transient displacement and the ancillary revenues and profits generated. Over the past few years some hotels have also transitioned to dynamic pricing, where the rate is set as a percentage off the rate of the day.

➤ Contract

The contract room segment mainly consists of airline crews that require a fixed number of rooms per night, 365 days a year. Generally, the segment is only relevant in hotels that are located near an airport. Determining the correct price for this segment is dependent on the arrival and departure times of the crew and the amount of transient displacement that will occur by taking the business. In addition, the segment is generally price sensitive and highly competitive as it provides occupancy throughout the year, including soft time frames. In most markets, there is a reciprocal agreement that either party can exit a contract with a 60-day notice period.

➤ Transient

◆ *Transient Sub-Segments*

■ *Retail*

The predominant segment in your hotel's mix is the portion of rooms that are purchased for general sale or "off the shelf." Rooms sold through the hotel's distribution **channels** for general sale are commonly referred to as the retail rate or best available rate (BAR). Both transient and leisure travelers will book into the retail segment. In this next section we will review the components of retail rate pricing and the process required to position your retail rate against your competitive set.

■ *Special Corporate*

These are negotiated rates between a business (such as banks, law firms, consulting firms, retailers, etc.) and hotels in order to accommodate the business's out-of-town employees and clients. These rates tend to be negotiated for a fixed priced for one year or for a seasonal period, though other contracting terms might also be negotiated, such as set percent discount off retail rate, number of blackout dates, provisions for upgraded rooms, and guaranteed inventory in case of tight availability in the market. Generally, the revenue manager will set thresholds for the amount of discount based on the volume commitment and stay pattern of the account. In most cases, the discounts range from 10 to 25 percent off retail.

■ *Government*

The number one producing segment in the United States is the US government. This segment cannot be overlooked and can be valuable in most markets, depending on the per diem established for a set geographical area. While the vast majority of government travelers will not pay a premium over the set per diem, the rate is yieldable and thus can be turned away during high demand time frames. Therefore, a hotel's mix of government can be higher over low demand times.

- *Wholesaler*

These are contracts similar to special corporate but are instead between a hotel and a travel merchandiser, commonly referred to as a wholesaler, and often the source is international arrival. While corporate rates are negotiated for the company's internal use, the wholesaler would resell these rooms to travelers and include other services, such as air, car rental, tours, etc. These wholesalers will often have a block or allotment of rooms guaranteed at the hotel for a period of time, and rates tend to be much lower than other contracted rates. In recent years, some of this business has been shifted to online travel agencies (OTAs), and the segment has declined with an increase in bookings on the Internet.

- *Packages*

Similar to wholesalers, hotels also utilize the room inventory and add other services to it in order to entice customers to book. In general hotel packages include other services offered by the hotel, such as meals, spa, and golf, but these packages can also include services outside of the hotel, such as theater tickets, museums, etc. Generally the most effective packages are priced less than all the components priced individually while still providing the hotel incremental sales and profit. For example, a resort may offer a spa package with the intent of driving sales into the spa. To increase conversion of a spa package, the hotel must price it as a value to the prospective guest. If the spa was busy all the time, it still may make sense to offer the spa package at a discount, but only if the resort was struggling with occupancy. In this scenario, the resort's strategy is to increase room sales, rather than spa sales.

- *Qualified Rates*

There are other public or private rates that are offered to guests based on specific memberships. The most common ones are AAA and AARP rates, in which the guest needs to be a member and offer proof of membership at time of check in. Other qualifying rates may include employee and friends & family rates, where the company offers to its associates a deep discount price and often offers "distressed inventory" when the hotel is not expected to sell every room for a particular date.

RETAIL PRICING EVALUATION

Setting Your Benchmark Rate

The predominant segment in your hotel's mix is the portion of rooms that are purchased for general sale or "off the shelf." Rooms sold through the hotel's distribution channels for general sale are commonly referred to as the retail rate or best available rate (BAR). In this next section we will review the components of retail rate pricing and the process required to position your retail rate against your competitive set.

The retail rate or best available rate is also referred to in this pricing module as the "benchmark rate" as it provides the foundation of your pricing strategy. It not only communicates to the customer the actual price point; it also is designed to represent the amount of experience that should be expected compared to other hotels in a similar location. Value is created for a customer when the benchmark rate is perceived as fair when evaluating it against the anticipated experience that the hotel will provide.

➤ Value Creation

The expected price of a hotel room will vary greatly based on the property and market demand of the specific time frame requested by the customer, combined with the perceived experience that will be delivered. The concept of economic value can be useful to illustrate the customer's willingness to pay for a hotel room. The total economic value is the reference price (best alternative offer) plus the net differential value of the specific product or service as illustrated in Figure 2.2.

Value creation occurs when services and products are combined and priced in a manner that increases the perceived economic value for a unique set of customers. In this process a business develops the mix of products and services that will drive the economic value. By satisfying AND communicating the value drivers better than the competition, a corporation can increase its price as it elevates the economic value.

➤ Positioning against the Competitive Set

Positioning against the competitive set is the process of evaluating a hotel's experience (the combination of product and services) against other similar properties and then determining the appropriate rate premium or discount that will create economic value for a specific segment. In the graph shown in Figure 2.3, Hyatt (Comp 3) shows more value against the subject hotel as it is offering the same rate for more experience. The Hilton (Comp 2) shows the least amount of value as it has a higher room rate and provides less experience.

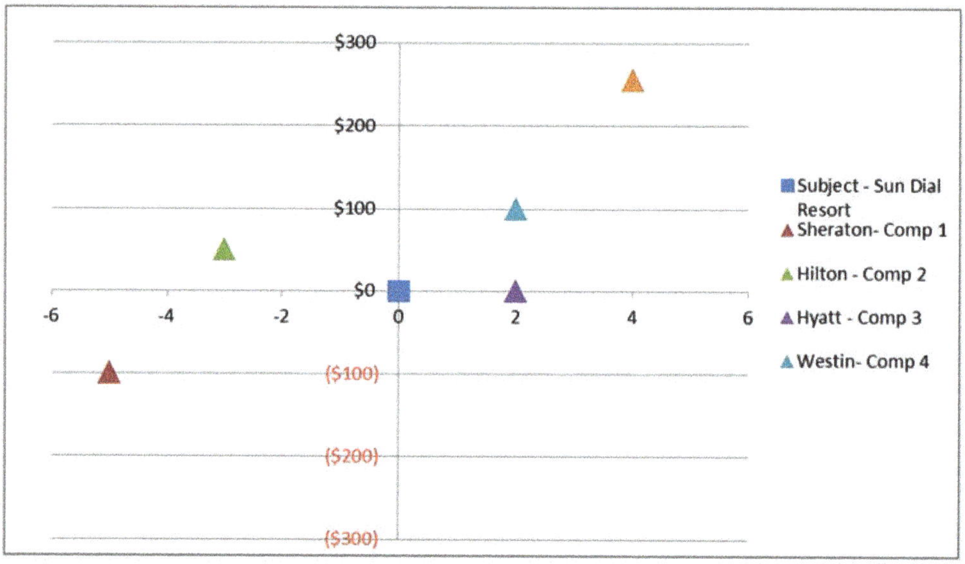

Figure 2.3: Competitive Pricing Analysis.

QUESTIONS TO CONSIDER

- Does the comp set seem reasonable? Are there any hotels that do not seem to belong with the group? Why or why not?
- Is the subject hotel priced appropriately? Are there any hotels that offer more value?
- How can you increase the value for price paid based on the chart data?
- What hotel investments do you recommend if financially feasible?
- Which hotel seems to be a threat to capturing more guests based on current positioning?

If the Hyatt is formidable and competes head on with the subject hotel, the subject hotel should consider positioning its price point lower or adding services or enhanced product offerings. This process can be completed by following the steps in Figure 2.4.

Price Positioning Process	
Step 1	Determine hotel's most critical segments. A hotel in a city center may choose leisure, business, and corporate group
Step 2	Select a competitive set (up to five) for each segment by asking guests and clients for feedback
Step 3	Pinpoint value drivers for each segment (which service and product offers matter the most)
Step 4	Evaluate subject hotel's experience level for each value driver
Step 5	Mark each of the subject hotel's experience score as ZERO for each value driver
Step 6	Evaluate comp set's relative experience level against the subject hotels (better or worse), range of 1-3
Step 7	Shop hotel and comp set and record the most frequently quoted rates for a specific season
Step 8	Mark price for subject hotel as ZERO and mark the competitors as the difference from the subject hotel
Step 9	Graph the experienc e differentaila scores on the X axis
Step 10	Graph the room rate diff erentials on the Y axis

Figure 2.4: Price Positioning Process

SPREADSHEET EXERCISE 2.1

TO DO: Review the pricing and experience of a hotel and its competitive set. Prior to analysis, select a specific market segment, such as family leisure or individual business traveler. Select any hotel that caters to the market you selected and determine its comp set utilizing shop data from various sources. Choose attributes that contribute to the desired experience for the market segment. Utilize the Internet for your research. Examine pricing, photos, descriptions, reviews, and service ratings. Utilize the Excel positioning tool to chart your results.

Answer the following questions:

1. Does the comp set seem reasonable? Are there any hotels that do not seem to belong with the group? Why or why not?
2. Is the subject hotel priced appropriately? Are there any hotels that offer more value?
3. How can you increase the value for price paid based on the chart data?
4. What hotel investments do you recommend if financially feasible?
5. What hotel seems to be a threat to capturing more guests based on current positioning?

➤ Pricing Level

While a hotel's published rack rate (a fixed price for the year or per season) is the highest rate the hotel can *legally* charge for a room to a guest (and in some states, it is required to be posted on the back of the door of each room), in practice the pricing strategy is far more fluid. The BAR rate is initially set based on competitive positioning and season but then is increased or decreased on an individual date basis depending on the demand.

Pricing changes on a daily basis, in some cases, by the hour, as revenue managers would update this price point based on a combination of factors, such as projected hotel occupancy, remaining capacity, competitor's pricing and availability, changes in price elasticity, and booking window. On a weekly basis, the hotel should meet and discuss the demand and pricing for the next 90 days and make strategic changes accordingly.

➤ Sample Pricing Review Critical Points

Timeframe	Review	Format
Daily	Daily Pick-Up	Review pick up trends and competitor pricing trends with focus on next 4 weeks
Weekly	Weekly Pick-Up	Lead hotel's pricing review meeting and examine next 90 days
Monthly	Projections Review	Analyze projection changes and shortfall for next 6 months and adjust pricing
Annual	Budget Process	Revenue Manager reviews segment pricing for annual budget and business plan

Figure 2.5: Sample Pricing Review: Critical Points.

➤ Rooms Mix

Most hotels have a selection of room types to accommodate the different needs of its customers. Having the right rooms mix can be crucial in ensuring the hotel is successful. For example, without rooms that can accommodate four people, the hotel will have a difficult time attracting families and filling up during leisure periods. For a luxury hotel, having premium suites is necessary to attract the affluent traveler. However, pricing multiple room types can be cumbersome and tedious depending on the systems and the process. Generally, the easiest and most effective way is to keep it simple. Designating a fixed or percent price differential from the standard room can be effective and relatively easy to implement (see Table 2.1).

In this manner, the revenue manager can adjust the benchmark rate (BAR), and then the other room types can be automatically adjusted. In today's environment, with the capability of complex data analysis, the fixed or percent differentials can be tweaked based on demand and seasonal patterns. In addition, the revenue manager can utilize room mix to yield out less profitable business when demand warrants pushing for premium room sales. Often, special corporate accounts will have **last room availability (LRA)** only for the lower/standard rooms. When the revenue manager restricts the sale of standard rooms, the special corporate accounts will be forced to purchase a premium room either at a higher negotiated rate or at retail rate (See Figure 2.6).

Table 2.1: Segmentation Mixes

	Segmentation - Rooms	
Transient:	**Rooms**	**Transient Mix**
Premium Retail	6,205	5%
Standard Retail	24,820	20%
eChannel Retail	12,410	10%
Special Corporate	18,615	15%
Government	12,410	10%
Wholesaler	6,205	5%
Other Discount	43,435	35%
Total Transient Rooms	124,100	100%
Segmentation - Rooms		
Transient:	**Rate**	**Revenue**
Premium Retail	$650	$4,033,250
Standard Retail	$500	$12,410,000
eChannel Retail	$440	$5,460,400
Special Corporate	$375	$6,980,625
Government	$212	$2,630,920
Wholesaler	$300	$1,861,500
Other Discount	$200	$8,687,000
Total Transient Rate	$339	$42,063,695

Seasonal Pricing Chart	start date	end date	Low BAR	Med BAR	High BAR	Super High BAR
Low Season	1/1/2018	3/1/2018	$245	$295	$325	$395
High	3/2/2018	6/23/2018	$295	$395	$425	$495
Moderate	6/24/2018	9/4/2018	$265	$325	$350	$425
Peak	9/5/2018	12/31/2018	$325	$425	$450	$545

Special Events	Low BAR	Med BAR	High BAR	Super High BAR
New Year's Eve	$550	$650	$750	$895
	$0	$0	$0	$0
	$0	$0	$0	$0
	$0	$0	$0	$0

Room Types	Number Rooms		
Standard (BAR)	700		
Corner King	30	$50	Supplement
Junior Suite	16	$100	Supplement
1 Bedroom Suite	8	$200	Supplement
2 Bedroom Suite	2	$400	Supplement
Presidential Suite	1	$2,500	Fixed

Figure 2.6: Seasonal Pricing Chart

PRICING TACTICS

- ***Static versus Dynamic Pricing***

Hotels can implement *static pricing*, or "fixed" pricing, for any segment for consistency and ease of operation. For example, the retail room rate may be set at one price point and changed infrequently. Or in another segment, such as special corporate, a static rate may be contracted and the business travelers would obtain the same rate every night of the year, regardless of the BAR rate. The trend, however, is increasingly moving towards *dynamic pricing* for all segments. In this case, the retail rate of a hotel generally would change more frequently with a large standard deviation across all dates of any given year. Another dimension of dynamic pricing is "floating" pricing. In this scenario, a room rate such as a qualified discount or special corporate account is set up as a percent discount off the BAR rate. Figure 2.7 shows an example of floating pricing.

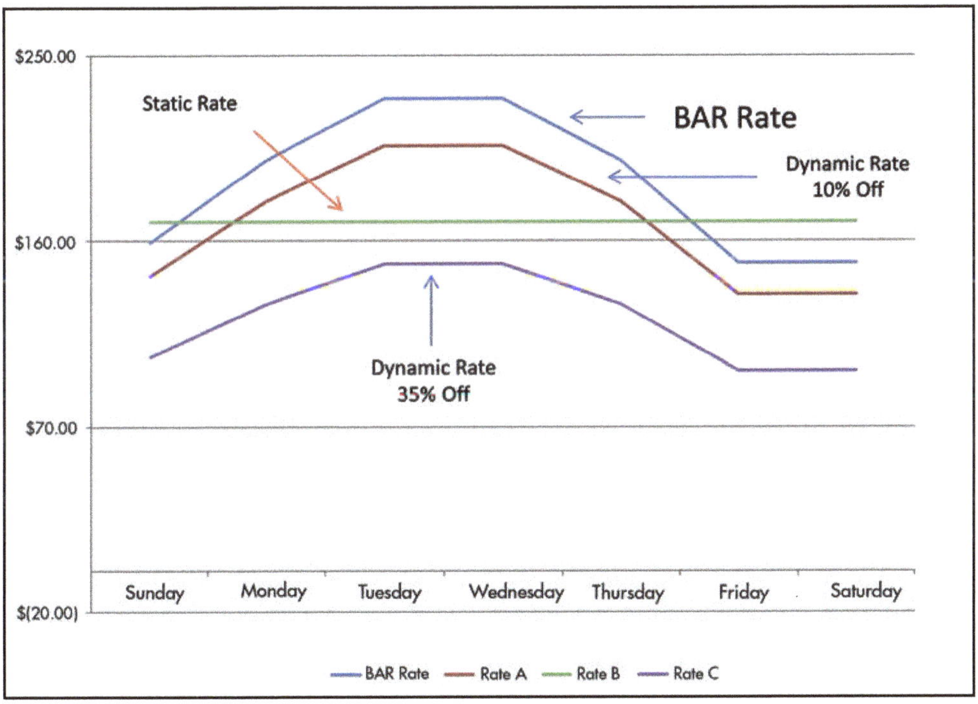

Figure 2.7: Floating Prices Example.

- **Static rates:** While room rates may change from time to time and by season, there are some rates that are guaranteed for a period of time, known as static rates. This means that regardless of when the customer is making the reservation, the rate would be the same, provided there is a room available to accommodate the guest. These rates can be either pre-negotiated (such as corporate, wholesaler, or group rates) or determined by other entities, such as government rates that are determined by the government based on average cost of hotel rooms in each county. Other examples of predetermined rates are branded discounts such as employee rates or other hotel special discounts.

- **Dynamic pricing:** More often than not, hotel rates vary by season, day of week, or even by the hour, depending on multiple factors, known as dynamic pricing, in which the hotel establishes the best available rate for the day. This BAR serves as a benchmark on which other rates are based. For example AAA rates are usually set up as 10 percent off the rate of the day, which means AAA members are guaranteed a specific discount on the rate rather than a fixed price. This dynamic pricing model has gained more popularity for both hotels and corporate partners so that some corporate accounts are now also based on a percentage basis of the rate of the day. In this scenario, the client is able to take advantage of discounted rates when the hotel prices the rooms below the negotiated agreement.

SEEING FURTHER

Dynamic pricing is a concept that has become a more common practice in recent years, especially in some markets where high demand has pushed revenue managers to think creatively.

- How do you think this practice will affect a hotel in low demand with a highly price competitive environment?
- Who benefits the most on high versus low demand?
- With increased price transparency in all channels, does decreasing the rate often lead to an increase in sales and profits for a single hotel? Why or why not?

- ***Differential Pricing through Booking Parameters***

The booking window for a hotel varies widely by location, property type, seasonality, etc. Resort and leisure destinations tend to get bookings further ahead than other non-resort locations because leisure customers plan their vacations further ahead than, say, a corporate customer. Leisure customers tend to book rooms outside of 30 days as this is often done in conjunction with air travel. Corporate customers, on the other hand, tend to book inside of 21 days as their travel plans tend to change constantly based on their business needs. Understanding the booking cycle for each market segment is extremely critical as these segments do not pay the same rates or have the same tolerance for increase in pricing.

Advanced sales are a pricing modality that has been around for a long time and is very common in the hospitality industry. Often hotels use additional discounted pricing in order to attract early bookers at traditionally higher rates than what they would otherwise sell rooms for to other contracted business, corporate accounts, and wholesalers. In this case, the hotels would offer a discount on their current public retail pricing (i.e., 10 to 30 percent off) for early bookings outside of the traditional booking window, for example, more than 21 or 30 days in advance. The tradeoff, however, is that the customer often would have to pay for the room in advance and may not be able to make any changes to the reservation after completing the booking process.

- ***Transparent versus Opaque Pricing***

Unlike the prior modality to sell rooms early as a discount on the public pricing, this concept is designed to sell rooms at a much lower pricing, however, through channels that allow for the rate not to be publicly displayed as such. The reason for this is because hotels would want to preserve their public pricing but still have unused inventory that they would want to sell. There are various ways the hotels can do this. Websites such as Hotwire are perfect examples of this practice, wherein the name of hotel is only disclosed after the guest has completed the booking process; therefore, the hotel is opaque and allows the hotel to maintain pricing integrity among other channels. This practice is also geared toward the shorter booking window, traditionally less than 3 days to arrival. Hotel rooms are perishable in that each room that is not sold on a particular day represents lost revenue opportunities. So, our goal is to sell each room at the highest revenue before the end of the day (See Figure 2.8).

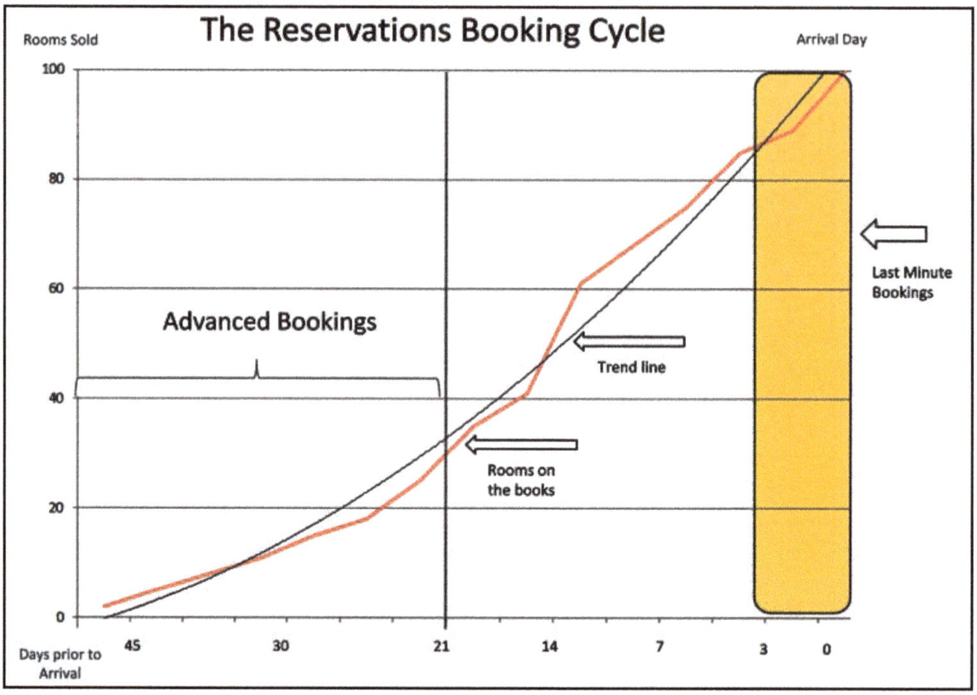

Figure 2.8: The Reservations Booking Cycle.

- ***Rate Parity and Channel Distribution***

In the US most hotel companies have "Best Rate Guarantee" or "Look No Further" policies, which highlight the company's commitment to maintaining the best (or equal) price on their website since the channel of distribution is much lower as opposed to a third-party website that often includes a commission to be paid to the OTA for the booking transaction. These policies may have consequences for the individual hotels that violate the policy, knowingly or not. When a guest finds a lower rate on a different website other than the company's own website, the guest is able to obtain benefits such as discount on the rate they found on the site, points toward the company rewards program, or other concessions. In addition, the hotel may have to pay the company additional penalty fees for guest recovery and/or for violating the policy. These policies are in place to discourage hotels from engaging in exclusive deals with online travel partners outside of a brand master agreement. It is important to highlight that some European countries, such as France, have recently enacted laws preventing the rate parity clauses that make it okay for brands to offer rates lower than on the OTA sites.

- ***Evaluating Pricing Effectiveness***

Pricing the retail rate at the right price point is not 100 percent scientific, and therefore, measuring the pricing effectiveness can also sometimes be somewhat nebulous. However, there are some industry norms that can directionally infer if the pricing strategy is sound and profitable. Certainly, healthy market share, with a premium in both occupancy and rate, can be indicative of proper price positioning. In addition, as the retail rate is the foundation of many segments in a hotel's transient mix, success also can be inferred with a strong non-qualified mix. What percentage of transient rooms did the hotel sell at retail/BAR? If a hotel is overpriced, it is assumed that the conversion will be low and the hotel will have to sell more discounts to fill the hotel.

Related to that is the rate efficiency metric that compares the overall transient average daily rate (ADR) with the retail ADR. If a hotel sells a lot of discounts, it can be assumed that the rate efficiency would be lower than optimal. Certainly, as the primary objective is to drive room sales, evaluating overall retail revenue can be relevant. All of these are more meaningful when expressed in comparison to prior year, budget, or last month. As size of hotel, type of hotel, and location of hotel can all yield different optimal metrics, often the trend of its own performance and goals is the only relevant indication. The important lesson is that to drive RevPAR, a revenue manager must balance both occupancy and ADR. Raising retail rates across the board is not the method to drive ADR. In fact, in some cases, lowering the retail rate can grow the non-qualified mix and, thus, overall transient ADR, given that generally the retail rate is the highest rated segment.

Pricing Effectiveness Calculations

Non-Qualified Transient Revenue = Revenue of all Retail Transient Rated Rooms Sold

Non-Qualified Mix = Total Retail Rated Transient Room/Total Transient Rooms

Retail ADR – Revenue of All Retail Transient Rooms/Total Retail Transient Rooms Sold

Rate Efficiency = Total Transient ADR/ Retail ADR

Individual Exercise:

Please refer to the segmentation (Table 2.1) and calculate each Pricing Metric.

- Do you think the hotel is priced effectively? Why?
- What additional analysis may be required? What data is missing for evaluation?

- ***Price Sensitivity***

Price sensitivity can also be referred to as the customer's reaction to pricing changes. In general, a revenue manager's role is to maximize revenues for the hotel, which often comes with a bias for higher prices. On the other hand, guests would favor lower rates or a perceived high value for the price paid. However, not all guests have the same price sensitivity. Consider this: a family of four going to visit friends for a weekend might choose the hotel based on the lowest rate available in the area even if they have to drive a bit more since they are paying for their room themselves. A business traveler, on the other hand, might choose the hotel for its proximity to the office or to his clients, and since the company will eventually reimburse travel expenses, the price of the room is less relevant to the traveler making the decision to book. Now consider what would happen if the hotel decided to increase the rates by $10–$20 for the same room the same day. What is the likelihood that the family would continue shopping for a cheaper room or that the business traveler would book the same room?

Similar to the examples above, each guest, market segment, and time frame has a different tolerance for price increases. In general, the higher the rate, the more likelihood that the guest would not book the room. Revenue managers often test these reactions to rate changes through price testing in that the rates are increased or decreased at different times of the booking cycle in order to figure out customer behavior. The percentage of customers booking versus not is often referred to as the conversion ratio, or the number of guests that were converted to sales as opposed to no sales.

Another factor in price sensitivity and conversion is availability. As referred to before, hotels often price their rooms based on their competitors. While higher prices tend to have a negative reaction to conversion ratios, this also depends on the available inventory. In periods of high demand, such as conventions in town, sporting events, graduation weekends, etc., the dynamic between supply and demand chain changes, which means there are more guests who want to stay in the area than there are hotel rooms available. In this case increase in demand would cause hotel room rates to temporarily increase for this time period. This also means that guests would be competing with each other for the available rooms. Those willing to pay more and book early would be able to reserve the rooms.

SPREADSHEET EXERCISE 2.2

TO DO: Your ownership has asked you to increase revenues and profit by at least 5 percent for the following year. Based on pricing principles in this chapter and price sensitivity for different market segments, you will have the opportunity to make strategic changes to rates or increase production to key market segments. Find the best combination of strategic changes to achieve the best possible profitable outcome.

Exercise: On the next tab, you will see different market segments. Columns F & G will allow you to make strategic changes for specific market segments. Corporate Accounts & Social Meetings will allow changing production through the sales efforts, positive or negative. For RACK, Opaque, and Corporate Meetings, you will be able to change rates up or down. As you make strategic changes, you will notice it will have an effect on either the production or the rate for each segment.

Notes: The changes also take into consideration fixed versus dynamic rates based on real-life practice. There are some market segments that have a relationship to each other, such as the BAR rate will also impact Brand.com, OTA, and packages. Other market segments might have a relationship on production, whereby increasing one, they would also decrease the other based on available inventory.

Goal: Your goal is to find the optimal combination of rate changes (positive or negative) as well as production between the market segments. Once you find the optimal revenue and profit growth, make a summary of your decisions and the rationale behind your decisions...

- ***Computer-Generated Sensitivity Models***

As you can see, the explosion of big data and the proliferation of different channels of distribution make these computer-generated models more and more common each day. Over the past few years the modern revenue manager has evolved and is quickly transitioning into a strategic statistician. However, at the same time, it becomes more important to place more emphasis on interpreting the information and acting upon the demand of their market, rather than only gathering facts and reporting against them.

Given the complexity of the retail pricing, over the past few years there has been a proliferation of computer-generated pricing models that have been created to assist a revenue manager in determining the optimal pricing for the hotel. Most of these pricing models are built into more elaborate revenue management systems since they integrate hotel demand, historical performance, available inventory, etc. One of the most commonly used systems is Duetto, which is an independent revenue strategy system that focuses on independent and small brands and which connects to the central reservation system (CRS) or property management system (PMS). Major hotel brands also utilize these pricing models that have been developed specifically to work with their systems and have been embedded to other existing tools.

REAL PEOPLE

Calvin Anderson is the Vice President of Managed Services for Duetto, and he explains that these sophisticated pricing response models are designed by providing a statistically relevant formula for determining optimal pricing at hotels and involves a vast amount of calculations that a human brain might not be able to compute as effectively and in the time required to make an impact. Duetto, in particular, is built on an open pricing model that focuses on the principle that all channels should be open and flowing at all times. This means there are no capacity restraints on any channel, but rather the pricing, room type, or the length of stay is adjusted based on the elasticity and demand for that specific channel or market segment, said Anderson.

Duetto also uses other nontraditional sources of data to determine the optimal price point, such as weather forecast, flight and train forward-looking aggregate data, reviews and reputation scores from different websites, as well as competitor pricing from online travel agent sites. The seamless integration of all these data points allows the system to suggest price positioning where the revenue manager can trust and push out the recommendation or make overrides to the recommended strategy. Another key to their success is their business analytics platform, which provides the revenue manager with the transparency on how and why the system is making recommendations. This allows the revenue manager to look at all the facts and make an informed decision, which improves their efficiency.

Question 1:

While the system-generated forecast is sophisticated, are there any instances that may require user intervention? What market or property data may be hard for the system to recognize?

Question 2:

Describe how an unexpected increase in the confirmed group forecast may impact the total hotel rooms forecast. What processes should be evaluated to minimize the frequency or large variances?.

DISCUSSION QUESTIONS

Question 1: How is value created? Think of a specific hotel or restaurant that you have experienced. How could it add more value for you? Do you think your list of enhancements would be the same for your mother or father? Why?

Question 2: Describe two distinct market segments and describe any differences in buying behavior.

Question 3: Assume you are the opening revenue manager for a new resort. List the steps that you would take to define a comp set and determine its benchmark rate.

Question 4: If a hotel has more demand than supply for a given time frame, what pricing strategies can be considered to increase profits?

TEAM ACTIVITY

NEW BUILD HOTEL—The Courtyard by Marriott Brand

Courtyard by Marriott is one of the most successful lodging brands in the hotel industry. It offers an affordable price for a mix of products and services that cater to the business traveler "road warrior." So who thought of the concept?

Marriott International actually used conjoint analysis to determine which offerings would provide the biggest bang for its buck for this new brand. The process involves consumers expressing satisfaction levels for numerous combinations of offerings or "profiles" at different price points. The process allows the marketing research analyst to identify that services and features are worth the most to the customer. In the case of Courtyard, the exercise was so successful that the brand is often referred to a as "the hotel designed by the business traveler."

As a group, discuss a new product or service that would cater to students on campus.

Brainstorm on the different attributes (or features) that may increase the preference of the product or service, understanding that it is likely that you cannot include all of them.

Without research, ask each other the following questions:

1. What features do you think are most important to the student?
2. What price range do you think is appropriate to capture the most sales and profit?

Generate five different combinations of attributes at three different price points (for a total of 15 profiles).

Send out a survey to at least 25 students that asks him or her to rate each profile (1 lowest, 7 highest).

Analyze the results and ask the following questions:

1. What features are most important for the students? Does this match up with your hypothesis prior to research?
2. Is there price sensitivity for any of the features?

3. Are you certain that you have identified the correct profiles? Why not?
4. What will your product or service include and what price will you charge?

Source: Wind et al., 1989.

INTERNET ACTIVITY

Select an upcoming high demand date in your city, such as a graduation weekend, citywide conference, sports event, or celebration. Now select 3 hotels near the event and shop their rates for 1-, 2-, and 3-night stays during their peak dates. Now do the same exercise for the date one month after the event and compare the rates.

- Is there a significant difference in rates between the two dates?
- How much premium has the hotel applied for these high demand dates?
- Why do you think that is?
- Are there any other dates you can think of that would apply to these concepts?

APPLICATIONS

Case 1

Examine the spreadsheet represented below to answer the following questions:

1. Are there trends in the data by day of week?
2. What price increases would you recommend for the revenue manager to implement immediately?

Hotel Capacity		**295**			
Date	**DOW**	**Projected Occupancy**	**Rooms on the Books**	**Rooms Left to Sell**	**Remaining Demand**
May 1	Sunday	72%	175	120	40
May 2	Monday	92%	225	70	50
May 3	Tuesday	98%	250	45	75
May 4	Wednesday	98%	275	20	75
May 5	Thursday	92%	225	70	45
May 6	Friday	86%	200	95	55
May 7	Saturday	98%	225	70	75
May 8	Sunday	80%	175	120	65

Hotel Capacity		295			
Date	**DOW**	**Projected Occupancy**	**Rooms on the Books**	**Rooms Left to Sell**	**Remaining Demand**
May 9	Monday	92%	175	120	100
May 10	Tuesday	98%	200	95	135
May 11	Wednesday	98%	225	70	115
May 12	Thursday	82%	175	120	70
May 13	Friday	80%	145	150	94
May 14	Saturday	98%	195	100	124

Case 2

Examine the spreadsheet represented below to answer the following questions:

1. Is the subject hotel being consistent on its pricing strategies weekday vs weekend?
2. Competitors A & B show the same differential weekday vs weekend. What are the advantages and disadvantages of this strategy?
3. What recommendations might you have for the focus hotel to implement moving forward regarding its pricing differential?

WEEKDAY	**Traditional Standard**	**Premium View**	**Premium Suite**	**View Differential View vs Standard**	**Suite Differential Suite vs Standard**
Focus Hotel	$ 100.00	$ 125.00	$ 140.00	$ 25.00	$ 40.00
Competitor A	$ 120.00	$ 145.00	$ 175.00	$ 25.00	$ 55.00
Competitor B	$ 110.00	$ 120.00	$ 150.00	$ 10.00	$ 40.00
Competitor C	$ 115.00	$ 135.00	$ 190.00	$ 20.00	$ 75.00
Competitor D	$ 125.00	$ 150.00	$ 185.00	$ 25.00	$ 60.00
Average	**$ 114.00**	**$ 135.00**	**$ 168.00**	**$ 21.00**	**$ 54.00**
WEEKEND					
Focus Hotel	$ 95.00	$ 120.00	$ 130.00	$ 25.00	$ 35.00
Competitor A	$ 119.00	$ 144.00	$ 174.00	$ 25.00	$ 55.00
Competitor B	$ 89.00	$ 99.00	$ 129.00	$ 10.00	$ 40.00
Competitor C	$ 109.00	$ 119.00	$ 159.00	$ 10.00	$ 50.00
Competitor D	$ 99.00	$ 119.00	$ 149.00	$ 20.00	$ 50.00
Average	**$ 102.20**	**$ 120.20**	**$ 148.20**	**$ 18.00**	**$ 46.00**

GLOSSARY

Brand.com – The main reservation booking website for the hotel or chain.

Channel/source – Platform or engine responsible for delivering a booking transaction. This could range from the hotel/brand call center, the hotel website, an online travel agency (OTA), a global distribution service (GDS), or the internal hotel sales team.

Competitive set (comp set) – A group of similar and directly competing lodging properties to which an individual hotel's operating performance is comparable and compete for the same business.

Last room availability (LRA) – A condition granted to special corporate accounts in which their negotiated rate is automatically available if the hotel is selling standard inventory.

Rate parity – The identical retail rate is quoted across all channels.

Remaining demand – Number of rooms the hotel can expect to sell with unlimited physical capacity.

Remaining supply – Number of rooms available for sale.

Retail rate/best available rate (BAR) – The rate a customer pays "off the shelf," often referred to as "best available."

Unconstrained demand – Total demand in a segment or overall in the absence of any constraints.

REFERENCES

Belobaba, P.P. (1987, May). Airline yield management: An overview of seat inventory control. *Transportation Science, 21* (2), 63-73.

Cross, R.G. (1997). *Revenue Management: Hard-Core Tactics for Market Domination.* New York, NY: Broadway Books.

Cross, R.G., Higbie, J.A., & Cross, D.Q. (2009, February). Revenue management's renaissance: A rebirth of the art and science of profitable revenue generation. *Cornell Hospitality Quarterly, 50* (1), 56-81.

Haley, M. & Inge, J. (2004, Fall) Revenue Management: It really should be called profit management. *Hospitality Upgrade.* Retrieved from https://ishc.com/wp-content/uploads/art_rm04.pdf

Hayes, D.K. & Miller, A.A. (2011). *Revenue Management for the Hospitality Industry.* Hoboken, NJ: John Wiley & Sons, Inc.

Kimes, S.E. & Chase, R.B. (1998). The strategic levers of yield management. *Journal of Service Research, 1* (2), 156-166.

Nagel, T.T., Hogan, J.E., & Zale, J. (2016). *The Strategy and Tactics of Pricing, A Guide to Growing More Profitably* (6th ed.). New York, NY: Routledge.

Smith, B.C., Leimkuhler, J.F. & Darrow, R.M. (1992, January/February). Yield Management at American Airlines. *Interfaces, 22*(1), 8-31.

Wind, J, Green, P.E., Shifflet, D. & Scarbrough, M. (1989, February). Courtyard by Marriott: Designing a Hotel Facility with Consumer- Based Marketing Models. *Interfaces 19*(1), 25-47.

CHAPTER 3

Evolving Hotel Segmentation

Roy Madhok and Theresa Doherty

OVERVIEW

Establishing segmentation strategy allows revenue managers to define and optimize the composition of travelers coming to the hotel. Revenue managers must understand their hotel's mix of business as well as the competition's mix of business. They must also understand the role and profitability of all distribution channels in the hotel's revenue strategy. This module also investigates the current and future trends in hotel segmentation.

LEARNING OBJECTIVES

After studying this module, you should be able to:

- Define major segments used by hotels
- Outline the progression and future of segmentation
- Explain the role of fencing discounts
- Rank segments by their price sensitivity
- Determine profitability of different segments
- Identify the importance of group, contract, and special corporate evaluation
- Analyze a hotel's mix of business

OUTLINE

Evolving Hotel Segmentation

- Defining Segmentation
- Evolution of Segmentation
- Littlewood's Rule

Fencing Segments

- Methods of Fencing Segmentation
- Ethical Issues with Fencing
- Varying Levels of Price Sensitivity
- Profitability within Segments

Contract Segment

- Special Corporate/Negotiated Segment
- Analyzing Mix of Sales

Discussion Questions and Applications

EVOLVING HOTEL SEGMENTATION

Defining Segmentation

Market **segmentation** or **mix of sales** is inherently a marketing function, wherein marketers classify and target customers in specific groups based upon their characteristics, behaviors, and preferences (Tallury & van Ryzin, 2004). For market segmentation to exist, it needs to be clear that the market for the product is not homogeneous, that the market can be divided into groups, and that not all customers for the product are the same (McDonald & Dunbar, 2012).

Revenue managers go to great lengths to accurately segment or categorize their customer base. More importantly, market segmentation allows hotels to lower the purchase price for particular guests and also helps revenue managers identify which groups of consumers are worth targeting at different times. In Figure 3.1 below, you can see that offering one price point is simple, but having multiple segments allows revenue managers to offer rates at differing levels, therefore increasing occupancy because of lower paying guests, increasing ADR (average daily rate) because of capturing guests that would pay more, and therefore increasing overall revenue and profit.

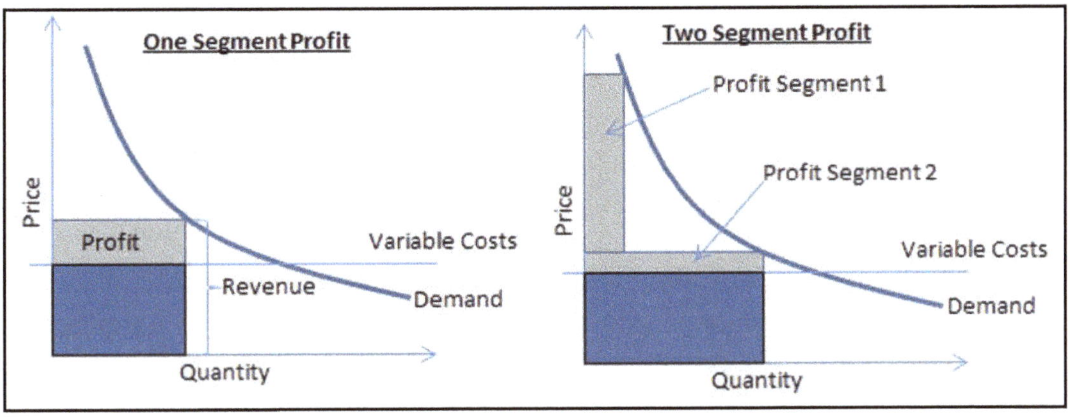

Figure 3.1: One-Segment Profit versus Two-Segment Profit.

SO WHAT?

- What are the benefits of offering different price points to different guests? Why would it be a bad idea to offer one price point to all guests?

EVOLUTION OF SEGMENTATION

In 1956, Wendell R. Smith published an article introducing the idea of market segmentation for all industries. Smith argued that the current marketing method of **product differentiation**, where marketers would modify or add supply/products to better adapt to demand, was only enough to skim the surface of how much of the market could be penetrated. Smith made the claim that expanding the number of consumers for a product would produce depth of "market position in the segments that are effectively defined and penetrated," or market penetration (Smith, 1956).

THINK HISTORICALLY

In 1956, most industries that used market segmentation strategies did not realize that they were in fact utilizing market segmentation. J. W. "Bill" Marriott, the founder of Marriott International, was working at his family's hotel in 1957, the Twin Bridges Motor Hotel, later known as the Twin Bridges Marriott. He sold his hotel rooms from a drive-up window and charged extra for each additional guest in each room. If his hotel was going to sell out, he would assess which cars had the most guests and then proceeded to turn away cars with one guest (Kotler, Bowen, & Makens, 2010).

Bill Marriott was using segmentation by understanding that turning away his lowest-rated segment, one occupant, would allow him to gain more revenue for the night.

Question:

- List other ways that segmentation has been put to use in various industries.

The official advent of segmentation in the travel industry was in 1972 when Ken Littlewood of British Overseas Airways Corporation created Littlewood's rule, arguably the first revenue management model.

Littlewood's rule stipulated that a discounted segment should only be accepted if the revenue from the discounted segment would exceed the expected revenue of future bookings from the higher-rated segment (McGill, 1999).

LITTLEWOOD'S RULE

Accept a discount reservation if:
$S_2 \geq S_1 \times \text{Probability}(D_1 > x)$
S1: High-rated segment
S2: Low-rated segment
D1: Demand for high-rated segment
X: Remaining inventory to sell

Littlewood's rule shows that a hotel should accept a low-rated segment if the expected revenue from a higher-rated segment would be less than if the hotel were to keep the lower-rated segment open.

Littlewood's rule is still in use today; as the question of "do we want to take this piece of business?" still comes up when evaluating whether to accept a discount segment, channel, or group over a particular set of dates.

QUESTIONS TO CONSIDER

How would you measure the probability that the demand for a lower-rated segment is greater than the amount of inventory remaining? What are problems with this method?

Hotel segmentation unofficially started when hotels would ask their guests upon check-in whether the guest was traveling for business or pleasure. The practice of tracking and actually segmenting guests began with the three fundamental segments still in use today: Transient, Group, and Contract. In order to more precisely target segments, hotels narrow down the these fundamental segments to Retail, Government, Opaque, **SMERF** (Social, Military, Education, Religious, Fraternal), Groups, Corporate Groups, etc.

Table 3.1: Various Market Segment Examples

Market Segment	Description
Retail	The rate a customer pays "off the shelf," often referred to as "best available"
Special Corporate/Business Transient (BT)/Negotiated	Corporate travelers booking their negotiated rate with a hotel
Qualified Discount	Any discount that a consumer must be qualified for, such as senior discount, AAA discount, student discount, etc.
Online Travel Agent (OTA)	Rooms booked via online travel agents, such as Expedia and Booking.com
Government Group	Discounted group rates for government officials on either the local, state, or federal level.
Government Transient	Individual government travel for officials on the local, state, or federal level
Rewards or Points	Those guests who accumulate enough points with their preferred brand to redeem a room night

These market segment examples have continued to evolve, moving from macro-segments and then becoming more granular as time progressed. In Figure 3.2 Transient Segments, AAA and OTA can be broken out further into **micro-segments** that can be considered as groups of consumers who share a similar level of interest in a set of features (McDonald & Dunbar, 2012). In the Online Travel Agent (OTA) segment for example, a consumer may fall into the segment of those people who are looking for **bundled travel**, or reservations where multiple travel services are combined, such as flight and hotel. Revenue managers continue to create and identify micro-segments as the addition of a new micro-segment may increase the amount of reservations booked, and the subtraction of a micro-segment may allow room for higher-rated segments.

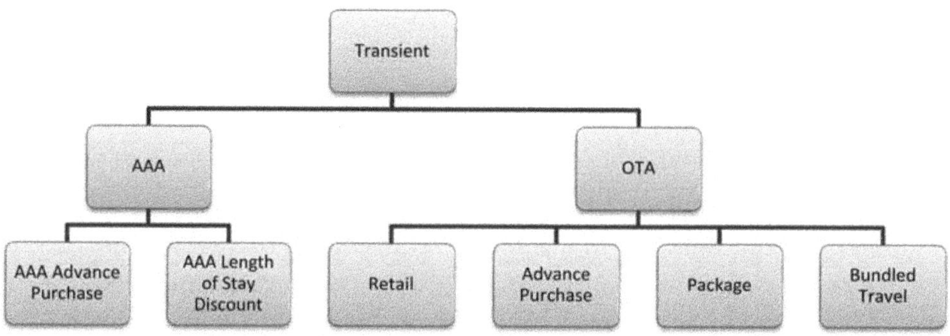

Figure 3.2: Macro- to Micro-Segmentation.

As market segmentation becomes more complicated, it becomes increasingly challenging to segment guests accurately. The current method of segmenting consumers is called **clustering**, in which a heterogeneous consumer market is divided into homogenous groups. One problem is that often times the natural groupings do not exist and information is then lost because the segments containing those consumers do not accurately fit. This problem arises when a guest booking a **retail rate** may be a business guest, a leisure guest, or both. Similarly, a guest booking via **opaque**, in which the hotel is not disclosed until the nonnefundable reservation is made, also may be traveling for either business or leisure.

SEEING FURTHER

It has recently been suggested that hotels should move past segmenting via transactional characteristics, such as lead time, but instead move towards behavioral segmentation, where the consumer's behavior and lifestyle is categorized (Kimes, 2010). Hotel revenue managers can price more accurately once they understand the value proposition the guest is looking for. For example, understanding a guest's spending patterns can help a revenue manager ascertain how to target that particular segment.

- What are some behavioral and lifestyle characteristics that revenue managers should track in order to understand, price, and target their consumer?

As revenue managers learn to accurately segment guests, the task becomes optimizing segment levels in the hotel. Revenue management focuses its efforts on creating value and increasing those segments that have the highest ADR and profitability. As segmentation evolves, we understand that e-commerce and marketing initiatives are necessary to target the appropriate guests depending on levels of demand. For example, hotels go to great lengths to target periods like Valentine's Day with display marketing featuring packages that attract higher-rated guests.

In the same light, revenue managers identify times where discount reservations will help grow occupancy and will therefore spend marketing dollars on OTA **Pay per Click (PPC)** ads or offer discounted rates to **Frequent Independent Traveler (FIT)** partners. Therefore, the evolution of segmentation has gone from identifying segments to developing and optimizing those segments that will help hotels during both high-demand and low-demand dates.

FENCING SEGMENTS

The purpose of segmentation is to be able to charge different consumers different prices for essentially the same product. However, it is impossible to offer a lower rate to different consumers without restrictions, or fences, on the purchase.

METHODS OF FENCING SEGMENTATION

There are multiple methods of **fencing,** or **segmentation hedges** that allow hoteliers to control the reservations they are willing to accept based upon the price being paid. **Price discrimination**, offering various prices to various consumers, can only exist when practical fences are in place.

There are five basic forms of rate fences; these include physical, controlled availability, customer characteristics, transaction characteristics, and product line (Dolan & Simon, 1996).

Table 3.2: Five Basic Forms of Rate Fences

Fence	**Description**
Physical	Offering varying room types, such as king-bedded rooms, suites, two beds, etc.
Controlled Availability	Setting an advance purchase window of 90+ days with a 20 percent discount to entice early bookers looking for a discount
Customer Characteristics	Offering discounts to leisure guests through qualified affiliations or status
Transaction Characteristics	Making a reservation fully nonrefundable upon booking
Product Line	Offering different versions of the same product, i.e. king room with breakfast versus without

Source: Based on Dolan & Simon, 1996.

For a rate fence to be considered strong, there are four key requirements (Smith, 2012):

1. Correlation: The fence must correlate with the consumer's perceived value proposition. Rate fences that effectively sort guests by their level of price sensitivity are the most effective as they make the mix of sales better defined and allow strict price discrimination.
2. Information: The information conveyed in the rate fence should be clear to both the consumers and employees. A rate fence without clarity results in confusion, lack of enforceability, and acceptability

on the part of the consumer. Additionally, too much information required is a deterrent on the ability to capture a booking.

3. Enforceability: The rate fence must be easy to enforce. If a rate fence is open to interpretation the rate fence is then rendered useless and fails to achieve its purpose of enabling price discrimination.
4. Acceptability: The consumer has to understand and perceive the fence as fair. A rate fence that is perceived as unfair could also be perceived as illegal or unethical.

QUESTIONS TO CONSIDER

- What are some rate fences that you have come by when purchasing items, hotel rooms, flight tickets, etc.?
- What are some risks that organizations face when using various rate fences?

ETHICAL ISSUES WITH FENCING

The four requirements for creating effective rate fences all can bring upon ethics issues. During high-demand periods, such as nearby sporting events or concerts, hotels often will raise rates and keep a 100 percent nonrefundable policy. For example, *Travel* magazine highlights the 2015 Superbowl as a period where "some hotels in the region are price-gouging even more as the big game day approaches" (Kehrli, 2015). The nonrefundable rate fence tied to the higher rate alters the perceived fairness of rate fencing. Hotels and airlines alike often have customers who talk to each other about the price they paid and can potentially disagree with the fence instituted. For example, if a lower price point is relegated to bookings made on mobile devices only, customers can complain about the price they paid because it is not fair to those who booked via traditional means.

VARYING LEVELS OF PRICE SENSITIVITY

In economics, price discrimination or the idea of segmentation can only exist when appropriate fences are in place and when an organization (or hotel) can charge different prices to different customers for a similar product

(Smith, 2012). Since hotel guests are all willing to pay different prices, revenue managers set fences to lower the rate of entry into the hotel for some guests while raising the rate for others. The economical idea is that by offering one price point, there is only one profit margin involved, but offering various price points allows a hotel to profit from the volume of lower-priced rooms and from customers who purchased the higher-priced room.

Within each segment there is an obvious level of price sensitivity whereby the leisure AAA traveler is more price-sensitive than the retail guest but less price-sensitive than most corporate guests. Economists naturally suggest determining **price elasticity** of each market segment, or the market segment's willingness to purchase a room depending on the rate amount. Once the price elasticity has been determined, one would then set the rate accordingly (Pigou, 1932). In practice this is difficult because of the dynamism in revenue management, where each day has different travelers and each of these travelers has a different reason for traveling (Elmaghraby & Keskinocak, 2003).

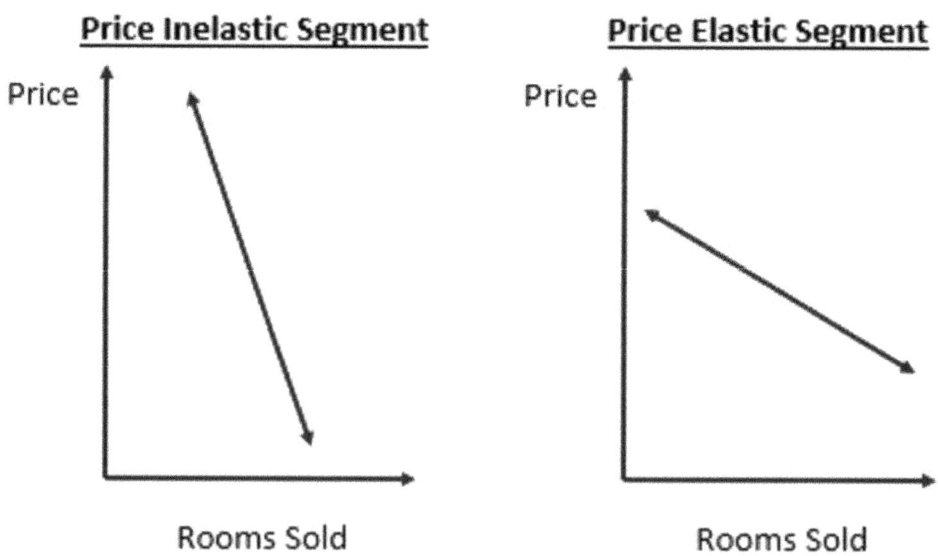

Figure 3.3: Price-Inelastic Segment versus Price-Elastic Segment.

Instead, demand for any given segment is seasonal and contains forecast error. Revenue managers look historically and assess competitor mix of sales to understand which of their segments are most **price inelastic**, or less sensitive to rate changes. Figure 3.3 shows that in a price inelastic segment, dramatic price drops will not result in significantly more volume but may dilute price to the point where the rate drop only hurts overall revenue. A dramatic price drop in the price-elastic segment, however, could yield significantly more volume of rooms sold and therefore more revenue.

REAL PEOPLE

Heather Raffetto*, Director of Revenue Management, works in New York City and looks to industry tools to measure how well she priced particular segments over dates that have passed. The industry tool she uses show a hotel's occupancy percent versus that of the market over a span of dates. To better understand price sensitivity, look at the segments in Figure 3.4 showing ADR for both Heather's hotel and the market's segment ADR. The relationship is shown below:

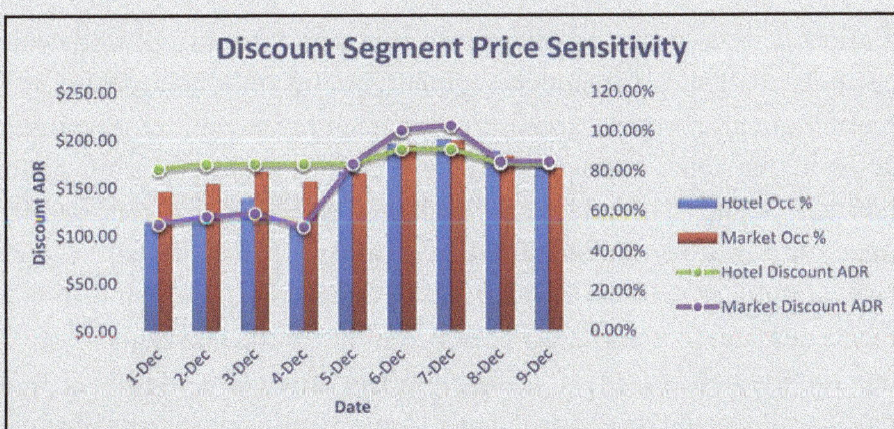

Figure 3.4: Discount Segment Price Sensitivity.

*Name has been protected

QUESTION

- Over what set of dates would you suggest that the discount segment price sensitivity is high? Why? How else could you measure price sensitivity within segments?

PROFITABILITY WITHIN SEGMENTS

Revenue managers are involved in many decisions that impact the segmentation of the hotel. These decisions occur based upon the **booking window** of the various segments. For example, Group and Contract decisions can be made anywhere from one year to five years prior to the date of arrival. Decisions regarding contracts for Special Corporate/Negotiated rates are normally made in the fourth quarter of the prior year. Understanding the profitability of each segment is therefore critical when making decisions that commit the hotel to volume in these segments well in advance. Segment costs need to be understood as each segment has a cost associated with booking. All segments incur different costs, and those segments that discount and have high costs pose a double-whammy on a hotel's profitability. For example, Group business more often than not requires labor because sales managers sell group business; OTA rooms come with commission costs; breakfast packages incur the cost of serving breakfast at the hotel; and all other segments have different costs because of the cost it takes to acquire any particular segment.

Earlier in this chapter, Littlewood's rule was introduced. Littlewood's rule stipulated that a discounted segment should only be accepted if the discount segment revenue exceeds the expected revenue of future bookings from the higher-rated segment. This concept is central to decision-making around the Group, Contract, and Negotiated/Special Corporate segments to ensure the most profitable business is booked for the hotel. "The current generation of revenue management systems in the lodging industry performs demand forecasting and optimization for the individual customer segment of the hotel business" (Hormby, Morrison, Dave, Meyers & Tenca, 2010). This allows the revenue manager to apply restrictions to ensure availability for the most profitable business for dates in the future.

"The next generation, referred to as total hotel revenue management systems, will span the entire hotel, including both meeting space and guest rooms, and will optimize both individual and group demand segments" (Hormby et al. 2010).

There are two pieces to evaluating a piece of Group business: the profit the group will deliver to the hotel and the **displacement cost.** The displacement cost is the value of other business that will be turned away if the group is given the necessary inventory. The role of revenue management in the sales process is to ensure that the profit a group delivers is greater than the displacement cost of the opportunity.

QUESTION TO CONSIDER

- Under what circumstances would it make business sense to confirm a Group booking where the profit from the group is less than the displacement cost?

SPREADSHEET EXERCISE 3.1

TO DO: The hotel has received a new Group opportunity. Use the Group Evaluation worksheet to determine the profitability of this potential group:

The group would like to confirm 150 guest rooms arriving on Monday, May 09 for 3 nights

- The group will spend $10,000 per day in food and beverage associated with this meeting.
- Their budget is $275 per night.
- The transient rate that would be displaced on those nights would be $350.

Fill in the data in the yellow highlighted boxes with the information above.

- Would this group be profitable for the hotel?
- What recommendations do you have for the sales manager to propose to the group to make the group more attractive for the hotel?

There are several factors that must be taken into consideration when evaluating the profit contribution of a Group opportunity:

- How much will the group spend in addition to rooms?
- What is the profit on the additional amount spent? Catering dollars deliver significantly less profit than room revenue, so this must be calculated at a much lower profit percentage.
- Is there meeting room rental or audio visual revenue with the group?
- Are there rebates or commissions to be paid to the group?

Hotel Capacity:	400							
Group Name:			Example					
Arrival:	5/11/2016							
Day of Week	SUN	MON	TUE	WED	THU	FRI	SAT	
Date	5/8/16	5/9/16	5/10/16	5/11/16	5/12/16	5/13/16	5/14/16	
Transient Demand	150	325	325	325	250	280	350	
Forecasted Group Definites	50	75	75	75	50	50	50	
Total Demand	200	400	400	400	300	330	400	
New Group Opprtunity Room Nights		150	150	150				450
Total	200	550	550	550	300	330	400	
Estimated Roomnight Displacement	0	150	150	150	0	0	0	450
New Catering Revenue			$30,000	$30,000	$30,000			$90,000
Summary:	Rooms	ADR	Revenue	Profit %	Profit			
New Group:	450	$275	$123,750	75%	$92,813			
Displaced Transient	450	$350	$157,500	75%	$118,125			
Rooms Profit					-$25,313			
New Group F&B			$90,000	30%	$27,000			
Meeting Room Rental			0	90%	0			
Total Group Profit					$1,688			

Spreadsheet Exercise 3.1

CONTRACT SEGMENT

The Contract segment for hotels is business that guarantees room nights on a contracted basis over an extended period of time. This segment is typically comprised of airline crew rooms but could also include college dorm rooms or extended project business.

Analysis of Contract opportunities also involves comparing the profit opportunity to the displacement cost. Due to the extended nature of a contract (normally covering 6 months to a full year or more), the hotel revenue forecast is used as a basis for determining displacement over the duration of the contract. The revenue gained from the opportunity is compared to the displaced revenue for the nights that the hotel is forecasting to have high demand.

A contract piece of business, such as an airline crew, can provide a lift in incremental occupancy and appear lucrative from a revenue perspective. It is critical to incorporate the **CPOR**, or cost per occupied room, for the Contract segment to the incremental room nights to ensure that the profit picture is appropriately represented. While the airline crew will deliver additional rooms to the hotel, there is a cost associated with occupying the additional rooms that would not otherwise have been occupied.

PROS & CONS

- What are the various pros and cons of taking Contract business from a revenue and profit perspective in addition to those already mentioned?

SPECIAL CORPORATE/NEGOTIATED SEGMENT

There are a number of terms used to describe the segment that includes the Negotiated rates that companies receive in exchange for volume. These include Special Corporate, Business Transient (BT), Corporate, and Negotiated, to name a few. Careful analysis must be done within this segment to ensure that companies are not given special discounts at the expense of higher-rated segments.

The factors to consider in this type of analysis are:

- Day of week pattern: Tuesday and Wednesday are the highest demand nights in many business transient markets. If accounts are only producing business on the strong demand nights, they are likely not providing incremental value to the hotel. If they are producing on **shoulder nights,** their business is more valuable to the hotel.

- Monthly/seasonal production: Similar to the day of week pattern, the seasonal pattern of an account is an important consideration. If the account produces in the slower season where the hotel does not sell out as often, it is likely producing incremental revenue for the hotel.
- Last room availability: An account that has been granted **last room availability (LRA)** is able to book their discounted rate as long as the hotel is selling standard rooms, regardless of how strong demand is for a given date. This impacts the profitability of the segment because it allows the account to displace higher-rated business competing for the same inventory on sold-out nights.

  (Additionally the concept of "non-last room availability" status allows the hotel to restrict availability as needed to yield out demand from this discounted segment and preserve availability for higher-rated business. Availability can be used as a negotiation tool to drive higher rates in this segment. In high-demand markets, last room availability will command higher rates because greater availability will be afforded to the account's travelers. Price-sensitive accounts can get more favorable rate terms in exchange for allowing their rate to be restricted during times of high demand.)

QUESTION TO CONSIDER

- In what situation would you accept an account with last room availability?

ANALYZING MIX OF SALES

In an ideal world, a hotel would fill with the most profitable segments possible to drive the most revenue potential available to the hotel. Hotels can model the optimal mix of sales based upon demand trends by segment to establish a strategy that pursues this optimal mix.

SPREADSHEET EXERCISE 3.2

TO DO: Review the mix of business trends at the hotel (see Table 3.3). Use the following assumptions to model the proposed segmentation for next year:

- Goal is to achieve 6% revenue growth.
- Occupancy will not exceed 80% due to seasonality constraints.
- Market will support 5% retail rate lift with comparable volume.
- Reduction in Contract rooms will translate into 60% lift for other segments (if you reduce Contract by 1000 rooms, it will translate into 600 rooms shifted into another segmentation due to the incrementalism).

QUESTIONS

- Goal is to achieve 6% revenue growth.
- Outline the mix strategy changes the hotel should make in order to achieve the 6% revenue growth goal.
- Which market segments will be most important for the hotel's success?

Table 3.3: Mix of Sales, This Year versus Last Year

	Roomnights			Mix of Total Roomnights			Average Rate			Revenue		
Segment	**TY**	**LY**	**% Chg**	**TY**	**LY**	**% Chg**	**TY**	**LY**	**% Chg**	**TY**	**LY**	**% Chg**
Retail	11000	13000	−15.4%	15.1%	18.3%		$300	$280	7.1%	$3,300,000	$3,640,000	−9.3%
Business Transient	15000	12000	25.0%	20.5%	16.9%		$225	$220	2.3%	$3,375,000	$2,640,000	27.8%
Government	8000	7000	14.3%	11.0%	9.9%		$180	$175	2.9%	$1,440,000	$1,225,000	17.6%
OTA	9000	8000	12.5%	12.3%	11.3%		$215	$210	2.4%	$1,935,000	$1,680,000	15.2%
Advance Purchase	6000	5000	20.0%	8.2%	7.0%		$199	$189	5.3%	$1,194,000	$945,000	26.3%
AAA	5000	5000	0.0%	6.8%	7.0%		$179	$175	2.3%	$895,000	$875,000	2.3%
Group	12000	14000	−14.3%	16.4%	19.7%		$215	$215	0.0%	$2,580,000	$3,010,000	−14.3%
Contract	7000	7000	0.0%	9.6%	9.9%		$159	$159	0.0%	$1,113,000	$1,113,000	0.0%
TOTAL	73000	71000	2.8%				$216.88	$213.07	1.8%	$15,832,000	$15,128,000	4.7%
Occupancy	80.0%	77.8%										

Optimal mix is a dynamic concept because no day, month, week or year is alike. During low seasons, it is important to build upon efforts to drive profitable segments, but it is equally important to understand that while Business Transient plays into the optimal mix on most weekdays, on a Friday during the coldest time of the year the optimal mix will be different. Revenue management professionals therefore identify their optimal mix for all periods of the year and then communicate that information so that the hotel can strategize to optimize their mix of sales at all times.

Hotels therefore emphasize a particular segment's percentage contribution, or a segment's room volume, as a percentage of total rooms sold. Revenue managers who focus their efforts on increasing the percentage contribution of profitable segments can therefore help increase the hotel's overall profit margin.

QUESTION TO CONSIDER

- What factors could have contributed to the decline in Retail mix versus the prior year? Which segment saw the largest % growth in room nights versus the prior year? What strategic decisions were behind this change in mix? (Refer to Table 3.3.)

DISCUSSION QUESTIONS

Question 1: Of the five varieties of rate fences, which do you think are the easiest and hardest to enforce? Why? What kind of problems may arise with a weak rate fence?

Question 2: Knowing that every minute there are reservations being made, how would you measure price elasticity for each market segment? How would you measure price sensitivity of guests who have not yet made a reservation? Are there any challenges with your method?

Question 3: There are industry tools available to measure the segmentation in the market or in the competitive set. What are other ways that you can identify potential segments of business?

Question 4: How can you use the internet to help obtain your optimal mix of sales?

Question 5: What are the costs associated with various segments? Is it worth taking in high-cost segments? What costs could be associated with low-cost segments that are not apparent, such as Retail, AAA, Government, etc.?

Question 6: What are potential ways to make a Group opportunity more profitable if the displacement cost exceeds the profit generated by the group?

APPLICATIONS

1. The Minneapolis City Center Hotel

The Minneapolis City Center hotel has been underperforming the comp set in occupancy over the last 6 months. The hotel executive team is discussing the potential to gain business from the Mall of America, a major demand generator in the market.

- What segments(s) of business would come from the mall?
- What type of discounts or promotions would you recommend they use to generate room nights?
- What fencing considerations would you use in order to minimize trade down from existing business?

2. Revenue Manager Comparison

Revenue managers A & B manage competing hotels with identical products and services. Using the information below, calculate the rooms, ADR, and revenue of each segment and the total rooms occupied, ADR, and revenue for the day for each hotel.

(This exercise should preferably be completed in spreadsheet software.)

Revenue Manager A

- Retail: 50 rooms, $12,500 revenue
- Business Transient: $200 ADR, $8,000 revenue
- Government: 25 rooms, $170 ADR
- OTA: 40 rooms, $6,400 revenue
- Group: 35 rooms, $180 ADR
- Contract: 20 rooms, $120

Revenue Manager B

- Retail: 70 rooms, $240 ADR
- Business Transient: 50 rooms, $9,750 revenue
- Government: 5 rooms, $850 revenue
- OTA: $9,100 revenue, $130 ADR
- Group: 40 rooms, $160 ADR
- Contract: The revenue manager decided not to pursue any contract business

Which hotel managed their mix of sales better?

What could manager A have done better? What could manager B have done better?

Which manager likely materialized the most profit? Why?

TEAM ACTIVITY

Your hotel's sales team is in the process of negotiating several Special Corporate deals with the top producing accounts in the neighborhood. Your budget for next year is to keep volume flat in the segment YOY but grow the average rate by 5 percent. The sales manager has presented the following scenarios from your top two accounts:

Company ABC is your top account, producing a third of your total Special Corporate segment volume. Their RFP (request for proposal) indicates that they wish to remain flat in rate YOY (year over year). Their negotiated rate was $175 this year. They expect that their business needs to remain flat for the following year. Fifteen percent of their volume falls on shoulder nights.

Company XYZ is your next highest volume account, producing just over 25 percent of your total Special Corporate volume. Their RFP does not have any indication of their rate expectations at this point. Their negotiated rate was $180 this year. They expect their business volume to grow by 20 percent next year because a new division is moving into the market. They expect to have relocation business in addition to their normal midweek business demand. Twenty-five percent of their volume falls on shoulder nights.

As a team, develop a strategy for the rates and conditions your hotel will offer to these accounts. Outline the strategy behind your offer and any risks you have identified in your approach.

INTERNET ACTIVITY

Visit the online pages of two independent hotels (hotels without any brand affiliation) and the websites of two branded hotels in major markets. Be sure to check the Facebook, Twitter, Instagram, and Pinterest pages of each hotel in addition to their regular website.

- What segments are being targeted at each hotel?
- What strategies are being employed by each hotel to appeal to the various segments?
- Based upon what you see, is the hotel missing out on any particular segment? Why?
- How could the hotel do a better job of targeting various segments?
- Do the hotels do a good job of targeting discount segments during times of need? Do they do a good job of targeting segments during peak periods?

GLOSSARY

Booking window – The time horizon prior to arrival that a segment typically makes reservations.

Bundled travel – Reservations in which multiple travel services are combined, such as flight and hotel.

Clustering – Where a homogenous consumer market is divided into homogenous groups based upon?

Cost per occupied room (CPOR) – This cost represents the expenses associated with occupying and servicing a room for one night. It includes costs such as labor (front office and housekeeping), cleaning supplies, linen, and utilities.

Displacement cost – The value of the business that will be turned away because the inventory has been committed to another segment (group, contract, etc.).

Fencing/segmentation hedges – Methods of control used by revenue managers to manage which reservations they are willing to accept based upon the price being paid.

Frequent independent traveler or foreign independent tour (FIT) – Prepaid packaged tours for individual travel.

Last room availability (LRA) – A condition granted to Special Corporate accounts wherein their negotiated rate is automatically available if the hotel is selling standard inventory.

Micro-segments – Segments that can be further broken out in order to more precisely group together those that share a similar level of interest in a set of features.

Opaque – Where a guest books and is unaware of which hotel they are booking until the non-refundable reservation is made.

Pay per click (PPC) – Ads that are placed on websites that cost a certain amount per each click on the ad itself.

Price discrimination – Offering various prices to various consumers.

Price elasticity – A consumer's willingness to purchase a product depending on the level of price.

Price-inelasticity – Where a customer is less sensitive to a change in price.

Product differentiation – How marketers modify or add supply in order to better adapt to demand.

Qualified discount – Any discount that a consumer must be qualified for such as senior discount, AAA discount, student discount, etc.

Retail rate/best available rate (BAR) – the rate a customer pays "off the shelf", often referred to as "best available"

Segmentation/mix of sales – How revenue managers and marketers classify and target customers in specific groups based upon their characteristics, behaviors, and preferences.

Shoulder night – A night before or after the peak arrival date, where total hotel demand is not strong enough to reach capacity.

SMERF groups – Any form of Group business relating to Social, Military, Education, Religion, or Fraternity.

REFERENCES

Dolan, R. J. & Simon, H. (1996). *Power Pricing: How Managing Price Transforms the Bottom Line.* New York, NY: The Free Press.

Elmaghraby, W. & Keskinocak, P. (2003). Dynamic Pricing in the Presence of Inventory Considerations: Research Overview, Current Practices, and Future Directions. *Management Science, 49*(10), 1287-1309.

Hormby, S., Morrison, J., Dave, P., Meyers, M. & Tenca, T. (2010, January-February). Marriott International Increases Revenue by Implementing a Group Pricing Optimizer. *Interfaces, 40*(1), 47-57.

Kehrli, K. (2015, January 26). Phoenix Hotel Rates Soar for Super Bowl 2015. *Travelmag.com.* Retrieved from https://www.travelmag.com/articles/hotels-super-bowl-2015/

Kimes, S. E. (2010). *Strategic Pricing through Revenue Management.* Retrieved from Cornell University, School of Hospitality Administration site: http://scholarship.sha.cornell.edu/articles/346.

Kotler, P., Bowen, J.T. & Makens, J. C. (2010). *Marketing for Hospitality and Tourism* (6th ed.). Upper Saddle River, NJ: Pearson, 2010.

McDonald, M. & Dunbar, I. (2012). *Market Segmentation: How to Do It and How to Profit from It* (4th ed.). Chichester, UK: John Wiley & Son Ltd.

Mcgill, J. I & van Ryzin, G.J. (1999, May). Revenue Management: Research Overview and Prospects. *Transportation Science 33*(2), 233-256.

Pigou, A. C. (1932). *The Economics of Welfare* (4th ed.). London: Macmillan and Co.

Smith, T. J. (2012). *Pricing Strategy: Setting Price Levels, Managing Price Discounts, & Establishing Price Structures.* Mason, OH: South-Western Cengage Learning.

Smith, W. R. (1956, July). Product Differentiation and Market Segmentation as Alternative Marketing Strategies. *Journal of Marketing, 21*(1), 3-8.

Talluri, Kalyan T., and Garrett Van Ryzin. The Theory and Practice of Revenue Management. New York, NY: Springer, 2005.

CHAPTER 4

Key Hotel Distribution Channels

Elyana Falk and Calvin Anderson

OVERVIEW

Channel distribution is one of the fastest changing segments in the hotel industry, with no stagnation in sight. This chapter will discuss channel distributions at length, but in short, channel distributions are the methods and/or platforms to book a hotel room.

LEARNING OBJECTIVES

After studying this module, you should be able to:

- Recognize the key hotel distribution channels
- Differentiate the benefits and detriments for the various distribution channels
- Formulate the booking process
- Explain what drives the evolving changes in distribution channels

OUTLINE

Introduction

Future of Distribution Channels

- Think Historically: Edgemere Hotel

Closer Look: Distribution Channel

- Drive Direct Practices
- Distribution Channel Challenges

Closer Look: Online Travel Agencies (OTAs)

Closer Look: Rate Parity and Best Rate Guarantee

- Rate Parity Legal Problems
- Real People: Director of Revenue Reflection of Rate Parity

Closer Look: Connectivity among Distribution Channels

Future of Channel Distributions

- Continued Mergers and Acquisitions among Key Players
- Increased Involvement of Social Media
- Cross Device Sharing Platforms
- Sharing Economy

Closing

Discussion Questions and Applications

INTRODUCTION

There are many ways to book hotel rooms, and the landscape has changed dramatically in the past 20 years. For example, the first online travel website with real-time reservations launched in 1994 (Warner, Quadri-Felitti, Chandnani, 2010), and by 2014 the average customer visits 6.5 websites through various devices before booking their hotel room (Vivion, 2014). Revenue managers must understand the distribution channel network and create a distribution strategy based on their hotel's needs.

An easier way to understand distribution channels is to relate them to clothing stores. Customers have the choice of Bloomingdales, TJ Maxx, a Levi's storefront, Amazon mobile app, Levi's sales phone line, etc. In each of these places they can buy the same exact pair of jeans—or in the hotel industry, a hotel room. But because customer preferences vary widely, people choose different booking methods.

Customers are the greatest influence on distribution channels, and the changes in technology, competition, and devices continue to impact distribution channels. A revenue manager must understand all distribution channels and the exciting changes that are happening to continue to be relevant.

A **distribution channel** is the chain of businesses or intermediaries through which a good or service passes until it reaches the end consumer; in the hotel industry distribution channels are the methods through which a customer can purchase a hotel room. There are many places where customers can purchase hotel rooms—from calling the hotel front desk to booking online through a third-party website. A revenue manager creates a successful distribution strategy by first understanding the distribution channel landscape and evaluating each channel's benefits, costs, and implications. Having a solid knowledge of distribution channels can lead to a successful distribution strategy that balances the costs of distribution channels by maximizing the booking sales at the hotel's ideal **average daily rate** (**ADR**).

SO WHAT?

Understanding distribution channels is a foundational element of hotel revenue management. A hotel can have one distribution channel or over twenty. Knowing and understanding the various distribution channels leads a revenue manager to optimize their mix and make the most revenue.

- What do you think are the primary distribution channels? How do they vary? Do you think a hotel should use every possible distribution channel? Why or why not?

There are six primary distribution channels that require understanding and strategies. These channels can be fluid to the customer, and a hotel's distribution mix can vary greatly based on the strategies used.

1. Hotel website, or **brand.com**: The hotel's or parent chain's website where customers can directly book their hotel rooms.

2. Voice: Call center or 800 numbers where customers call to book their hotel room via the hotel's **central reservation system (CRS).**
3. Direct to hotel: Any booking handled on property, including walk-ins, calls directly to the property, groups, contract, etc.
4. **Global distribution channel (GDS)**: A worldwide computerized reservation network that provides transactions to travel agents, online reservation sites, and large corporations.
5. **Online travel agency (OTA)**: Third-party travel website that allows customers to easily compare hotels and book their hotel.
6. **Meta websites**: A search engine that aggregates hotel inventory from several sources (OTAs, hotel websites) and presents the compiled results in one list.

Customers do not differentiate between the various distribution channels, and many times use multiple methods during their booking process. For example, a customer may start their research on an OTA, then visit the hotel's website for more information, and actually book the room via an 800 number. Therefore, while it is important for hoteliers to understand each channel and their differences, they must also consider customer dynamics and see how the channels are woven together.

In addition to looking at the interconnectivity of distribution channels, it is important to know that the distribution mix can look very different at each hotel. Distribution mix differences can be due to the nature of the specific hotel. For example, a roadside motel off the freeway will likely index higher on direct to hotel due to a higher likelihood of walk-ins. The mix can also vary due to specific strategies hotels put in place to increase or decrease specific channels. When building a smart distribution strategy or mix, Kelly McGuire notes to "replace less-profitable business." By this McGuire refers to a hotel reducing airline crew contracts (direct-to-hotel channel category) due to the low price and typical add-ons of breakfast with OTAs, which can yield higher profitability (McGuire, 2016).

Now, with an understanding of exactly what the primary channel distributions are, let's review how we got to today and how the industry morphed and evolved to these distribution channels.

EVOLUTION OF DISTRIBUTION CHANNELS

As noted at the start of the chapter, distribution channels have changed dramatically in the past 20 years. However, for the longest time, hotel distribution was rather simple: the majority of bookings came directly from guests either walking through the front door or calling the hotel. From the 1950s to 1990, the foundation for technology was being created that enabled the distribution boom that started in the mid-1990s. Below are highlights of what changed from 1950 to 1990 (Warner et al., 2010):

- **1958**: Sheraton introduced the first automated electronic reservations system and toll-free number.
- **1959**: A *global distribution system* (GDS) created for American Airlines to track airline reservations (American Airlines Inc, 2015).
- **1970**: Westin Hotels developed Westron, first hotel reservation system.
- **1976**: The Sabre Corporation (a travel technology company) was introduced for the first time to travel agencies. It took until the mid-1980s for its widespread implementation (over 10,000 travel agency offices).
- **1980**: The central reservation system (CRS) was developed.
- **1987**: Hilton HHonors®, a guest reward program, is introduced as the first hotel rewards program.
- **1994**: The first online website for real-time hotel reservations launched, TravelWeb.com.

1995 was the start of the "dot-com" boom—or the rapid growth the internet sector (Cassidy, 2002). During this time there was also immediate acceleration of distribution channels. Choice Hotels International led the way to be the first company to offer "real-time" access to its CRS (Warner et al., 2010). The first OTA, Travelocity.com, was introduced in 1996, which was quickly followed by Expedia, a Microsoft brainchild. By 1997, 42 percent of all hotel reservations were booked by travel agents or corporate travel departments (Use Our Lodging, 2010).

THINK HISTORICALLY

Newspapers, including the New York Daily Tribune, previously were a hotel distribution channel. As seen below, the Edgemere Hotel advertised that they are open for the season and gave instructions on how to book their hotel.

NEW-YORK DAILY TRIBUNE, SUNDAY, JULY 5, 1903.

SUMMER RESORTS. SUMMER RESORT

HOTEL CHAMPLAIN

Golf.

ADIRONDACKS.
STAR LAKE INN, Star Lake P.O., N.Y.

WAWBEEK and COTTAGES

ADIRONDACKS.

ADIRONDACKS.
THE SAGAMORE.

Paul Smith's
ADIRONDACKS

MORLEY'S

ST. HUBERT'S INN
ADIRONDACKS

The Windsor

EDGEMERE HOTEL,
EDGEMERE, LONG ISLAND, NEW YORK,
NOW OPEN.

STAMFORD
NEW YORK.
"QUEEN OF THE CATSKILLS"

Richfield Springs, N. Y.

HOTEL EARLINGTON

E. M. EARLE & SON.

THE BERKELEY-WAIONTHA,
AT RICHFIELD SPRINGS, N. Y.

THE INN AT HIGH POINT
Port Jervis, N. Y.

CASCADE LAKE HOUSE.

WHERE all is life and movement, the man of affairs forgets the cares, the anxiety and complications of his daily grind in the compelling force of the fascination of the things that arouse, attract and enchain his attention. Herein lies the superlative value of

SARATOGA

with its brilliant, kaleidoscopical and yet restful life, with its ceaseless round of entertainments, its many sports and pastimes, its delightful climate and bracing air.

Go thither, ye brain-fagged men of affairs and get a new lease on life!

The finest and fastest trains, including the superb SARATOGA LIMITED which makes the trip from New York in less than 4 hours, are now running to Saratoga over the New York Central and Delaware and Hudson.

The Best Hotels:

UNITED STATES CONGRESS HALL
KENSINGTON AMERICAN-ADELPHI

For Cottages apply to LESTER BROS. or S. H. MYERS & CO.

The Popular Springs:

CONGRESS.

THE LINCOLN.

THE SPOUTING CARLSBAD.

SARATOGA VICHY.

SARATOGA SELTZER.

Don't fail to visit the Natural Carbonic Gas Company's Works on South Broadway, and NEWMAN'S at the Lake.

President of Business Men's Association.

Source: New-York Tribune, July 5, 1903.

QUESTIONS

- Do you think newspapers could be an effective distribution channel today? Why or why not?
- There are many distribution channels that have come and gone. Why do you think that is?
- What are potential future distribution channels you can invasion?
- What do you think the role of travel agencies will be in the future?

A CLOSER LOOK AT DISTRIBUTION CHANNELS

With the historical background known, let's review the key distribution channels again. There are many different ways hoteliers can further categorize distribution channels. For example, online versus offline, direct (voice, brand.com, property direct) versus indirect (OTA, GDS). It is also helpful to categorize distribution channels by their cost and benefits.

Let's review the associated costs of each distribution channel. These costs estimates are from a TravelClick®'s data launched in May 2015 (Mahmoud, 2015). Some of the costs are easier to identify, such as, for example, a fee per booking, while others are not as easy to track, such as the associated cost of a sales team. It is very important to understand all costs of channels because although shifting share to increase occupancy is positive, it may not yield to higher profits. It is paramount to focus channel mix to maximize profits, rather than revenue.

Table 4.1: Distribution Channel Analysis

Channel Distribution	Definition	Pros	Cons and Estimated Cost
Hotel Website/ brand.com	A hotel's own website or parent chain's website For example, Marriott.com, Choice.com, or Hilton.com	Once created, a hotel website is very cost-effective. Startup costs are much more expensive for independent hotels v. branded websites since they are creating their site from start. Flexibility: The hotel is in full control of its website. Therefore a hotel can create a website that is the best reflection of the hotel. Hotel brands invest huge amounts in marketing.	Hotel brand websites: \$2 – \$5 per booking. Independent hotels and resorts: \$8.50 – \$12.50 per booking. There are many other costs that are included in this channel but not reflected in the per-booking cost. Independent hotels face website fees, maintenance fees, and website analytics. Brands face management, royalty, and/ or licensing fees.
Voice Channel	Call centers and/ or 800 numbers booked via the hotel's CRS. CRS is a computerized backend system of a hotel's booking engine.	Call centers have to engage the customer and can use the opportunity to upsell more effectively. CRS pros: Basic tool to help manage a hotel's ever-changing rates and availability.	Hotel brands: \$6 – \$10 per booking. Independent hotels and resorts: \$10 – \$15 per booking. Bookings directly through the CRS have declined in recent years as consumers shift to digital channels. (Green & Lomanno, 2015).

Table 4.1: (Continued)

Channel Distribution	Definition	Pros	Cons and Estimated Cost
	A CRS is very conventional and is almost a necessary system if a hotel wants to have an online profile.		
Property Direct	Any booking handled on property, including walk-ins, calls directly to the property, groups, contract, etc.	The direct channel is the most cost-effective. The customer satisfaction of property direct is completely driven by the hotel.	\$3.25 – \$13 Difficult to compare to other distribution segments because it is a mixture of multiple bookings. Many times because property direct is the most cost-effective, hoteliers drastically decrease their ADR on this channel, which can lend it to be less profitable. The customer acquisition cost continues to rise, so that while the per-transition cost is the lowest, it is very expensive to drive property direct overall.
Global Distribution System (GDS)	A worldwide computerized reservation network that provides transactions to travel agents, online reservation sites, and large corporations. The GDS is dominated by transient business travelers.	Many OTAs and other internet-based travel services are connected to the GDS. So if a hotel does not want to directly partner with an OTA, for example, they still may be able to be listed via the GDS and typically at a lower cost. GDS channels specialize in corporate rates and complex leisure packages (travel including air, hotel, attractions, car) This segment continues to grow.	\$4.50 – \$6 PLUS 10% travel agent commission There is no content editing by the GDS, and content is driven only by the hotel. The hotel does not have control over the customer booking experience.
Online Travel Agent (OTA)	OTAs are a third-party travel website allowing customers to	OTAs have a broad reach of customers in varying countries, with multiple languages, and differented	The price varies by contract, OTA, and model but typically ~20% As OTAs revenues grow, they

Table 4.1: (Continued)

Channel Distribution	Definition	Pros	Cons and Estimated Cost
	easily compare hotels and book their hotel. There are three basic OTA models: 1) merchant; 2) agency; 3) opaque. (OTAs are outlined further later in this chapter.)	buying preferences. Hotels are able to tap into this huge customer base without making the huge investments necessary. OTAs spend huge dollars marketing their channels and travel overall. Significant access to smart data and market trends. OTAs can provide this data directly to hotels to help make smarter pricing strategies and targeted promotions (McGuire, 2016).	have larger budgets and better technology platforms to find new ways to reach customers and gain market share away from hotels. Hotel has limited control over the customer booking experience.
Metasearch Engine	Search engine that aggregates hotel inventory from several sources (OTAs, hotel website) and presents as one compiled result.	Meta sites deliver on the customer desire of price transparency and clarity and have grown in popularity in recent years. Reinforce the idea behind rate parity. (Rate parity is further discussed later in this chapter.)	Cost is defined by the website channel the customer chooses on the meta. In definition, a meta site incorporates multiple parts that allows for a greater chance of problems (i.e., if one of the search sites the meta site is pulling from is down, and the customer will see that). Customer base is price-sensitive; the primary differentiating factor between the aggregated sites is price. The hotel does not have control over the customer booking experience.

Source: Based on Mahmoud, 2015.

QUESTIONS TO CONSIDER

- Can you think of an additional distribution channel cost that was not listed in the above chart?
- Categorize each of the distribution channels as direct versus non-direct and online versus offline.

DRIVE DIRECT PRACTICES

By definition, property direct distribution has the least amount of associated costs for a hotel. Therefore, there has been a longstanding goal to drive more direct business. A hotel "drives direct" by focusing strategies to increase their direct channel mix; Duetto Research notes a comprehensive revenue strategy is anchored by "driving as much direct business as possible" (Duetto Research 2016). To help encourage revenue managers to focus on drive direct, many hotel management companies include hotel direct mix share as a part of the hotel's goals.

There are various methods hotels can use to drive direct business, including (but not limited to) targeted discounts, television advertising, targeted offers, upgrades, mobile investments, responding to online reviews, and even general guest encouragement to join the loyalty program.

In February 2016, Hilton launched its largest global marketing campaign ever, called "Stop Clicking Around," encouraging guests, via a 10 percent discount, to become a Hilton HHonors loyalty member. Early results were very positive—including HHonors members representing 56 percent occupancy, which was a 400 bps (basis points) year over year increase (Hilton Worldwide Holdings, Inc., 2017). Many other brands, including Marriott, Hyatt, and Wyndham were quick to follow with their own drive direct campaigns.

However, driving direct business has an associated cost. Hilton's "Stop Clicking Around" campaign Hilton will not disclose the total advertising and/or associated cost of the campaign), but it was noted as their most expensive campaign in their history (Hilton Worldwide Holdings, Inc., 2017). Additionally, a 2014 study revealed that hotels' costs to acquire a guest consistently have risen more than their revenues have increased (HAMA Study, 2014). Drive direct costs can also include free internet, discounted rates, free nights, etc. Therefore, it is important to evaluate the full costs of a suggested drive direct platform. But as property direct is the most cost-effective segment, it will be an inherent goal of hotels to drive more business through this channel.

DISTRIBUTION CHANNEL CHALLENGES

As seen, there is a wide diversity of travel 'parts' that work together to appear to be one experience for the customer. One constant problem hoteliers face is that if one of the parts fail (i.e. the CRS is down for 2 hours), the customer experience fails. Another theme you may have noticed in Table 4.1 are the multiple costs a hotel can incur for one reservation. For example, when a reservation is booked on an OTA, a hotel can pay 20 percent of the total rate, plus $10 to the CRS system.

Other major challenges of distribution channels include:

- Big data: All of these online distribution systems and channels are able to provide an enormous amount of data. However, big data is not helpful. It is important to change big data to *smart data*. Smart data is digestible and actionable.
- Proliferation: The rapid growth of distribution channels leads to some negative implications. First, hotels need to decipher which channels they should use, and there is not always not a clear choice. It is important for hotels to base their choice on the channel's return on investment (ROI). Second, the multiple distribution channels lead to more overhead of managing the various channels. While there are systems that can help with management, these come at a cost. Third, paradox of choice. As customers continue to have more choices of where to book, it can cause more confusion and actually interfere with a customer's booking.
- Fragmented distribution network: There are many moving parts that are not connected in distribution channels. While there are systems in place to provide a connection to the various parts (at a cost to the hotel), it does not always work smoothly. For example, a hotel's CRS may connect to two OTAs but not to a third. If a hotel works with all three OTAs, they need to consider if they would want to manage the third OTA by 1) additional connectivity system, 2) manage online directly with the third OTA, or 3) decide to not work with the third OTA.

QUESTIONS TO CONSIDER

- How would you research a new distribution channel? What are the important aspects a hotelier would need to know before adding a new distribution channel?

SPREADSHEET EXERCISE 4.1

TO DO: Review the provided spreadsheet and answer the following:

1. Calculate the total revenue the hotel would collect.
2. Calculate the net profit the hotel would receive.
3. As a business executive focused on profit, would you modify the segmentation for this hotel? How would you change your segmentation strategy and how would that affect your distribution strategy?

CLOSER LOOK: ONLINE TRAVEL AGENCIES (OTAs)

OTAs have seen significant growth since their start in 1996, and their prominence has exploded since the 2000s. For example, OTAs' share of guest-paid room revenue in economy and midscale hotels jumped 7.8 percent in 2011 to 15.8 percent in 2014; this means a 108 percent growth for OTAs in the economy to midscale in less than four years (Mahmoud, 2015). When talking with customers, we find that OTAs like Expedia and Priceline are considered the primary ways to book their hotel rooms (Duetto Research, 2016).

There are two major benefits of OTAs that many times are not heavily considered. First is the access to the data that OTAs can provide. OTAs have huge access to big data. For example, OTAs can easily see marketwide trends, leisure compression, and booking trends, etc. OTAs can provide this data to hotels to help suggest data-driven strategies and opportunities for the hotel. The second benefit is access to customers. Not only do OTAs have a wide net of customers who likely would not find the hotel otherwise, some OTAs are very prominent in specific areas or countries. For example, Wotif is the largest online hotel website in Australia (Expedia Inc., 2015), and if a hotel wants to target the Asia Pacific market, the hotel manager can work with Expedia (who owns Wotif) to increase their share very quickly and relatively cheaply.

However, while these are two benefits, these benefits are not the same among different OTAs, and OTAs are not created equal. Therefore, hoteliers will find some OTAs work better for their hotel than others. For example, a hotel may evaluate the four different OTAs they work with and realize 90 percent of their business comes from one of the OTAs, and therefore the hotel may choose to only work with that one OTA for simplicity. Other examples include if an OTA does not have a large hotel management team and therefore a hotel may have an ongoing distribution challenge with the specific OTA that goes unfixed – this could cause a hotel to no longer work with an OTA. Conversely, a hotel may choose to focus strategy to a specific OTA due to date they can provide or that they are easy to work with.

For general grouping of OTAs, there are three basic models OTAs can work with hotels, outlined below.

- Merchant: The OTA collects payment from the customer directly, and the hotel receives the net rate after the intermediary is compensated, based on the pre-negotiated deal. The hotel records the net room rate.
- Agency: The hotel collects payment directly from the customer, and the intermediary (the OTA) is compensated after, based on the pre-negotiated deal. The hotel records the gross or total room rate.
- Opaque: In the bidding method, the customer does not know the hotel until after the sale. The hotel receives a pre-negotiated rate, and the OTA keeps the difference between what the guest pays and the pre-negotiated room rate.

QUESTIONS TO CONSIDER

- What are the impacts to a hotel when they record the net rate (merchant model) or the gross rate (agency model)?

A controversial benefit of OTAs is the **billboard effect**. In 2009 the Cornell Center for Hospitality Research published an article finding that "hotels that are listed on third-party distributors' websites, commonly known as online travel agents, gain a reservation benefit in addition to direct sales" (Anderson, 2009). The study found that hotels had between a 7.5 percent to 26 percent uplift in direct bookings when listed in Expedia. However, Kalibri

Labs found that this billboard effect is also enjoyed by other channels as well, not just OTAs (O'Neill, 2014). While many hoteliers may see the billboard effect at their property, there is the question if it is diminishing. Metasearch websites clearly diminish the billboard effect since customers are beginning their booking process at a meta site rather than at the OTA. Additionally, the rise of customers booking on mobile apps lends to a different booking trend. Anderson at Cornell contemplates this:

> "As phone/tablet usage grows, we may see a different story. Let's say consumers switch to having higher conversion ratios on mobile devices. Then they probably won't shop in an app and then call the hotel directly. They will instead shop and purchase via the app. So the billboard effect may be reduced." (O'Neill, 2014).

QUESTIONS TO CONSIDER

- Do you think the billboard effect still exists?

SPREADSHEET EXERCISE 4.2

You work at an OTA and are pitching to a hotel to sign up. You will find general stats of a similar comp hotel that currently works with your OTA.

To Do: Create or complete the Excel spreadsheet based on the data of the comp hotel and answer the questions that follow. When creating the Excel spreadsheet, use formulas and reference cells in the 'Facts' tab (do not hardcode the spreadsheet). This will allow you to continue to reuse the spreadsheet for future hotels of various sizes.

1. How much revenue will your OTA bring the hotel?
2. What will be the costs of the OTA?
3. As a business executive focused on profit, would you modify the segmentation for this hotel? How would you change your segmentation strategy and how would that affect your distribution strategy?

CLOSER LOOK: WHOLESALE/FIT (FREE INDEPENDENT TRAVEL)

Wholesalers and FIT companies (often used interchangeably) existed long before the OTA model and often served as a discounted alternative to booking retail rates directly through brand or GDS channels. To the hotelier, FIT and wholesale companies brought incremental rooms by selling bundled deals (i.e. packaged air, dining, rental car, sightseeing) to individual customers or through small tour groups. Because FIT rates (net + markup) were not publically available, there was no maximum or minimal competition with the merchant's standard distribution channels. Using the merchant model, FIT companies such as Tourico, Hotel Beds, or Gulliver's would negotiate discounts such as 20 percent to 30 percent off a property's average retail rate in exchange for a commitment to fill a prenegotiated daily allotment of rooms. Wholesalers would then launch large marketing campaigns to sell hotel packages in order to re-sell room nights for more than the negotiated discount and pocket the difference as compensation.

As OTAs began to move into the discount space, wholesalers were forced to evolve in order to sustain their business model and eventually created rate and inventory direct-connections in order to source retail rates right into wholesaler websites, much like an OTA. Today, FIT companies still bundle and package deeply discounted rates using the merchant model, but they have added additional hidden rate channels to their repertoire of bookings streams, such as discounted offerings made to various fenced loyalty groups and airline or credit card point redemption merchandise. Pre-sold allotments have become rare in the industry, and instead hoteliers have been given the ability to restrict and loosen inventory and discount levels more dynamically through direct internet connections. One of the challenges with many wholesalers that exist today is the ability to regulate public pricing parity. Most FIT contracts state that the wholesaler cannot underprice the hotel, but as the same block of hotel rooms can often be sold from one wholesaler to the next with small commissions taken off the top with each trade, the origin of the initial contractor can become difficult to track down should a public rate be found at a lower price than the brand offering. Often times, a hotelier will have to book the miscellaneous rate themselves in order to track the rate code on the reservation back to the primary FIT company in order to prove a breach has occurred. In many ways, today's traditional FIT companies have had to expand beyond their initial business models and beyond traditional wholesale methods and have grown to emulate modern OTAs more than anything else.

CLOSER LOOK: RATE PARITY AND BEST RATE GUARANTEE

The rise of multiple distribution channels, OTAs, and the transparency of rates on the internet have caused a larger focus of **rate parity**. Rate parity is defined as maintaining the same rate for the same product on all distribution channels. While rate parity existed long before OTAs and the internet because it made management of distribution channels much easier, it became an industry standard in 2004 (Aggarwal, 2013). There are reasons why a hotel may be in favor for or against rate parity.

PROS: Rate parity agreements allow hotels to remain in control of their pricing and ability to set a minimum rate for bookings; rate parity removes price when customers are choosing distribution channel; rate parity avoids customer confusion; rate parity simplifies prices for revenue managers.

CONS: Hotels are paying various commissions based on distribution channel but have the same rate across all channels, therefore generating less profit than if the customer h booked on their direct site; all customers are treated the same way, although customer behavior may be different between distribution channels; a hotel may want to reward or further incentivize a strong distribution channel but are unable to.

Additionally, even if a hotel is hoping to maintain rate parity, there can be roadblocks. These roadblocks can include 1) human error—such as a hotel accidentally loading lower rates on a distribution channel; 2) technology lag/caching—rate and/or inventory updates sent to distribution channels are delayed, causing rate discrepancies among channels; 3) third-party sites offering a self-funded discount that makes a hotel appear less expensive.

RATE PARITY LEGAL PROBLEMS

Rate parity faced legal challenges in the United States in 2014 and Europe in 2014 and 2015 (Freed, 2016). Rate parity came into legal scrutiny because of alleged violation of antitrust laws and consumer protection statuses.

While rate parity has survived in the United States so far, Europe has stricter antitrust laws. On July 9, 2015, the French National Assembly came to a final vote to remove rate parity clauses from contracts between hoteliers and OTAs. This law had been named the "Macron Law" after France's then Minister of Economy, Industry, and Digital Affairs, Emmanuel Macron. The Macron Law was designed to eliminate barriers to free competition in the hotel industry (Freed 2016). The results of rate parity removal are still unknown, but it will foster a more collaborative relationship between OTAs and hoteliers as rate parity is no longer a given in Europe.

QUESTIONS TO CONSIDER

- How do you think the removal of rate parity will affect hotels and their success in Europe? How do you think it will affect the OTAs?

REAL PEOPLE

Director of Revenue Reflection of Rate Parity

Rachel Cole,* a self-taught director of revenue, has worked in hospitality since 2004 and found her place in revenue in 2008. She has worked for multiple hotels, ranging from a 170-room hotel in New York City to a Starwood hotel in Long Beach, California. Her view on rate parity might surprise you and make you consider less obvious pros and cons.

What are your thoughts of rate parity among distribution channels?

Rate parity is a great idea in theory. But there are some channels and some customers you can pretty much predict their behavior. A brand loyal customer will always go to westin.com (or whatever brand.com website they are a member of). The same can be said on OTAs. The reason why they are booking on those channels is because they are that type of customer, they do not care about a hotel's brand; they are looking for the best price.

Because people shopping on Expedia (or any OTA) are not going to buy me on my website and they are shopping on Expedia because they are not loyal, and they want a good price. I need to be competitive in that market place. If I have a rate parity on all channels, I cannot sway the OTA customer to choose my hotel. I need to market myself towards to customer differently than the customer booking on my site. I am competitive on Expedia when I offer an exclusive deal. This helps my sort, and the customer's book when they see the tag.

Then compared to my brand site. Those customers are not a casual shopper. They want to have their preferences saved and they want their points. The customers will not behave the same. Given the choice, I would just throw it [rate parity] out the window.

Do you think rate parity is important to a hotel's success?

It is kind of not. Rate parity in the markets I have been in, no, it has not been important to the hotel's success. Varied pricing has been my success. For the larger markets, I think varied prices are really important, and it has led to a lot of the success I have created in the markets I've been in.

The thing that pushes rate parity is the brand. They have the fines, guarantees. They are slowly but surely making it more restrictive and making it worse when getting caught out of parity. But in the end, not enough customers know about BRG [Best Rate Guarantee] for it to really make an impact the brand wants to see. The amount of revenue you gain for being out of parity totally outweighs the fines you get for being out of parity. The positives significantly outweigh the ding. I know the brands don't like it; it is just way more too beneficial to have your rates be competitive.

Has anyone ever challenged your beliefs on rate parity?

Of course, many times ownership or asset managers have questioned me. One time I ran an exclusive deal on Expedia that booked over 200 room nights. To prove my point, I personally looked up each person in Marriott's system to see if they had an account. None of them did. These were all new customers. If anything, maybe there is a 2 percent overlap. But that's it. Customers that are brand loyal are not shopping on these sites. And to get those customers you need to target and price to them.

Consider the time that Rachel was not hitting her monthly budget, for the second month in a row. She was feeling a lot of pressure to hit her budget, as she was getting nervous about hitting her annual budget with her current gap.

Her general manager wants her to maintain rate parity, although her asset manager continues to pressure her about the budget. What should Rachel do? How would you convince the general manager that doing a special sale might help the hotel?

***Name changed**

CLOSER LOOK: CONNECTIVITY AMONG DISTRIBUTION CHANNELS

With the proliferation of distribution channels and rate parity still in play (at least in the United States and most other countries), hotels are faced with how to easily send their rates and availability to distribution channels. The most basic simple/basic method a hotel can deploy to send their rates and inventory to a distribution channel is managing it directly via an **extranet**. Connectivity via an extranet is very manual and means the hotelier is logging into each distribution channel's extranet, loading their availability and rates. When the hotel receives a reservation, the distribution channels send over the reservation (typically via fax or email) and the hotel must manually input into their CRS. This works well for some hotels, especially if they are smaller and/or do not work with many distribution channels. But even with a smaller hotel this can be a very manual process that can lead to human error. Let's consider an eight-room bed and breakfast for example. The bed and breakfast likely has a different room type for each of their rooms. Managing so many room types can be very time consuming and leave too much room for error (double booking, for example).

Therefore, for the majority of hotels, direct connectivity systems have been created to solve for this manual process. While connectivity, the ability to connect two systems together (distribution system and hotel's CRS) for the purpose of conducting business and delivering reservations, seems simple, a lot more goes into it.

There are two overarching types of how systems are connected: push versus pull. Push is when a hotel reservation system pushes their **availability, rates, and inventory** (**ARI**) data out to their distribution channels. Pull is when the distribution channel requests (or pulls) the ARI from the hotel reservation system as consumers are shopping. A good analogy of the push versus pull comparison is the difference between a text message and a phone call. A text message is a push transaction, where someone is pushing a message (or data) to a recipient. In contrast, a phone call is a pull transaction, the caller (recipient of data, or distribution channel) is requesting the call (or data) (Barnby et al., 2011). Pull systems are typically employed by large hotel portfolios (or brands) with substantial volumes of data to maintain.

PROS: Push: Data workload with search requests is reduced many times, alleviating the need for further IT investment.
Pull: ARI data is accurate at the time of booking and allows for more granular control over factors that include last room availability and yield management restrictions.

CONS: Push: Data may not be as accurate.
Pull: Hotel reservation system must account for high volumes of shopping messages; typically can be more expensive.

Deciding between push versus pull is just the first step in connectivity. There are many of these third-party connection systems that all account for other variables. Third-party connectivity systems have different mapping requirements and ability of pricing strategies (i.e., if a hotel prices by length of stay, they will want a connectivity system that allows for that). These are both things hoteliers need to consider when choosing a connectivity system (also referred to as **channel manager**). Other considerations for mapping are extra person fees, tax calculations, currency differences, etc. Once all of these items are considered, a hotelier can find the right connectivity system and/or channel manager for their hotel. With the ever-growing distribution landscape, the right connectivity system for a hotel is vital.

PROS & CONS

- What are the pros and cons of directly connecting to your distribution channels?

FUTURE OF CHANNEL DISTRIBUTION

There a few themes when considering the future of channel distribution; however, the ultimate goal will continue to be balancing the costs of distribution channels by maximization of hotel's RevPAR. Future themes will continue to transform channel distribution include: 1) continued mergers and acquisitions among key players; 2) increased involvement of social media; 3) creation of technologies to decipher benefits of varying channels; 4) new distribution channel platforms; 5) sharing economy. There has been a huge acceleration in change for distribution systems since the 2000s, and while these are some of the upcoming disruptors, there will be others.

CONTINUED MERGERS AND ACQUISITIONS AMONG KEY PLAYERS

2015 was the year of merger frenzy in the hotel industry. In 2015, the industry saw huge mergers among hotel brands. There are a few causes of these mergers. First the hotel industry has had strong performance since the recession; growth in revenue per available room has been positive since March 2010 (STR, 2017). But as growth continues, hotels are considering ways to continue the growth, especially as new players such as the Airbnb sharing economy enters the game. A clear method of saving costs and therefore growing revenue is via economies of scale. Second, the mergers lend to greater brand recognition. As noted previously, the cost of customer acquisition continues to increase, and expanded loyalty programs and larger marketing budgets created by mergers help counteract this. Third, the hotel brand mergers help hoteliers negotiate contracts with other distribution channels, such as OTAs. Barry Sternlicht, founder and former CEO of Starwood Hotels & Resorts and current CEO of Starwood Capital, believes that huge hotel mergers are the best offense against Expedia and Airbnb because they creates scale (Weissmann, 2016).

QUESTIONS TO CONSIDER

- Are there other benefits of merging hotel brands?

From an OTA standpoint, consolidation has been happening since the early 2000s; there are now two major players, Expedia Inc. and The Priceline

Group. Throughout 2014 and 2015 Expedia Inc. acquired Wotif, Travelocity, Orbitz, Trivago, and Homeaway (Expedia Inc. 2015). The Priceline Group includes Booking.com, Priceline.com, Agoda.com, Kayak.com, and OpenTable (Priceline Group). A benefit of the mergers among OTAs is easier distribution to multiple sites when contracting with an OTA. However, as they merge, hoteliers are faced with individual OTAs harnessing more market share and therefore influence.

INCREASED INVOLVEMENT OF SOCIAL MEDIA

When asked about social media, Sternlicht acknowledged it is "critical," adding that if social media aren't used well, a hotel is "in danger of losing a generation" (Weissmann, 2016).

While social media is an important factor for hotels, there is also the future potential of social media actually entering the distribution game. George Corbin, VP eCommerce Strategy & eMarketing at Marriott International, contemplates the potential of Google, Apple, Facebook or "non-travel-players leveraging their platforms to drive into travel and hotel space" (Green & Lomanno, 2015). These websites already have a huge consumer base, and if we look at Facebook, for example, they are doing more to adapt their site to keep consumers there. Therefore, it becomes a natural extension when a Facebook users posts they just booked their flight for Facebook to recommend hotels.

"When asked if hotels should do social media, my answer usually isn't just 'yes,' it's 'Hell, yes!' says Tim Peter, of Tim Peter Associates (T. Peter, March 2016). Tim acknowledges that social media may work better for certain types of hotels than others; for boutique properties and resorts versus economy chain properties, for instance, "social [media] plays an integral role in helping hotels connect directly with their customers early in their purchase funnel, during their stay, and post stay. Plenty of hotels see solid and consistent traffic growth and improving conversion rates from content posted on social sites such as Facebook, Twitter, Pinterest, and Instagram." (T. Peter, March 2016)

CROSS DEVICE CHANNEL PLATFORMS

Webtrends found that the average customer visits 6.5 devices and/or websites before booking their room (Vivion, 2014). The internet and ability to research and book hotels is everywhere. There are about 13.4 billion internet-connected devices in the word. This means 2 internet-connected devices for every person on the planet (Hoisington, 2014). As consumers continue to visit multiple sites before booking and the number of devices increase, hoteliers need to consider where they want to be shown and how. The highest level for a hotel reservation system to be cross-channel, platform, and functional.

OTAs have invested heavily to ensure their continued presence on all new channels. For example, Expedia rolled-out Scratchpad in 2014. Expedia's Scratchpad allows customers to return to any logged-in device and instantly see the hotels, flights, and packages most recently viewed; Scratchpad creates a seamless cross-device experience (Kim & Bhutani, 2014). This is an inherent benefit of working with an OTA. While an individual hotel may not have the IT infrastructure to invest in a wearable app (such as a smartwatch), Expedia Inc. has, and your hotel is now listed on wearables.

Marketing consultant Tim Peter notes that mobile is not a trend, it is here to stay; in fact, Peter states, "It's almost impossible to overstate the impacts we will continue to see from mobile over the next several years . . . guests never 'go online;' they are online. Everywhere. All the time" (T. Peter, March 2016). A TripAdvisor study in 2015 revealed that 42 percent of travelers use a smartphone to plan or book their trip (Tripadvisor, 2015). Additionally, Annalect conducted a six-month study to examine the impact of technology on millennials' relationship with brands. Most notable for distribution channels, smartphone-owning millennials (ages 19 33) are more likely to expect brands to have mobile-friendly website or app (55 percent) than a social media presence (39 percent).

When considering mobile further, it is important to consider its impact to the guest. Peter speculates potential impacts include "guests continually shopping for lower rates whenever and wherever they happen to be even after they've booked their stay; decreased use of concierge services and room service; and third-parties offering enhancements to the on-property experience using mobile apps or messaging as a marketing and service delivery channel" (T. Peter, March 2016).

Therefore, while hotels may rely on OTAs to be displayed on the cutting-edge channels, a hotel should heavily consider mobile friendly websites and apps if they want to see continued growth in brand.com business.

SEEING FURTHER

Consider you are a director of revenue management (DORM) at a hotel. Your general manager (GM) does not want to pay to create a mobile-friendly website.

- How would you convince him that it makes sense to invest in mobile? What would your mobile specific strategy be?

SHARING ECONOMY

The sharing economy is another trend of the 21st century with the rise of companies like Uber, Lyft, Airbnb, HomeAway, Couch Surfers, etc. Airbnb is a very hot topic among hoteliers. Niki Leodakis, CEO of Commune Hotels + Resorts said, "I think we better be eyes wide open about Airbnb … It's reminiscent of 2001, 2002, 2003 when we were all watching the OTAs and going 'holy crap these guys are going to chew up our business'" (Peter, 2015). While it is unseen if Airbnb will chew up hotel business, there is nothing to say that it will not.

Peter recommends to "stay nimble, stay humble, stay focused"—and avoid commoditization. Peter goes further and commands hotels to be clear on what makes your hotel special and know that a hotelier can offer their guests an experience no one else can (Peter, 2015).

CLOSING

As we look into the future, we can only expect that distribution channels will continue to grow and morph. The hotelier's goal is to increase share in their least expensive channels and partner with channels that provide benefits they cannot create on their own.

DISCUSSION QUESTIONS

Question 1: You are the general manager of a 20-room independent hotel in the remote Rocky Mountains. Right now you only accept walk-ins and reservations via the phone. What other distribution channels would make sense for your hotel and why?

Question 2: Why do you think the customer cost of acquisition has increased?

Question 3: You are a hotel located about 5 miles from downtown Hartford, CT. You are currently independent and are considering flagging with a brand. What would be the distribution benefits of using a brand?

APPLICATIONS

Application 1

You are opening a new 60-room hotel in Bend, Oregon. While Bend, Oregon, is known by outdoor enthusiasts, it is a relatively small city.

- Go through the process of reviewing the 2 likely distribution channels and indicate the pros and cons of each.
- Should the hotel use a push or pull connectivity system and why?
- How can the hotel be ahead of its competition?

Application 2

You are a hotelier of an independent hotel in France.

- What are the benefits of being independent versus branded?
- Will you have the same prices across all channels?
- What will be the partnership impact to their distribution channels?

TEAM ACTIVITY

A new distribution channel has been created, Geo-Trip. Geo-Trip allows customers to book adventures bundled with hotels. Geo-Trip claims to be a game changer by providing a huge millennial consumer base across the world.

Split up the class into pairs. Each pair will conduct a negotiation—one student pitching Geo-Trip and one student representing the hotel.

The following questions should guide the negotiation:

- What are the benefits to the hotel for signing up?
- What are the costs associated with Geo-Trip?
- How will the hotel connect to Geo-Trip?
- How will Geo-Trip affect the hotel's other distribution channels?
- Will Geo-Trip affect the operations at the hotel? If so, how?

INTERNET ACTIVITY

Go to http://www.expediaquickconnect.com/content/eqc-preferred-program.

- Do you think it makes sense to use a preferred connectivity vendor? Why or why not?

Research three of the preferred vendors.

- Find three unique qualities of each vendor you research.
- Find out what their competitive edge is.

GLOSSARY

Average daily rate (ADR) – Rooms revenue divided by rooms sold, displayed as the average rental rate for a single room.

Availability, rates, and inventory (ARI) – Referred to by connectivity systems.

Billboard effect – In the Cornell study, the billboard effect is the marketing and advertising benefits experienced by hotels when they're listed on online travel agent websites.

Brand.com – The main reservation booking website for the hotel or chain.

Channel manager – A connectivity third-party system that pushes a hotel's ARI to a distribution channel.

Central reservation system (CRS) – A computerized backend system of a hotel's booking engine.

Distribution channel – The chain of businesses or intermediaries through which a good or service passes until it reaches the end consumer; in the hotel industry distribution channels are business or intermediaries through which a customer can purchase a hotel room.

Extranet – A connectivity system website where hotel's upload their rates and availability to display on the associated third-party website.

Global distribution system (GDS) – A worldwide computerized reservation network that provides transactions to travel agents, online reservation sites, and large corporations.

Metasearch engine – Travel website that uses data from multiple search engines (OTAs and brand.com) to produce a compiled result.

Online travel agent (OTA) – Travel website allowing customers to plan and book travel.

Rate parity – Identical retail rate is quoted across all channels.

REFERENCES

Aggarwal, S. (2013, May). *The Uncovered Interest Rate Parity Puzzle in the Foreign Exchange Market* [Scholarly project]. NYU Stern School of Business. Retrieved from http://web-docs.stern.nyu.edu/old_web/economics/docs/workingpapers/2013/Aggarwal_ParityPuzzle_May2013.pdf

American Airlines Inc. (n/d). *History of American Airlines.* Retrieved from https://www.aa.com/i18n/customer-service/about-us/history-of-american-airlines.jsp

Anderson, C. (2009, October 2). The Billboard Effect: Online Travel Agent Impact on Non-OTA Reservation Volume. Center for Hospitality Research Publications. Retrieved from https://scholarship.sha.cornell.edu/cgi/viewcontent.cgi?referer=&httpsredir=1&article=1001&context=chrpubs

Barnby, C., Bruno, T., Harasymiw, Kiker, C., Neal, R., Noble, T., Revelle, D., Troudi, N & Unwin, T. (2011) Push and Pull Connectivity Models for Hotel Distribution. [White Paper] Retrieved from https://c.ymcdn.com/sites/www.hedna.org/resource/resmgr/HEDNA_Push_Pull_White_Paper.pdf

Cassidy, J. (2002). *Dot.con: the greatest story ever sold.* Allen Lane: The Penguin Press.

Duetto Research. (2016). *The Ultimate Guide to Hotel Revenue Strategy,* 1-66. Retrieved from http://go.duettocloud.com/revenue-strategy-guide

eMarketer. (2014, December 19). Travel Planners Migrate to Mobile. Retrieved from https://www.emarketer.com/Article/Travel-Planners-Migrate-Mobile/1011734

Expedia Inc. (2015). 2014 Annual Report. Transcript.

Expedia Inc. (2016). 2015 Annual Report. Transcript.

Freed, J. (2016, July 7). Rate Parity Issues Keep Hotel Lawyers Busy. Retrieved from https://www.duettocloud.com/library/rate-parity-issues-keep-hotel-lawyers-busy

Green, C. E. & Lomanno, M. V. (2015). *Distribution Channel Analysis: A Guide for Hotels. An AH&LA and STR Special Report.* Retrieved from https://www.hotelnewsnow.com/media/File/PDFs/DCA%20Executive%20Summary.pdf

HAMA Study. (2014). *Retail Commissions Only.* Kalibri Labs.

Hilton Worldwide Holdings, Inc. (2017). Q4 2016 Earnings Call. Transcript.

Hoisington, A. (2014, December 22) 5 Hotel Marketing Trends for 2015. *Hotel News Now.* Retrieved from http://www.hotelnewsnow.com/Articles/24707/5-hotel-marketing-trends-for-2015

Kim, J & Bhutani, A. (2014, March 31). *A Technical Look: How Expedia is Simplifying Travel Planning.* Retrieved from Expedia Blog https://viewfinder.expedia.com/a-technical-look-how-expedia-is-simplifying-travel-planning/

Mahmoud, A. (2015, June 12). *Hotel ADR Rise vs. Distribution Channel Cost, What Hoteliers Need to Calculate.* Retrieved from https://www.hospitalitynet.org/opinion/4070604.html

Marsh, P. (2015, January 28). #GenerationTech: Millennials & Technology. Annalect. Research Study. Retrieved from http://www.annalect.com/generationtech-millennials-technology/

McGuire, K. A. (2016, August 11). Building a Smart Distribution Strategy. Cornell Hotel Research. Retrieved from https://sha.cornell.edu/faculty-research/centers-institutes/chr/blog/building-a-smart-distribution-strategy/

O'Neill, S. (2014, May 22) Does the Expedia Billboard Effect Still Exist for Hotels? [Originally published on tnooz]. Retrieved from https://www.phocuswire.com/Does-the-Expedia-billboard-effect-still-exist-for-hotels

Peter, T. (2015, June 9) How Safe Are Independent Hotels from Airbnb. Retrieved from https://www.timpeter.com/2015/06/09/how-safe-are-independent-hotels-from-airbnb.

Priceline Group. (2016) 2015 Annual Report. Transcript.

STR AMER Lodging Data. (2017, January). Unpublished raw data.

Ting, D. (2016, May 16) Comes to Pushing Direct Bookings. Skift. Retrieved from https://skift.com/2016/05/16/hotel-ceos-wont-back-down-when-it-comes-to-pushing-direct-bookings/

TripAdvisor Study (2015, June 30). Retrieved from http://ir.tripadvisor.com/news-releases/news-release-details/tripadvisor-study-reveals-42-travelers-worldwide-use-smartphones

"Use Our Lodging/Hotel Industry Database of Internet Marketing Articles." Hotel Internet Marketing, Hotel Web Site Design by Milestone. Retrieved from <http://www.milestoneinternet.com/hdml/article-databse-lodging-industry.asp>

Vivion, N. (2014, September 2). How Many Websites and Devices Does a Consumer use to Research Travel? [Originally published on tnooz.] Retrieved from https://www.phocuswire.com/How-many-websites-and-devices-does-a-consumer-use-to-research-travel

Warner, M. & Qaudri-Felitti D. & Chandnani, P. (2010). A History of Travel Distribution: 1915 – 2009. *HEDNA*. Retrieved from https://corsi.unibo.it/magistrale/emt/bacheca/2013-05-seminario-in-revenue-management-the-distribution-dilemma/5a3e53f2148447caa7b55cf3d80d1f2b

Webtrends Recommends Best Practices to Help Travel Sites Increase Bookings. (2014, August 26). *Webtrends*. Retrieved from https://www.globenewswire.com/news-release/2014/08/26/1130302/0/en/Webtrends-Recommends-Best-Practices-to-Help-Travel-Sites-Increase-Bookings.html

Weissmann, A. (2016, January 16). OTAs Driver Hotel Mergers. *Travel Weekly.* <http://www.travelweekly.com/Travel-News/Hotel-News/Barry-Sternlicht-power-OTAs-driving-hotel-mergers>

CHAPTER 5

Competitive Analysis in Hotel Revenue Management

Theresa Doherty and Leslie Lew

OVERVIEW

Knowing and understanding competition is key to growing revenue and market share. This chapter will present the processes used to determine and evaluate the most appropriate **competitive set.** It will also cover the tools available to monitor and analyze competitor performance in order to improve a hotel's revenue results.

LEARNING OBJECTIVES

After studying this module, you should be able to:

- Design a competitive set for an individual hotel
- Create a SWOT analysis (strength, weaknesses, opportunities, threats) to compare an individual hotel and its competitors
- Prepare a competitive set value offering analysis
- Construct a rate value matrix to validate the hotel's strategy
- Identify business opportunities by understanding competitor performance
- Apply competitive assessment methodologies to hotel development feasibility studies

OUTLINE

Introduction

Defining Your Competition

- Validating the Set
- Determine Competitive Positioning within Competition

Inverse SWOT Analysis

Competitive Grid Analysis

Segment Performance

Positioning Statement

Rate Value Matrix

Discussion Questions and Applications

INTRODUCTION

Defining Segmentation

The specific objectives of competitive intelligence are basically to manage and reduce risk, achieve profitable knowledge, ensure information security, and avoid information overload (Myburgh, 2004). This means that managers need to understand their customers and competitors better to build a competitive advantage. Therefore, a vital component in strategic planning and management is to gather a variety of information, which allows companies—by analyzing the strengths and weaknesses of competitors—to anticipate market developments, as they can predict what will happen in their competitive environment.

SO WHAT?

Hotel managers need to understand their customers and competitors better to build competitive advantage. Understanding your competitors is key to understanding your market and available opportunities.

- Why is it not enough to understand your own business? Why do you need to understand your competitive landscape?

DEFINING YOUR COMPETITION

A competitor can be defined as one selling or buying goods or services in the same market as another. In the hotel world, the definition goes further than just offering services within the same market. In order to identify a hotel's true competitors, the hotel team must determine what other hotels are targeting the same customers. The group of hotels that are considered competitors is referred to as the **competitive set**.

The typical considerations for defining a competitive set are:

- Location: Location is one of the primary factors that are used to establish direct competitors. It goes beyond the city. Hotels are considered competitors depending upon proximity to **demand generators** within a city. Demand generators apply to all segments. They can include corporate offices, government agencies, tourist/leisure attractions, and convention centers.
- Hotel Services/Tier: Hotel competitors typically fall within the same or similar class of service or tier. This holds true because customers can usually be differentiated by the hotel tier they tend to select. This can also be a function of the price range that hotels fall into within a given tier and the budget considerations of the various segments.
- Customer **Segmentation**: Hotels typically have several main business segments that drive their success. Understanding the segmentation of the competitors helps to determine which hotels share the same segmentation and are true competitors. Segmentation can include comparable group profiles, special corporate accounts, government business, and leisure travelers.
- Market: A market is typically defined by geographic proximity. It can be based upon geographic considerations or market segmentation. Some hotels look at competitive data through a segmentation lens without the location parameter. For example, a large convention hotel may create a competitive set that includes hotels from other cities that compete for large group business. Another example is a resort location that competes for leisure customers with other resort destinations.
- Online Information: There is also plenty of data online, such as ratings and commentary, to provide insight from a consumer's

perspective. OTA sites provide information on other hotels that customers reviewed during their search and other hotels that customers booked after viewing a given hotel. As hotels assess their competitors, reading customer reviews can provide critical insight into the actual customer experience at the other hotels.

VALIDATING THE SET

How do you know if a competitive set is appropriate? Oftentimes there is disagreement between the property and owners/asset managers on the appropriate set for a hotel. The key is to have a set where revenue growth performance is a realistic barometer for comparison purposes.

PROS & CONS

While competitive sets are easily defined in theory, it is oftentimes more difficult to establish an ideal set based upon the makeup of the other hotels in a given market. For example, there could be a 4-star hotel with only select service competitors in the immediate vicinity. The next closest 4-star hotel is located 15 miles away, fed by a different set of demand generators.

- As you consider this situation, is it better to select a select service competitor or the more distant 4-star hotel as a competitor for performance and opportunity measurement purposes?

Source: Google map showing location of hotels.

THINK HISTORICALLY

History of STR

Smith Travel Research is the leading global provider of competitive benchmarking, information services, and research to the hotel industry. Randy and Carolyn Smith founded STR from their kitchen table in 1985, and to this day the company remains a privately held family business with a long-term vision. From its headquarters outside of Nashville, Tennessee, the company currently gathers performance data from over 63,000 hotels located in more than 180 countries.

Consider the below example dated September 2002:

- Why would hotels have signed up to participate in this type of service?
- Explore www.str.com and discuss how its reporting services have evolved.

Hotel Anywhere
789 East Main Street
Oakland, CA 95071-4981
United States
Telephone: (615) 824-8664

Star Summary Report · September 2002

STR * 1234
Chain ID: OAK 2323
Open Date: 198201

Mgt Co: None
Owner: None
Total Rooms: 490

Operation Franchise
Market Oakland Ca
Tract: Oakland-Berkeley

10/24/02
e-star_summary
1.01

Segment		Occupancy Percent	% Chg	Average Room Rate	% Chg	RevPar	% Chg	Room Revenue % Chg	Rooms Available % Chg	Rooms Sold % Chg	Occupancy Percent	% Chg	Average Room Rate	% Chg	RevPar	% Chg	Room Revenue % Chg	Rooms Available % Chg	Rooms Sold % Chg
		Monthly Performance									**Year To Date Performance**								
Hotel Anywhere		66.9	17.6	$138.52	1.2	$92.65	19.0	19.8	0.6	18.3	62.2	-13.7	$138.32	-7.0	$86.08	-19.7	-19.0	0.9	-12.9
Market:	Oakland, Ca	59.5	-1.2	$89.42	-1.7	$53.20	-2.8	2.6	5.5	4.3	60.5	-12.9	$99.84	-7.9	$54.98	-19.8	-16.4	4.3	-9.2
Market Price:	Luury	61.3	11.1	$125.44	-4.6	$76.87	5.8	11.9	5.7	17.3	61.7	-5.2	$127.25	-12.7	$78.47	-17.3	-14.4	3.4	-2.0
Tract:	Oakland Berkeley	62.5	7.8	$104.41	-1.5	$65.28	6.1	11.0	4.6	12.7	60.9	-11.2	$104.50	-7.6	$63.64	-18.0	-13.0	6.1	-5.9
Tract Scale:	Upscale Chains	68.3	15.2	$122.23	-3.3	$83.45	11.4	28.8	15.7	33.2	65.3	-6.8	$123.20	-9.8	$80.47	-15.9	-3.4	14.9	7.1
Competitive Set:	Competitors	64.0	11.3	$123.75	-3.6	$79.18	7.2	7.2	0.0	11.2	63.0	-11.4	$125.01	-7.2	$78.71	-17.9	-17.9	0.0	-11.5

12 Month Performance

Segment		Occupancy Percent	% Chg	Average Room Rate	% Chg	RevPar	% Chg	Room Revenue % Chg	Rooms Available % Chg	Rooms Sold % Chg
Hotel Anywhere		62.4	-15.6	$139.63	-5.1	$87.10	-19.9	-19.1	1.0	-14.8
Market:	Oakland, Ca	59.9	-15.8	$90.71	-7.4	$54.37	-21.9	-18.5	4.4	-12.0
Market Price:	Luxury	60.1	-10.2	$128.22	-12.3	$77.11	-21.2	-18.9	2.9	-7.5
Tract:	Oakland-Berkeley	60.1	-14.5	$105.03	-5.9	$63.07	-19.6	-13.7	7.2	-8.4
Tract Scale:	Upscale Chains	64.5	-9.3	$124.11	-8.9	$80.07	-17.3	-2.6	17.8	6.9
Competitive Set:	Competitors	61.7	-15.2	$126.40	-6.1	$78.00	-20.4	-20.4	0.0	-15.3

Census/Sample - Properties & Rooms

Segment	Census		Sample		Sample % (Rooms)
	Properties	Rooms	Properties	Rooms	
Market	213	22795	129	18479	81.1
Market Price	29	5778	26	5473	94.7
Tract	56	6633	33	5695	85.9
Tract Scale	8	2167	8	2167	100
Competitive Set	9	2550	9	2550	100

Figure 5.1: Sample STAR Summary Report, Smith Travel Research

QUESTIONS TO CONSIDER

The 2016 version of the STAR report includes running 3 month data.

- Why do you think STR included running 3 month data? Why do you think STR added Supply, Demand, and Pipeline data to the modern version of the report?

2016 STAR Summary

Tab 3 - STAR Summary - My Property vs. Comp Set and Industry Segments
TS Hotel 200W 67h St Austin, TX 78704 Phone: (512) 565-1999
STR # 430 CheinID: None MgtCo: Major Hotel Group Owner TLCP Development
For the Month of March: 2016 Date Created: April 30, 2016 Monthly Competitive Set Data Excludes Subject Property

	Occupancy (%)								Supply			
	Current Month	**% Chg**	**Year of Date**	**% Chg**	**Running 3 Month**	**% Chg**	**Running 12 Month**	**% Chg**	**Month % Chg**	**VID % Chg**	**Run 3 Mon % Chg**	**Run 12 Mon % Chg**
TS Hotel	88.0	-1.5	87.0	31	87.0	3.1	83.0	2.4	0.0	1.1	1.1	0.3
Market Austin. TX	82.9	1.0	81.6	35	68.7	3.5	75.5	3.3	1.0	1.1	1.1	1.2
Market Class Luxury Class	80.2	0.4	75.2	14	75.2	1.4	80.6	-0.8	11.8	11.8	11.8	9.8
Tract: Austin. TX	79.1	0.4	74.7	29	74.7	2.9	80.7	0.1	3.1	3.6	3.6	1.4
Tract Scale: Independents	70.0	-0.7	71.4	1.3	71.4	1.3	77.1	-0.3	10.9	10.9	10.9	6.4
Competitive Set Competitors	85.8	9.5	81.7	7.6	81.7	7.6	85.8	0.3	0.0	3.7	3.7	0.9

	Average Daily Rate								Demand			
	Current Month	**% Chg**	**Year of Date**	**% Chg**	**Running 3 Month**	**% Chg**	**Running 12 Month**	**% Chg**	**Month % Chg**	**VID % Chg**	**Run 3 Mon % Chg**	**Run 12 Mon % Chg**
TS Hotel	310.98	4.0	300.84	5.1	300.84	5.1	237.68	17.2	-1.5	4.2	4.2	2.7
Market Austin, TX	256.45	4.1	252.45	5.4	117.79	5.4	127.58	9.2	2.0	4.6	4.6	4.6
Market Class Luxury Class	187.91	-3.3	182.45	-1.6	182.68	-1.6	214.34	7.0	12.2	13.3	13.3	8.9
Tract: Austin, TX	162.72	0.2	156.35	2.6	156.35	2.6	177.56	9.9	3.5	6.6	6.6	1.5
Tract Scale: Independents	144.59	-0.6	139.97	2.1	139.97	2.1	163.50	10.3	10.1	12.3	12.3	6.0
Competitive Set Competitors	206.12	-3.3	200.04	-1.5	200.04	-1.5	230.08	7.8	9.5	11.6	11.6	1.2

	RevPAR								Revenue			
	Current Month	**% Chg**	**Year of Date**	**% Chg**	**Running 3 Month**	**% Chg**	**Running 12 Month**	**% Chg**	**Month % Chg**	**VID % Chg**	**Run 3 Mon % Chg**	**Run 12 Mon % Chg**
TS Hotel	273.66	2.4	261.73	8.3	261.73	8.3	197.27	20.0	2.4	9.5	20.4	
Market Austin, TX	88.00	5.1	80.90	9.0	80.90	9.0	96.26	12.9	6.2	10.2	14.2	
Market Class Luxury Class	150.70	-2.9	137.38	-0.2	137.38	-0.2	172.79	6.1	8.5	11.5	16.5	
Tract: Austin, TX	126.76	0.6	116.75	5.6	116.75	5.6	143.34	10.0	3.7	9.3	11.5	
Tract Scale: Independents	112.85	-1.4	99.91	3.4	99.91	3.4	126.10	9.9	9.4	14.7	16.9	
Competitive Set Competitors	176.88	5.9	163.52	6.1	163.52	6.1	197.37	8.1	5.9	10.0	9.1	

	Census/Sample Properties & Rooms					Pipeline			
	Census		Sample		Sample %	Market: Austin, TX			
	Properties	Rooms	Properties	Rooms	Rooms	Under Construction		Planning	
Market Austin, TX	271	26693	206	23880	89.5	Properties	Rooms	Properties	Rooms
Market Class: Luxury Class	12	1596	12	1596	100.0	7	617	22	3684
Tract: Austin, TX	53	9994	35	8809	88.1	See Help page for pipeline definitions.			
Tract Scale: Independents	26	2340	17	1974	84.4				
Competitive Set Competitors	5	1024	5	1024	100.0				

The STR STAR Report is a publication of STR, Inc. and STR Global, Ltd. and intended solely for use by paid subscribers. Reproduction or distribution of the STR STAR Repot, in whole or part, without written permission is prohibited and subject to legal action.
If you have received this report and are NOT a subscriber to the STR STAR report, please contact us immediately. Source: 2016 STR, Inc. / STR Global, Ltd. trading as "STR".

Figure 5.2. Example STAR Summary Tab, Smith Travel Research

DETERMINE COMPETITIVE POSITIONING WITHIN COMPETITION

A **SWOT analysis** is a four-quadrant table organized by your organization's greatest strengths, weaknesses, opportunities, and threats. The purpose of the analysis is to validate your organization's operating position of strengths and weaknesses and identify external opportunities and threats to build a strategy plan.

Strengths are unique internal characteristics of your organization that provide an advantage over your competition. These characteristics can be tangible, like a landmark location that is inimitable or unique, or intangible, like brand recognition when the positive attributes cannot be measured.

What do you do better than anyone else?

What are the positive unique qualities you offer that no one else can replace or copy?

Weaknesses are negative detractors of your organization that disallows it from reaching its peak potential. Often these detractors are also strengths of your competition.

What does your business lack in order to reach peak revenue or profitability?

Why do consumers buy from your competition instead of your organization?

Opportunities are unrealized potential for your organization to gain/prosper in.

Is there a change in business drivers that can increase demand for your product or market?

Are there existing customers who are buying from the competition who can be better served by your organization if these potential customers understood your product?

Threats are negative external factors that impact your organization and that you have little ability to control or anticipate when these factors will materialize.

Are there transportation regulation changes that can reduce the number of travelers to a destination?

Is there significant new supply anticipated for the market after years of strong performance above the national average growth?

Consideration	**Strengths**	**Weaknesses**	**Consideration**
• Internally influenced • Differentiator from competitor • Competitor cannot easily replicate	• High repeat guest rate and satisfaction from over 30 years of operation • The tallest hotel with ocean views in the market. Local zoning prohibits another high-rise hotel in the city.	• High guest amenity costs from ordering local vendors with low economies of scale • High training costs from high employee turnover • Guest satisfaction scores are trending negatively in the last six months	• Internally influenced • Can be unfeasible to resolve, i.e. historic building with limited scope to change
Consideration	**Opportunities**	**Threats**	**Consideration**
• Externally influenced • Outside of the organization's control • Can change your business plan • Unexpected	• Air Traffic is expected to grow 25% in five years bringing new travellers to the city. • New professional sports team stadium will open this year and is located three blocks from the hotel.	• New supply to enter market • Limited in-market talent pool due to lack of like product • Construction zone near hotel for new public transit center to open in three years	• Externally influenced • Outside of the organization's control • Can change your business plan • Unexpected

Figure 5.3: SWOT Analysis Template

QUESTION TO CONSIDER

If your hotel and its competitors share the same strength, then it is not unique to your hotel.

- How would you differentiate your hotel if the shared strength is an oceanview location?

A SWOT analysis is structured to assess your organization relative to the marketplace. By design it is an introspective assessment of your organization. You can take the SWOT approach further and prepare a SWOT that compares your organization directly with a specific competitor to identify the strategy strengths, weaknesses, opportunities, and threats. Refer to Table 5.1. This table examines how a competitor hotel would prepare a SWOT analysis when compared against the subject hotel.

Table 5.1: Inverse SWOT Analysis

Competitor Hotel # 2:	**The Grand Hotel, 3 Star 80 Key**
What are the key competitive attributes of this competitor?	**What are your selling strategies against these attributes?**
• Guestrooms have 13 ft high ceilings vs our 10 ft high ceiling. • Location is 3 blocks (vs 6 blocks) closer to leisure attractions. • Hotel has 5K sq ft. meeting space, but can utilize adjacent building with 10K sq. ft meeting space.	• Grand Hotel rooms have higher ceilings but are outdated. Last room renovation occurred 12 years ago. • Our hotel guest rooms all have windows and natural lighting. Grand Hotel has rooms with light-well only. • In-house gym, restaurant, coffee bar, bar.
What business segments do you compete with this competitor for?	**How will you position yourself against this competitor to win a customer?**
• Transient Leisure • Transient Corporate • Tour & Travel	• After a $15 million dollar renovation our organization will be repositioned to a full-service four-star hotel, which is one full star category up from the competition. • Two award winning F&B outlets vs Roosevelt's third-party operated average restaurant. • Our guest room size is 25% larger (375 sq ft. vs 300 sq ft.).

QUESTION TO CONSIDER

The subject hotel's guest room size is 25 percent larger than the average competitor.

- How can the hotel promote this compelling product feature?

COMPETITIVE GRID ANALYSIS

A **competitive grid analysis** is a tactical tool to evaluate the product and service offering for the hotel and its competitors. This is different from the SWOT analysis that is focused on assessing the hotel's strengths, weaknesses, opportunities, and threats to determine strategy. The competitive grid analysis is a quantified comparison of the subject hotel and its competitors for product, service, facilities, and location. By quantifying the product and services offered, the hotel can use the competitive grid analysis to identify entries for the hotel's SWOT analysis.

Site Location: What is the competitors' distance to the subject hotel and major attractions as measured by walking distance in blocks or miles?

Facilities: Food and beverage outlets, meeting space, spa.

Services and Pricing: Valet parking, self-parking, concierge, business center.

Property Condition or Age: Year built, year of last renovation, condition of product.

SPREADSHEET EXERCISE 5.1

Another aspect of positioning relative to the competitive set is rate positioning. One way of evaluating a hotel's pricing is to look at the ratio of the subject hotel to the weighted average of the competitor's rates. This determines the rate position index for the hotel.

Rate position index = subject hotel rate / weighted average rate for comp set

If the index is greater than one, the hotel is priced at a premium over the comp set. If the index is less than one, the hotel is priced at a discount to the comp set. Over time, a hotel can determine what index is appropriate during various demand times and use this measurement to determine if retail pricing is appropriate.

In the Excel document, update the hotel's pricing and comp set's pricing based upon the grid below. The weightings for each of the competitors are also listed in the grid. Once this information has been entered into the spreadsheet, answer the following questions:

- What is the rate position index for each date?
- Is the hotel priced at a premium over the competitive set?
- What other competitor information would you like to have in order to validate what the appropriate rate position index is for this particular hotel?
- What are two potential strategy changes the hotel could make based upon the rate position index alone?

	3/2	4/15	5/17	6/20	Weight
bject Hotel	$ 250	$ 269	$ 289	$ 325	
ompetitor A	$ 240	$ 240	$ 275	$ 299	20%
ompetitor B	$ 250	$ 275	$ 285	$ 305	35%
ompetitor C	$ 225	$ 225	$ 225	$ 225	15%
ompetitor D	$ 240	$ 240	$ 280	$ 280	15%
ompetitor E	$ 250	$ 260	$ 280	$ 300	15%

COMPETITIVE SET

Hotel	Competitor 1	Competitor 2	Competitor 3	Competitor 4	Competitor 5
Property Image					
Property Summary	Formerly the Queen and Crescent Hotel, 4 stars. Recently completed a new building with additional guest rooms. Independent.	New Building with emphasis on contemporary design. 3.5 star. Part of Trust Hospitality.	Historic, boutique hotel, located within the New Orleans CBD. 2014- TripAdvisor Certificate of Excellence. 3.5 Star. Part of the Ascend Hotel Collection.	Opened in 1999. Formerly a bank. 3.5 star. Boutique hotel with buildings original architecture. Part of Interstate Hotels & Resorts and the New Orleans Hotel Collection.	Newly renovated, the 3.5 -star Blake Hotel New Orleans, a part of the Ascend Collection Hotels.
Website Address					
Geographic Location [what's nearby?]	Located withing CBD, In between FD and Warehouse District.	Located on Lee Circle in the Warehouse District.	Center of the CBD. Two blocks from the French Quarter and Warehouse District.	Located within the CBD. 4 blocks from the Old No 77 Hotel. Centrally located in FD, Warehouse and Superdome.	Stands along Poydras and St. Charles in the CBD.
* *French Quarter*	2	7	1	4	5
* *Convention Center*	7	4	7	8	6
* *Major Companies*	1	3 to 4	1	1	1
Management / Ownership	Aimbridge Hospitality	Trust Hospitality	Ascend Hotel Collection [Choice Hotels]	Interstate Hotels & Resorts	Ascend Collection Hotels
Year Built	1993	n/a	1933	1909	n/a
Renovation	2014	n/a	2003	2013	2003
Number of Rooms (Including Suites)	196	135	86	93	122
Fitness Center	In adjacent building	Yes, fully equipped	Hotel guests can use the fitness center at the Blake hotel, 3 blocks away	Yes, limited equipment	Yes, fully equipped
COMPSET					
Hotel	Competitor 1	Competitor 2	Competitor 3	Competitor 4	Competitor 5
Parking	Valet / $34 overnight	Valet/ $33 overnight	Valet/$29.95 overnight	Valet/ $34 overnight	Valet/$34 overnight
Restaurant(s)	Lobby restaurant – all local ingredients	Tivoli & Lee	Chophouse Restaurant	Bistro	Café at the Square
Bar / Lounge	Lobby bar – all local inspirations	Belle epoque	Chophouse Bar	Restaurant Bar	Restaurant Bar
Meeting Space	In adjacent building – Square footage TBD	750 sq.ft.	None. Located next to New Orleans Board of Trade that hosts meetings and meetings	One meeting space with 470 sq ft.	1,275 sq ft of meeting space
Other Facilities	None	None	Sister Property: the Blake Hotel	New Orleans Hotel Collection, Le Marais	Sister property – St James hotel
Sales / Catering Team	DDS, 1 Sales Manager and 1 Sales Coordinator	DDS. 1 sales Manager and 1 Sales Coordinator	1 Sales Manager, 1 Sales Coordinator	1 Sales Manager	DDS, Sales Manager and Sales Coordinator
Market Mix	Group, Smerf Group, Corporate, Transient, Leisure	Group, Smerf Group, Corporate, Transient, Leisure	Group, Smerf Group, Corporate, Transient, Leisure	Group, Smerf Group, Corporate, Transient, Leisure	Group, Smerf Group, Corporate, Transient, Leisure
Published Rate Range	$109-$329	$109-$299	$119-$329	$109-$259	$109-$299
Clientele / Top Accounts	Entertainment, Citywides, Local Corporate	Fashion & Entertainment, Citywide Blocks	Weddings, Corporate, and Citywide Blocks	Transient, SMERF, Tour & Travel, they are currently adding Transient Corporate	Transient corporate from nearby buildings Smerf, Citywides
TripAdvisor	3.3	3.9	4.3	3.7	4.5
Concierge	Yes	Yes	Yes	Yes	Yes
# of Elevators	2	2	2	2	2
Spa	Yes	Yes	Yes	Yes	Yes
TV/Entertainment Set-Up / Apple TV	Flat Screen with Local Cable	Flat Screen with Local Cable	Flat Screen with Local Cable	Flat Screen with Local Cable	Flat Screen with Local Cable
Rituals / Events / Signature Happenings	Happy Hours Specials	7 pm Happy Hour	None	None	None
Local Affiliations / Partnerships	Local culinary treats at the Lobby bar. No partnerships ate this time	Local artist participates in the Cocktail and Fashion Week.	None	None	None
Reservation (In-House)	Yes	Yes	Yes	Yes	N/A (offsite)
Other Notes			Refreshed their rooms in 2004 and are in the middle of expanding and updating the lobby		
Breakdown in Room Types	King Queen, Superior King and Queen	Small, Medium, Large rooms, Double, Junior Suites	Standard, Enhanced, Deluxe guest rooms and suites	Superior King, Queen, Double-Double, Premium King and Queen suites	Standard Queen, Double-double, double-queen, Interior deluxe queen-queen. Executive double queen, Deluxe King.

QUESTIONS TO CONSIDER

- What are the significant variances when it comes to location and why should location matter?
- What product or services does your competitor offer that is a competitive disadvantage to you and how can you overcome?

SEGMENT PERFORMANCE

There are industry tools that allow revenue managers to evaluate their results compared to the competition from a segment perspective. This information sheds valuable light on where there are opportunities relative to the competitive set. It can help you validate the depth of demand in various segments and aid in modifying segment strategies to improve performance versus the competitive set.

Some segment information is more general and only goes as far as Group, Transient, and Contract. This can be beneficial in establishing strategies and sales deployment, particularly in the Group and Contract segments. It can also be beneficial in determining potential transient rate strategies, depending upon rate performance relative to that of the competitive set.

More detailed segment intelligence is available for purchase from industry vendors in order to determine more specific transient opportunities and strategies. Below is a sample data set reflecting detailed property and competitive set segmentation over the course of several months. Review the information provided and answer the questions below the chart.

		Jan	Feb	Mar	Apr	May	Jun
Total	Hotel Occupancy	58.3%	73.7%	90.2%	85.6%	86.4%	88.5%
	Comp Set Occupancy	63.3%	59.6%	82.2%	84.5%	90.0%	90.8%
	Occupancy Index	92	124	110	101	96	97
	Hotel ADR	$172	$176	$229	$253	$273	$275
	Comp Set ADR	$160	$169	$219	$240	$253	$257
	ADR Index	107	104	105	105	108	107

		Jan	Feb	Mar	Apr	May	Jun
	Hotel RevPAR	$100	$130	$207	$217	$236	$244
	Comp Set RevPAR	$101	$101	$180	$203	$228	$234
	RevPAR Index	99	129	115	107	104	104
Group	Hotel Occupancy	20.3%	39.5%	52.5%	37.0%	43.2%	46.3%
	Comp Set Occupancy	26.4%	17.0%	38.3%	32.9%	42.5%	43.2%
	Occupancy Index	77	232	137	112	102	107
	Hotel ADR	$155	$174	$224	$264	$272	$271
	Comp Set ADR	$164	$191	$219	$250	$246	$260
	ADR Index	95	91	102	106	111	104
	Hotel RevPAR	$31	$69	$118	$98	$117	$125
	Comp Set RevPAR	$43	$33	$84	$82	$104	$112
	RevPAR Index	72	212	140	119	112	112
Retail	Hotel Occupancy	9.4%	9.7%	11.5%	12.0%	10.6%	11.4%
	Comp Set Occupancy	6.5%	7.4%	6.9%	8.5%	7.8%	7.5%
	Occupancy Index	145	131	165	141	136	152
	Hotel ADR	$250	$248	$340	$374	$429	$432
	Comp Set ADR	$190	$191	$274	$284	$354	$325
	ADR Index	131	130	124	132	121	133
	Hotel RevPAR	$23	$24	$39	$45	$45	$49
	Comp Set RevPAR	$12	$14	$19	$24	$27	$24
	RevPAR Index	191	170	205	186	165	202
Special Corporate	Hotel Occupancy	5.5%	4.1%	5.3%	6.9%	4.4%	6.3%
	Comp Set Occupancy	8.1%	8.9%	9.7%	10.3%	8.8%	9.4%
	Occupancy Index	67	46	54	67	50	67
	Hotel ADR	$226	$214	$270	$293	$301	$298
	Comp Set ADR	$207	$212	$269	$299	$319	$319
	ADR Index	109	101	101	98	95	93
	Hotel RevPAR	$12	$9	$14	$20	$13	$19
	Comp Set RevPAR	$17	$19	$26	$31	$28	$30
	RevPAR Index	74	46	54	65	48	63

QUESTIONS TO CONSIDER

- How does the hotel perform overall in occupancy compared to the comp set during the months of January through June?
- In what segments does the hotel outperform the comp set? In what segments does the hotel underperform the comp set?
- What opportunities can you identify for this hotel to improve its performance relative to the competitive set?

SPREADSHEET EXERCISE 5.2

Your hotel is struggling with occupancy index that is causing the hotel to lose RevPAR index. You have determined that your shortfall in occupancy is in the Negotiated segment.

NEGOTIATED:	Jan	Feb	Mar	Apr	May	Jun	Jul	Aug	Sep	Oct	Nov	Dec
Subject Occ	3.0%	2.6%	3.7%	1.8%	3.4%	2.8%	2.4%	2.3%	2.2%	2.6%	3.2%	3.4%
Comp Set Occ	7.2%	5.9%	9.1%	6.6%	7.9%	7.7%	6.3%	6.5%	6.3%	4.9%	6.6%	6.7%
Occ Index	42	44	41	27	43	36	38	35	35	53	48	51
Subject ADR	$150	$150	$152	$154	$141	$150	$161	$151	$138	$154	$156	$151
Comp Set ADR	$135	$137	$134	$141	$124	$136	$140	$139	$125	$149	$144	$146
ADR Index	111	109	113	109	114	110	115	109	110	103	108	103
Subject Rev PAR	$5	$4	$6	$3	$5	$4	$4	$3	$3	$4	$5	$5
Comp Set Rev PAR	$10	$8	$12	$9	$10	$10	$9	$9	$8	$7	$10	$10
Rev PAR Index	46	48	46	30	49	40	44	38	39	55	53	52

Utilizing the monthly data, determine how many additional rooms your hotel will need to sell in this segment in order to gain your fair share of occupancy.

In the Excel document, enter the month occupancy levels in the Negotiated segment for your hotel and for the competitive set. Enter the supply represented by your hotel (450 rooms). Enter the supply represented by the competitive set (2100 rooms). Identify the amount of additional rooms your hotel will need to sell in the Negotiated segment in order to get to your fair share.

- What strategies can you put into place in order to drive additional occupancy in this segment?
- What observations can you make about the competitor's strategy that is allowing them to garner more share in this segment?

POSITIONING STATEMENT

A hotel's **positioning statement** is a concise proclamation of the hotel's product and service offering that fulfills consumer demand in the market. It is generally prepared by a small group of senior leaders of the hotel that include the general manager, director of sales, and marketing or revenue manager and may involve corporate office leadership. The positioning statement identifies the unique opportunity the hotel can serve to meet a specific market niche. The hotel's product and service philosophy should align to deliver the positioning statement.

GUIDELINES FOR AN EFFECTIVE POSITIONING STATEMENT

1. The statement should be concise and limited to one to three sentences.
2. Provide an easy-to-understand message of what the brand stands for.
3. Address why this brand is different from other similar businesses.

How to write a positioning statement:

"For [insert **Target Market**], the [insert Brand] is the [insert **Point of Differentiation**] among all [insert **Frame of Reference**] because [insert **Reason to Believe**]." (Stayman, 2015)

REAL PEOPLE

"The first step in the valuation process is to perform a market study where the local hotel demand is quantified and allocated among the existing and proposed supply of lodging facilities. The allocation of room night demand is based on the relative competitiveness of all the hotels in the market. The end result is a projection of demand captured by the proposed subject hotel, which is then converted into an estimate of annual occupancy. A similar procedure is used to project the average room rate.

"The second step is to project the hotel's operating revenue and expenses based on the previously estimated occupancy and room rate.

This results in an estimate of annual net operating income. Most consultants use a five- to 10-year projection period, so this process needs to be repeated for each year.

"The last step is to convert the projected NOI (net operating income) into an estimate of value using a weighted cost of capital discounted cash flow procedure. The end result is an estimate of economic value that can be compared to the total project cost." (Rushmore, 2011)

QUESTIONS

- How do you project the occupancy and ADR performance for a unique hotel concept that is incomparable to the existing hotel performance metrics in the market?
- How do competitive analysis tools and methodology incorporate into underwriting a future hotel's performance?

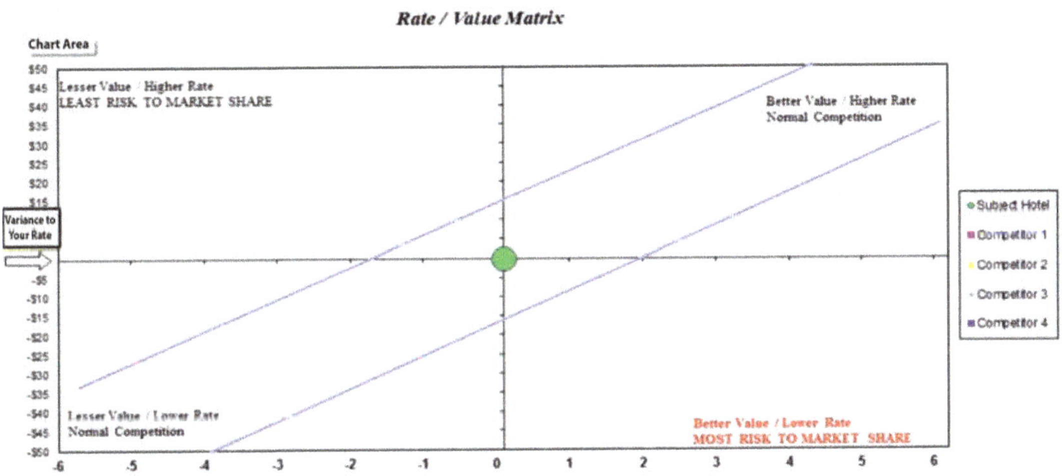

Figure 5.4: Rate/Value Matrix

RATE VALUE MATRIX

Step 1: After completing the competitive set value offerings assessment, establish a value for each category along the X-axis of the rate/value matrix relative to the subject hotel. A positive value reflects that the competitor is stronger in that measurement. A negative value means the subject hotel is superior. Fill in all categories for all competitors.

Step 2: Conduct price shops to determine the more representative price point for each hotel on the same date. is exercise can be done for di erent segments, such as weekday for business and weekend for leisure. For the purpose of this assessment, use weekday price shops to evaluate weekday business positioning. Using the predetermined price-points for each hotel, calculate variances for each competitor from the subject hotel and position the result along the corresponding value of the Y-axis. Matching this to the X-axis designation found in the prior step will provide the final placement for each hotel on the matrix.

Step 3: Review the results on the resulting chart. Hotels that fall within the two diagonal lines are properly positioned based upon price differential and the relative quality rating. Hotels that fall above the upper diagonal line are not of concern because they are considered lesser quality but are priced higher than the subject hotel. The hotels to consider closely are those that fall below the lower diagonal. These hotels are considered a greater value than the subject hotel because they are higher in quality but are priced at or below the subject hotel.

DISCUSSION QUESTIONS

Question 1: How can you use the rate value matrix to design your business strategy?

Question 2: How does online reputation influence the perception of value for price paid?

Question 3: How much influence should the SWOT analysis factor into pricing strategy?

Question 4: Do you assume that all categories on the SWOT analysis are equally important?

SEEING FURTHER

How do online guest reviews impact competitive analysis?

Historically hotel star ratings and price have been used as an indicator of hotel quality. The assumption is that a hotel with a 5-star designation and a rate that is significantly higher than a 4-star hotel must equate to the quality and service differential in the experience.

The star rating is at best a general indicator and is used when comparing one star category to another, but it fails to provide value when comparing hotels within a similar star category. In addition, star categories, whether official accreditation or an unofficial appointment, is also ineffective for comparing hotel products given the lack of a universal delineation on the criteria for a star category.

Online guest reviews have a growing impact on booking, pricing, and financial performance of a hotel, and the importance of online guest reviews is changing the historical approach of competitive analysis to determine a hotel's product and service offering. The historical approach of comparing a hotel's product and services to determine a price positioning is being disrupted by the rise of online guest reviews, providing a quantitative score on the guest experience and real-time customer feedback on their experience.

Studies have found that guest reviews have a direct impact on hotel conversion rate; when given equal pricing, customers are 3.9 times more likely to book the hotel with higher ratings (Mulligan, 2014).

Questions:

- How does hotel star ratings educate the consumer on expectations for product and guest service?
- What tools and tactics can a hotel utilize to improve their online reputation?
- If a hotel has high guest satisfaction scores, how can the hotel merchandise the accolades to outperform its competitors?

Companies increasingly use social media to communicate and interact with customers. Much information is thereby generated and is available to everybody, including competitors. Firms need to analyze what their customers say and interact with them.

APPLICATIONS

Case 1:

You are the new revenue manager at the Anderson Hotel. You have been asked to reevaluate the competitive set for the hotel. Your hotel is a 350-room 3-star hotel that is heavily leisure but also attracts transient business customers. You have the following potential hotels to select from for your competitive set. Select three competitors from this list and provide your reasons for selecting these as the most appropriate hotels to benchmark off of:

- Hotel A: 775-room 4-star hotel one block from your hotel. 60% group hotel with 55,000 square feet of meeting space.
- Hotel B: 125-room 5-star boutique hotel across the street from your hotel. Strong transient base. Retail rates average $100 to $125 above your hotel.
- Hotel C: 300-room 3-star hotel 2 miles from your hotel. Similar type of customer base but different corporate demand generators.
- Hotel D: 500-room 3-star branded hotel 4 blocks from your location. Very strong brand loyalty program that gives them a significant distribution advantage over your hotel.
- Hotel E: 425-room 3.5-star historic hotel. Three blocks from your hotel 40% group mix. Also strong in leisure transient.
- Hotel F: 280-room 3-star hotel. One mile from your hotel. In a less desirable neighborhood than your hotel, more remote from the major demand generators in the market.

Which 3 hotels would you select for the competitive set? (And why?)

Case 2:

You recently joined a hotel development company and are tasked with creating a new hotel concept and positioning statement for a new-build hotel in a secondary city market with an existing convention center that will double in size from 60,000 sq ft to 120,000 sq ft in two years. City-wide group conventions account for 125,000 annual room nights or 25% of annual hotel room nights in this market. To complete this assignment, you are asked to evaluate the existing five hotels in the market to identify a new hotel concept that fulfills a market niche that is not being served today. What hotel concept would you develop and what is the positioning statement of that hotel?

- Hotel 1: 100-room 4-star branded hotel with 2,000 sq ft of meeting space located next to the convention center.
- Hotel 2: 120-room 3.5-star Upscale independent hotel with 3,000 sq ft of meeting space located five blocks from the convention center.
- Hotel 3: 130-room 3-star upper midscale branded hotel with 5,000 sq ft meeting space located twenty blocks from the convention center.
- Hotel 4: 80-room 5-star luxury hotel with 1,000 sq ft of meeting space located four blocks from the convention center.
- Hotel 5: 110-room 4-star independent hotel with 2,000 of meeting space located six blocks from the convention center.

TEAM ACTIVITY

Competitive Research to Produce Competitive Grid Analysis

Formulate a team of four to five students and assign a subject hotel. The student team is to determine 4–6 potential competitor hotels with consideration to product offering, price position, and star category. Each student is responsible for conducting individual research and completing the competitive grid analysis spreadsheet.

INTERNET ACTIVITY

Select three hotels in a similar area in a city or destination. Thoroughly read the reviews on Trip Advisor and Expedia regarding the three hotels. Rank the three hotels in terms of product and service based upon customer feedback.

GLOSSARY

Competitive grid analysis – A tactical tool that evaluates the product and service offering for the subject hotel and its competitors.

Competitive set (comp set) – A group of similar and directly competing lodging properties to which an individual hotel's operating performance is comparable and compete for the same business.

Demand generator – Any event, sports area, hospital, military base, or business that creates lodging demand for a market.

Fair share – The proportional share of business assuming an even distribution of supply, revenue, and demand among all properties included within a competitive set.

Frame of reference – Describes alternative choices in the market today to set a baseline of existing expectations and further support the point of difference.

Inverse SWOT analysis – Conducting a SWOT analysis through the lens of a competitor.

Point of differentiation (POD) – The qualities separate the brand from its competitors.

Positioning statement – Statement of the hotel's product and service offering that address the target market it is trying to fulfil with a point of differentiation compared to existing substitute and includes a reason why this organization is able to deliver the promise made.

Reason to believe – Provides the context of how the business is able to deliver on its positioning statement.

Segmentation/mix of sales – How revenue managers and marketers classify and target customers in specific groups based upon their characteristics, behaviors, and preferences. The most common customer segmentations are Transient, Group and Contract.

Smith Travel Research (STR) – A global provider of competitive benchmarking, information services, and research to the hotel industry, with performance data from over 63,000 hotels and located in 180 countries.

SWOT analysis – A four-quadrant analysis to examine the subjects strengths, weaknesses, opportunities and threats.

Target market – The segment of customers the business it trying to reach.

REFERENCES

Mulligan, D. (2014). How online hotel reviews affect booking decisions: The research, stats, viewpoints & strategies. Cvent. Retrieved from http://hospitality.cvent.com/blog/cvb-internet-marketing-2.

Myburgh, S. (2004, March/April). Competitive Intelligence: Bridging Organization Boundaries. *Information Management Journal*, *38*(2), pp. 46-55.

Rushmore S. (2011, September 26.). *How to Test Hotel Feasibility.* HVS. Retrieved from https://www.hvs.com/article/5456/how-to-test-hotel-feasibility/

Stayman, S. (2015, March 201). How to Write Market Positioning Statements. Cornell Blog. Retrieved from https://blog.ecornell.com/how-to-write-market-positioning-statements/

CHAPTER 6

Hotel Revenue Management: Forecasting and Budgeting

Theresa Doherty and Carolyn Fredey

OVERVIEW

Understanding the principles and components of forecasting and budgeting is critical for the aspiring revenue manager (RM). A forecast can be best described as the best ***estimate*** of future performance and overall demand, while a budget is the ***desired*** future performance to meet the hotel's goals and objectives.

Hotel revenue management (HRM) focuses on how a hotel can produce the highest amount of "profitable" revenue given its fixed capacity and variable demand. The ratio between the demand and the capacity determines the hotel's potential for driving revenue for a specific time frame in the horizon. As demand increases, the expectation is to drive average daily rate. While there is a physical limit to the amount of rooms sold, average rate has less of a constraint.

It is the primary objective for the RM to formulate a revenue forecast for multiple time frames. A secondary goal, but equally important, is to communicate the forecast to various stakeholders. The forecast is utilized for both short-term needs and long-term planning and budgeting.

LEARNING OBJECTIVES

After studying this chapter, you should be able to:

- Explain the importance of the forecast and the impact it has on various stakeholders
- Describe the relationship between forecasting, price, and revenue maximization
- Compare the various mechanics and models behind a system-generated forecast
- Identify the economic indicators and market level information that impact hotel demand
- Interpret the system forecast with available market data to create a user forecast
- Forecast a group block
- Measure forecast accuracy
- Discuss the annual budget process

OUTLINE

Introduction

Impact of the Forecast

- The Reality of Seasonality and Impact On Operations
- Impact on the Revenue Strategy and Sales Deployment
- Impact on Hotel Valuation

Forecasting Fundamentals

- Different Time Horizons and Frequency
- Unconstrained Forecast vs Constrained Forecast
- Sources of Data for Demand Forecasting
- Building Blocks of the Constrained Forecast
- Calculating Forecast Error

Budgeting

- Internal and External Expectations
- Execution

- Communication
- Impact on Goal Setting and Compensation

Discussion Questions and Applications

SO WHAT?

Imagine you just graduated from school and are named hotel manager for a busy hotel. You arrive to work on your first day and realize you are the only manager on duty and you cannot find a forecast of any kind.

As hotel manager, how would you answer these questions without a forecast?

- How much staff will you require? How much food will you purchase?
- How many rooms will need to be cleaned?
- How is your sales team's performance?
- A forecast is generated to assist in operational planning and to set baseline of performance.

INTRODUCTION

Hotel forecasting and budgeting generally falls under the combined responsibility of finance and revenue management. It is necessary for the RM to prepare the revenue forecast in order for the finance department to complete the expense and profit forecast.

In nearly all cases, the RM may prepare the rooms revenue forecast for the hotel.

In addition, for some properties, the catering forecast is also completed by the RM rather than catering sales or operations.

PART ART AND PART SCIENCE—THAT IS THE REALITY

The demand forecasting process for a hotel is a combination of both art and science. While extensive modeling is available and utilized, it is never enough.

There are several external factors that are nearly impossible for any system to completely understand.

For example: severe weather, competitor renovations, special events, and any shifts in holiday placement.

Questions to Consider:

What other difficult to forecast factors can you think of?

How would you find out this information easily and how would you track?

Conversely, what data would be easier and faster for a system to manage?

IMPACT OF THE FORECAST

The Reality of Seasonality and Impact on Operations

Operations rely very heavily on forecast information to maintain expense and productivity targets. Department profitability is a major focus for department heads and executives. Detailed planning takes place based upon the projected business volume established by revenue management. This can be particularly impactful with hotels where demand varies seasonally.

Think about a hotel that runs 80 percent occupancy annually in a seasonal market. There will be months/seasons where the hotel runs 65 percent occupancy and other months/seasons where the hotel will run 90 percent occupancies. Revenue management must forecast each day/week/month appropriately in order for the operational departments to plan accordingly and run their areas effectively.

Over forecasting business levels can result in overspending due to over staffing and purchasing more supplies than necessary. On the flip side, under forecasting can result in poor guest experience and unnecessary costs such as overtime.

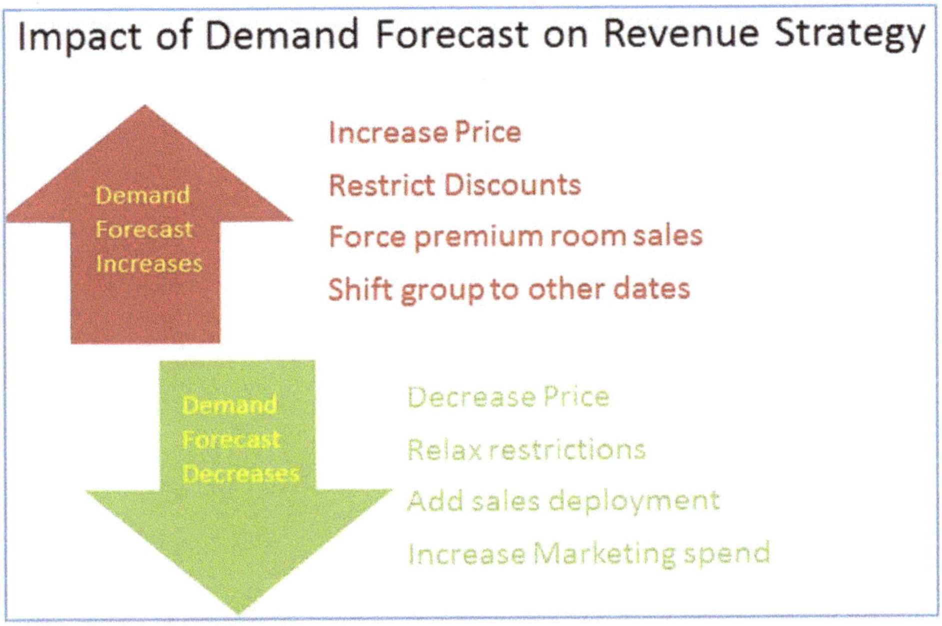

Figure 6.1: Impact of Demand Forecast on Revenue Strategy

Impact on the Revenue Strategy and Sales Deployment

The forecast is central to the revenue strategy for the hotel. The RM establishes pricing and restriction strategies based upon forecasted demand levels. As forecasted demand increases, rates and restrictions increase and lower priced business is turned away. As forecasted demand decreases, prices are reduced and restrictions are relaxed in order to ensure stronger conversion on lower demand.

The forecast is used to determine deployment of sales resources and marketing dollars based upon anticipated business levels and business needs. In the short term, promotions are developed to impact shoulder and need times as outlined in the forecast. Longer term, sales resources are deployed to various business segments and booking windows depending on where needs are identified.

A CASE IN POINT—GROUP CANCELLATION

Please work with one or two other students and review the following scenario:

A typically busy resort located near several tourist attractions was nearly sold out for Memorial Day Weekend, and had been for several weeks.

Less than 3 months to arrival, the revenue manager had increased the rates and closed out all discounts to allow for the average rate of the hotel to grow with the sale of its remaining rooms.

However, things changed 1 month out when a group canceled its room block. Now instead of a handful of rooms left, there were more rooms left to sell than the hotel can typically pick up.

QUESTIONS TO CONSIDER:

Should the revenue manager adjust the forecast?

What rate and restrictions changes should be made?

What other strategies can be explored and implemented?

Impact on Hotel Valuation

The exercise of hotel valuation begins with the estimation of the property's operating cash flow into the future. Market demand and supply trends are used to establish market occupancy and rate trends which are then applied to the hotel in question. An optimistic view of current and future market conditions can lead to an inflated projection of cash flow and over valuation of a given hotel or prospective hotel opportunity.

FORECASTING FUNDAMENTALS

In this section, we will review the critical processes, the mechanics, and the art of forecasting a hotel's rooms demand. While a RM will heavily rely on the modeling of a computer generated system, he or she must apply expertise and make adjustments when necessary. Behind the scenes, there are a lot of numbers and calculations that a general manager would not understand completely but expects the RM to distill this information into a hotel forecast and formulate a strategy to maximize revenue.

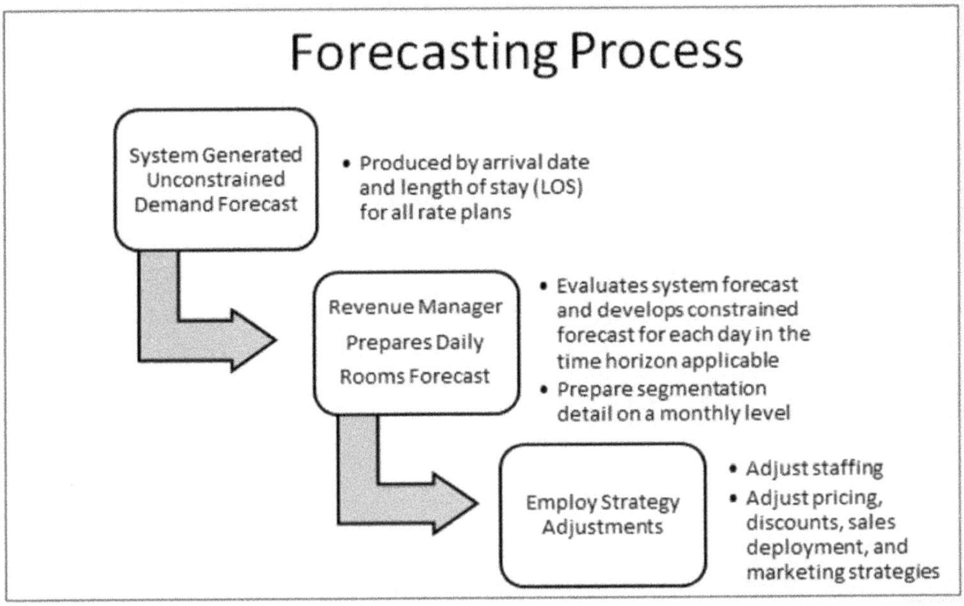

Figure 6.2: Forecasting Process

Different Time Horizons and Frequency

There are various types of forecasts to satisfy both short-term and long-term needs for multiple stakeholders. Usually, the following schedule is followed:

1) *Weekly Forecast:* Each week the RM will update the current month (at least 2 weeks) for staffing updates. This is completed based on current data on the books and expected transient pick up (the addition number of rooms and revenue). Generally, assumes no group pick up.
2) *Long Range Projections:* Each month the RM will update the next 3–6 months for planning purposes and to communicate with various stakeholders, including ownership. Prior to submission, it is recommended that the projections are reviewed with the general manager and director of sales to ensure alignment. The long range projections will include an unconstrained forecast for all three major segments: contract, group, and transient.
3) *Annual Budget:* Each year the RM will plan for the following year to assist in goal setting and resource planning.

Unconstrained Forecast Versus Constrained Forecast

Forecasting is problematic with the reality of variable demand throughout the year and across a given week of time. Furthermore, it is important to understand that the RM must look beyond the constraints of the hotel capacity and occupancy history for future demand calculations. Instead, the starting point to any projection or strategy begins with the unconstrained forecast. If a hotel had unlimited amount of rooms, how many rooms could be sold? As you can see in the example below, there is more demand than capacity on Tuesday, Wednesday, and Saturday. Hence, an **unconstrained demand** forecast aims to estimate the total rooms demand, either by arrival date or stay date.

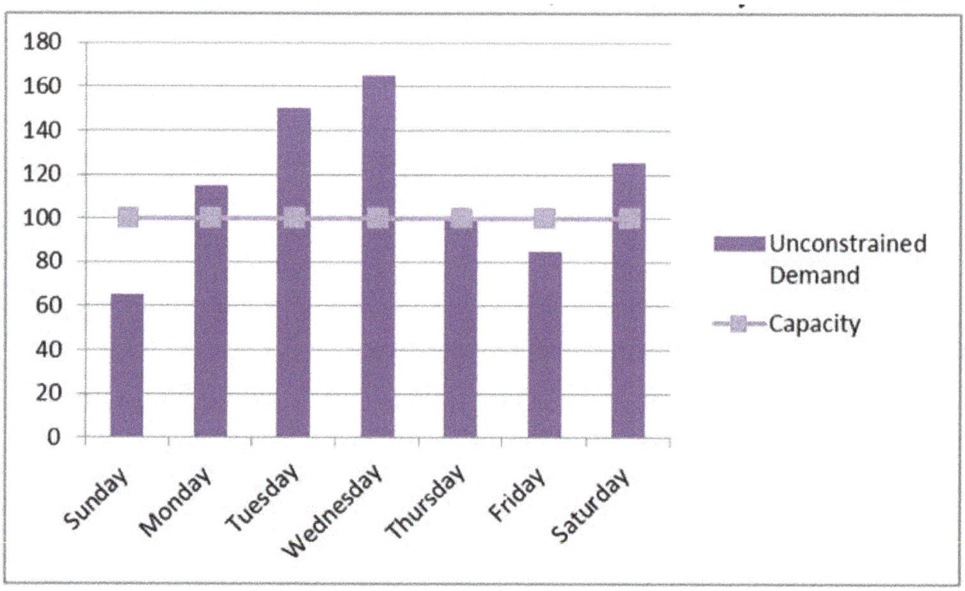

FIGURE 6.3: Unconstrained Demand

Sources of Data for Demand Forecasting

In today's environment, most RMs will rely on both an automated revenue management system and their own knowledge and data integration about the hotel and market. The RM will have to override or adjust the system's inputs when necessary, based on the market data and any anomalies in the historical data. The combined output will generate both an unconstrained demand forecast to allow for the revenue maximization strategy and the necessary constrained transient forecast to allow for a revenue forecast for the hotel operations.

The RM has two primary forecasting methodologies to integrate with the system. The first method group being based strictly on internal historical property data such as occupancy history, called endogenous. The second method group is based on both internal and external variables called exogenous and may include such items as market trends and special events (Based on Legohérel, 2013, p. 59).

Both groups of data can be divided into three buckets that are easy to understand. All are critical pieces of information to compile and consider in the development of the forecast.

Data Sources for Demand Forecasting

Property Data – Historical	Property Data – Current	Market Data
Occupancy statistics of hotel	The number of rooms available to sell	Changes or new demand generators such as a new stadium or nearby office park
Average Daily Rate (ADR) statistics of hotel	The number of transient rooms booked and ADR	Economic indicators that may increase or decrease travel and rooms demand
Unaccommondated demand history (denials)	The number of group rooms reserved and ADR	Unpredictable factors such as a snow storm or construction
Cancellation and no show history	Recent improvements in the hotel's services or products	
Guest Satisfaction trends	Additional sales deployment	Planned renovations of hotels, new hotels, or closures

Figure 6.4: Data Sources for Demand Forecasting

The system forecast will most likely use a combination of statistical modeling to predict future demand. Figure 6.5 (Weatherford & Kimes, 2003) illustrates the Various Forecasting Methods used in Revenue Management.

Revenue management forecasting methods		
1. Historical	A.	Same day, last year
	B.	Moving average
	C.	Exponential smoothing
	D.	Other time series (ARIMA, etc.)
2. Advanced Booking	A.	Additive
		1. Classical pickup
		2. Advanced pickup
	B.	Multiplicative
		1. Synthetic booking curve
	C.	Other time series
3. Combined	A.	Weighted average of historical and advanced booking forecasts
	B.	Regression
	C.	Full information model (Lee, 1990)

Figure 6.5: Forecasting Methods

Historical models only consider the final number of rooms or arrivals on a particular stay night. Advanced Booking models solely include the buildup of reservations over time for a particular stay night. In practice, it is typical that a hotel may best utilize a combination of both the historical forecast and an advanced booking forecast. Generally, this can be implemented using a regression model or a weighted average of a historical forecast and an advanced booking forecast to develop the forecast (Weatherford and Kimes, 2003).

The flow chart below describes the process of the integration of the system and the available market data that enable the revenue forecast and strategy recommendations.

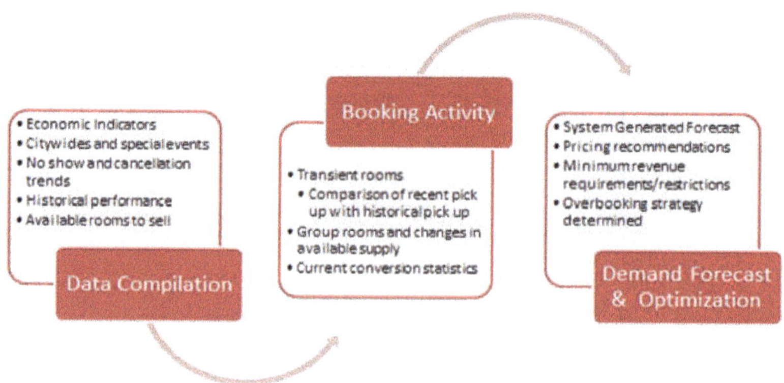

Figure 6.6: Methodology to Forecasting

THINK HISTORICALLY

The evolution of distribution channels in has changed dramatically over the years.

A century ago only mail and phone enquiries (see article) existed for rooms reservations. However, in the 1960s, technology began to accelerate, first with the airlines' development of electronic distribution and eventual migration of the technology to travel agencies via the Global Distribution System (GDS) in the 1970s. The next step was the development of the Centralized Reservation System (CRS) in 1980 that improved efficiencies for hotel chains (Warner, M.; Quadri-Felitti, D.; Chandnani, P. V.—A History of Travel Distribution: 1915–2009, 2010).

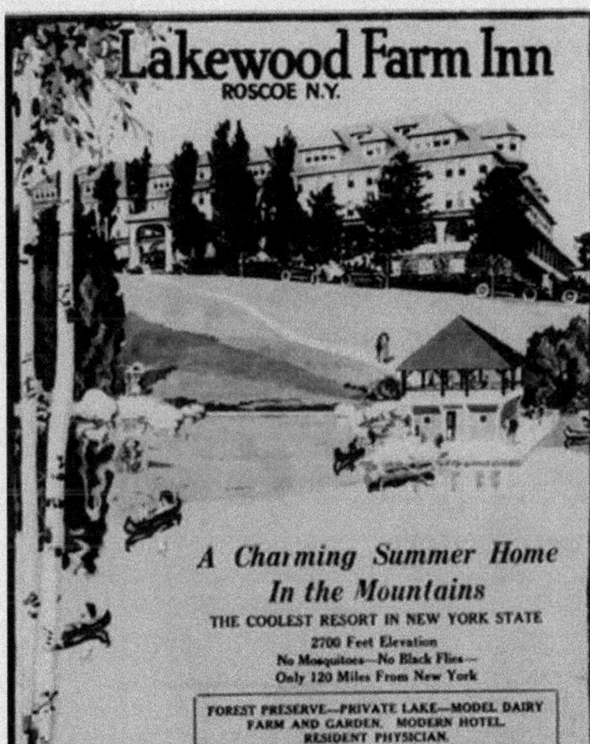

Source: New-York Tribune, June 11, 1922, Graphic Section, Part Seven.

However, it was the 1990s and the advent of the Internet that exponentially changed distribution and subsequently made forecasting demand a real problem to solve. Think about it. In 1924, rate comparison shopping was cumbersome for the consumer. Sales enquiries tended to be more qualified and buyers more apt to purchase. Today, there are numerous travel sites and rate comparison shopping is widespread. Consumers are likely to shop several sites before making a purchase. It is more complex to validate how much demand exists and data assumptions must be made by systems and forecasters.

Questions to Consider:

List all the different ways a hotel room can be booked.

Why would more distribution channels make it more challenging to forecast demand?

How can systems adapt to the changes in distribution mix?

The Building Blocks of the Constrained Forecast

While the system forecast is extremely valuable in forecasting transient cancels and demand yet to be realized, it requires the RM to estimate the number of rooms already committed, and ultimately assemble constrained forecast for the stakeholders. In this section, we will outline these steps with concentration on the group forecast which requires the most intervention.

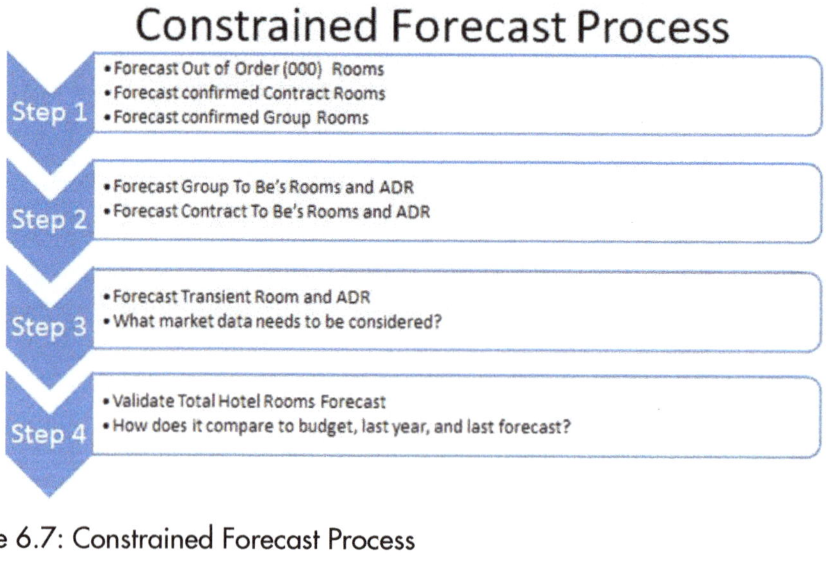

Figure 6.7: Constrained Forecast Process

Step 1: Forecasting Group and Contract Confirmed

While the system forecast is extremely valuable in forecasting demand yet to be realized, it requires user input to estimate the supply of rooms already committed, and ultimately the published constrained forecast for the stakeholders. This generally will include out of order rooms (out for renovation or repair) that cannot be utilized, confirmed group, and confirmed contract. In this case of group and contract, a hotel sales manager has negotiated a room rate for a specified number of rooms called a group or contract block for a specific time period. Generally, a contract (airline crew most common) will utilize nearly all the rooms requested as it reserves a fixed number of rooms for each night based on precise needs and schedules. However, a group's needs are not as clear at the time of booking, and there are fluctuations between contract and actual pickup.

A cutoff date, the time the reservation details are due to the hotel, is agreed at the time of booking between the sales manager and the meeting planner. While there are variances based on type of booking and lead time, 3 weeks prior to arrival is fairly typical and provides the hotel enough notice of any rooms not filled by the group to sell to transient. However, due to the knowledge that most groups do not utilize all rooms requested, it is prudent for the RM to forecast each individual group block with some slippage or fall off. Different types of groups will behave differently based upon the nature of the segment (Figure 6.8).

Type of Group	Slippage Behavior
Tour and Travel	Typically contracts allow for cancel 60 days out so forecast conservatively unless there is history with hotel Guidance : 25-50% slippage
Social	The meeting planner (such as a bride) generally will not guarantee rooms and thus will ask for more rooms than necessary so actual pick up can be Guidance: 40- 50% slippage
Association	While attendees are responsible for payment, generally there is good history of annual events and attendance is predictable Guidance: 15-20% slippage
Corporate	Generally, attendance is expected and rooms are paid by the corporation so pick up is stronger than most groups. Guidance: 10-15% slippage

Figure 6.8: Anticipated Slippage by Sub-segment

It is a good practice to use guidance slippage percentages at the time a group is contracted. The next step is for the event manager to obtain pickup and intelligence from the meeting planner to update the group projection. Depending on the source of lead and billing method, the group block will be either call-in, where the group attendees make their own reservations, a rooming list, where the meeting planner collects the names of the attendees, or housing bureau link, where an electronic feed is sent to the hotel with the reservation details at a set time before arrival.

Group Block Forecast Example

In this example, a simple percent off peak forecast is used. After a partial rooming list or call-in block, the event or reservations manager records the pick up by day for the group. The manager can then determine the peak day of the block and calculate the percent off peak for each pre-day and post-day of the group. Then based on the type of group, and the remaining days before cutoff, and any history, the manager can determine a forecast for the peak. In this case, the manager is predicting the bookings to grow from 30 peak to 45 peak. The surrounding days are a simple percent off the peak.

	Thursday	**Friday**	**Saturday**	**Sunday**
	2-Mar	3-Mar	4-Mar	5-Mar
Contract	50	50	50	50
Reservation Booked	10	20	30	15
Percent off Peak	33%	67%	100%	50%
Forecast	15	30	45	23

SPREADSHEET EXERCISE 6.1

Interpreting Property Reservations Data to Generate a Group Forecast:

Calculate a group room block forecast for the following group. Assume that cutoff date is already passed and you expect a 10 percent slippage of what is already booked. In other words, rather than additional pickup, the bookings will actually decrease.

	Sunday 7-May	Monday 8-May	Tuesday 9-May	Wednesday 10-May
Contract	25	25	25	25
Reservation Booked	0	15	25	20
Percent off Peak				
Forecast				

- Do you think the group was contracted correctly?
- Do you expect your overall rooms forecast to grow or decline since the group was first contracted?
- What stipulations would you demand for the group to book again for next year?

Step 2: Forecasting Group To Be's

After the existing groups are forecast, the next step is to predict the remaining group rooms to be picked up by sales. This is not a scientific process typically as historical trends are not as consistent as transient. Whiles systems may attempt to forecast, most often the RM is responsible for the majority of the heavy lifting of this task. The information used to estimate the to-be's is based partially on past history of pick up and the remainder on any group leads, or prospects that may be in the sales System.

Step 3: Validating Transient Forecast

After the contract and group forecast is complete, the last step is to validate the transient system forecast and make any adjustments. The system will calculate the transient forecast based on the **remaining unconstrained demand and supply**. However, due to market data that may not be inherited in the system forecast, the RM will adjust. Ideally, this should be done in the unconstrained transient forecast phase so this task is not necessary. Today it is more common to override the forecast in the final phase.

Step 4: Validating Total Hotel Forecast

After Steps 1 through 3, the RM must validate the total hotel forecast to ensure that it makes sense. Often when you forecast the individual parts, it is easy to overlook the final result and check for errors in areas of pattern, holiday placement, or unusual booking activity. In addition, the RM must consider the impact on the stakeholders and ensure that too much risk or too little risk is in the forecast. Generally, a good strategy to manage expectations is to be slightly conservative in the forecast. This allows the RM to increase the projection at a later date with a positive response from stakeholders. Compare and report the forecast to budget, last year, and last projection. Finally, ensure you communicate the forecast to all relevant stakeholders and include notes for any time periods that have changed dramatically. Explain why the forecast has changed and include any action items that may be helpful in improving the results.

SPREADSHEET EXERCISE 6.2

To Do: Review the market and transient demand information in the instructions tab of the student supplement spreadsheet. Populate the transient rooms forecast by day for the month based upon the data provided. Review the full month projection on the summary tab of the file.

Answer the following questions:

- How is the hotel forecasted to perform compared to the budgeted expectations? What factors are affecting the hotel's performance compared to budget? How is the hotel forecasted to perform versus last year?

SEEING FURTHER

Assume you are the revenue manager of a large resort in the Pacific.

Due to a sharp slowing of the economy in East Asia, booking pace for the hotel is significantly down. Prudently, you decide to bring down the revenue projections for the remainder of the year.

1) What stakeholders need to be notified?
2) What strategies may be adjusted or employed to offset the decline?
3) Would you expect your system-generated forecast to require adjustments and why?

CALCULATING FORECAST ERROR

With the importance of forecasting, given the direct relationship of the unconstrained demand projection and the revenue strategy, accuracy is critical. Both the system forecast error and the RM's constrained forecast should be measured to track progress. Generally, tracking accuracy over long periods of time is more meaningful as there may be anomalies in shorter periods of time. If the forecast error increases, there may be a change in the trend, incorrect data, or human error. As the system forecast plays such an important role and relies on user inputs and overrides, it is recommended that goals be established and managers held accountable. In statistics, there are generally three common measurements used to test the accuracy of forecasting modeling: MAD, MSE, and MAPE (Minitab, n/d).

Mean Absolute Deviation

$$MAD = \Sigma \mid Actual - Forecast \mid / n$$

Mean Squared Error

$$MSE = \Sigma (Actual - Forecast)^2 / n$$

Mean Absolute Percentage Error

$$MAPE = (100 \Sigma^{n}_{i=1} \mid Actual_i - Forecast_i \mid / Actual_i) / n$$

Mean absolute percentage error (MAPE) expresses accuracy as the average percentage of error across a number of instances. It can be easier to understand than the other statistics. For example, if the MAPE is 6, on average, the forecast is off by 6 percent.

Let us review in a worksheet for ease of understanding (Table below):

Date: DOW	Rooms Revenue Forecast	Actual Rooms Revenue	Difference	Absolute Error	MAD	MAPE	MSE
6-Mar Sunday	$18,500	$19,140	$640	$640	$640	3%	$409,600
7-Mar Monday	$33,750	$35,680	$1,930	$1,930	$1,930	5%	$3,724,900
8-Mar Tuesday	$40,425	$40,095	($330)	$330	$330	1%	$108,900
9-Mar Wednesday	$40,425	$42,075	$1,650	$1,650	$1,650	4%	$2,722,500
10-Mar Thursday	$32,625	$33,180	$555	$555	$555	2%	$308,025
11-Mar Friday	$16,675	$14,200	($2,475)	$2,475	$2,475	17%	$6,125,625
12-Mar Saturday	$23,925	$25,905	$1,980	$1,980	$1,980	8%	$3,920,400
Total	$206,325	$210,275	$3,950	$9,560	$9,560	5%	$91,393,600
					$2,390	6%	$13,589,194

While the revenue difference added together for the week is only off by 2percent, from an absolute error perspective, there is a variance of 5 percent. The negatives do not offset the positive variances.

PROS & CONS

There is always a margin of error in any forecast. The goal is to be as accurate as possible, in order to give the best guidance with the forecast.

Is it better to under forecast or over forecast?

What are the implications of each?

What impact does it have on the operation as well as the profitability of the hotel?

BUDGETING

The hotel annual budget is an extension of the forecasting process. The RM first forecasts the rooms' revenue expectations for the following year. Total hotel sales and profit goals are determined based upon this rate and occupancy projection. The budget goals are ultimately spread through every department of the hotel to give the department leaders the targets they must achieve for success. Business plans are established to outline how these targets will be achieved.

REAL PEOPLE

Sloan Dean is the Vice President of Revenue Optimization for Ashford.

He has provided insight into the impact of budgeting and forecasting from an owner's perspective:

> *Budgets & Forecasts are paramount for public companies like Ashford, especially for REITs and C Corps that provide forward guidance to the investor community. Revenue Budgets have wide ranging implications such as CAPEX investment, disposition & hold strategies and management company performance incentive clauses that impact an owner's EBITDA.*

Regarding CAPEX, budgets influence how much CAPEX owners can allocate for future years. Most public owners allocate future CAPEX as a percentage of total revenue; thus, if the Revenue Budget is not accurate, then an owner cannot properly plan for major renovations, etc. Because large capital spending requires 12–18 months of planning, the spend is typically based on budgets. Currently, most public lodging REITs are spending 8–11% of their Budgeted Revenues as owner funded CAPEX to improve their hotels. With less revenue comes less reinvestment.

Regarding disposition strategy, if a hotel's budget & forecast is bleak, the owner is going to be more apt to sell the asset than hold it in the interim albeit debt allocations and where we are in the lodging cycle also play a large influence in the selling of hotels.

Regarding management contracts with companies like Marriott, Hilton, Interstate, etc., many of the management incentives paid by the owner to the manager are driven by performance versus budget. An inaccurate budget can cost either party a lot of money.

Lastly, and maybe most importantly, many companies provide forward RevPAR growth performance for future quarters, which is based on Budgets & Forecasts. If these guidance's are missed, a company's stock can get pummeled.

QUESTIONS

Given the issues outlined above, if you were an owner, would you prefer to see an aggressive budget or a conservative budget? List at least three factors that support your position.

As an operator, are you better off with an aggressive budget or a conservative budget given the perspective of ownership? List at least three factors to support your position.

Internal and External Expectations

In many cases, hotels teams are challenged to establish aggressive goals to meet corporate and/or ownership growth goals. Revenue expectations for individual hotels are compared with market expectations established by market "experts" such as PKF and STR Global. Corporate leaders, owners, and asset managers want to ensure that the growth target for the hotel will lead to market share growth based upon these market expectations unless valid conditions exist where a hotel may not be able to grow share (i.e., renovations, impact of one time event in the previous year, etc.).

Execution

Creating a budget starts with the same fundamentals as a long range forecast. The forecasted sales for each month or period are estimated based upon anticipated market conditions and group booking pace information. Transient segmentation is modeled based upon expected market demand applied to historical trends along with any strategic changes the hotel plans to make. The end result is a projection that reflects occupancy and rate expectations for the following year that will be used as the basis for the total hotel budget. Revenue management will also typically outline the budget for catering sales based upon booking pace in group and local catering as well as trends in pickup within the year of arrival.

Review the sample hotel budget below:

	Jan	Feb	Mar	Q1
Budget Occ	51.6%	66.3%	74.7%	64.1%
Last Year	47.9%	61.2%	69.1%	59.4%
Budget Rooms	5600	6500	8100	20200
Last Year	5200	6000	7500	18700
% Chg	7.7%	8.3%	8.0%	8.0%
Budget Rate	$165.00	$172.00	$179.00	$172.87
Last Year	$167.00	$179.00	$185.00	$178.07
% Chg	–1.2%	–3.9%	–3.2%	–2.9%
Budget Revenue	$924,000	$1,118,000	$1,449,900	$3,491,900
Last Year	$868,400	$1,074,000	$1,387,500	$3,329,900
% Chg	6.4%	4.1%	4.5%	4.9%

QUESTION TO CONSIDER

How does the hotel expect to increase revenue during the first quarter based upon how they have budgeted these months?

List strategy changes that the hotel potentially made versus the prior year that would lead them to budget the numbers above.

Communication

The budget is first reviewed by the property team to ensure the RM, general manager, sales leader, and director of finance are in agreement. The subsequent review process for the budget will depend upon the company approach as well as the engagement level of the ownership group in the budget process. Oftentimes there is a formal meeting with the management organization and ownership organization to review the assumptions used to develop the budget to ensure that target is appropriate to achieve market expectations as well as the expectations of the organizations involved.

Impact on Goal Setting and Compensation

Budgeted sales are typically used as the basis for compensation for sales, revenue management, and the executive leadership in the hotel. The goal could be top-line sales, or it could also be the bottom line house profit driven from budgeted sales. Sales manager goals are typically derived from the budgeted sales for the segment targeted by the sales person (group, business transient, etc.). Establishing unrealistic targets can have a significant impact on the compensation of a number of managers within the hotel.

QUESTION TO CONSIDER

How does the budgeted target impact the behavior of revenue managers and sales executives?

DISCUSSION QUESTIONS

Question 1: While the system-generated forecast is sophisticated, are there any instances that may require user intervention? What market or property data may be hard for the system to recognize?

Question 2: Describe how an unexpected increase in the confirmed group forecast may impact the total hotel rooms forecast. What processes should be evaluated to minimize the frequency or large variances?

Question 3: Assume you are the RM of a relatively new hotel and rely heavily on the system-generated forecast due to lack of history and expertise. You have noticed that in recent weeks that the system-generated forecast accuracy is declining. The occupancy is coming in much stronger than the forecast.

As a result, you have set up an appointment with the programmers that are responsible for the system forecast. What questions would you have for the programmer and what could be negatively impacting the accuracy?

Question 4: Why is the annual budget process critical to a hotel?

Question 5: Describe how a sharp reduction in the forecast impacts the overall value of the asset?

APPLICATIONS

Case 1: Forecast Accuracy

A busy convention hotel has been struggling with over forecasting. Subsequently, the hotel has incurred unnecessary costs due to overstaffing and over purchasing food items. In addition, the hotel has lost rooms revenue due to the RM over restricting discounts due to the inflated forecast.

You have been asked to see if there was a trend to the forecast accuracy shortfalls.

	Rooms Forecast	**Rooms Actual**
Sunday	1,050	1,008
Monday	1,400	1,372
Tuesday	1,400	1,372
Wednesday	1,400	1,386
Thursday	1,250	1,138
Friday	1,150	1,047
Saturday	1,350	1,323
Sunday	1,075	1,032
Monday	1,350	1,323
Tuesday	1,350	1,323
Wednesday	1,350	1,337
Thursday	1,200	1,092
Friday	1,175	1,070
Saturday	1,300	1,274
Sunday	975	936

	Rooms Forecast	Rooms Actual
Monday	1,200	1,176
Tuesday	1,300	1,274
Wednesday	1,300	1,287
Thursday	1,200	1,092
Friday	1,200	1,092
Saturday	1,400	1,372

Questions:

What is the MAPE for the time frame provided?

Are there trends in the data by day of week?

Case 2: Budgeting

You are the new RM for a hotel in a major city. The hotel team has been working on their budget for the upcoming year. You have done your research and found out the following facts about the market conditions for next year:

- Several new hotels will open in the market. One of the new hotels is a 400 room hotel located 2 blocks from your hotel. It is slated to open in February.
- Two large annual conventions that are held during the shoulder season are not going to be held next year due to budget constraints.
- An international airline will start new direct service from a major gateway city to your city starting in April.
- Your hotel's group booking pace is behind by 3 percent compared to the same time last year.
- Your hotel had a significant renovation last year and the owners are expecting strong returns on their investment.

Questions:

- The owners expect the budget to reflect occupancy performance equal to the current year. Do you agree with their assertion? Why or why not?
- How does the impending new supply impact expectations for rate and occupancy for the hotel?

TEAM ACTIVITY

Work with at least two other students in this team activity. Research a Citywide event in your local area or a nearby city center. Select one hotel to analyze and choose four other hotels of similar experience level. Compare pricing and availability for the peak event dates against a time period of low demand.

Please discuss the following with your team:

Based on the information available, do you expect the forecasted results to differ and why?

Does pricing fluctuate similarly between the two different time frames for all the hotels or are there exceptions?

When forecasting occupancy and rate for the dates over the Citywide, what property data would you analyze?

INTERNET ACTIVITIES

Research a market—find five things that would influence the forecasted results for the following year (new supply, change in **demand generators**, change in infrastructure, air lift, investment in the market, convention center, leisure attractions, etc.).

- Outline the five demand influencing factors.
- Rank them in order of impact from highest impact to lowest.
- Explain how these factors will impact demand, positively or negatively.

GLOSSARY

Citywide – event in the market that results in lodging demand adequate to fill the vast majority of all hotels.

Demand generator – any event, sports area, hospital, military base, or business that creates lodging demand for a market.

Remaining demand – number of rooms the hotel can expect to sell with unlimited physical capacity.

Remaining supply - number of rooms available for sale.

Unconstrained demand - total demand in a segment or overall in the absence of any constraints.

REFERENCES

Belobaba, P. P. (1987, May). Airline Yield Management: An Overview of Seat Inventory Control. *Transportation Science, 21* (2), 63–73.

Cross, R. G. (1997). *Revenue Management: Hard Core Tactics for Market Domination.* New York, NY: Broadway Books. 1997.

Cross, R. G., Higbie, J. A., & Cross, D. Q. (2009). Revenue Management's Renaissance: A Rebirth of the Art and Science of Profitable Revenue Generation. *Cornell Hospitality Quarterly, 50* (1), 56–81.

Haley, M. & Inge, J. (2004, Fall) Revenue Management: It Really Should Be Called Profit Management. *Hospitality Upgrade Magazine.* Retrieved from https://ishc.com/wp-content/uploads/art_rm04.pdf

Hayes, D. K. & Miller, A. (2011). *Revenue Management for Hospitality Industry.* Hoboken, NJ: John Wiley & Sons, Inc.

Legohérel,P., Poutier,E. & Fyall, A. (Eds.). (2013). *Revenue Management for Hospitality and Tourism.* Woodeaton, Oxford. Good Fellow Publishers Ltd.

Minitab.com (n/d). Retrieved from https://support.minitab.com/en-us/minitab/18/help-and-how-to/modeling-statistics/time-series/how-to/trend-analysis/methods-and-formulas/methods-and-formulas/

Warner, M., Qaudri-Felitti D. & Chandnani, P. (2010). A History of Travel Distribution: 1915–2009. HEDNA. Retrieved from https://corsi.unibo.it/magistrale/emt/bacheca/2013-05-seminario-in-revenue-management-the-distribution-dilemma/5a3e53f2148447caa7b55cf3d80d1f2b

Weatherford, L. R. & Kimes, S. E. (2003/9). *A Comparison of Forecasting Methods for Hotel Revenue Management.* The Scholarly Commons. Cornell University School of Hotel Administration.

CHAPTER 7

Performance Analysis in Hotel Revenue Management

Roy Madhok and Leslie Lew

OVERVIEW

Hotel revenue management (HRM) has grown over time as a function of front office operations to a highly analytical practice based upon dynamic data-driven decisions. Hotels operate around the clock, and reservations are made and cancelled at all times of the day for different days often multiple years into the future. This wide net of data continues to grow and as it grows revenue management has had to learn how to appropriately record data, gain new metrics, establish goals, and ultimately critique performance in order to grow the business

LEARNING OBJECTIVES

After studying this chapter, you should be able to:

- Analyze the depth of key performance indicators for revenue management
- Apply performance metrics to create and measure the effectiveness of a strategy
- Identify opportunities in pace statistics in order to drive market share results
- Practice inventory utilization and common yielding strategies
- Examine the impact of customer perception on HRM performance
- Recognize the emerging metrics for the hospitality industry (cost of acquisition, digital marketing, and e-commerce)
- Evaluate performance utilizing a strategy critique and establish measurable goals that can be monitored over time

OUTLINE

Key Performance Indicators

- Industry Metrics
- Market Share
- Pace Reports Available within Hotel Revenue Management
- Inventory Management
- Emerging Profitability Metrics
- Digital Marketing and e-Commerce

Strategy Planning Utilizing Key Performance Indicators

- Strategy Critique
- Establishing Goals
- Monitor and Evaluation over time

Discussion Questions and Applications

KEY PERFORMANCE INDICATORS

In its most basic form, revenue management involves putting "heads in beds," or occupying as many rooms as possible. Basic room statistics have evolved from there and have since established the core three KPIs: occupancy percentage, average daily rate (ADR), and revenue per available room (RevPAR)

BASIC KPI CALCULATIONS:

Occupancy percentage = sold rooms/available rooms

Average daily rate = total room revenue/total rooms sold

RevPAR = Average daily rate × occupancy percentage

or

RevPAR = Room revenue/available rooms

RevPAR is the relationship between occupancy and ADR, where alone occupancy and ADR both have significant limitations. A hotel that runs 100 percent occupancy could be giving away its rooms for very little whereas a hotel with an extremely high ADR could likely be missing out on the opportunity to sell more inventory.

RevPAR allows hoteliers to balance ADR and occupancy in order to ultimately capture more revenue. Nonetheless, RevPAR is a KPI with its own limitations as it does not give a holistic picture of a hotels success.

SO WHAT?

What is the point of introducing new metrics? Why should revenue management professionals expand their data sets?

RevPAR itself measures room revenue alone; hotels encompass much more than room revenue and expand into areas such as banquets, conferences, food and beverage, and so on. Scholars have argued that since RevPAR is an incomplete picture, hotels should instead focus on **Total Revenue per Available Room**, or **TrevPAR** (Dickens, 2006; Lado-Sestayo et al., 2017). **TrevPOR or Total Revenue per Occupied Room** came into existence to understand how much revenue a hotel makes in total. For example, hotels evaluate groups and take into consideration more than the room rate. A group that requests sleeping rooms, meeting rooms, and food could potentially bring in more revenue than a group requesting just sleeping rooms. Despite the advent of TrevPAR, hotels have not widely adopted this metric and have instead started to gravitate more toward profit-driven metrics.

A hotel or business can spend copious amounts of money on labor, advertising, marketing, guest/consumer satisfaction, and more in order to drive revenues, but those hotels would gain revenue at the expense of Profit and **Profit Margin**. Therefore, revenue managers and hoteliers have increasingly moved focus onto Gross Operating Profit per Occupied Room (GOPPOR) or Gross Operating Profit per Available Room (GOPPAR). The notion of callously growing revenue without any regard for cost is a relic of the past. Revenue management professionals have to now measure whether their efforts drive revenue while reducing costs.

Market Share

Despite the addition of new metrics, HRM still has a major focus on growing market share; the hotels performance against defined competitors. Market share reports are provided by a variety of companies and are the report card for revenue managers.

While the reports have started to incorporate new KPIs, they still tend to center around Occupancy Index (Market Penetration Index or MPI), ADR Index (Average Rate Index or ARI) and RevPAR Index (Revenue Generation Index). Revenue managers judge their performance against competitors with these reports and then break into further detail in order to see how they can further shift market share their way.

> Occupancy Index (MPI) = Hotel Occupancy Percentage/Competitive Set Occupancy Percentage
>
> Example: .87/.92 = 95.0%
>
> ADR Index (ARI) = Hotel ADR/Competitive Set ADR
>
> Example: $306.87/$260.62 = 117.7%
>
> RevPAR Index (RGI) = Hotel RevPAR/Competitive Set RevPAR
>
> Example: $267.41 / $239.03 = 111.9%
>
> Percentage Change = [(Current Value–Previous Value)/Previous Value] × 100
>
> Rank: Where a hotel falls amongst its defined competitive set in any KPI (i.e., 2 of 8 in ADR)

Percentage change is of relevance because hotels are consistently looking to grow share in Occupancy, ADR, and RevPAR. Market share reports and tools show daily, weekly, monthly, quarterly, and yearly performance for hotels that subscribe to the third-party service. The reports often show segment performance like the hotel's group occupancy on a particular day versus the competitive set.

Table 7.1: Shahawk Hotel Market Share Report March 6th 2016–March 12th 2016

Sample Market Share Report			% Change
Occupancy	Property	87.1%	0.0%
	Comp Set	91.8%	2.0%
	Index	94.9%	-2.0%
	Rank	3 out of 4	
Rate	Property	$306.87	2.0%
	Comp Set	$260.62	0.0%
	Index	117.7%	2.0%
	Rank	1 out of 4	
RevPAR	Property	$267.28	2.0%
	Comp Set	$239.25	2.0%
	Index	111.7%	0.0%
	Rank	3 out of 4	

The hotel lost valuable Occupancy share (-2.0%) which potentially further decreased its occupancy rank amongst competitors.

A 3 of 4 rank in RevPAR indicates that the hotel had room to grow in RevPAR despite having achieved a 111.7% RevPAR Index

Table 7.1 has a significant amount of data in the form of a market share report. The hotel had an occupancy percentage of 87.1 percent and was flat year over year. Overall, the hotel underperformed in occupancy (87.1 percent versus competitors at 91.8 percent) while also ranking near the bottom of the competitive set at 3 of 4.

The hotel in Table 7.1 achieved success in RevPAR Index, but lost occupancy share and ultimately was ranked 3 of 4 in RevPAR. Revenue managers look both backward and forward at market share to search for alternative ways to grow occupancy, ADR, and RevPAR more than their competitors. The hotel in Table 7.1 should also understand recurring trends; if they are consistently losing occupancy the revenue manager has to put strategies into place and articulate to sales and operations the new points of emphasis in order to gain back lost share.

THINK HISTORICALLY

Data on market share reports today provide significantly more detail by segmentation and day of week compared to a sample market share report from 2002 that only provided summary data. Without the segmentation or day of week, hotels had to speculate on market share drivers instead of analyzing data to prepare a strategy plan to improve results.

STAR Summary Report - September 2002

Hotel Anywhere 789 East Main Street Oakland, CA 95071-4 United States Telephone: (615) 824	**STR #: 1234** Chain ID: OAK2323 Open Date: 198201		MgtCo: None Owner: None Total Rooms: 490	Operation: Franchise Market: Oakland, Ca Tract: Oakland-Berkeley	10/24/02 e-star_summary 1.01

Segment	Occupancy Percent		Average Room Rate		RevPar		Room Revenue	Rooms Available	Rooms Sold	Occupancy Percent		Average Room Rate		RevPar		Room Revenue	Rooms Available	Rooms Sold
		% Chg		% Chg		% Chg	% Chg	% Chg	% Chg		% Chg		% Chg		% Chg	% Chg	% Chg	% Chg
	Monthly Performance									***Year To Date Performance***								
Hotel Anywhere	66.9	17.6	$138.52	1.2	$92.65	19.0	19.8	0.6	18.3	62.2	-13.7	$138.32	-7.0	$86.08	-19.7	-19.0	0.9	-12.9
Market: Oakland, Ca	59.5	-1.2	$89.42	-1.7	$53.20	-2.8	2.6	5.5	4.3	60.5	-12.9	$90.84	-7.9	$54.98	-19.8	-16.4	4.3	-9.2
Market Price Luxury	61.3	11.1	$125.44	-4.6	$76.87	5.8	11.9	5.7	17.3	61.7	-5.2	$127.25	-12.7	$78.47	-17.3	-14.4	3.4	-2.0
Tract: Oakland-Berkeley	62.5	7.8	$104.41	-1.5	$65.28	6.1	11.0	4.6	12.7	60.9	-11.2	$104.50	-7.6	$63.64	-18.0	-13.0	6.1	-5.9
Tract ScaleUpscale Chains	68.3	15.2	$122.23	-3.3	$83.45	11.4	28.8	15.7	33.2	65.3	-6.8	$123.20	-9.8	$80.47	-15.9	-3.4	14.9	7.1
Competitive Competitors	64.0	11.3	$123.75	-3.6	$79.18	7.2	7.2	0.0	11.2	63.0	-11.4	$125.01	-7.2	$78.71	-17.9	-17.9	0.0	-11.5

	12 Month Performance								
Hotel Anywhere	62.4	-15.6	$139.63	-5.1	$87.10	-19.9	-19.1	1.0	-14.8
Market: Oakland, Ca	59.9	-15.8	$90.71	-7.4	$54.37	-21.9	-18.5	4.4	-12.0
Market Price Luxury	60.1	-10.2	$128.22	-12.3	$77.11	-21.2	-18.9	2.9	-7.5
Tract: Oakland-Berkeley	60.1	-14.5	$105.03	-5.9	$63.07	-19.6	-13.7	7.2	-8.4
Tract ScaleUpscale Chains	64.5	-9.3	$124.11	-8.9	$80.07	-17.3	-2.6	17.8	6.9
Competitive Competitors	61.7	-15.2	$126.40	-6.1	$78.00	-20.4	-20.4	0.0	-15.3

Census/Sample - Properties & Rooms

Segment	Census		Sample		Sample % (Rooms)
	Properties	Rooms	Properties	Rooms	
Market	213	22795	129	18479	81.1
Market Price	29	5778	26	5473	94.7
Tract	56	6633	33	5695	85.9
Tract Scale	8	2167	8	2167	100
Competitive Set	9	2550	9	2550	100

Figure 7.1: Sample STAR Summary Report, Smith Travel Research

QUESTIONS:

How can a revenue manager use segmentation data to create a strategy plan to improve results?

Why is it important to examine performance by day of week?

Aside from overall Occupancy, ADR, and RevPAR, the revenue manager needs to look at the market share report along with other data to see where there is room to gain back share and to improve performance. It is common for a revenue manager to align their **mix of sales** or **market segmentation** with their market share report to see what changes to segmentation could have been made to improve results.

Table 7.2: Shahawk Hotel Segmentation March 6th 2016–March 12th 2016

March	03/06/16 Sun	03/07/16 Mon	03/08/16 Tue	03/09/16 Wed	03/10/16 Thu	03/11/16 Fri	03/12/16 Sat	TOTAL
Paid Occupied Rooms	145	190	184	185	180	140	195	1219
Available Rooms	200	200	200	200	200	200	200	1400
Paid Occupancy %	72.5%	95.0%	92.0%	92.5%	90.0%	70.0%	97.5%	87.1%
ADR	$269.24	$285.84	$355.09	$354.97	$282.00	$283.14	$304.22	$306.9
REVPAR	$195.20	$271.55	$326.68	$328.35	$253.80	$198.20	$296.62	$267.2
Rooms Revenue	$39,040	$54,310	$65,336	$65,670	$50,760	$39,640	$59,323	$374,079
TRANSIENT								
Retail	65	80	90	90	80	80	98	
	$280.00	$305.00	$379.00	$379.00	$299.00	$299.00	$335.00	
	$18,200	$24,400	$34,110	$34,110	$23,920	$23,920	$32,830	
Business Transient	10	50	60	60	40	5	2	
	$269.00	$279.00	$349.00	$349.00	$275.00	$265.00	$329.00	
	$2,690	$13,950	$20,940	$20,940	$11,000	$1,325	$658	
Government	10	10	10	10	10	5	5	
	$289.00	$289.00	$289.00	$289.00	$289.00	$289.00	$289.00	
	$2,890	$2,890	$2,890	$2,890	$2,890	$1,445	$1,445	
Online Travel Agent	40	30	20	20	40	40	85	
	$249.00	$259.00	$299.00	$299.00	$255.00	$255.00	$269.00	
	$9,960	$7,770	$5,980	$5,980	$10,200	$10,200	$22,865	
Group	20	20	4	5	10	10	5	
	$265.00	$265.00	$354.00	$350.00	$275.00	$275.00	$305.00	
	$5,300	$5,300	$1,416	$1,750	$2,750	$2,750	$1,525	

QUESTIONS TO CONSIDER

Refer to Tables 7.1 and 7.2 to understand the segmentation of the market share week where the hotel was ranked 3 of 4 in RevPAR.

What days did the hotel perform well on? What helped the revenue manager achieve their 117.7% ADR index? What segments could the hotel have targeted in order to further build occupancy? Which segments were discounted too much?

The weekly market share report tells an abbreviated story of how the hotel did during the entire week. Revenue managers have a depth of market share data and can therefore drill down even further to isolate areas of opportunity within the day, week, month, or year.

Table 7.3: Sample Market Share Analysis Progression

1. Forward Looking Market Share Reports
• Revenue manager adjusts pricing based upon forward looking market share reports
2. Weekly Market Share Report
• The hotel lost in occupancy index and lost overall RevPAR share for the week
3. Daily Market Share Analysis
• The hotel looks to see what days of the week underperformed in occupancy
4. Daily Market Segment Analysis
• Revenue manager identifies of occupancy, ADR, and revenue opportunity in the mix of sales. • Revenue manager communicates opportunities and need for strategies to fill gaps

Pace Reports Available within HRM

Each revenue manager looks to perform better than last year, at least in market share. In a simple scenario, a market growing 3 percent year over year for a particular month likely means that a hotel's competitors are growing 3 percent as well. The hotel therefore must strategize to grow more than 3 percent in order to gain share. Outgrowing competitors or declining less than competitors is called gaining share. Similarly, if a hotel has lost more year-over-year than competitors, it would be referred to as having lost share.

Tracking performance versus last year, called **pace**, is mostly done in comparison to the same time last year on a day by day, month by month, and quarter by quarter basis. For example, a hotel pacing behind same time last year for a month where competitors are expected to grow is a warning sign that the property may be underperforming in pricing, segmentation, or a multitude of areas.

Pace data are used in a variety of ways, but mostly via the overall rooms occupied, ADR, and revenue over a defined period of time (OTB) and via segment pace to understand which segments are performing well and which ones are underperforming. Each type of pace data can be dissected to a detailed level of days versus same time last year to weeks, months, and yearly pace.

Table 7.4: Daily Pace versus Same Time Last Year

DOW	March 2016				SDOW March 2015			Variances		
	Date	**Rooms**	**ADR**	**Revenue**	**Rooms**	**ADR**	**Revenue**	**Rooms**	**ADR**	**Revenue**
Sun	03/06	90	$134.00	$12,060.00	85	$150.00	$12,750.00	5	($16.00)	($690.00)
Mon	03/07	130	$217.00	$28,210.00	105	$200.00	$21,000.00	25	$17.00	$7,210.00
Tue	03/08	120	$295.00	$35,400.00	100	$250.00	$25,000.00	20	$45.00	$10,400.00
Wed	03/09	110	$295.00	$32,450.00	105	$245.00	$25,725.00	5	$50.00	$6,725.00
Thu	03/10	100	$169.00	$16,900.00	135	$169.00	$22,815.00	-35	$0.00	($5,915.00)
Fri	03/11	120	$159.00	$19,080.00	145	$150.00	$21,750.00	-25	$9.00	($2,670.00)
Sat	03/12	130	$159.00	$20,670.00	155	$175.00	$27,125.00	-25	($16.00)	($6,455.00)
		800	**$205.96**	**$164,770.00**	**830**	**$188.15**	**$156,165.00**	**-30**	**$17.81**	**$8,605.00**
							% Pace	**-3.61%**	**9.47%**	**5.51%**

Daily pace is often looked at to see how months are performing and where areas of opportunity lie. In Table 7.4, a revenue manager would be able to assess that Monday, Tuesday, and Wednesday are all up in Occupancy and ADR to STLY. However, Sunday, Thursday, Friday, and Saturday are all areas of opportunity. Similarly, this report can be run for a particular segment and can also be shown to illustrate a month's performance by segment (Table 7.5).

Table 7.5: Monthly Segment Pace

Segment	Mar-16			Mar-15			Variances		
	Rooms	**ADR**	**Revenue**	**Rooms**	**ADR**	**Revenue**	**Rooms**	**ADR**	**Revenue**
Retail	2,480	$199.00	$493,520.00	2,790	$179.00	$499,410.00	-310	$20.00	($5,890.00)
Business Transient	1,240	$189.00	$234,360.00	620	$179.00	$110,980.00	620	$10.00	$123,380.00
Government	155	$165.00	$25,575.00	310	$165.00	$51,150.00	-155	$0.00	($25,575.00)
	3,875	**$194.44**	**$753,455.00**	**3,720**	**$177.83**	**$661,540.00**	**155**	**$16.61**	**$91,915.00**
						% Pace	**4.17%**	**9.34%**	**13.89%**

While pace statistics have been a core of HRM, new business intelligence software are pushing the boundaries of what revenue managers look at. Hotels more and more are able to understand how airfare impacts travel, whether prices will decline as the arrival date approaches, how long the booking window is for each week, and more.

SEEING FURTHER

Hotel revenue managers use a conjunction of reports to understand how effective pricing and discounts are in terms of both occupancy and ADR. A common combination of the evolving technology in HRM is the surfacing of rate shops combined with forward looking segment penetration. In the example below rate shops are shown for retail and **qualified segments**, or travel associated with a membership discount. The occupancy penetration is also shown for each of those dates against the Comp Set. Hotels use these tools along with others to understand how effective their retail pricing and discounting has been.

Rate Shops

Date	DOW	Retail Rate	CS Retail Rate	Qualified Rate	CS Qualified Rate
3/6/2016	Sun	$179.00	$169.00	$143.20	$101.40
3/7/2016	Mon	$199.00	$189.00	$189.05	$170.10
3/8/2016	Tue	$249.00	$229.00	$236.55	$206.10
3/9/2016	Wed	$249.00	$229.00	$224.10	$206.10

Forward Looking Segment Penetration

Date	DOW	Retail Occ	CS Retail Occ	Retail Index	Qualified Occ	CS Qualified Occ	Qualified Index
3/6/2016	Sun	24.00%	35.00%	68.57%	15.00%	25.00%	60.0%
3/7/2016	Mon	29.00%	40.00%	72.50%	12.00%	15.00%	80.0%
3/8/2016	Tue	37.00%	45.00%	82.22%	12.00%	15.00%	80.0%
3/9/2016	Wed	30.00%	42.00%	71.43%	15.00%	15.00%	100.0%

How can this hotel adjust their retail pricing? Their qualified pricing?

Why could it be ok that the hotel isn't capturing their fair share in retail/qualified occupancy?

Where does it appear that the hotel is doing well? What other reports would you want to see in addition to this?

Inventory Management

In order to increase market share and influence future dates, hotels need to be able to price and manage their inventory appropriately. Inventory management encompasses the total hotel inventory and managing inventory on the segment level. Strong inventory management skills allow hotels to limit low rated channels during periods of excess demand and the ability to open the funnel when the hotel would be willing to take more types of business.

Hotel revenue managers are therefore responsible for controlling **unconstrained demand**, or demand that is in excess of the hotels capacity. See Table 7.6, where the revenue manager had excess demand of 40 rooms Tuesday and Wednesday. The challenge comes into play where the revenue manager must manage the occupancy pattern and rate to maximize revenue for the week.

The hotel in Table 7.6 could have had a number of issues that resulted in not materializing another 10 percent of occupancy on Monday and Thursday along with the 20 percent occupancy lost for Friday. The revenue manager likely sold out too early for Tuesday, Wednesday, and Saturday, resulting in the inability to sell more rooms on Monday, Thursday, and Friday.

Table 7.6: Unconstrained Demand and Occupancy Losses at Hotel A

	Sunday	Monday	Tuesday	Wednesday	Thursday	Friday	Saturday
Available Rooms	200	200	200	200	200	200	200
Occupied Rooms/ Realized Demand	120	160	200	200	160	140	200
Occupancy %	60.00%	80.00%	100.00%	100.00%	80.00%	70.00%	100.00%
Unconstrained Demand (Room Nights)	120	180	240	240	180	180	200
Occupancy % Lost	0.00%	10.00%	0.00%	0.00%	10.00%	20.00%	0.00%

Also, looking back at market share, hotels sometimes cannot make swift changes to their segmentation in order to increase their performance. It requires creativity and an understanding of inventory management to capture all unconstrained demand and additional revenue opportunities.

Table 7.7: Inventory Control Methods

Inventory Control	Definition
Open	Accepting reservations or free sell
Closed	No longer accepting reservations
Minimum length of stay (MLOS)	Requiring particular reservations to stay multiple nights. Mostly requiring the arriving reservation to stay multiple nights
Maximum length of stay (MXLOS)	Restricting the amount of time to a maximum amount of dates. Mostly requiring the arriving reservation to stay a maximum amount of nights
Allotment	Allocating the maximum number of rooms sold
Closed to arrival (CTA)	Not allowing reservations to arrive on a particular day but allowing reservations on previous days to stay through

Each of these basic inventory controls comes into play when managing unconstrained demand, where the same hotel in Table 7.6 could have more effectively captured occupancy on **shoulder dates**, or dates the fall on the sides of peak demand dates. Take for example the following 7 Day Period (Table 7.8) with varying levels of unconstrained demand at a hotel with the same number of rooms and same amount of unconstrained demand.

Table 7.8: Inventory Controls to Control Demand at Hotel B

	Sunday	**Monday**	**Tuesday**	**Wednesda**	**Tyhursday**	**Friday**	**Saturday**
Available Rooms	200	200	200	200	200	200	200
Unconstrained Demand (Room Nights)	120	180	240	240	180	180	200
Inventory Control	Open	Open	MLOS 3 night	MLOS 2 night	Open	MXLOS 1 night Discounts	MLOS 2 night
Additional Inventory Control	80 room discount allotment	20 room discount allotment	0 room discount allotment	0 room discount allotment	20 room discount allotment	20 room discount allotment	0 room discount allotment
	Sunday	**Monday**	**Tuesday**	**Wednesda**	**Tyhursday**	**Friday**	**Saturday**
Available Rooms	200	200	200	200	200	200	200
Unconstrained Demand (Room Nights)	120	180	240	240	180	180	200
Inventory Control	Open	Open	MLOS 3 night	MLOS 2 night	Open	MXLOS 1 night Discounts	MLOS 2 night
Additional Inventory Control	80 room discount allotment	20 room discount allotment	0 room discount allotment	0 room discount allotment	20 room discount allotment	20 room discount allotment	0 room discount allotment

The revenue manager applied minimum lengths of stay on the entire day for Tuesday, Wednesday, and Saturday. The purpose of applying a minimum length of stay to peak demand dates is to make sure that the full amount of demand is captured on shoulder dates. To more precisely target days where there is lesser unconstrained demand, the hotel set an allotment on discount segments in hopes of realizing as much demand as possible. Similarly, excess demand Tuesday, Wednesday, and Saturday prompted the hotel to not allow any discount reservations therefore protecting higher rated reservations.

Despite these inventory controls, one can argue that the hotel is turning away high rated business on Tuesday, Wednesday, and Saturday by not offering one night rates. Many hotels therefore offer discounts based upon length of stay. For example, a hotel can offer a discounted rate for any set of nights it desires in order to allow discounts over soft dates and then only offer premium rates touching peak demand dates Table 7.9.

Table 7.9: Length of Stay Pricing to Manage Demand

	Sunday	Monday	Tuesday	Wednesday	Thursday	Friday	Saturday
Available Rooms	200	200	200	200	200	200	200
Unconstrained Demand (Room Nights)	120	180	240	240	180	180	200
Premium Rate	1234567	1234567	1234567	1234567	1234567	1234567	1234567
Discount Rate	1267	14567	34567	34567	124567	134567	234567

To take advantage of unconstrained demand requires utilizing pricing power, restrictions, and an in-depth knowledge of segmentation.

However, execution of basic inventory management also includes the necessity of understanding group inventory and short-term inventory cancellations, no-shows, and early departures. Revenue managers are responsible for understanding that a group that contracts 30 rooms will likely only occupy 10, and they should therefore forecast to sell 20 more rooms that what the group would be holding.

QUESTIONS TO CONSIDER

As a revenue manager, how would you know how to forecast how many rooms a group will utilize?

What are the implications of over-forecasting how much a group will pick up?

What are the implications of under-forecasting how much a group will pick up?

On a day where demand is high, leaving 1 room empty can be very costly as the ability to sell a room at a high price is gone as a new date rolls in. Hoteliers must gain a thorough understanding of cancellation, early departure, and no show history to understand how much to oversell by, or how far to set their overbooking limit (Phumchusri & Maneesophon, 2014). For example, see Table 7.10, a hotel that averages a $300 ADR for all Tuesdays and Wednesdays in the year and each Tuesday/Wednesday has more demand than hotel capacity.

Table 7.10: A Case for Overbooking (Assuming no Show Reservations are at the ADR for the Day)

Hotel Rooms available	200
Tuesdays and Wednesdays in 2016	104
Total rooms sold	20,800
Tuesday/Wednesday ADR	300
Total revenue with zero overbooking	$6,240,000.00
Additional rooms sold @ 5 overbooking	520
Additional revenue from overbooking	**$156,000.00**
Total revenue with 5 overbooking	$6,396,000.00

When a hotel takes an aggressive stance on overbooking it can see immediate gains in revenue, in this example a gain of 2.5 percent or $156,000!

SPREADSHEET EXERCISE 7.1

Assume the hotel only gets the opportunity to overbook rooms for each Tuesday, Wednesday, and Saturday of May 2016 and that each day of week is consistent in terms of Occupancy, ADR, and Revenue.

With No Show ADR equal to the ADR of the Day:

With a five room overbooking limit on Tuesday, Wednesday, and Saturday, how much more revenue would the hotel gain in no shows for the month of May 2016 versus no overbooking limit (assuming that each room overbooked yields a paid no-show)?

- What would the hotels new ADR for the month of May be?
- What are the added benefits of overbooking beyond no-show revenue?
- How can setting the overbooking limit too high be detrimental to the hotel's success?

May	05/01/16 Sun	05/02/16 Mon	05/03/16 Tue	05/04/16 Wed	05/05/16 Thu	05/06/16 Fri	05/07/16 Sat	TOTAL
Paid Occupied Rooms	145	190	200	200	180	140	200	1255
Available Rooms	200	200	200	200	200	200	200	1400
Paid Occupancy %	72.5%	95.0%	100.0%	100.0%	90.0%	70.0%	100.0%	89.6%
ADR	$269.24	$285.84	$357.00	$356.78	$282.00	$283.14	$304.99	$308.8
REVPAR	$195.20	$271.55	$357.00	$356.78	$253.80	$198.20	$304.99	$276.8
Rooms Revenue	$39,040	$54,310	$71,400	$71,355	$50,760	$39,640	$60,998	$387,503

May	05/01/16 Sun	05/02/16 Mon	05/03/16 Tue	05/04/16 Wed	05/05/16 Thu	05/06/16 Fri	05/07/16 Sat	TOTAL
Paid Occupied Rooms	145	190	200	200	180	140	200	1255
Available Rooms	200	200	200	200	200	200	200	1400
Paid Occupancy %	72.5%	95.0%	100.0%	100.0%	90.0%	70.0%	100.0%	89.6%
ADR	$269.24	$285.84	$357.00	$356.78	$282.00	$283.14	$304.99	$308.8
REVPAR	$195.20	$271.55	$357.00	$356.78	$253.80	$198.20	$304.99	$276.8
Rooms Revenue	$39,040	$54,310	$71,400	$71,355	$50,760	$39,640	$60,998	$387,503

Emerging Profitability Metrics

While market share speaks to a revenue manager's effectiveness against competitors, a revenue manger must remain focused on cost effective ways to drive revenue in addition to increasing profitability. To effectively measure Gross Operating Profit per Available Room (GOPPAR) revenue managers must understand the major components of cost that diminishes house profit. Traditional operating costs include guest services: labor, food and beverage outlets; room product: amenities, linen, laundry; administration and general: utilities, insurance. Beyond these traditional operation costs, revenue managers continue to become more sophisticated in managing profitability by managing **cost of acquisition**, the cost of acquiring the revenue through distribution, marketing and commission fees.

Distribution fees: costs incurred during the reservation process.

Example: A travel agent makes a reservation in utilizing the Global Distribution System (GDS). This incurs a GDS pass through fee that is paid to the GDS company. That reservation is then delivered to the Central Reservation System (CRS) which may incur a transaction fee with the CRS company for receiving a new booking. In this case, there are two layers of fees: (1) GDS (2) CRS transaction.

Marketing fees: The cost of a marketing campaign or affiliation that generated the reservation.

Example: Digital pay-per-click banner ad on a website that costs $1.50 per click.

Commission fees: a predetermined fee paid to an agent or business for completing a reservation booking.

Example: American Automobile Association (AAA) charges 10% of actualized room revenue post guest stay from bookings made by AAA distribution channels that includes travel agents, call center, or website.
Distribution fees: costs associated with the reservation transaction.

The cost of acquisition has quickly become a critical topic for the hospitality industry as these costs on an industry average are growing faster than revenue growth. Between 2009 and 2012, total customer acquisition costs increased 23 percent, brand allocation fees increased 37 percent, and third-party commission fees increased 34 percent (HTrends, 2013). Cost of acquisition is changing how hotels are deploying their direct sales, marketing and distribution strategies in order to yield maximize profit.

PROS & CONS

Group segment business can be extremely costly when you factor in the labor (group sales director, managers, and coordinators) and administration (legal contract review, billing, reservations) in order to acquire group business. There are hotel companies that purposely select to forgo the group segment and save on the costs of labor and administration. Do you think the cost savings outweighs the risks of not deploying direct sales efforts to book group? Why?

QUESTIONS TO CONSIDER

Hotel Saint Petersburg has an in-house reservation staff of five agents that costs $250,000 per year in wages and benefits. The hotel averages 82,000 voice bookings a year. Hotel Saint Petersburg is considering eliminating the in-house operations department and outsource call-in reservations to a third-party company that charges $3.00 per reservation transaction.

Do you recommend Hotel Saint Petersburg to eliminate the in-house reservation department and outsource to a third-party?

What is difference in annual cost to keep the reservation in-house instead of a third-party company?

What is the impact on conversion rate and guest experience by moving reservation to a third-party company?

SPREADSHEET EXERCISE 7.2

Calculate the Mix % of Transaction Volume for each channel as a percentage of the total.

Calculate RevPAR for each Channel for the 550 room hotel in a 365-day year.

Calculate the Net RevPAR—Distribution Costs.

Which Channel yields the highest Net RevPAR?

Note: Your instructor will provide the expanded version of the table illustrated below for calculation.

Channel	Transactions	Mix %	Room Nights	ADR	Revenue	RevPAR	Net RevPAR-Distribution Costs
GDS	30,000		42,000	$250.00	$10,500,000		
Website	50,000		70,000	$280.00	$19,600,000		
Call Center	15,000		21,000	$300.00	$6,300,000		
OTA	10,000		14,000	$240.00	$3,360,000		
Property Direct	25,000		35,000	$260.00	$9,100,000		
Total	130,000	100%	182,000	$268.46	$48,860,000	$243.39	

QUESTIONS

1. Does the highest ADR channel always yield the highest Net RevPAR?
2. What channel mix changes can the hotel execute to increase Net RevPAR?
3. How does Net RevPAR change if the hotel decides to take zero Property Direct reservations?

Digital Marketing and e-Commerce

HRM has begun its transition from simple room and ADR calculations to understanding how often hotel websites are visited, how well a hotel converts clicks to reservations, and overall how well the hotel does in the e-commerce landscape. Digital and e-commerce are integral to moving business from less profitable channels to more profitable channels.

In e-commerce, it is well known that ranking at the top of a search engine results in more visibility and in more website **visits.** Similarly, hotels ranked at the top of OTA search results receive, on average, 2.39 times more **clicks** than those compared with hotels ranked second and 3.42 times more than those ranked third (Ghose et al., 2014). Clicks result in more website visits which in turn result in more reservations and revenue. A hotel with poor visibility will automatically suffer in terms of clicks, visits, and ultimately reservations.

Aside from rank order and the page the hotel falls on, information about the hotel such as the picture, price, hotel class, rating, and review count all play a major role in a hotel that receives a click, or a **conversion,** where the consumer has completed the payment in the online session (Ghose et al., 2014).

The concept of **conversion rates** and **click through rates (CTR)** are integral in understanding whether marketing initiatives, guest satisfaction, rank, and pricing are effective.

BASIC HOTEL WEB ANALYTICS

Conversion Rate = Bookings/Visits

Click Through Rate (CTR) = Clicks/Impressions

Cost Per Click (CPC) = Total Ad Cost/Clicks

A hotel with a low CTR means that very few consumers are clicking the hotel despite the hotel accumulating **impressions**, or times that hotel has been shown. Likewise, a hotel with a low conversion rate is a hotel that is often clicked but does not convert well. For luxury hotels, a drop from the number one rank to the number five rank leads has shown to lead to a 75 percent decline in CTR (Ghose et al., 2014).

REAL PEOPLE

Mika Nayak (name has been protected) works at a management company in New York City that handles both branded and independent hotels ranging from 2 to 5 stars. Mika often notices on reports that many hotels of the same star rating and brand have vastly different click through rates.

- Aside from rank, what are some reasons a hotel would have a low click through rate?
- What are some reasons a hotel would have a low conversion rate?

The rise of the Internet has increased accessibility to large amounts of data, with analytics rapidly moving toward its interpretation and practical use. However, the influx of excessive information has been found as impractical and unusable as a source of competent decision making, where additional data points do not directly relate with a better mathematical answer. Industry trends are moving away from this earlier idea of Big Data analytics, toward more practical approaches with comprehensive models (McGuire, 2017).

Strategy Planning Utilizing Key Performance Indicators

Strategy planning requires key performance indicators to determine the effectiveness of the strategy plan to validate the strategy is yielding the intended result. Now that we have established the common performance indicators in revenue management we can apply performance analysis techniques to evaluate strategy effectiveness.

Strategy Critique

The Strategy Critique is a tool to document a strategy with an intended result for a defined period of time to evaluate the effective of the strategy by using key performance indicators for revenue management established in this chapter (Occ, ADR, RevPAR, and market share indices). Documenting the strategies allows for evaluation over time to track key performance indicators are trending favorably or unfavorably to the goal.

Results	**Market Segment**	**ADR Focus**	**Occ Focus**	**Strategy to Drive Performance**	**Comments**
Booked 50 RNs $12.5K Rev from Emails YTD Q1 2016. Resulted in 0.3% RevPAR Index growth.	ALL	x	x	**Pre-Stay Messaging** -50% discount on Premium upgrade cost	Launched 01/01/16
Increased upsell revenue by 20% vs Same Time Last Year. Resulted in 0.15% RevPAR Index	ALL	x		**Room Upsell: FD Agent incentive,** Select standard room bookings with high ADR to entice them to	Generated $47K in FY 2015. 10% off early depature or late check out, 10% of any
Increased sell-out efficiency to 99% fro 98% vs STLY. Occupancy Index increased by 0.4%	ALL	x	x	**Walk in Incentive:** FD Agent incentive to sell walkins—help secure +95% Occupancy	Generated $363K in FY 2012 Agents receive 10% of any walk-in (first night
Booked 80 RNs $18K Rev YTD Q1 2016. Resulted in 0.4% RevPAR Index growth.	Package		X	Corner room package loaded, open over weekends Corner room at the price of a standard	New offer. Launched 01/01/16

Establishing Goals

In any organization strategic objectives are set in which goals are based upon. Revenue management professionals must understand their hotels and therefore understand realistic goals and expectations that the team can be unified around. Setting goals typically revolves around a budget; where a hotel should be accurately assessed in terms of revenue potential, market penetration capabilities, mix of business, and more.

The process at arriving at a hotels goals starts with understanding competitors, the strategic advantages and disadvantages of the hotel, the previous results, and intentions for the upcoming period. Hotel Revenue managers set goals for their optimal mix of sales, forecast accuracy, market share, channel mix, and more.

Monitor and Evaluate Over Time

The process of establishing goals and key metrics is immediately followed by monitoring and evaluating the goals over time. In Table 7.11 see that each goal has corresponding processes for evaluation; hotels set their targets for market share, if goals are not met, market share reports need to be analyzed in conjunction with pricing levels, segmentation, inventory management, and the sales process in order to regain the targeted market share.

TABLE 7.11: Monitoring Process of Goals

Market Share	• Receive Results • Analyze and make changes to pricing, segments, inventory management, and the sales process
Forecast	• Monitor Daily, Weekly, and Monthly forecasts over time • Modify forecasting assumptions and procedures going forward
Establish Optimal Mix	• Receive reservations, track segment pick-up, use pricing and inventory management to manage mix • Analyze past and future mix of sales and modify strategies to move back towards optimal mix goal

The aforementioned goals are concrete that are written and established; however, goals can exist in many forms. Some hoteliers set targeted discount percentages, website contribution percentages, segment contributions, commission levels, and more. Revenue managers must therefore maintain a delicate balance of achieving each goal but most of all creating operating profit for the hotel.

DISCUSSION QUESTIONS

Question 1: What are some issues with market share reports? How can a hotel read a market share report and incorrectly claim success or declare failure?

Question 2: What kind of reporting do you think would be useful to hotel revenue managers in the future?

Question 3: How would you measure unconstrained demand using technology and the Internet?

Question 4: If a hotel has more demand than supply for a given time frame, what pricing strategies can be considered to increase profits?

APPLICATIONS

Case 1:

The hotel below was able to acquire data on their display marketing initiatives and total website production.

	Display Marketing		Totals
Impressions	71,420	Bookings	400
Clicks	110	Property Visits	6,200
Click through Rate (CTR)	x	Conversion Rate	z
Spend	$100		
Cost per Click (CPC)	y		
Revenue Booked	$2,550		
Bookings	17		

1. Solve for x, y, and z
2. Based upon this data, is it worthwhile for the hotel to increase the amount spent on display marketing? Why?

Case 2:

You are a member of a hotel development group that is underwriting The CDB Hotel, a new-build luxury five-star hotel with 300 all-suite guest room with 525 sq. ft. average. This hotel is the only all-suite hotel in the luxury segment with the competitive set guest room 350 sq. ft. average. As a result of the new-build guest rooms with a significant size and finish premium to the competitive set, The CDB Hotel is expected to yield a 130 ADR Index in Year 1 compared to the five existing luxury hotels in the market.

What is the projected ADR for The CDB Hotel if the comp set is projected to grow ADR by 4.5 percent in Year 1?

Assume that Occupancy Index is 100, what is the RevPAR Index for The CDB Hotel if Occupancy for the comp set stays flat in Year 1?

Comp Set Actual figures for previous year: 88.0 percent Occupancy, \$503.13 ADR, \$442.75 RevPAR.

TEAM ACTIVITY

Using data to improve results is a critical skill for revenue managers. Review the following Pace table that indicates Retail and Government segment is behind same period last year that is resulting in unfavorable pace by \$31.5K.

Questions:

How can the hotel improve pace in Retail and Government segments?

What other ways can the hotel improve revenue pace?

Table 7.12: Sample Pace Table

Segment	Mar-16			Mar-15			Variances		
	Rooms	**ADR**	**Revenue**	**Rooms**	**ADR**	**Revenue**	**Rooms**	**ADR**	**Revenue**
Retail	2,480	\$199.00	\$493,520.00	2,790	\$179.00	\$499,410.00	-310	\$20.00	(\$5,890.00)
Business Transient	1,240	\$189.00	\$234,360.00	620	\$179.00	\$110,980.00	620	\$10.00	\$123,380.00
Government	155	\$165.00	\$25,575.00	310	\$165.00	\$51,150.00	-155	\$0.00	(\$25,575.00)
	3,875	**\$194.44**	**\$753,455.00**	**3,720**	**\$177.83**	**\$661,540.00**	**155**	**\$16.61**	**\$91,915.00**
						% Pace	**4.17%**	**9.34%**	**13.89%**

INTERNET ACTIVITY

New Year's Eve in the Times Square neighborhood of New York, NY is one of the best examples of unconstrained demand for a single night. Many Times Square hotels put a minimum length of stay restriction to yield longer length of stay on shoulder dates to maximize RevPAR. In addition to length of stay restrictions, hotels can enforce prepaid or nonrefundable policies to maximize the high unconstrained demand. For this activity, pick a large national chain hotel in Times Square, New York. Shops for rates and availability for New Year's Eve for one-night length of stay.

Questions:

1. Does the hotel allow one-night length of stay? If not, does the website tell you the minimum length of stay or alternative dates you can stay?
2. Is there a special cancellation, prepaid or nonrefundable policy?
3. If you project high unconstrained demand of 130 percent of the hotel's sellable inventory for New Year's Eve, but project 80 percent occupancy on the pre and post shoulder dates, what yielding tactics can you implement to maximize RevPAR?

INTERNET ACTIVITY 2

Find five different revenue management tools and services with different purposes to help revenue managers understand past and future performance. Which do you think are the best? What tools or services were you unable to find and how would those new tools help revenue managers?

GLOSSARY

Click – when a consumer clicks on a link.

Click through rate (CTR) – percentage of clicks on a link or advertisement out of the amount of times the link or advertisement was shown.

Cost of acquisition – fees, commissions, and expenses attributed to each booking from third party distributors or internal payroll including

GDS commissions, OTA commissions, direct marketing expenses and all customer acquisition payroll.

Conversion – when a consumer has completed the payment in an online session.

Conversion rate – percentage of visits that resulted in bookings.

Impressions – the amount of times an ad or link has been shown.

Mix of sales/market segmentation – how revenue managers and marketers classify and target customers in specific groups based upon their characteristics, behaviors, and preferences.

Pace – tracking performance versus a previous period, mostly done to compare to the same moment in time as last year. For example, how many rooms were sold at this point last year for the upcoming month versus how many are sold today for the upcoming month?

Profit margin – percentage of profit out of total revenue.

Total revenue per available room (TrevPAR) – total revenue that a hotel accumulates coming from rooms, F&B, and all other outlets per each available room in the hotel.

Total revenue per occupied room (TrevPOR) – total revenue that a hotel accumulates coming from all outlets per the occupied rooms in the hotel.

Qualified segment – a segment that requires some type of membership identification in order to qualify to receive the discount.

Shoulder dates – dates that fall on the sides of peak demand dates.

Unconstrained demand – total demand in a segment or overall in the absence of any constraints.

Visit – a visit is when a consumer accesses and has an interaction with a website.

REFERENCES

Dickens, M. (2006, June 15). Benchmarking Bugbears. *Caterer & Hotelkeeper, 196* (4429), 22.

Ghose, A., Ipeirotis, P. G., & Li, B. (2014). Examining the Impact of Ranking on Consumer Behavior and Search Engine Revenue. *Management Science, 60* (7), 1632–1654.

HTrends. Com (2014, August 20). *Hama Study Documents Growing Acquisition Costs Outpacing Hotel Revenue Growth.* Retrieved from https://www.htrends.com/trends-detail-sid-79384.html

Lado-Sestayo, R., Vivel-Búa, M. & Otero-González, L. (2017). Determinants of TRevPAR: Hotel, Management and Tourist Destination. *International Journal of Contemporary Hospitality Management, 29* (12), 3138–3156.

Lindt, M. (2006, August 17). RevPAR Needs an Overhaul. *Caterer and Hotelkeeper, 196* (4438), 16.

McGuire, K. A. (2017). *The Analytic Hospitality Executive: Implementing Data Analytics in Hotels and Casinos.* Hoboken, NJ: Wiley.

Phumchusri, N. & Maneesophon, P. (2014). Optimal Overbooking Decision for Hotel Rooms Revenue Management. *Journal of Hospitality and Tourism Technology, 5* (3), 261–277.

CHAPTER 8

Market Data for Hotel Revenue Management

Calvin Anderson, Elyana Falk, and Nicholas Catalfamo

OVERVIEW

Of the many contributing elements to a successful revenue strategy, there is no single factor more important than market data. This is because the industry standard for measuring top line success is Revenue per Available Room (RevPAR) index or revenue per available room as compared to the average of your nearest competitors. In many instances, the RevPAR index contest is similar to a NASCAR race. Both scenarios function in a series of constants: a race car encounters the same turns as it speeds around the circular track just as the market brings similar highs and lows year after year. Just as such permanencies exist in our analogy, so do certain variables: those being external conditions and competitor position. In a race, external conditions such as temperature, humidity, and precipitation can dramatically impact speed and traction. Similarly, in navigating revenue strategy, external conditions such as customer reviews, weather patterns, and airline flight volume can both accelerate or decelerate pace to prior year. The final external variable, and perhaps most important, is competitor position. Visibility into competitor positioning allows one to measure market elasticity on a far broader scope than what would be possible individually. Such a vantage point is key because it is impossible to perfectly navigate the future markets based merely on one's running pace and prior year trends alone. Competitor pace not only signals unusual opportunity to compress rates and restrict yielding, but also serves as a preliminary warning to a variance in prior year trends that ultimately will demand a change in strategy. In many ways, a revenue strategy without market data is much like racing a car with no windows—if you cannot see the competitors next to you, you are likely to have an accident.

LEARNING OBJECTIVES

After studying this chapter, you should be able to:

- Differentiate between the two design purposes of data modeling: reporting and analysis
- Recognize the pitfalls of utilizing only internal pace data and trends
- Interpret historic competitive set benchmarking data to explain hotel performance
- Source forward-looking market benchmarking intelligence to derive sound revenue strategy
- Appreciate the consumer's growing level of market visibility through technology and its impact on artificial rate elasticity
- Identify the broad array of alternative market data that can and will be used to improve hotel revenue pricing, yielding and digital marketing efforts
- Communicate data as a story according to your audience

OUTLINE

Introduction

Two Purposes of Data: Reporting and Analysis

- Modeling Internal Booking Data
- The Four Booking Pace Quadrants
- The Four Lenses of Segmentation

Benchmarking Performances as an Industry Standard

- Standards of Benchmarking
- Forward-Looking Benchmarking Data
- OTA Market Data
- Pricing Market Data

Non-Traditional Market Data

- Consumer Sentiment Converted into Data
- Air Traffic

- Tracking Website Regrets and Denials Through Custom Tags

The Future of Market Analytics

- Speaking to Data

Discussion Questions and Applications

INTRODUCTION

Revenue management exists nowhere more prominently than in a business where both supply is static, fixed costs are high, variable costs are low, and demand for goods sold is elastic. No surprise, hotels become the perfect candidate for this function as neither a hotel's rooms can be suddenly grown to accommodate short-term demand surges nor can they be reduced to minimize static expenses such as a mortgage or maintenance when occupancies are low. As a result, the most successful business strategies in the hotel space center is filling as many rooms as possible each day at the maximum price the market will bear. If demand is less than the available number of rooms at a given property, pricing will likely drop in order to garner the additional bookings needed to cover business costs. An optimized revenue strategy can often keep a full workforce employed over short downturns to be sure the property is able to quickly turn and service a sold-out hotel when demand resumes. As demand increases, rates ought to increase in parallel to obtain the highest rates customers are willing to pay. While the concept is simple, successfully selling a hotel at the most optimal combination of occupancy and rate requires tremendous insight into market demand trends, guest preferences, and price elasticity. The combined understanding of these elements creates sound revenue strategy that will consistently yield growth and improved market share. In this chapter, we will further review the importance of market data, discover industry best practices for both measuring and optimizing demand, and finally explore what the future holds for predictive analytics as technology advances our capabilities.

SO WHAT?

Revenue management has been one of the most powerful resources within the airline, car rental, and hotel industry since the 80s due to their high fixed costs and low variable costs, but are these the only candidates that could benefit from revenue management? If not, what other industries could adopt the principles of revenue management and what sort of market intelligence would they need in order to be successful?

TWO PURPOSES OF DATA: REPORTING AND ANALYSIS

Before digging into the many modeling formats of market data, it is important to note that data is commonly structured to solve one of two primary purposes: reporting or analysis. In the context of this chapter, reporting will be understood to mean data that is rolled up into a series of metrics to convey a performance trend. Reporting is commonly used in a corporate infrastructure to measure the health of the business and create informational awareness. Because reporting is typically macro in nature, its primary function is to alert as opposed to divulging detailed causation. By contrast, data formatted to derive analysis is designed to offer the user micro-insights that can be directly leveraged to impact change or relay attribution. Analysis is action-oriented and compliments the work of the practitioner. While both reporting and analysis-based models can overlap at times, appropriately navigating the design purpose of a data model will expedite the delivery of a desired outcome. Monthly aggregate data often "reports up" to alert the user of broader trend that will need to be "analyzed down" to solve or optimize. Both models are required to successfully optimize a business. Most traditional data models relay business intelligence with the primary purpose of reporting. If a reporting model exists alone, the practitioners can be left guessing at potential solutions for lack of concrete proof of causation; this meaning that one may understand a trend to exists, but is ill-equipped to derive how said trend came to be. As access to "big data" has grown, so have analytical data models, greatly empowering the work of the practitioner.

Modeling Internal Booking Data

In the 80s, while revenue management was introduced to airlines, the hotel industry was starting to realize the importance of segmenting their business. No longer was a room just a room; it was a booking sold to a leisure guest, a corporate traveler, or a large group of which each category had distinct buying behaviors. As it became apparent that the behaviors of each customer segment were predictable, hoteliers utilized financial engineering to create a series of top line reports to track internal trends and the behavior within each customer segment to better predict future behaviors. Most internal booking data falls into one of four quadrants related to booking pace: monthly pace, monthly pickup pace, daily pace, and daily pickup pace as illustrated below.

Table 8.1: Four Booking Pace Quadrants.

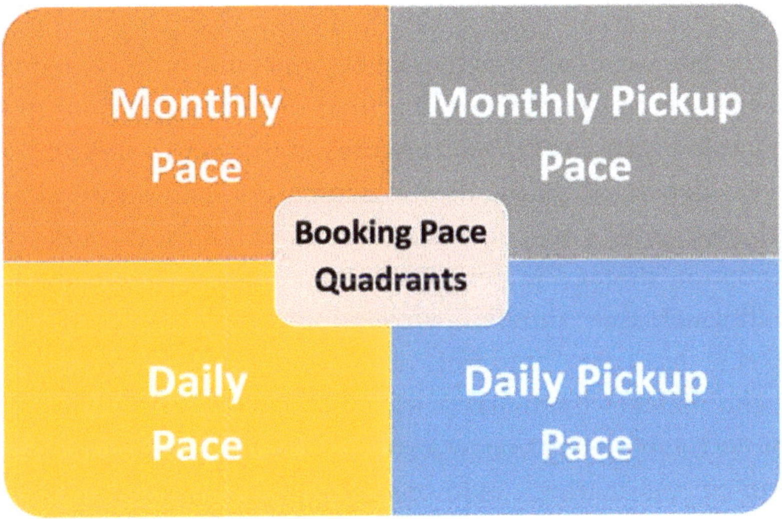

Source: Provided by Calvin Anderson.

- **Monthly Pace:** Net bookings and cancellations committed currently for a given stay month as compared to the net bookings and cancellations committed same day (by numbered date) prior year.
- **Monthly Pickup Pace:** Net bookings and cancellations committed within a set booking period (i.e., last 7 days) for a given stay month as compared

to the same net bookings and cancellations that occurred over the same booking dates (by day of week) prior year.

- **Daily Pace:** Net bookings and cancellations committed currently for a given stay date as compared to the net bookings and cancellations committed same day (by numbered date) prior year.
- **Daily Pickup Pace:** Net bookings and cancellations committed within a set booking period (i.e., last 7 days) for a given stay date as compared to the same net bookings and cancellations that occurred over the same booking dates (by day of week) prior year.

The four booking pace quadrants all represent booking data filtered differently by stay period and booking period with the intent of answering two important questions for a subject stay month or date. On the books pace answers: "How am I positioned versus the same time last year?" while pickup pace answers: "Am I making my current position better or worse versus the same time last year?" On the books pace relays a roll up of all bookings to date versus all bookings at the same time prior year. Because on the books pace is a bi-product of all actualized booking periods, the rooms and average daily rate (ADR) achieved are not necessarily indicative of what the market will bear currently. Thus, it is important to contrast on the books pace with pickup pace to gauge customer response to the current pricing and distribution strategy. In periods of compression, market conditions are apparent through lower purchasing resistance to higher prices. By contrast, if a market is decompressing, reservations will trend fewer until pricing is lowered and matches the markets willingness to pay. In order to continually improve booking position, a strategist should shape his or her pricing strategy to current market conditions which are best noted in pickup pace as opposed to on the books pace. While all four quadrants are insightful, monthly on the books pace tailors toward a rolled-up reporting model and monthly pickup pace, daily on the books pace, and daily pickup pace serve a more actionable analytics-based purpose.

Within the measures of the four booking pace quadrants lie multiple dimensions that the hotel property management system (PMS) commonly attributes to each reservation. These dimensions typically include a market segment which is linked to the segmentation found on the hotel profit and lost statement (P&L), the booking channel or source, the room type booked, the guests assigned to each reservation, and many more. With these dimensions in mind, a revenue strategist can begin to view each of the booking pace quadrants through a different perspective in order to more fully understand a hotel's booking behavior through the lens of each unique dimension. There are four key lenses that a strategist should seek to understand internal booking through: the channel or source from whence the booking came, the cost of acquiring the booking, the demand elements surrounding the product type sold, and the booking path or patterns taken prior to transacting.

Table 8.2: Four Lenses of Segmentation.

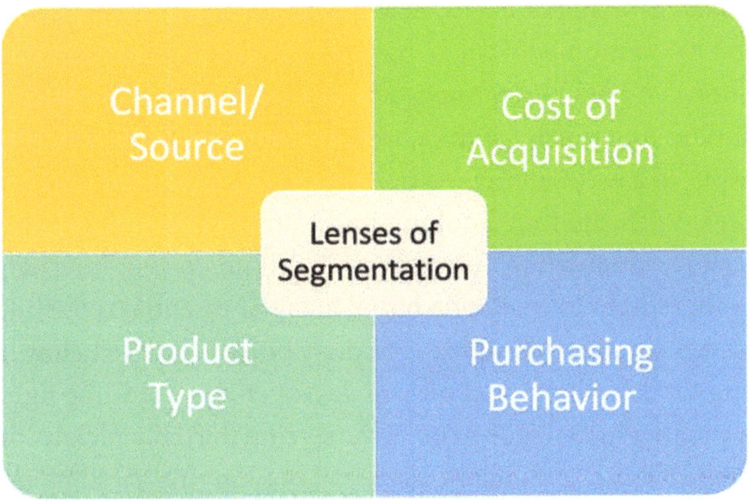

Source: Provided by Calvin Anderson.

- **Channel/Source:** The platform or engine responsible for delivering a booking transaction. This could range from the hotel/brand call center, the hotel website, an online travel agency (OTA), a global distribution service (GDS), or the internal hotel sales team.
- **Cost of Acquisition:** The fees, commissions, and expenses attributed to each booking from third party distributors or internal payroll including GDS commissions, OTA commissions, direct marketing expenses, and all customer acquisition payroll.
- **Product Type:** Defined narrowly as the room type, package element, or booking policy attached to the reservation or more broadly as the length of stay or lead time dimension. This meaning, that a product can be defined both by the physical attributes, such a premium room type or package ele-

ment, just as much as it can be considered an accommodation available for purchase at the very last minute in a compressed market.

- **Purchasing Behavior:** Common purchasing patterns found within a given group of bookers including price sensitivity, responsiveness to various types of advertisement, propensity to cancel, and customer loyalty.

The four lenses of segmentation are not singular dimensions in themselves as much they are perspectives to guide the analytical mind as its review of the physical booking attributes tracked by the PMS. And just as one lens may have multiple applicable dimensions, one dimension can speak to many lenses as well. For example, a booking channel such as a wholesaler may exhibit a common booking behavior with one commission model (cost of attribution). Where by contrast, a brand website could deliver bookings through multiple channels (mobile, web, and app platforms) offering various product types to a series of buying behaviors (i.e., advanced purchase versus last-minute). With the four booking pace quadrants analyzed through the four lenses of segmentation (using booking dimensions), internal booking data is the ingredient to making a broad array of essential reporting models that span from simple to complex. The daily booking curve below illustrates the running total of segmented pickup day-over-day shedding light on how and when each segment came to be. In analyzing the daily pickup, one is able to understand where to dynamically yield booking restrictions in order to create balanced stay patterns as well as price according to internal demand directly affecting the property.

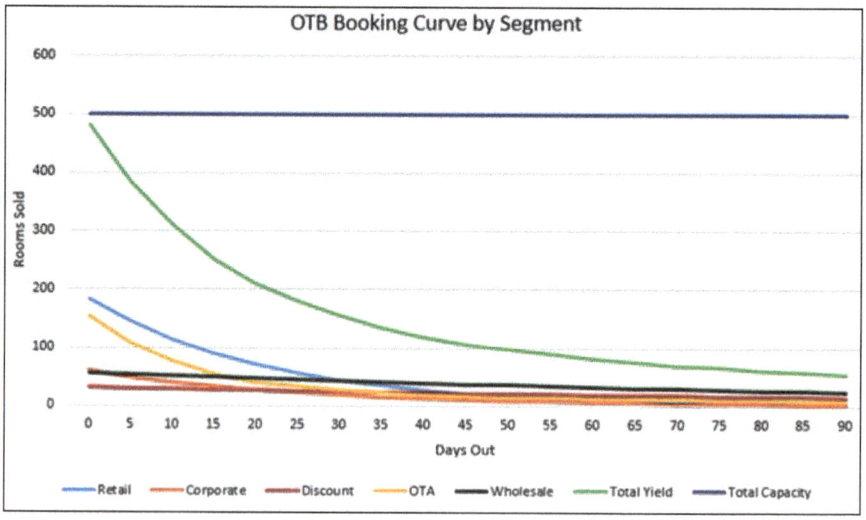

Figure 8.1: Booking Curve

Author generated booking curve of a 500-room hotel showing internal buildup of bookings into day of arrival.

QUESTIONS TO CONSIDER

Referencing the above graph, which market segment has the longest booking window? By contrast, which has the shortest window?

While the importance of internal booking data cannot be overestimated, fundamentally, there is an Achilles' heel: internal booking data is isolated to one property within a broader market. If prior year performance is poor compared to the rest of the market while the hotel is experiencing growth toward the competition's current year's median, then an isolated viewpoint might conclude that year-over-year (YOY) growth was highly optimized. The truth, in this case, would be that the property performed at a sub-par level one out of two years. This one-dimensional viewpoint can result in consistent underachievement to what the market can deliver year-upon-year. In the same vain, if a market is in recession and the subject hotel understandably declines to prior year, it could be falsely concluded that revenue strategy was poorly executed when, in fact, all competitors lost revenues due to downward market conditions. While internal growth may have been the most important metrics years ago when hotel ownership was private, today's publically traded companies are deemed successful relative to market conditions represented by aggregate competitive data. Thus, exclusive use of internal booking data is no longer sufficient to consistently outmaneuver the market and thus data that provides visibility into the broader market is required. The goal of revenue a revenue strategist has, thus, transformed from achieving year-over-year growth to the pursuit of holding a premium revenue index to the aggregate of one's competitors whether that amount is more or less than prior year.

REAL PEOPLE

Jane Henderson*, is the brand new Director of Revenue Management at a four-star hotel in Midtown Manhattan and she has just attended her first budget meeting. The new owners have asked Jane to grow the property's RevPAR 10 percent in the coming year.

Jane feels this is very high compared to the projected market growth for Midtown Manhattan, which is only expected to increase by 4 percent. Is it possible that the expectations for Jane's hotel are, in fact, fair and logical? If so, what logic would you use to explain to Jane how it is possible that her goals are set so much higher than most of her competitors?

*Name has been concealed.

SPREADSHEET EXERCISE 8.1

Unpacking Big Data

Internal booking data can hold the secrets too many impactful booking behaviors and trends that a revenue manager would benefit from knowing. Most property management systems (PMS) can export raw booking data into an Excel format, but gaining insight out of such data is not automatic. Thus, it is important to be able to format data in order to unlock booking behaviors and trends which could lead to more informed revenue strategy decision making.

Open the attached booking data extract for a boutique hotel in midtown Manhattan for the month of October and use Microsoft Excel functionalities (i.e., pivot tables and v-look ups) to build a presentation-worthy dashboard illustrating average customer lengths of stays, booking lead times, day-of-week patterns and room type preferences. In your observation of the data, determine two additional elements that might be useful to note and display the observed trends alongside the above list.

BENCHMARKING PERFORMANCE AS AN INDUSTRY STANDARD

With the rapid commercialization of the hotel industry and the rise of major brands, the need to benchmark competitive performance became undeniable. In the mid-1980's, a company called Smith Travel Research Global (STR) answered this need and remains one of the industry's top resources for historic performance benchmarking. STR provides micro-economic environmental scans offering aggregate benchmarking performance metrics of self-selected competitors. By aggregating the data, STR provides context to the ups and downs of the market without revealing confidential competitor performance. Jan Freitag, Senior Vice President, Lodging Insights, STR, Inc., notes that while STR is not the only company to aggregate competitive data (there are regional competitors), STR remains one of few GLOBAL bench markers (J. Freitag, personal communication, January 4, 2016). Regardless of service provider, almost all hotel feasibility studies include competitor benchmarking data in support.

Carolyn and Randy Smith of Hendersonville, TN began STR (formerly known as Smith Travel Research) in the basement of their home in 1985. Randy had worked for Laventhol and Horwath (L&H), a dominant hospitality consulting company of the day, where he had been introduced to the idea of benchmarking. L&H didn't choose to pursue the business leaving the opportunity open for the Smith family. Randy and Carolyn saw strong growth after an endorsement by the American Hotel and Lodging Association shortly after starting the company (J. Freitag, personal communication, January 4, 2016).

Prior to STR, hotel benchmarking was generally conducted very poorly and ineffectively. Night auditors used to drive to other hotels parking lots and count cars or perform a "nightly call around" asking if the competitor was full and inquiring about pricing. Reported data was often incorrect as people would exaggerate the stats and there was no way to know if the exaggeration was greater or less than the actual performance. With STR, came solid numbers, finally. Today STR's global presence is prominent; there are few hotel feasibility studies that occur without STR data behind them. Originally, data processing was managed through reams of print outs with data collection coming by way of faxes and even letters (methods that are still used by some properties today). No surprise that data processing has much improved in domestic hotels and throughout the world due to technology. As STR expands internationally, and competitor benchmarking with it, the issue of selling a benchmarking product requires trust, which is often earned slowly. Often branded hotels take STR into a marketplace first. Additionally, former employees of branded hotels who move into the independent arena often become key influencers when it comes to STR adaptation and it is through them that private ownership groups become participants (J. Freitag, personal communication, January 4, 2016).

THINK HISTORICALLY

While the process of counting cars in competitor hotel parking lots or calling around to ask nightly may have been a bit archaic, it was one of the few ways to estimate competitor business occupancies prior to benchmarking services. Can you think of some alternative (legal) methods you might have used to gauge the level of business your competitors were experiencing prior to benchmarking technology?

Standards of Benchmarking

The most widely known benchmarking report that STR distributes is the STAR report, which is available for historical data daily, weekly and monthly. In alignment with industry standards, the reported data points used are the following:

- **Occupancy:** Rooms sold divided by rooms available multiplied by 100. Occupancy is always displayed as a percentage of rooms.
- **Average Daily Rate (ADR):** Room revenue divided by rooms sold, displayed as the average rental rate for a single room.
- **Revenue per Available Room (RevPAR):** Room revenue divided by rooms available.
- **Segmented Data:** Rooms sold and revenue data broken down by source of business (transient, group, contract) and source of revenue (room, food and beverage, other).

With the above listed data points, STAR reports benchmarking metrics according to:

- **Index (Occupancy, ADR, RevPAR):** Property performance divided by competitive set performance multiplied by 100. Internationally, indexes are also referred to as MPI—Market Penetration Index (Occupancy Index), ARI: Average Rate Index (ADR Index), and RGI—Revenue/RevPAR Generation Index (RevPAR Index).
- **Percentage Change (% Chg.):** Amount of growth—up, down, or flat— this period versus same period last year (day, week, running 28 days, running month-to-date). Calculated as ((TY-LY)/LY)*100.

- **Rank (Occupancy, ADR, RevPAR, % Chg.):** Property performance ranked versus hotels in the competitive set (e.g., a "3 of 6" ADR ranking means the subject hotel's absolute ADR is third highest of the six competitors).

In Figure 8.2, the monthly glance tab from a sample STAR report is given. The data in the first row and first column begins with the monthly (February, 2013) performance of the subject property; in the second column, the aggregate performance of the competitive set for the same period (excluding subject property); and finally, the index of the subscriber to the competitive set in the third. Indexes can refer to occupancy by Market Penetration Index (MPI), ADR by Average Rate Index (ARI) or Revenue/RevPAR by Revenue/RevPAR Generation Index (RGI). An index over 100 represents a performance higher than the average or greater than "fair share" to the competitive set. Preceding rows include performance periods of year-to-date, the most recent running three months, ending with "current" month, and the same running 12-month period, also ending with the "current"s month. The second subset of rows refer to the percentage change verses same month prior year allowing the reader to compare the growth of the subject hotel to the growth achieved by the competitive set over the same period. In this case, one would refer to MPI, ARI, and RGI followed by "percentage change" or "% Chg." MPI, ARI, or RGI % Chg represent the shift in market share to or away from the subject hotel. While one should aspire to perform at an index above 100, the growth in share year-over-year (YOY) can also represent a winning revenue strategy.

Tab 2 - Monthly Performance at a Glance - My Property vs. Competitive Set
Any Hotel 123 Any Street Any City, Any State 99999 (555) 555-5555
STR # 98765 Chain ID: 999999 MgtCo.: None Owner: None
For the Month of: February 2013 Date Created: April 09, 2013 Monthly Competitive Set Data Excludes Subject Property

February 2013									
	Occupancy (%)			*ADR*			*RevPAR*		
	My Prop	Comp Set	Index (MPI)	My Prop	Comp Set	Index (MPI)	My Prop	Comp Set	Index (MPI)
Current Month	69.0	68.9	100.2	164.66	147.37	111.7	113.59	101.48	111.9
Year To Date	69.6	63.1	110.3	160.04	145.90	109.7	111.32	92.04	120.9
Running 3 Month	68.9	62.9	109.5	144.43	136.25	106.0	99.53	85.74	116.1
Running 12 Month	72.5	71.2	101.8	139.09	127.51	109.1	100.78	90.76	111.0

February 2013 vs. 2012 Percent Change (%)									
	Occupancy (%)			ADR			RevPAR		
	My Prop	Comp Set	Index (MPI)	My Prop	Comp Set	Index (MPI)	My Prop	Comp Set	Index (MPI)
Current Month	7.0	6.5	0.5	3.7	3.2	0.5	11.0	9.9	1.0
Year To Date	5.3	6.9	-1.5	3.5	3.3	0.1	9.0	10.4	-1.3
Running 3 Month	7.1	5.1	2.0	5.5	5.8	-0.3	13.0	11.1	1.7
Running 12 Month	5.5	4.6	0.9	0.4	2.5	-2.0	6.0	7.2	-1.2
						Smith Travel Research, Inc			

Figure 8.2: STAR Monthly Glance Tab

Glance Tab—note how Year to Date RevPAR Index runs a premium to the competitive set at a 120.9 RGI, but is losing -1.3 RGI % Chg as the set is growing faster YOY than the subscriber (Courtesy of STR).

QUESTIONS TO CONSIDER

Is the subject property in this example achieving positive year to date results? If so, what is the greatest contributor to this success? Did the subject in the property before better indexes to the competitive set this year or last? What element (ADR or occupancy) was responsible for this shift?

When looking to interpret and action against STAR data, J. Freitag suggests it is imperative to have the correct comp set and understand what that set represents; to really get a sense of who you're competing with and in what arena. One of the best tools STR offers to help clients identify competitors is a Reverse Comp Set showing who has chosen you as their competitor. This brings context to one's decision when understanding their market. Second, the RevPAR % Chg. number is key because it encompasses both ADR change and Occupancy change and the other is RevPAR Index Growth % Chg. that allows one to measure gain or loss in market share relative to the competitor's gain or loss (J. Freitag, personal communication, January 4, 2016).

While the STAR is most well-known benchmarking product offered by STR, there are many more offerings. For years, STR has been providing the Hotel Operating Statistics Almanac (HOST Almanac) report that offers benchmarked full P&L perspective revealing everything from department expenses, to NOI, to GOP. While STR is able to offer this level of detail on a monthly basis, most clients have not expressed an interest. As STR evolves, the company is constantly wrestling with the difference between interesting and actionable data and thus products that point to areas of revenue opportunity and greater profitability will take priority. Currently, STR plans to take the HOST Almanac globally, bring deeper segmentation data to the market and grow the usage of the F&B STAR in order to give better insights into outlet, room service & banquets revenues (J. Freitag, personal communication, January 4, 2016).

SPREADSHEET EXERCISE 8.2

STAR Analysis

One of the problems with Big Data is that there is often too much of it. The most important data points are those that can be actioned and affected. In order to find such points, one must read the data almost like a story, often beginning with the more macro points and then by following the peculiar trends down the data trail to discover the source of the behavior. It is then important to be able to critique (both spoken and written) your findings concisely and convincingly so that your audience can both agree and remember your analysis.

Using the sample STAR report, determine one positive and one negative trend within the February 2013 performance. Once you have determined which two performance indicators best highlight your success and opportunity, select data points from the many tabs that may help to explain what happened.

Take your findings and write two paragraphs—one on each point. Explain the success and the opportunity in your own words while referencing data points from the report to support your arguments. Your paragraphs should be easy to read (much like a spoken explanation), but also concise and well supported.

Forward Looking Benchmarking Data

While the value of historic benchmarking is irreplaceable to the industry as a whole, the ability to see these same trends as they book into future dates allows revenue strategists to directly compete with an understanding of trends while they are unfolding. Much like STR's STAR report is the industry household name for historical benchmarking, so is TravelClick®'s Demand360® business intelligence (BI) tool the same for forward-looking benchmarking. Demand360® allows revenue managers to understand compression in their comp-set or market to make more informed decisions. Understanding bookings by segment or channel ensures a hotel knows how to optimize its mix and drive maximum revenues and promotes confidence in decision-making. The concept was originally brought to market by The Rubicon Group in 2008 and was distributed reporting via email much like STR. In 2011, TravelClick® acquired the Rubicon Group and has since evolved the data into a powerful online suite of dashboards. Katie Moro, Global Director of Business Intelligence Product, TravelClick®, explains that Demand data is a collaboration between TravelClick® and the data providers. The data comes directly from hotel's PMS or Data Warehouse, thus ensuring that the data is accurate, reliable and real. It provides a full year into the future and a full year into the past, broken out by day. The data is segmented into Group and Transient as well as Retail, Discount Negotiated, Wholesale, and Qualified rates and is broken into booking channel—Online Travel Agents, brand websites, Global Distribution Systems, and hotel direct reservations. One of the reasons there are so few competitors in this space is because every brand and every hotel does business in a different way, so normalizing and making the data consistent is not an easy task (K. Moro, personal communication, January 15, 2016).

Prior to demand data, hotels used and continue to use historical data, internal reporting, convention calendars, and event and airline data to make smart decisions. While that data is still relevant, Demand360®'s historical and forward looking data allows hotels to understand the full picture for future dates, and make decisions that can make a real-time impact, and further analyze historical data to see trends (K. Moro, personal communication, January 15, 2016).

TravelClick and Demand360 are registered trademarks of TravelClick, Inc.

The power of converting data into online dashboards is evident in that the user is no longer restricted to the Excel export and would be forced to build timely pivot tables in order to pursue perspectives beyond the original output. Within the application, there are three main areas of focus—transient by segment, transient by channel, and group. In order to begin auctioning the data, revenue managers would first look at future months to find key periods where compression exists in the comp-set and make sure strategy is in place to account for the situation.

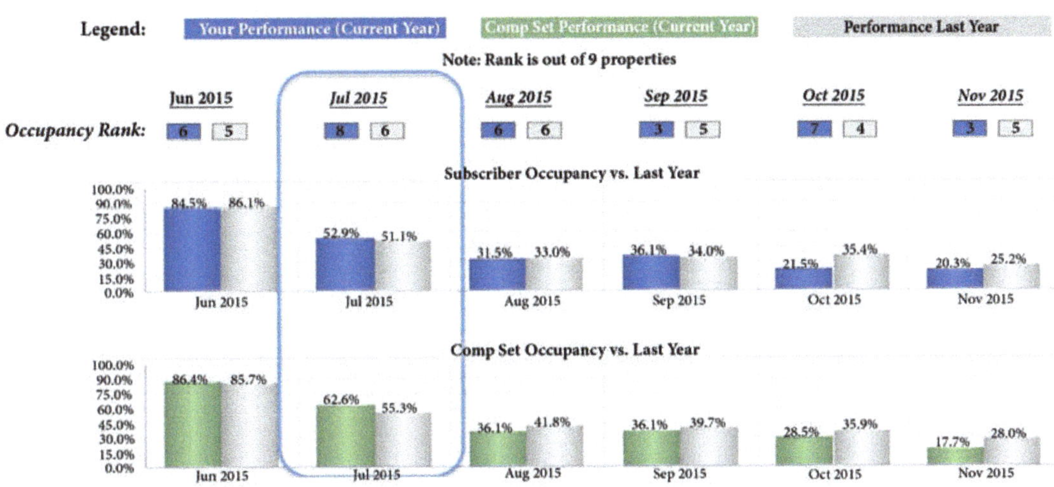

Figure 8.3: TravelClick® Overview Tab

Overview Tab—note how July 2015 runs nearly 10 percent below the comp set in occupancy indicating an area requiring strategic action. Courtesy of TravelClick®.

> **QUESTIONS TO CONSIDER**
> Referencing the above graph, which month is the subject lagging behind the set competitively the most? Which month is ahead the most?

This high-level overview often calls out periods of group need and offers insight allowing for more confident group pricing, a feature benefiting both the sales and revenue team. Good group base business for most hotels is critical to success.

Stay Date	Subscriber Total Occupancy	Subscriber ADR-All Sold Rooms	Non-Group Occupancy	Group Committed Occupancy	Group Sold Occupancy	Comp Set Total Occupancy	Non-Group Occupancy	Group Committed Occupancy	Group Sold Occupancy	Group Committed Occupancy Index	Group Committed Index Variance vs. Last Year	Group Committed Index Change vs. Last Week
01-May-2016 Sun	0.0%		0.0%			7.1%	0.1%	7.0%			(107)	0
02-May-2016 Mon	0.0%		0.0%			8.1%	0.0%	8.1%	0.1%		(107)	0
03-May-2016 Tue	0.0%		0.0%			6.4%	0.0%	6.3%	0.1%		(456)	0
04-May-2016 Wed	0.0%		0.0%			4.6%	0.0%	4.5%	0.1%		(92)	0
05-May-2016 Thu	0.8%		0.0%	0.8%		8.6%	0.0%	8.6%	0.2%	9	(52)	(1)
06-May-2016 Fri	3.8%		0.0%	3.8%		10.9%	0.0%	10.8%	0.1%	35	(114)	(4)
07-May-2016 Sat	14.6%		0.0%	14.6%		11.3%	0.0%	11.3%		129	115	(11)
08-May-2016 Sun	29.9%		0.0%	29.9%		25.2%	0.1%	25.1%		119	119	(1)
09-May-2016 Mon	29.1%		0.0%	29.1%		28.0%	0.1%	27.9%		104	104	0
10-May-2016 Tue	29.1%		0.0%	29.1%		30.2%	0.1%	30.1%		97	97	0
11-May-2016 Wed	29.1%		0.0%	29.1%		32.1%	0.1%	31.9%	0.1%	91	91	0
12-May-2016 Thu	24.5%		0.0%	24.5%		36.5%	0.1%	36.4%	0.2%	67	49	(1)
13-May-2016 Fri	7.3%		0.0%	7.3%		17.3%	0.2%	17.1%	0.2%	43	(2)	(2)
14-May-2016 Sat	0.8%		0.0%	0.8%		9.7%	0.3%	9.5%	0.1%	8	(47)	(1)

Figure 8.4: TravelClick® Group Penetration

Courtesy of TravelClick®.

Group Tab—note that the competition is averaging nearly 30 percent group base over a period where the subscriber property has nothing. This means that the subscriber might be able to command a higher price on group business over the shown period knowing that group market is already saturated in the set.

When it comes to transient strategy over dates closer in (to day of arrival), there are several options to pursue. One could choose to analyze channel strategy (the source of the business, i.e., Expedia, Government, AAA, brand website) in order to understand if there are need-periods that require marketing support. Without forward-looking aggregate data, hotels could only see their own position, which may not necessarily be reflective of the deficiencies they may be carrying to the market. Once opportunities are identified, promotions can be run through the brand, the GDS or individual OTA channels in order to recover lost territory. After such actions have been implemented, the results can be measured by observing whether or not week-over-week share increases to the set in the targeted channel. Again this sort of analysis is superior to internal data because the subscriber is now measuring market share shift as opposed to just seeing if gains are made to historical pace.

Pace Tab—tracks weekly pickup for both the subscriber as well as the aggregate of the set by day with filters options for both market segments and contributing source. One can measure if an improvement is being made in each area and over exactly what period said improvement is occurring.

QUESTIONS TO CONSIDER

Referencing the above graph, which day is the subject property best positioned to the competitive set and why?

From the segmentation side, hotels can find opportunities where retail business is compressing and begin to close out discounts in order to shift the mix of business away from high-cost distribution channels. Similarly, from a negotiated standpoint, there may be need periods where corporate accounts can help to fill a gap that would otherwise leave rooms empty. For each hotel, the mix of business will be different, but thanks to forward looking aggregate market data, revenue managers can make sure they are hand-selecting

Tue Jun-23-2015
0 of Days (Max 90)
00
Apply

Transient
Sub-Segment
(All Column Value
Apply

(All Column Value
Sub-Channel
(All Column Value
Apply

• Competitive Set
Primary

Sold/Committed
Committed
Sold

Hotel Elegance
Booking date updated as of Jun 15, 2015

Booking Performance for committed Room Nights by Stay Date
As of June 15, 2015

Stay Date	Subscriber Occupancy	Comp Set Occupancy	Difference	Index	Occ Rank	Subscriber Room Nights	% Growth vs. Last Year	Comp Set % Growth vs. Last Year	Occupancy Index Variance vs. Last Year	Subscriber Room Nights Pickup vs. Last Week	Subscriber Room Nights % Pickup Since Last Week	Comp Set Room Night % Pickup Since Last Week	Occupancy Index Change Since Last Week	Subscriber ADR	ADR Rank	Subscriber RevPAR	RevPAR Rank
23-Jun-2015 Tue	58.6%	57.8%	0.9	101	4 of 9	153	(0.6%)↓	10.8%	(1)	6	4.1%	17.9%	(14)	$279	5 of 9	$163	5 of 9
24-Jun-2015 Wed	53.3%	59.6%	(6.4)	89	5 of 9	139	2.2% ↑	15.7%	(1)	1	0.7%	18.1%	(16)	$276	5 of 9	$147	6 of 9
25-Jun-2015 Thu	53.6%	52.7%	0.9	102	4 of 9	140	13.8% ↑	0.4%	1	(2)	(1.4%)	15.4%	(17)	$237	6 of 9	$127	6 of 9
26-Jun-2015 Fri	52.9%	50.2%	2.7	105	4 of 9	138	7.8% ↑	(14.8%)	1	17	14.0%	10.2%	3	$235	2 of 9	$124	5 of 9
27-Jun-2015 Sat	59.0%	52.9%	6.1	111	4 of 9	154	21.3% ↑	(3.5%)	2	32	26.2%	7.1%	16	$241	2 of 9	$142	3 of 9
28-Jun-2015 Sun	41.4%	46.5%	(5.1)	89	5 of 9	108	54.3% ↑	55.7%	0	27	33.3%	13.8%	13	$184	5 of 9	$76	6 of 9
29-Jun-2015 Mon	46.4%	47.1%	(0.7)	99	3 of 9	121	86.2% ↑	68.1%	1	35	40.7%	23.6%	12	$176	5 of 9	$82	6 of 9
30-Jun-2015 Tue	41.4%	35.8%	5.6	115	3 of 9	108	44.0% ↑	38.0%	0	35	47.9%	28.4%	15	$186	5 of 9	$77	3 of 9
01-Jul-2015 Wed	39.8%	32.5%	7.4	123	3 of 9	104	76.3% ↑	31.4%	3	31	42.5%	25.2%	15	$181	6 of 9	$72	3 of 9
02-Jul-2015 Thu	54.4%	50.9%	3.5	107	4 of 9	142	51.1% ↑	35.3%	1	23	19.3%	10.6%	8	$270	5 of 9	$147	5 of 9

Figure 8.5: TravelClick® Pace

Source: Courtesy of TravelClick®.

the best of what is obtainable before the results are in (K. Moro, personal communication, January 15, 2016).

OTA Market Data

A secondary resource used by hoteliers to better understand macro-market trends comes from online travel agencies (OTAs). Because OTAs facilitate and distribute a strong share of the most leisure markets, their transaction data carries with it incredible insight into market dynamics of demand and compression. While such data is never "open source" for private use, most OTA partners are glad to offer insight to hoteliers upon request. It is also important to note that this data typically varies from both STR and TravelClick®'s resources in that the aggregation of competitors extends across an entire market as opposed to a smaller 5-10 competitor aggregate.

There are three particular instances where a hotelier may choose to look to an OTA partner for insight into market trends: (1) estimating the impact of large first-time events like as a Super Bowl or the Olympic games; (2) garnering insight into unusual macro-market changes such as a burst in supply growth; (3) comparing broader customer trends such as average booking lead time and country of origin to one's internal characteristics.

For large first-time events, OTAs have the ability to show how the market is broadly trending in comparison to non-affected historical patterns in prior years. This is useful because it is often difficult to price and yield optimally when the scale of demand is unknown. Because the goal of revenue management is to get the best of what can be gotten within one's market, OTA Insight is a company forward-looking buying behaviors and market pricing is especially necessary when a region enters into "unknown territory." In these cases, a strategic meeting with one's OTA partners helps to better understand the unique demand characteristics surrounding a special event allow the revenue manager to posture strategy accordingly. In such situations, a revenue strategist might request insight into the patterns that occurred during the same event in other cities, historically. If short-term cancellations for a particular event were heavy, one might respond by implementing an aggressive overbooking strategy. Understanding whether average market occupancies run above, below or parallel the city, as a whole, may bring pricing insight and elicit a change in one's current hotel strategy in order ensure competitive indexes.

Much like first-time events, macro-market changes also become difficult to understand without a broader view. If rooms supply grows materially over a given year, the strategies formerly used to elicit strong performance may no longer prove successful. In order to adjust to new dynamics, a revenue strategist would be prudent to elicit macro-behaviors seen by the all-seeing eye of the OTA. In understanding changes such as slowed booking pace or lower average ADR's captured within similar booking windows allows for strategy correction before the negative impacts are uncorrectable.

Finally, regarding broader customer trends, often times OTAs are the first to see when a material shift in customer buying behavior occurs. If short-term cancellations begin to grow, an OTA partner can confirm to individual hoteliers that the behavior they are seeing exhibited by their own guests is not a microcosm unique to just one property. When global currencies change valuations, the OTAs typically notice the corresponding change in destination-based booking behaviors. Understanding these insights allows a revenue strategist to more successfully target promotions by destination.

Figure 8.6: Shifts in Star Rating and ADR YoY, Trends Over Rolling 3 Months

Star Rating Shift—an example of OTA market data generated by the authors. This displays room night shift between star ratings in a market.

Notice how 4 star hotels are losing noticeable share from 3.5 and 5 star hotels. This observation should cause a revenue strategist to re-asses his or her true competitors, understanding that one's "target customer" may be shifting up or down a level for various reasons.

QUESTIONS TO CONSIDER

Referencing the above graph, do you believe it is more likely that the 3.5 Star set or the 5 Star set is absorbing "share" from the 4 Star set? Explain.

In addition to serving hotels as a distribution partner, it's clear that OTAs can also be used as a strategic partner in the sharing of broad market data. Often times, this contribution is overlooked, but if used appropriately, the insights can greatly contribute to a hotel's success.

Pricing Market Data

While shopping and benchmarking competitor pricing is not new to the hotel industry, how we look at this data is. Historically, competitor pricing was mined by calling competitors' call centers or front desks and asking what the rate of the day was (or for any period in question). Because pricing was typically static, a few shops across the market seasons would give a pretty solid visual as to where the market was priced. As the Internet evolved and websites, OTAs and meta search became prevalent, so came dynamic pricing (pricing that fluxes based on booking time and stay period) and a call around was no longer sufficient. With that came multiple service providers who offered daily shopping services of competitors for as far out as the 365-day window, but reporting was delivered in excel workbooks which could be painful to pull trends from. Today, the most advanced processes used are live shoppers that output to a digital dashboard. Instead of showing data in a grid format, pricing typically follows a daily booking curve as is shown below:

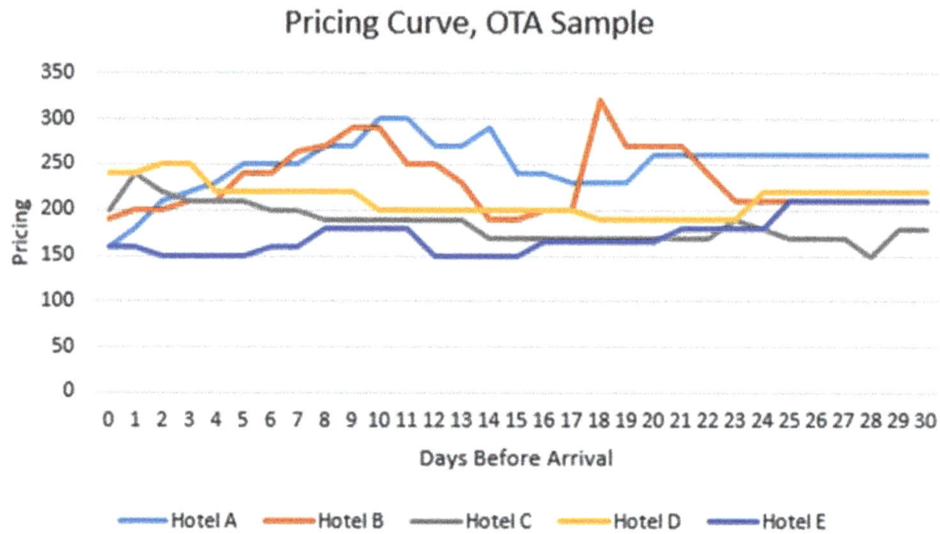

Figure 8.7: OTA Pricing Curve
Source: Author generated sample.

Pricing Curve—one can track the pricing behavior on the above graph for each competitor noting the pricing behavior leading into day of arrival. An average trend that grows into day of arrival would suggest that the market is filling and compressing while the opposite would lead one to believe that hoteliers are chasing demand down in order to shift business to themselves with more competitive price points.

QUESTIONS TO CONSIDER

Referencing the previous graph, do you believe demand is compressing the city (meaning demand is outpacing supply) as day of arrival grows closer or that the city is decompressing (that demand is falling below supply)? Explain.

While market pricing is only one of many factors that should affect a revenue strategy, it is often reflective of competitor strategy and within a like-competitive set, should indicate what the range of rates being booked into your market is currently.

NON-TRADITIONAL MARKET DATA

In this chapter, we've discovered the importance of internal data, aggregate market data and pricing data. Aligned management of all will ensure that a property outperforms to prior year as well as supersede the market in times of growth. When demand is soft, the same principles can guide one to lose the least in the market. Next, however, we will explore some newer and less traditional market data resources that promise to drive revenue optimization to even higher levels including consumer sentiment, air traffic, and website **custom tags**.

Consumer Sentiment Converted into Data

For years, consumer sentiment has been digitally recorded and displayed by companies like Yelp and TripAdvisor. Even non-review-centric businesses have created their own internal platforms from hotel distributors such as Expedia and Booking.com to those in the restaurant business such as Seamless and Open Table. Regardless of the product, reviews are part of our purchasing process; we trust our fellow shoppers and want to vet their opinions prior to investing personally. Unfortunately, however, the process wherein a variety of people write static reviews over a vast timeline doesn't always lend itself to determining if a service-driven product is a fit or not. Unalike consumers who perceive value differently can skew reviews. Also, outdated reviews can haunt a business whose management has changed. The consumer isn't the only one that can be misled by these flaws. Revenue managers struggle to unite all strains of consumer consent into an actual metric that speaks the **price elasticity of demand (PED)** for their product at any given point.

That said, there is still tremendous value in extracting general consumer sentiment from the muck of reviews that exist out there and that's exactly what RJ Friedlander, CEO and founder of ReviewPro, has done. RJ believes that intuitive hoteliers understand that revenues are directly impacted by guest satisfaction and this consumer sentiment impacts the price they can charge to both repeat and new guests related to online reviews and word-of-mouth experiences. RJ's product, ReviewPro, not only converts multi-platform reviews into data for the hotelier's own property(s), but also provides the same for one's competitors allowing the ability to analyze and understand the value differentiators and where to prioritize improvements.

Essentially, ReviewPro produces a real-time guest satisfaction report card and the global review index score (GRI) that is updated every three hours. This data is further segmented through multi-language semantic analysis, department indexes, channel indexes, language, and country indexes. The GRI of a hotel can, and often does, change by day. Data is compiled from 160 online travel agencies and review sites pulling from 45 languages. Uniquely, the score is not an average and instead, attempts to closely track the user-generated content that is impacting both individual and business travelers at a given point in time. Thus, the purpose is to offer the most comprehensive and timely guest review data across the industry (RJ Frielander, personal communication, January 06, 2016).

In order to action the data, the product offers tools for hoteliers to prioritize improvements so they can affectively move the needle where the needle can be moved. That meaning, a complaint regarding location will most likely not be resolved by hotel staff as the location is set, whereas an issue with room cleanliness can be addressed promptly in order to turn the tide of guest sentiment. ReviewPro reporting creates a tangible bridge between direction of revenue strategy and those at a property level that actually have the possibility of impacting the guest experience. Daily GRI scores allow revenue managers to cross-analyze reputation and ADR in order to annotate "optimized" vs. "underperforming" segments and source channels in order to charge optimally according to demand. Ultimately a strong property reputation can be used to curate more direct bookings valued for their lower cost of acquisition. By contrast, a declining GRI score could be used to bring visibility to an increased dependency on OTA mix of business (RJ Frielander, personal communication, January 06, 2016).

Air Traffic

Especially for primary and secondary markets, air traffic volume serves as an excellent indicator of future hotel occupancies because a large percentage of arriving guests do not live in the city they are visiting. The notion of foresight also applies because airline tickets are commonly booked before hotel reservations are made. Thus, a spike in airline activity will tie hand-in-hand to compression surrounding hotel room bookings. The two most important metrics to the hotel community are arrivals and PAX, or passengers on the ground. Arrivals are the number of arriving aircrafts and a heavy number of them produce a surge in PAX that typically stay multiple nights. If the number of arrivals in a given period exceeds the number of departures, a compression bubble can be identified and this bubble will affect hotel demand positively. By contrast, the opposite scenario (heavy departures followed by fewer arrivals) often foretells a softening in hotel demand.

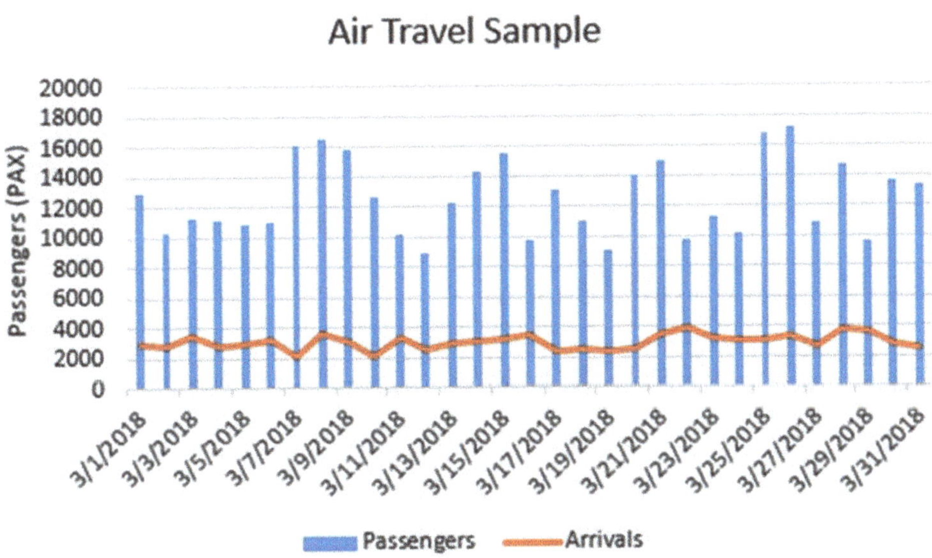

Figure 8.8: Air Travel Arrival Patterns

Air Traffic Arrivals & PAX On the Ground Chart.

Another perspective when looking to the airlines for market trends is the variance in arrivals year over year. If arrivals are not directly tied to a citywide event, this compression can go unnoticed to the hotel economy until the reservation cycle begins. The benefit of alternative market data such as airline traffic data is that the subscriber can intuit the trend before it affects both themselves and the market.

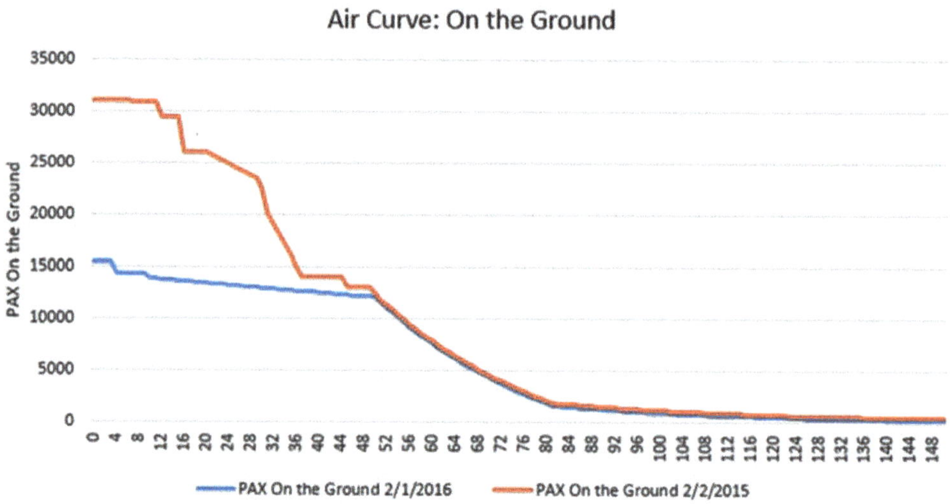

Figure 8.9: Air Curve OTG
Source: Author generated graph.

Air Curve on the ground (OTG)—notice how the example date above is carrying only half of the PAX OTG as same time last year. This negative trend first became apparent 50-days prior to arrival and grew dramatically worse beginning at the 40-day window where last year arrivals surged, but this year arrivals virtually plateaued.

PROS & CONS

Alternative market data can serve a valuable purpose when seeking to understand future demand and price elasticity, but no single factor can tell the whole picture. Airline data can be misleading, as there is currently no way to consistently link individual flight bookings to hotel reservations. Consumer sentiment is relative to the individual and does not guarantee that each guest perceives the values your hotel vs. the competition the same way you do. List one pro and one con of using both airline and consumer sentiment data to support your revenue strategy.

Tracking Website Regrets and Denials Through Custom Tags

A final alternative source of market data that has proven immensely valuable to revenue strategists is the ability to track regrets and denials. A website regret occurs when an individual selects and searches a series of dates in the booking widget, but fails to transact. Essentially, the assumption stands that something, namely the price, was not attractive enough to compel the customer to finalize his or her booking. Hence opportunity to covert a shopper into a paying customer has failed and the occurrence is registered as a regret. In the same vein a denial occurs when a shopper similarly selects a series of dates and searches for rooms, but receives and message stating that there is no availability over the selected dates. This could be due to a yielding restriction that is purposefully in place or because the hotel has sold out over the shopped dates. Regardless, the failed transaction is registered as a denial to the customer for the shopped dates as the hotel is unable or unwilling to accommodate the request. The technology that allows one to track regrets and denials is called a custom tag. Website developers can build these tags over the booking widget in order to encapsulate recurring tasks. This same behavior can also be tracked by subscribing one's website to Google Analytics with many additional features offered.

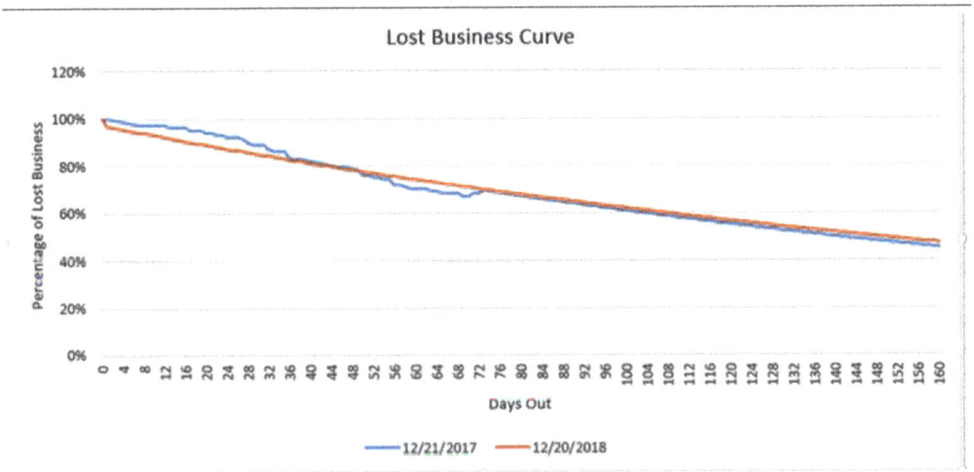

Figure 8.10: Lost Business Curve
Source: Author generated graph.

Lost Business Curve: Regrets & Denials—notice that the percentage of Final Lost business occurring throughout the booking curve for Dec 8th of 2016 virtually mirrors that of same day, 2014 with a small divergence in the 8–35 day window and the 50–75 day window. When trends are similar, it suggests that both market conditions and hotel yielding/pricing strategy are likely similar YOY as well.

If the hotel is sold out over a select date and the combination of regrets and denials spikes, then it is possible that the property sold out too quickly and could have taken advantage of guests later in the booking curve who may have been willing to pay more than those that booked earlier.

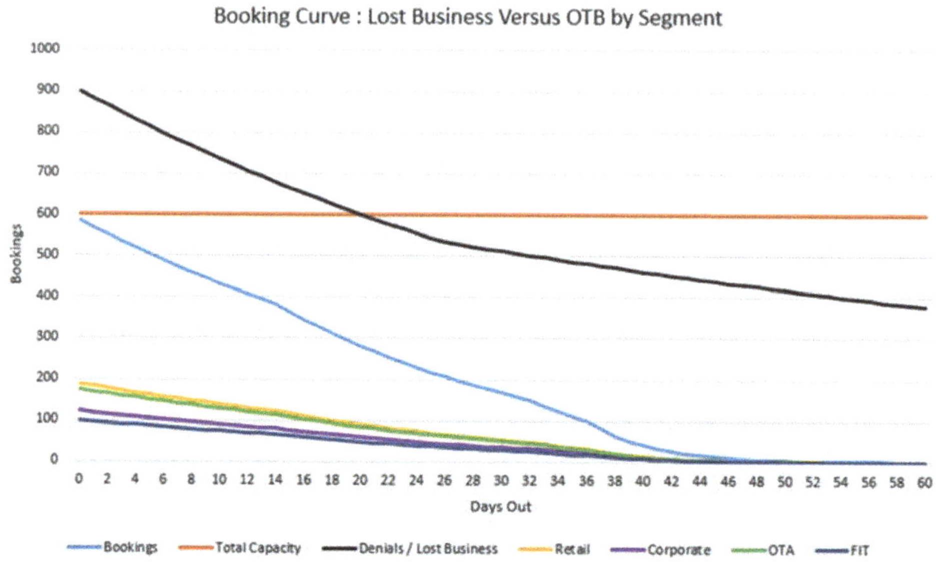

Figure 8.11: Regret and Denial Booking Curve

Regrets & Denials Lain Over Booking Curve—In the above example, a multi-graph showing regrets & denials set over the booking curve can easily illustrate the level of market demand as the property reaches capacity and regrets and denials similarly spike within the same short-term window. Content generated by the authors.

QUESTIONS TO CONSIDER

Referencing the above graph, if one observed a consistent pattern where regrets and denials spiked as the hotel sells out, would it be beneficial to have priced higher or lower further out into the booking window?

If a hotel is not sold out, but determines a yielding restriction to optimize the long-term occupancy potential is necessary, a spike in demand may validate this strategy assuming the longer length of stay books through as expected. If, however, the regrets and denials spike over the peak date while the extended date series fails to book, one could determine that the demand only centers on the peak date and a strategy of raising rate for the one night might be more optimal.

THE FUTURE OF MARKET ANALYTICS

While today's use of market analytics has advanced dramatically over the last ten years, it is almost certain that the next ten will evolve the industry to a near-unrecognizable state. This is not to say that the principles of market analytics will change, only that the level of human interaction with the data will evolve. More time will be spent prioritizing and auctioning the data vs. compiling and filtering it. Here is a list of predictions to keep an eye out for and to be sure you are updating your skillset with:

1. Standard excel usage will be replaced by data visualization tools such as Tableau, Spotfire, Raw, or Power Editor. If you are skilled in these tools, your use of data will look like wizardry compared to an Excel pivot table.
2. All data will be live and two-way. This will close the dark space of attribution modeling and will clearly link the entire purchasing process together.
3. Forward-looking aggregate benchmarking will diversify into many more channels, it will adapt forecast/regression modeling and will source live data feeds.
4. Customer sentiment will be segmented in order to connect like-reviewers with like-customers. It will answer the question: "What do people like me think of this place?" Reviews will first become time-sensitive and eventually will begin to forecast user experience levels. This will bring more weight than ever to customer sentiment indexes and may completely upset our current understanding of price elasticity. Lastly, reviews will span far beyond the current written format and will source anonymous location tracking data and alternative crowd sourcing indicators such as music tagging.

5. Through future mergers in the travel industry, loyalty programs will connect travel behavior throughout the entire trip greatly increasing the reliability of air, train, and even automobile traffic patterns giving clear indicators of demand and compression.

The world of revenue analytics as it relates to market data is in the midst of an exciting world of change. The core fundamentals covered in this chapter are applicable across any free market and obtaining a solid skillset therein will make you both relevant and valuable in your career.

SEEING FURTHER

Today many new technologies are in the blossoming stage that will become key sources for mining market data. Often times the data is a by-product of the prime-product. For example, apps like Shazam and SoundHound initially started as tools to help users discover new music they were enjoying, but could not identify. The data behind such tools is now able to spot burgeoning sounds and tracks as they take off and with the application of predictive modeling, can identify the level of success a new track will have even before it hits the market. Name a product/app/service we use today that may eventually produce data to serve a completely different purpose tomorrow?

Speaking to Data

While the primary reason any business should embrace "big data" is to perceive trends and action the content into perceptive management of pricing, yielding and marketing strategy, it is also crucial to be able to clearly speak to the data. This is necessary in order to gain team alignment and create buy-in surrounding a proposed process or direction. The below Data Analytics Flow Cycle illustrates the natural flow of 1) compiling the numbers 2) shaping context around metrics 3) creating visuals of the behaviors you are tracking and 4) communicating those trends to a broader audience. By embracing this cycle, one is sure to purvey the story behind the data in a way that creates alignment, support and ultimately inspires action.

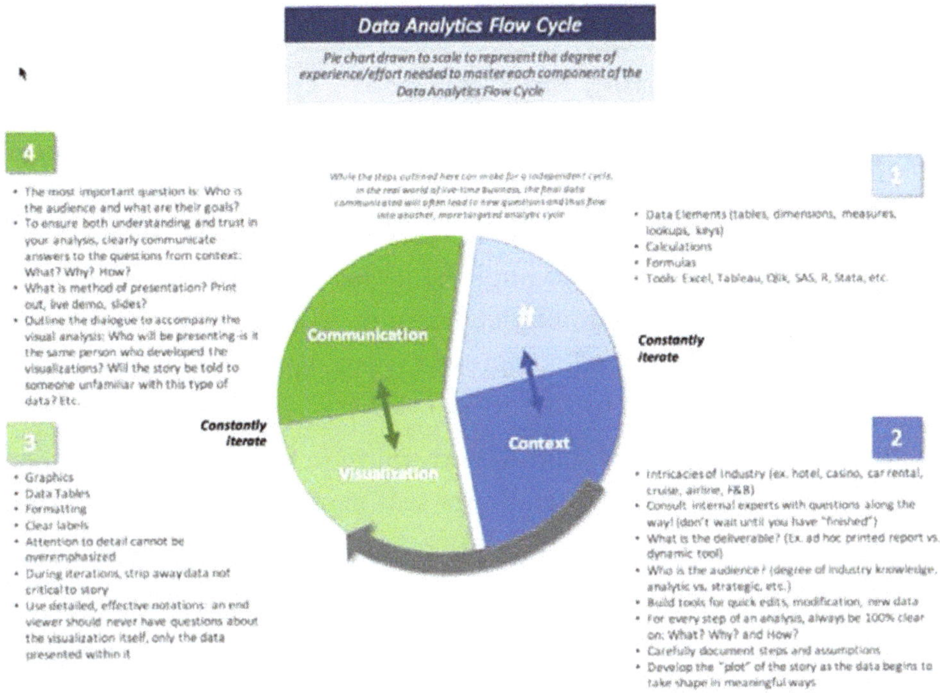

Figure 8.12: Data Analytics Flow Cycle

Data Analytics Flow Cycle—four steps to cultivating raw numbers into actionable team-lead direction. Provided by Chris Chambers.

DISCUSSION QUESTIONS

Question 1: Of all the forms of reporting and market data covered in the chapter, what do you believe is the most useful when seeking to create an impactful revenue strategy? Explain your choice.

Question 2: Are there any forms of market data not covered in this chapter that you believe would be beneficial for hoteliers to incorporate in the future? Explain how you would use this data to optimize your revenue strategy.

Question 3: Market data is not only integral to revenue strategists attempting to price and yield a hotel, but it is also valuable to marketing teams. What data source would you recommend marketers use in and how might they use it to bring more business to a hotel?

APPLICATIONS

Selecting the Right Data

It is September in New York City and Robert is the newly hired Director of Revenue Management at a notable Midtown Manhattan hotel. Robert has been instructed to prioritize the implementation of a pricing strategy that targets the coming slow season of January and February while also preparing the hotel for the expected compression coming as a result of the Super Bowl which will be hosted by the city in February.

(1) What sort of data should Robert utilize in order to price the hotel appropriately for the overall slow season of January and February?

(2) Should Robert be using multiple data sources to understand how the market will behave?

(3) What resources should Robert use to build out a pricing and yielding strategy for the one-time compression event, the Super Bowl?

(4) Are there any data sources that will be useful in both situations?

Explain the data sources you have chosen for each event and correlate their use into actions Robert should take (i.e., reviewing historic Star data over last year's Jan and Feb will give Robert a general sense the obtained ADR's across the stated season and thus Robert should ensure his rates do not exceed the observed cap.)

Explaining a Loss

During Emily's first week on the job at a popular Miami hotel where she was recently hired as the Director of Revenue Management, the property received a terrible weekly STAR report showing a loss in RevPAR to prior year, with a below 100 percent RevPAR Index (RPI) and a negative shift in RPI % Chg to the competitive set. While Emily was not employed as the Director of Revenue Management at the time the losses occurred, she has been asked to explain what caused the poor performance.

Create a list of the data sources Emily should use in order to understand how the hotel performed poorly to the average of its competitors. List the reports in the order Emily should review them in so that the line-up tells a story.

TEAM ACTIVITY

As a class, identify a major hotel in a primary U.S. hotel market (NYC, LA, SF, Chicago).

In groups of 3–5, use the maps feature of a search engine to locate similar hotels within the surrounding area of your subject hotel. Each group is to propose the most logical competitive set of six competitors which will best serve as an aggregate bench marker for both an official Star and Demand360® "comp set."

Each team is to prepare a power point presentation that will be delivered to the rest of the class illustrating why their "comp set" is the most relevant.

Students should be prepared to cover the following elements in their presentation:

1. Minimum of five competitive advantages and five disadvantages of your subject hotel
2. Minimum of five competitive advantages and five disadvantages of the selected competitors
3. An analysis showing why the balance of advantages and disadvantages merit competition
4. Minimum of two sources that prove inter-product similarity (e.g., Expedia lists "people who stayed at XXX also considered XXX.)

INTERNET ACTIVITY

Go to http://data2go.nyc and review the list of indicators and the sub-categories listed thereunder describing the geographic trends and characteristics of New York City. Identify three data elements that could be helpful in building a revenue strategy for pricing and marketing a hotel in the popular Times Square neighborhood. Identify three elements that would prove resourceful in optimizing revenue and marketing strategies for a hotel in the chic neighborhood of SoHo.

GLOSSARY

Average daily rate (ADR) – rooms revenue divided by rooms sold, displayed as the average rental rate for a single room.

Cost of acquisition – fees, commissions, and expenses attributed to each booking from third-party distributors or internal payroll including GDS commissions, OTA commissions, direct marketing expenses and all customer acquisition payroll.

Channel/Source – platform or engine responsible for delivering a booking transaction. This could range from the hotel/brand call center, the hotel website, an online travel agency (OTA), a global distribution service (GDS), or the internal hotel sales team.

Custom tags – are user-defined JSP language elements that encapsulate recurring tasks. Custom tags are distributed in a tag library, which defines a set of related custom tags and contains the objects that implement the tags.

Daily pace – net bookings and cancellations committed currently for a given stay date as compared to the net bookings and cancellations committed same day (by numbered date) prior year.

Daily pickup pace – net bookings and cancellations committed within a set booking period (i.e., last seven days) for a given stay date as compared to the same net bookings and cancellations that occurred over the same booking dates (by day of week) prior year.

Index (Occupancy, ADR, RevPAR) – property performance divided by competitive set performance multiplied by 100. Internationally, indexes are also referred to as MPI—Market Penetration Index (Occupancy Index), ARI—Average Rate Index (ADR Index), and RGI—Revenue/RevPAR Generation Index (RevPAR Index).

Monthly pickup pace – net bookings and cancellations committed within a set booking period (i.e., last seven days) for a given stay month as compared to the same net bookings and cancellations that occurred over the same booking dates (by day of week) prior year.

Monthly pace – net bookings and cancellations committed currently for a given stay month as compared to the net bookings and cancellations committed same day (by numbered date) prior year.

Price elasticity of demand (PED) – shows the relationship between price and quantity demanded and provides a precise calculation of the effect of a change in price on quantity demanded. The following equation enables PED to be calculated.

$$\frac{\textbf{\% change in quantity demanded}}{\textbf{\% change in price}}$$

Percentage change (% Chg) – amount of growth—up, down, or flat—this period versus same period last year (day, week, running 28 days, running month-to-date). Calculated as ((TY-LY)/LY) × 100.

Product type – defined narrowly as the room type, package element, or booking policy attached to the reservation or more broadly as the length of stay or lead time dimension. This meaning, that a product can be defined both by the physical attributes such a premium room type or package element just as much as it can be considered an accommodation available for purchase at the very last minute in a compressed market.

Purchasing behavior – common purchasing patterns found within a given group of bookers including price sensitivity, responsiveness to various types of advertisement, propensity to cancel, and customer loyalty.

Rank (Occupancy, ADR, RevPAR, % Chg) – property performance ranked versus hotels in the competitive set (e.g., a "3 of 6" ADR ranking means the subject hotel's absolute ADR is third highest of the six competitors).

Revenue per available room (RevPAR) – total rooms-related revenue per the number of available rooms in the hotel over a period of time: [Rooms Revenue / (Rooms Available * Number of Days)].

Segmented data – rooms sold and revenue data broken down by source of business (transient, group, contract) and source of revenue (room, food and beverage, other).

REFERENCES

Data Analytics Flow Cycle, Chambers, C. (2016, March 26).

Economics Online. (2016) *Price Elasticity of Demand.* Retrieved from http://www.economicsonline.co.uk/Competitive_markets/Price_elasticity_of_demand.html

Frielander, RJ. (2016, January 6). Telephone interview.

Freitag, J. (2016, January 4). Telephone interview.

Moro, K. (2016, January 15). Email interview.

Oracle. (2010) *The Java EE 5 Tutorial.* Retrieved from http://docs.oracle.com/javaee/5/tutorial/doc/bnaiy.html

CHAPTER 9

Restaurant Revenue Management: Basic Concepts

Kristin V. Rohlfs

OVERVIEW

Restaurant revenue management (RRM) focuses on how a restaurant can produce the highest amount of revenue possible for a certain time period. Every transaction includes elements of RRM and the use of many RRM strategies is most beneficial when a restaurant has demand that exceeds capacity. This chapter presents an overview of RRM theories and an introduction to RRM terms, tools, and techniques.

LEARNING OBJECTIVES

After studying this chapter, you should be able to evaluate a restaurant in the context of RRM. Specifically, you should be able to:

- Apply revenue management principles to restaurants
- Explain and calculate RevPASH (revenue per available seat hour)
- Analyze a food service operation as a system through which customers flow
- Calculate the throughput time and throughput rate for a simple service system
- Perform an RRM analysis for a restaurant by establishing the baseline, collecting data, and developing and implementing RRM solutions

OUTLINE

Introduction

Restaurant Revenue Management

- Conditions Necessary
- Operations Component
- RevPASH
- Duration and Price

RRM Program

- Establish the Baseline
- Collect Data
- Develop RRM Solutions
- Implement and Monitor RRM Solutions

Discussion Questions

Applications

- Tasty Banquets
- Muchacho

Team Activity

Internet Activity

Glossary

References

SO WHAT?

Mario Testa is a well-seasoned restaurant owner and operator of nine full-service outlets in the greater Philadelphia area. Mario has been thinking about the short conversation he just had with his son, Arturo, who grew up working in Mario's restaurants and recently graduated from an accredited Hospitality Management program.

Arturo was telling Mario about something called Revenue Management, which Mario recognized in practice (from making airline, car rental, and hotel reservations throughout his life) but had not heard of it being used in restaurants. From what Arturo was saying, restaurant revenue management (RRM)—the field of applying RM to restaurants—provides restaurant owners and managers with an operating framework focused on making more money without sacrificing customer service or satisfaction. Their conversation was interrupted by the start of a planned meeting but not before Arturo told Mario that RRM could help boost low demand, better manage high demand, optimize how Mario's outlets use space, and even find out which menu items should be removed.

What are some questions you think Mario has for Arturo about RRM and the strategies Arturo described?

INTRODUCTION

Revenue management (RM) principles were first applied to restaurants almost 20 years ago. The goal of using RM in a restaurant is to maximize the revenue it can generate over a certain time period. In theory and practice, RRM is a data-driven field that combines elements of both demand and supply management. On the demand side, the focus of RRM is on understanding demand and developing ways to profitably influence and respond to it. On the supply side, RRM focuses on how each unit of physical inventory of a restaurant currently and potentially generates revenue over time.

RRM has slowly gained prominence in the food and beverage industry. Savvy restaurateurs have realized that utilizing RRM principles and tools can uncover and capture revenue-enhancing opportunities that do not necessarily require huge investments. It has been reported that using RRM increased the revenue of various restaurants by 3–5 percent (Sinclair, 2010). This chapter discusses the theory behind RRM and outlines the data and metrics required to create and use an appropriate RRM program. It also provides basic tools and techniques for analyzing how the current operations of a restaurant generate revenue and for identifying areas for improvement.

RESTAURANT REVENUE MANAGEMENT

Because restaurant operations occur in real-time, service providers face the risk of not capturing all potential revenues if the capacity a restaurant has available does not match the demand for its service. When a restaurant's demand is too low to fill available seats, it uses sales and marketing techniques, like coupons or advertising, to attract additional customers. But when demand exceeds the capacity of the restaurant, the problem becomes more complicated. RM professionals and academics realized that RM could help restaurants solve this problem. In theory, if the restaurant cannot serve every customer, it would maximize its revenue by serving the most profitable customers—the classic RM problem—thus beginning the field of RRM (Kimes et al., 1998).

Although RRM principles can undoubtedly help streamline, refocus, and strengthen any F&B operation, not every restaurant benefits equally from using RRM. RRM provides the most benefit when a restaurant is operating at, or close to, capacity. This means that demand is greater than supply during some time periods.

SEEING FURTHER

As service businesses have realized the advantages of managing revenue and customers have become familiar with RM practices, the scope of RM has been transitioning (Cross et al., 2009). The newer approach to RM has a more strategic, customer-centric focus that is concerned not only with using existing supply to fulfill demand but also with creating and managing new demand. Many aspects of a service operation, including customer behavior, marketing, operations, technology, and design, can now be considered part of the RM problem, further demonstrating RM is an integrative, long-term operating strategy.

Another way RM has been progressing involves the proliferation of the digital world. The predominance of eCommerce has changed the RM landscape by creating new and diverse distribution channels, generating huge amounts of customer data, and opening the door for price optimization (McGuire, 2016). In addition, customer-generated information available through social media and review sites can impact purchase decisions and perceptions of value (Noone & McGuire, 2013b).

1. Your friend's 50-seat restaurant in Atlanta is operating at 80–90% capacity all six nights per week it is open. What aspects of RM could help her?
2. Another friend's 50-seat restaurant in New York City is only half full most of the time, including weekend nights. What aspects of RM could help him?

Conditions Necessary

The five conditions necessary for RM to be truly effective and successful are relatively fixed capacity, perishable inventory, predictable and time-variable demand, high fixed costs and low variable costs, and segmentable markets (Kimes, 1989). Restaurants commonly have four of these conditions (Kimes et al., 1998):

- Relatively fixed capacity: The capacity of a restaurant is substantially fixed. The footprint of the restaurant (the space allocated to the kitchen, dining room, restrooms, etc.) is not easily altered in a way that could considerably change the number of customers who can fit at any given time. However, restaurants have a higher level of flexibility in their capacity than many other services. If necessary, a restaurant can add another table or seat to its inventory to fulfill demand without incurring a significant additional cost.
- Perishable inventory: Every seat at a restaurant is capable of generating revenue for a certain time period—for instance, the pre-theater seating, the 5:00–6:00 p.m. hour, or the 12:00–12:15 p.m. quarter-hour. If the seat is not used in that time, the opportunity for that seat to generate revenue is lost forever. Although perishable inventory in a restaurant is usually thought of as raw food inventory in the back-of-house (BOH), RRM defines perishable inventory as front-of-house (FOH) seat and table inventory.
- Predictable and time-variable demand: Understanding when customers arrive at a restaurant and how much time they will occupy seats is vital to using RRM. The ability to forecast demand allows a restaurateur to use the most appropriate strategies to build demand where it is low and operate more effectively where demand is high.

Restaurant demand is also time-variable. Although customers generally want to dine at mealtimes (breakfast, lunch, and dinner), demand differs within meal periods and across days of the week and even seasons of the year.

- High fixed costs and low variable costs: Restaurants require a large initial outlay of funds and incur an amount of fixed costs every day in operation, regardless of whether any customers arrive. The variable cost of serving a restaurant customer is quite low in comparison.
- Segmentable markets: While every restaurant serves different market segments, the nature of restaurants does not easily allow customers to be segmented on the basis of purchasing behavior. Unless a restaurant sells the majority of its seats through reservations or relies heavily on a prix fixe menu, having segmentable markets is not generally a consideration when applying RM to restaurants.

PROS & CONS

The management team of Go's, a high-volume sushi restaurant, in a busy Manhattan transit station is having a lively discussion about capacity. Executive Chef Satoshi suggests that capacity is determined by the size of the kitchen because, after all, customers cannot buy food that does not get made. After adding that the sushi bar also makes food that customers buy, Sushi Chef Mei raises the point that no matter how big her prep area is, the amount of sushi that can be made is limited by the number of line cooks at work. If she doesn't have staff, she can't make sushi.

At this point, Rai, the Dining Room Manager, brings up the point that unless they switch to takeout only, the capacity of Go's is set by the number of tables on the floor and how many times they can turn those tables each day. Chef Mei reminds Rai that the sushi bar seats 20, bringing up the idea that seats are the best measure of capacity at Go's.

Restaurant capacity can be defined by kitchen size, staffing levels, number of tables, or number of seats. What are the pros and cons for defining capacity in each of these ways? How do you think restaurant capacity should be defined, and why?

Operations Component

Unlike airline and hotel revenue management, restaurant revenue management has a large operations component. This is due to the fact that the duration of the restaurant service—the time interval during which revenue is generated—is short. For instance, the time it takes for a dirty table to be bussed and reset impacts when that table can be resold. In a hotel, however, the 30 min it takes for a dirty room to be cleaned does not usually mean a revenue opportunity is lost, because rooms are sold by the night.

Like other services that use revenue management, restaurant revenue management focuses on FOH concerns and maximizing potential top-line revenue. Undoubtedly, BOH operations, including food cost and staffing, play a dynamic role in revenue and profit generation and must be taken into account when evaluating RM solutions. The strategic focus on the FOH allows operators to manage the FOH supply of physical inventory, plus manage and create demand, without having to make a significant investment in new kitchen equipment or reconfiguration.

RevPASH

In RRM, a metric that reflects both supply and demand management is RevPASH – revenue per available seat hour (Kimes, 1999). RevPASH measures how well each individual physical inventory unit generates top-line revenue each hour. Because the two primary components of a restaurant's revenue—utilization and price—are incorporated into the RevPASH metric, it allows for an apples-to-apples comparison across time and/or between different operations.

RevPASH is a function of occupancy (table or seat) and average check (per table or per person).

RevPASH = Average check × occupancy

If a restaurant has an average check per person of $18 and a seat occupancy of 50 percent, its RevPASH would be

$18 × 50% = $9.

RevPASH can also be calculated using total revenue.

RevPASH = Revenue/(# of seats × # of hours in operation)

If a 145-seat restaurant is open 360 days a year for 10 h a day and has a total annual revenue of $4,698,000, its RevPASH would be

$\$4,698,000/(145 \times [360 \times 10]) = \$9.$

This means that, on average, each seat in the restaurant generates $9 for every hour the restaurant is open.

SPREADSHEET EXERCISE 9.1

You are the owner of Root, a 200-seat restaurant that is open five nights a week, from 4:00 p.m. to 11:00 p.m. You recently heard a webinar on restaurant revenue management and decided to apply some of the concepts to your restaurant. You have pulled revenue figures from your POS system for last year. Assume average duration, including seating and bussing processes, is 1 h. A sample of the Excel data file is

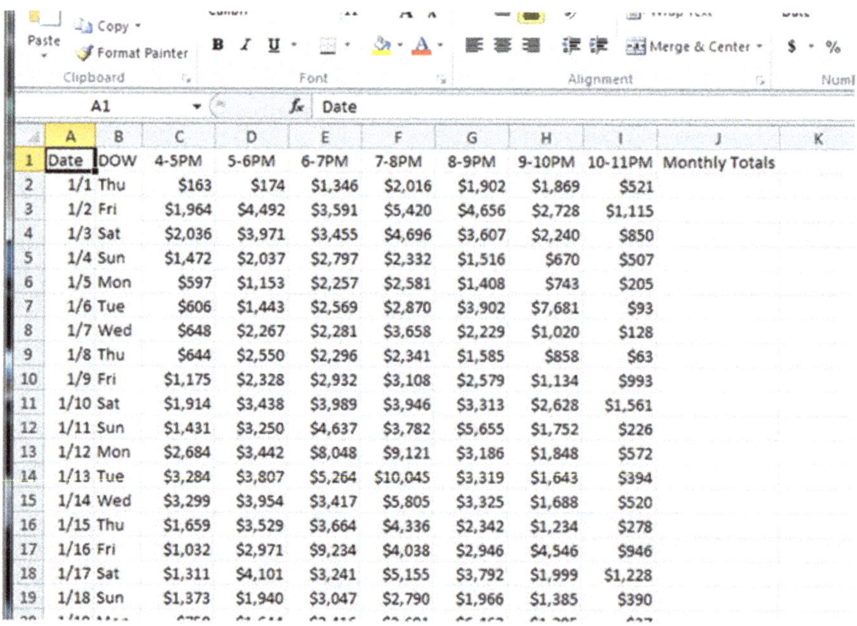

Date	DOW	4-5PM	5-6PM	6-7PM	7-8PM	8-9PM	9-10PM	10-11PM	Monthly Totals
1/1	Thu	$163	$174	$1,346	$2,016	$1,902	$1,869	$521	
1/2	Fri	$1,964	$4,492	$3,591	$5,420	$4,656	$2,728	$1,115	
1/3	Sat	$2,036	$3,971	$3,455	$4,696	$3,607	$2,240	$850	
1/4	Sun	$1,472	$2,037	$2,797	$2,332	$1,516	$670	$507	
1/5	Mon	$597	$1,153	$2,257	$2,581	$1,408	$743	$205	
1/6	Tue	$606	$1,443	$2,569	$2,870	$3,902	$7,681	$93	
1/7	Wed	$648	$2,267	$2,281	$3,658	$2,229	$1,020	$128	
1/8	Thu	$644	$2,550	$2,296	$2,341	$1,585	$858	$63	
1/9	Fri	$1,175	$2,328	$2,932	$3,108	$2,579	$1,134	$993	
1/10	Sat	$1,914	$3,438	$3,989	$3,946	$3,313	$2,628	$1,561	
1/11	Sun	$1,431	$3,250	$4,637	$3,782	$5,655	$1,752	$226	
1/12	Mon	$2,684	$3,442	$8,048	$9,121	$3,186	$1,848	$572	
1/13	Tue	$3,284	$3,807	$5,264	$10,045	$3,319	$1,643	$394	
1/14	Wed	$3,299	$3,954	$3,417	$5,805	$3,325	$1,688	$520	
1/15	Thu	$1,659	$3,529	$3,664	$4,336	$2,342	$1,234	$278	
1/16	Fri	$1,032	$2,971	$9,234	$4,038	$2,946	$4,546	$946	
1/17	Sat	$1,311	$4,101	$3,241	$5,155	$3,792	$1,999	$1,228	
1/18	Sun	$1,373	$1,940	$3,047	$2,790	$1,966	$1,385	$390	

TO DO

1. Use the data in the Excel spreadsheet to calculate RevPASH by hour for each day of the week at Root. When is RevPASH highest? When is RevPASH lowest?
2. You estimate that initiating an RRM program at Root will cost $100,000 and would likely increase revenues by 1% in 1 year. Assuming you would not amortize the program, would you adopt the RRM program if this were your restaurant? What if revenues increased by 2%?

Duration and Price

A significant amount of RRM research pertains to two strategic levers—duration and price—that restaurant operators can manipulate in an effort to influence demand (Kimes, 1999; Kimes et al., 1999; Kimes et al., 1998).

- Duration: If operators are able to control the time a customer occupies a seat at a restaurant, they can better manage RevPASH. Duration of any restaurant experience is unpredictable, although most restaurateurs would be able to provide a solid estimate of how long a meal takes. Duration management starts by analyzing the current duration and reducing variability. It also involves forecasting arrivals and assessing the procedures used to handle them. In some situations, duration management techniques could lead to an additional table turn.
- Price: If operators are able to manipulate the price charged to restaurant customers, they can also better manage RevPASH. Pricing strategies that restaurants commonly use include two-for-one specials, happy hour discounts, coupons, and early-bird specials. Demand-based pricing moves beyond these marketing-based promotions and instead uses rules, also known as price fences, which allow for more ongoing control over the prices charged.

THINK HISTORICALLY

Controlling dining duration and price are not new strategies to the restaurant business. Consider the following menus from two restaurants:

Dinner Menu

Fairport, New York *Wednesday, October 30, 1895*

Mushroom Soup *Mousseline of Clams*
Browned French Bread and Baked Cauliflower

Roast Mutton with
Potatoes and Bread-Fruit

Cheese and Wafers

Chocolate Custard with Cream

Tea and Coffee Service

80 cents per diner.

Dinner 6pm to 9pm. *Seats reserved 20 minutes only.*

Steve's Restaurant

•LUNCH Menu, Updated Weekly•
Served from 11-4 Daily
5¢ off from 2pm 'til dinner

Assorted Soup	10c	Stuffed Olives	25c
Oyster Stew	40c	Hearts of Celery	20c
		Cucumbers with Vinegar	25c
FULL LUNCHES			
Fried Oysters	50c	Hamburger Steak with Toast	50c
Chicken with French Fries	75c	Chicken Salad	40c
Pepper Roast	55c	Corned Beef Sandwich	50c
Spaghetti with Bread	40c	Creamed Mushrooms on Toast	70c
Steak Tenderloin	90c	Salad Vegetable Bowl with Dressing	65c

Saturday Minimum Charge in Booths 25c

Which one shows an example from a duration management strategy? Which one shows how a restaurant used price to influence the behavior of customers? These menus are from 1895 and 1945, respectively; how could these duration and price strategies be used today?

RRM PROGRAM

An RRM program is a set of analytical and operational tools tailored for an individual operation. In all RRM programs, historical data are collected and analyzed in order to develop strategies that will allow the restaurant to capture the maximum possible revenue over a certain time period using its existing physical capacity (Kimes, 1999). The techniques used to achieve those goals depend on several factors:

- The scope of the program: Is the RRM initiative for the corner bistro owned by you and your sister? A portfolio of corporate-owned, multibrand, multilocation, national restaurants? A quick-service restaurant you recently franchised? A coffee shop? An individually owned and operated upscale casual steakhouse?
- The focus of the program: Although RRM is rooted in research-based principles, it does not disregard the firsthand knowledge and instincts a manager, maître d', owner, or chef has regarding her

operation. An RRM program could focus on a specific issue already detected by an operator, such as why the dining room is only half full at 6:00 p.m. on Saturday night but overflowing at 7:00 p.m. Or how can more VIP customers be served at a casino buffet?

- The budget for the program: The total cost to initiate and execute an RRM program depends on whether or not an RM firm or analyst will be hired, if a new point-of-sale (POS) or RM system will be purchased, how many tangible items like tables and linens must be acquired, and how much time and payroll will be spent on training employees.

Establish the Baseline

The first step of any RRM program is to establish the baseline or develop a data-supported understanding of how a restaurant is currently performing (Kimes, 1999; Kimes et al., 1999). This involves the operations management area of process analysis, which simply means analyzing the current way inputs (hungry customers) are turned into outputs (satisfied customers).

In RRM, a restaurant operation is viewed as a system of processes that moves hungry customers through all the stages required to turn them into satisfied customers. Examples of FOH food service processes include seating, collecting payment, taking orders, and bussing. Some process analysis tools useful in establishing the baseline for an RRM program are a process flow chart, a process flow diagram, and a fishbone diagram.

Process Flow Chart

A process flow chart is a visual tool that can help focus attention on how a customer is moved through a service delivery system—and when that customer is waiting for and participating in the service. Flowcharts have long been used in industrial engineering, often for planning and quality control purposes and are so widely used that Excel has a built-in flowchart function (Gilbreth & Gilbreth, 1921; ASME, 1949). The symbols and descriptions for several categories of actions used in a process flow chart are as follows:

○	Operation – Activity in the system
⇨	Transportation – Movement through the system
□	Inspection – Pause for evaluation
▽	Storage – Waiting within the system
◇	Decision – Work requires a condition to be met/unmet before it can move on

An interesting aspect of a restaurant setting is that although both a customer and a customer's F&B order move through the service system, they often take separate paths. Figure 9.1 gives an example of a simple process flow chart for a service transaction at a coffee shop.

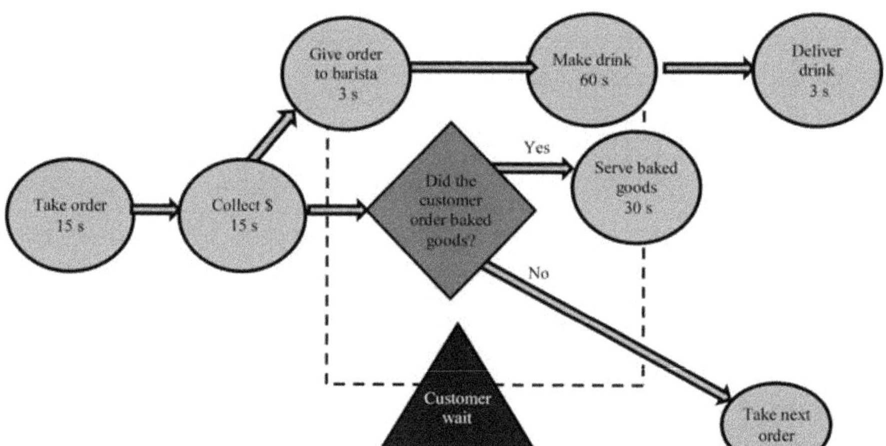

Figure 9.1: Simple Example of a Process Flow Chart for a Coffee Shop

A process flow chart can become extremely complex if all possible activities, processes, and decisions within a service delivery system are included. To illustrate, the process depicted in Figure 9.1 is considered simple not just because it only has five steps but also because it makes several significant generalizations like process times never vary and every customer orders a single drink. Although these assumptions are impractical, a simple process flow chart includes enough detail and to serve as a baseline picture of the core service system; complexity can be added and the simple flowchart can be augmented if needed.

For an RRM baseline analysis, the process flow chart should include at least every high-level, major activity that directly helps fulfill the needs of the customer. Constructing a process flow chart requires first observing the service system and recording process times. Robust F&B POS systems and spreadsheet skills can help estimate process times.

Throughput

In addition to providing a snapshot of how a system runs, the timings included in a process flow chart are used in determining two basic system metrics:

- Throughput time: The time a customer spends in a service system from enter to exit.
- Throughput rate: The number of customers that flow through a service system per unit of time.

Throughput time measures how long it takes for a pass through the system, while throughput rate measures the output of a system. These metrics reflect how effectively a service system processes customers.

Throughput time = Total time a customer spends in a system from the start of the first process to the end of the last process

In Figure 9.1, the throughput time for a customer who did not order baked goods = 15 s for order to be taken + 15 s to pay + 3 s waiting for the barista to get the order + 60 s waiting for drink + 3 s getting drink = 96 s.

The throughput time for a customer who ordered baked goods = 15 s for order to be taken + 15 s to pay + 3 s waiting for the barista to get the order + 30 s getting baked goods + 30 s waiting for drink (note: 30 of the total 60 s spent on waiting for a drink have already been accounted for in the 30 s spent getting a baked good) + 3 s getting drink = 96 s.

Throughput rate = 1/throughput time

For Figure 9.1, the throughput rate = $1/96 \times 60 = 0.0104 \times 60 = 0.625$ customers/min. This is the number of customers who can pass through the system per minute.

Transform this to determine the number of customers who can pass through the system per hour: Throughput rate (customers per hour) = Average covers per hour = 0.625 ×60 min/h = 37.5 customers/h.

A process flow chart is also useful in determining the system's bottleneck—the process that has the lowest throughput rate. The bottleneck sets the pace of the throughput rate of the system because it limits the number of outputs that can be produced. It is the slowest activity, process, or operation in the system. It sets the pace for the throughput rate of the system. To determine a bottleneck, calculate the throughput rate for every process.

For Figure 9.1, the throughput rate for each process in the coffee shop is as follows:

Activity >>	**Take order**	**Collect $**	**Give order to barista**	**Make drink**	**Serve baked goods**	**Deliver drink**
Throughput rate (customers/s)	1/15 = .0667	1/15 = .0667	1/3 = .3333	1/60 = .0167	1/30 = .0333	1/3 = .3333

The bottleneck is the make drink process because it has the lowest throughput rate. No matter how efficient the other steps in the process are, the system will always be held up at the bottleneck. Therefore, to move more through the system requires alleviating the bottleneck. This is done by increasing its capacity or decreasing its processing time. For the coffee shop example, to increase the number of drinks that can be made per second could be accomplished by adding another barista or streamlining and standardizing the make drink process.

For the coffee shop example, adding another barista to the make drink process results in the following:

Throughput rate = (1/throughput time) × # baristas = (1/60) × 2 = 0.0333 customers/s.

A throughput rate and bottleneck analysis is recurrent. This means that after the primary bottleneck is identified and alleviated, the system should be reexamined to determine what (if any) process is the new bottleneck. The coffee shop from Figure 9.1 would consequently have two bottlenecks: Make drink and serve baked goods.

Process Flow Diagram

Like a process flow chart, a process flow diagram is a visual tool that serves as an abstract of the restaurant system. A process flow diagram is a sketch of the actual system operations and traces how customers, employees, and other resources flow through the facility. Process flow diagrams are useful when movement is a large part of how the restaurant operates, like in a buffet setting, a self-service establishment, or a sequential-step/made-to-order service model. They also can be useful when movement within a restaurant is impeding efficient operation, such as if hosts, servers, and customers all share a narrow staircase to reach the dining room.

Flow diagrams aid in identifying potential failure points, which are the places in the system where operations are most likely to break down. Identifying potential failure points in a baseline analysis will ultimately help direct and prioritize RRM recommendations. Potential failure points often found using a process flow diagram include gaps in the service delivery system, unnecessary steps within processes, and redundancies across processes (Fitzsimmons and Fitzsimmons, 1999).

Constructing a process flow diagram for an RRM baseline analysis requires observation and customization, as each restaurant has its own unique operating characteristics. Figure 9.2 shows a simple process flow diagram for the entrance-to-seated process of a casino buffet restaurant.

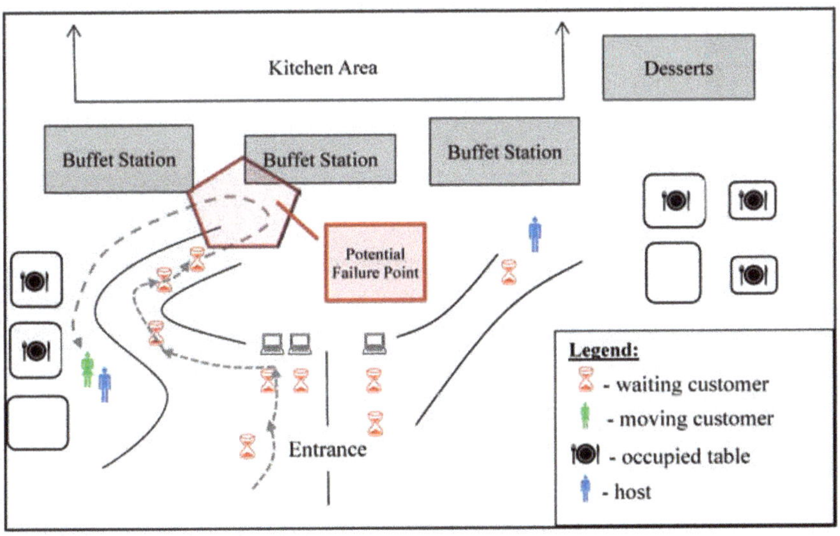

Figure 9.2: Process Flow Diagram for the Seating Process at a Casino Buffet

Fishbone Diagram

A fishbone diagram, also known as a cause-effect diagram, is a tool used to help identify possible causes for a problem (Ishikawa, 1968). In a fishbone diagram, the problem is put at the head of the fish, signaling that this problem is the "effect" of many potential "causes." Likely categories of the root causes are included on individual bones of the fishbone diagram, with possible sub-causes included as smaller bones.

The first step in constructing a fishbone diagram is to identify the problem by observing the situation, interviewing employees and perhaps even analyzing relevant data. The problem statement can range in complexity, from a clear problem of "too many no-show reservations" to a more layered problem of "better manage the flow of customers through a restaurant." The next step in building a fishbone diagram is to brainstorm the likely causes of the problem. Gather information on possible causes by observing the problem area if possible and interviewing both the management and the people closest to the problem (e.g., bussers, servers, cooks).

Figure 9.3 is an example of a fishbone diagram for a restaurant. The problem at the head of the fishbone is that customers experience a long line at lunch. Several possible causes and sub-causes are included in the branches of the diagram.

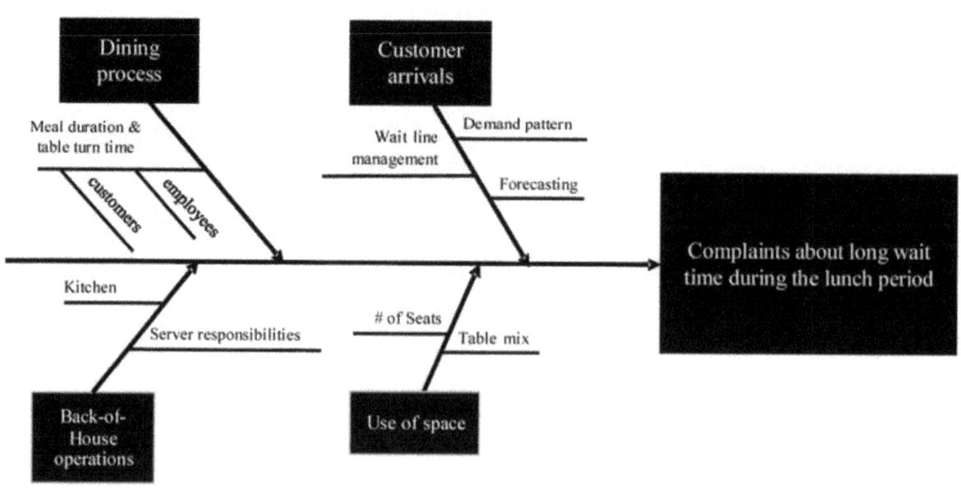

Figure 9.3: Example of a Fishbone Diagram

In addition to these three process analysis tools—process flow chart, process flow diagram, and fishbone diagram—several other measures should be calculated and analyzed to establish the baseline in a RRM analysis. These measures—arrivals, duration, occupancy, average check, and RevPASH—provide indications of how well an operation is using its physical resources to generate revenue.

Arrivals

The number of parties or customers arriving to a restaurant in certain time periods is referred to as arrivals. When graphed, arrival patterns show the timing of the flow of demand into the restaurant system. Peak demand periods and shoulder periods—the times of increasing/decreasing demand before/after peak—are generally times that benefit the most from RRM.

Arrivals data is easily obtained from newer table management systems. Getting arrivals data from older POS systems is not always straightforward. POS data often reflects the time a check is opened, which is not necessarily the time a party arrives to the restaurant. If a check is opened at 7:04 p.m., it is impossible to know the customer actually arrived at 6:30 p.m. More accurate arrivals information can be manually collected, but if no other information is available, POS check-open data can serve as a proxy for arrivals in an RRM baseline analysis.

Figure 9.4 shows the arrivals graph for Trader G's, a casual, family-run restaurant in Ithaca, New York, for the month of June. The number

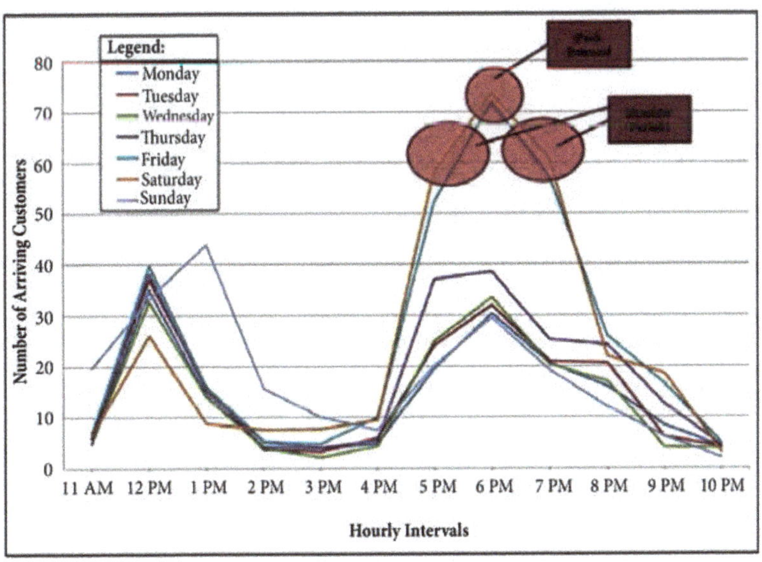

Figure 9.4: Graph of Arrivals for June

of customers arriving to Trader G's peaks around 6:00 p.m. every night and is markedly higher on weekend nights. Although a small spike in demand occurs for lunch, the peak demand period is at 6:00 p.m. and shoulder times are 5:00 p.m. and 7:00 p.m.

Dining Duration

The total amount of time a customer occupies a seat in a restaurant is referred to as dining duration. Total dining duration can be approximated by calculating the time from when a check is opened to when it is closed. However, check-open and check-close time measures do not necessarily reflect when a table is seated or when customers vacate the table. A more precise measure of duration could be obtained by performing a time study but duration data from a POS system is usually acceptable to use as a proxy for dining duration.

Once raw dining duration data has been gathered, a spreadsheet analysis is used to calculate the average and standard deviation of duration. The standard deviation measures the amount of variation in a system, so a low standard deviation indicates a high level of consistency in operations. Common ways in which dining duration data are examined include by party size, by steps in a meal, by hour, and by day of week. Figure 9.5 provides an example of a dining duration analysis.

	Duration by Time Period				Duration by Steps in a Meal			
	5:00 PM		6:00 PM		Seat-to-Entrée Delivery		Check Delivery-to-Exit	
Party Size	Average (min:sec)	Standard Deviation	Avg	Std Dev	Avg	Std Dev	Avg	Std Dev
1-2	55:28	28:45	58:27	30:04	20:17	9:35	10:12	6:05
3-4	62:40	31:07	64:19	32:22	23:41	11:53	14:29	7:16
5-6	68:44	36:23	71:21	35:40	29:25	14:51	14:08	7:29
7-8	70:13	20:19	72:55	39:03	36:26	15:40	16:26	8:07

Figure 9.5: Example of a Duration Analysis

Table Occupancy and Seat Occupancy

Occupancy measures how well the physical inventory of the restaurant is being used to satisfy demand. Both table and seat occupancies should be included in a baseline RRM analysis, often broken down by table size and time period. Although seats are the smallest physical/FOH inventory unit in a restaurant system (not considering ancillary operations like take-out services) that can generate revenue, they are situated at tables, which are the actual units sold in most restaurants.

Seat occupancy = Customers served/# of seats

If a 36-seat restaurant has 27 covers (customers) from 7:00 p.m. to 8:00 p.m., its seat occupancy for that time period = 27/36 = 75%.

Table occupancy = Parties served/# tables

If the restaurant has nine tables and eight checks (parties) from 7:00 p.m. to 8:00 p.m., its table occupancy for that time period = 8/9 = 88.9%.

Table occupancy by table type (i.e., two-top, four-top) is more difficult to calculate. A good POS system and an experienced spreadsheet user could determine table occupancy for table types using transaction-level data such as a table number/identifier, party size, and meal duration. Manual data collection of table occupancies could also be used. Figure 9.6 shows a summary of a spreadsheet analysis of seat and table occupancy.

Table Size	*2*	*4*	*6*	*8*	*Total*
Tables Available	3	4	1	1	9
Seats Available	6	16	6	8	36
Seats Used	5	11	5	6	27
Tables Used	3	3	1	1	8
Seat Occupancy (Seats Used / Seats Available)	83.3%	68.8%	83.3%	75.0%	75.0%
Table Occupancy (Tables Used / Tables Available)	100.0%	75.0%	100.0%	100.0%	88.9%

Figure 9.6: Example of an Occupancy Analysis

Seat occupancy will almost always be lower than table occupancy. This is because restaurants operate with table sizes (e.g., two-top, four-top, six-top, eight-top) that do not always match the sizes of parties (e.g., party of 1, party of 3, party of 5, party of 7). However, when table occupancy is much higher than seat occupancy, the restaurant usually benefits from an advanced RRM analysis of its table mix.

Average Check

Restaurant operators are familiar with the average check metric:

Average check = Revenue/customers

Average check measures not only the amount of money a restaurant is bringing in but also its price point, which helps in determining its competitive set and its marketing strategy. Average check is usually considered on an aggregate level but analyzing it in different ways can yield interesting information. For instance, the average check may differ depending on how many people are in a customer's party. Knowing that per person spend is higher for parties of 2 than for parties of 7 could help a restaurant in deciding whether or not to add four two-tops or one eight-top to its table inventory.

RevPASH

As previously shown, RevPASH can be calculated in two ways:

RevPASH = Average check × seat occupancy or

= Revenue / (# of seats × # of hours in operation)

A good beginning point for a RevPASH baseline analysis is to calculate hourly RevPASH by each day of the week. Figure 9.7 shows hourly RevPASH for the dinner period for a 212-seat seafood restaurant in Boston over the summer months.

	Sunday	Monday	Tuesday	Wednesday	Thursday	Friday	Saturday
5 PM	$4.73	$3.27	$4.38	$4.20	$4.22	$8.88	$5.01
6 PM	$5.61	$3.40	$5.87	$5.00	$4.90	$10.61	$9.76
7 PM	$7.17	$4.89	$6.75	$4.76	$6.00	$13.21	$15.64
8 PM	$7.42	$4.99	$6.71	$5.98	$6.76	$14.88	$15.97
9 PM	$5.92	$4.02	$6.23	$5.01	$5.17	$12.21	$14.59

Figure 9.7: Hourly RevPASH for Summer

Most restaurants already consider the metrics—number of table turns, dining duration, and average check—that make up RevPASH. The benefit of the RevPASH metric is that it provides an easier and more comprehensive way to evaluate how well the restaurant generates revenue.

QUESTION TO CONSIDER

1. Calculate the RevPASH for each restaurant below.
2. Which restaurant would you rather manage and why?

Restaurant	Seat occupancy	Average check per person	RevPASH
A	30%	$25	
B	40%	$21	
C	50%	$18	
D	80%	$11	
E	90%	$10	

SPREADSHEET EXERCISE 9.2

Ann Li is the general manager of Camellia, a 180-seat restaurant in Los Angeles hotel that is owned by a private equity group. Camellia is open from 8 a.m. to 10 p.m. every day of the year, including holidays. Next week, Ann will be attending the annual meeting of the investors, where she will be expected to discuss the performance of Camellia over the past year. Ann asked the assistant manager for a summary of last year's gross revenue figures and received the following:

Jan - $759,315	Jul - $657,627
Feb - $593,249	Aug - $684,046
Mar - $645,096	Sep - $729,807
Apr - $645,118	Oct - $686,490
May - $730,624	Nov - $633,192
Jun - $625,515	Dec - $783,785

TO DO

Explore the RevPASH Web App, found at http://www.bu.edu/revpash/.

Use the app to calculate and chart monthly RevPASH for the past year. What are the months with the highest RevPASH? What are the months with the lowest RevPASH?

Hints for using the app: Work in the Monthly tab, add rows, hours open is not the same each month.

Collect Data

RRM is a data-heavy discipline, so collecting and analyzing data is fundamental to using RRM (Kimes et al., 1999). Different RRM programs involve different amounts and types of data. Things that should be considered when determining data requirements include: What is needed? To what level of detail? How to get it?

Another concern in data collection is how many observations need to be used to ensure a statistically sound analysis. Much RRM analysis is concerned with the average and standard deviation of data sets. Because of this, a general guideline for the amount of data that should be used to ensure a statistically sound analysis is 30 observations, unless more data are available.

For instance, to determine the dining duration for Friday nights from 5:00 p.m. to 8:00 p.m. would require that roughly 30 tables were observed each hour, preferably over several different Friday nights, and duration data were recorded. However, if there is access to thousands of observations (for instance, through a POS system), much more data should be used. In addition, all data should also be "scrubbed" of incorrect or duplicate entries to ensure that only sound data are included in the analysis.

A strong baseline analysis could be conducted with the following data requirements:

What is Needed	**Levels of Detail to Consider**	**How to Get It**
Throughput time and throughput rate	- Monthly - Day of week - Time period (usually hourly or by 15-min intervals) - Party size - Steps in service delivery system	Do a time study and use covers (# of customers served) from POS
Arrivals	- Monthly - Day of week - Time period (usually hourly or by 15-min intervals) - Party size	Manually or from POS/wait mgt system
Dining duration	- Monthly - Day of week - Time period (usually hourly) - Party size - Steps in meal	Use check opened from POS or do a time study

What is Needed	Levels of Detail to Consider	How to Get It
Table occupancy	- Monthly - Day of week - Time period (usually hourly or by 15-min intervals) - Table size	Use POS or do manual data collection
Seat occupancy	- Monthly - Day of week - Time period (usually hourly or by 15-min intervals)	Use covers by time interval from POS
Average check	- Monthly - Day of week - Time period (usually hourly or by 15-min intervals) - Party size	Use revenue and covers from POS
RevPASH	- Monthly - Day of week - Time period (usually hourly or by 15-minintervals) - Party size	Use revenue

Develop RRM Solutions

The ongoing goal of a RRM program is to maximize RevPASH. Solutions for maximizing RevPASH depend on the issues uncovered during the baseline analysis, and many RevPASH solutions are time-based. During times that RevPASH is low, RRM strategies should be aimed at increasing occupancy. When RevPASH is high, RRM solutions should focus on increasing price and/or making occupancy more effective (Kimes et al., 1999; Kimes et al., 1998).

Usually, demand-based RRM solutions revolve around manipulating duration and price in an effort to influence the demand of a restaurant. Correspondingly, supply-based RRM solutions involve ensuring that a restaurant can effectively and profitably serve incoming demand.

As with any RM program, the RRM solutions chosen to help manage RevPASH must work well together. RRM solutions should not only help increase revenues but also preserve or enhance customer satisfaction. The following table shows a variety of RRM solutions:

High RevPASH	Low RevPASH
- Manage arrivals and altering the mix of reservations, walk-ins, and call-ahead seating customers so the most profitable ones are served - Overbooking, especially if reservations are not guaranteed or if there is not a penalty for no-shows - Smooth demand from peak periods to shoulder periods - Reduce dining duration - Minimize dining options by offering a limited menu - Consistently use overt, but not aggressive or obnoxious, cues to move diners - Ensure staffing is appropriate - Streamline and standardize service delivery - Pre-bus tables - Ensure check payment process is effective and quick - Optimize the mix of service inventory - Install (or develop) a technology system that has RRM capabilities	- Make price more variable - Traditional time-based discounting, like early bird weekday specials - Couponing and promotions - Upsell/suggestive selling - Create new demand - Marketing tactics - Use new distribution systems, such as OpenTable - Use group discounters such as Groupon - Create new services and products - Bundle offerings or group different items together and sell at a discounted price - Being a frequent diner club that offers incentives during off-peak hours - Cross-train employees to perform various functions

One progressive RRM solution that is useful in both high and low RevPASH scenarios is the use of electronic menus. Electronic menus allow operators to change menu offerings and vary prices in real-time, essentially enabling a restaurant to respond to almost any demand situation in a revenue-maximizing manner.

RRM solutions can range from tried-and-true RM methods to adaptive and creative untested ideas. Ultimately, the set of RRM solutions will be unique to most any operation. They will also be unique to a period of time since the solutions are derived using data from past performance. One thing every RRM program has in common, though, is that strong analytics serve as its foundation.

Implement and Monitor RRM Solutions

After establishing a restaurant's baseline and selecting a RevPASH-maximizing set of RRM strategies, the next step of an RRM program is to implement the solutions and make sure they are working appropriately. There are no long-established rules for implementing RRM solutions. Since an RRM program is customized for an individual operation, one solution or method of implementation that works at one facility may have no impact on RevPASH at another.

Brainstorming creative ideas for implementing an RRM program and talking with other RRM users can be beneficial. Whoever is assigned to lead the implementation of the RRM initiative—an owner, manager, or RRM consultant—will be responsible for managing the people and processes associated with the particular RRM program.

- Managing people: Employees are directly impacted by many RRM solutions. For example, decreasing dining duration potentially means that servers and bussers will have added responsibilities and cooks and dishwashers will have to work harder to produce more meals. Training helps employees understand their vital role in an RRM program. Putting the proper incentive and communication systems in place to ensure that the RRM program works as intended helps secure their support.
- Managing processes: Depending on the RRM solutions chosen, new and/or improved processes will need to be established, tested, and implemented. For instance, streamlining service delivery by retooling the check delivery and payment process requires a careful plan, good training, and a trial period to work out any problems. The process of purchasing and installing a new POS system capable of capturing RRM data would require a much different type of management.

One more thing every RRM program has in common is the need to monitor the program and update it when necessary. This is done by periodically recalculating metrics and analyzing processes again—essentially reestablishing the baseline. If RevPASH has not performed as well as anticipated after the last round of RRM updates, a fishbone diagram would be helpful in determining why.

REAL PEOPLE

John Singleton, the manager of a restaurant at a beachside resort in Panama City Beach, Florida, was upset when he first learned that the corporate office was beginning an RRM initiative. He insisted that an RRM program would erode his average check. His yearly bonus was tied to average check. Even though he heard something about bonuses being tied to something called RevPASH, he was not convinced that anything messing with his high average check is a good idea. Convince him that an RRM program is a good idea.

DISCUSSION QUESTIONS

1. Consider this scenario: The Cat Pub, a bar and restaurant in Hershey, PA, offers discounts on appetizers and drinks from 5 p.m. to 7 p.m. each night. These happy hour specials are quite popular, especially on the nights when the local ice hockey team plays nearby.

   Should the happy hour specials be offered every night? Why does offering the happy hour specials every night of the week represent a suboptimal solution to an RRM problem?

2. You are trying to determine if the cashier process or the kitchen process is the bottleneck of dinner service at Crazy Joe's Chickn n' Waffles Fast Food Truck. Crazy Joe's has one cashier who takes orders and payment and also hands out prepared meals and two cooks who prepare the meals. You know that the cashier can process 16 customers per hour and that each customer purchases 3 chickn n' waffles meals on average. You also know that the throughput rate of each cook is 25 meals per hour. Follow the steps below to gather more information about what is happening at Crazy Joe's to help you identify the bottleneck.
   - Determine how many meals customers demand in an hour.
   - Determine how many meals the kitchen can produce in an hour.
   - Calculate how many customers the kitchen can serve in an hour. This is the throughput rate of the kitchen or the number of customers the kitchen can serve in an hour.

Compare the throughput rate of the cashier to the throughput rate of the kitchen and determine the bottleneck. The process with the smaller throughput rate is the bottleneck, as it limits how many customers can be served in this simple scenario. Is the bottleneck's throughput rate significantly smaller than the other process? How does the significance of the difference between throughput rates of processes impact the solutions you would recommend to alleviate the bottleneck?

3. Explain why doubling the capacity of a bottleneck would not necessarily double the capacity of a system.
4. Using restaurant revenue management directly impacts the FOH operations, especially since RRM solutions often address elements like the types of customers FOH staff will serve, the busyness of a facility, and the layout of a dining room floor. Certainly, RRM practices also directly influence kitchen operations. For instance, a restaurant that issues a two-for-one entrée coupon is trying to build demand, but its kitchen must be ready with ingredients and staff to accommodate that greater demand. What are some other ways and scenarios that illustrate how FOH-centric RRM practices impact BOH operations?
5. For a busy restaurant that frequently has a wait, why would the POS data of time-check-opened not be a reliable source to determine arrivals?

APPLICATIONS

Tasty Banquets

Tasty Banquets has the following system in place for servicing banquet tables: Dinner plates are assembled (4 min per table), plates are loaded onto a tray (2 min per table), and trays are delivered to tables (5 min per table).

1. What is the throughput time for a table's food?
   What is the throughput rate (tables per hour) for the system?
2. Tasty plans to use two expediters, two helpers, and four servers. What is the throughput rate (tables per hour) for each task?
3. What is the throughput rate of the entire system now? What is the bottleneck activity?

Muchacho

The manager of Muchacho, a casual dining Mexican restaurant, is trying to reduce the mean time of weekend dinners. Develop a fishbone diagram to identify the possible causes of a long meal.

TEAM ACTIVITY

Imagine your team has been hired by McArdees, a gastropub in Chicago, as RRM consultants. McArdees has a sit-down, full- service restaurant area open from 5:00 p.m. to 10:00 p.m., and all menu items are also available in the large bar area. McArdees would like to know if it should expand its restaurant section. You are given the following information:

- McArdees has 15 two-tops, 14 four-tops, 2 six- tops, and 3 eight-tops
- A graph of its arrivals:

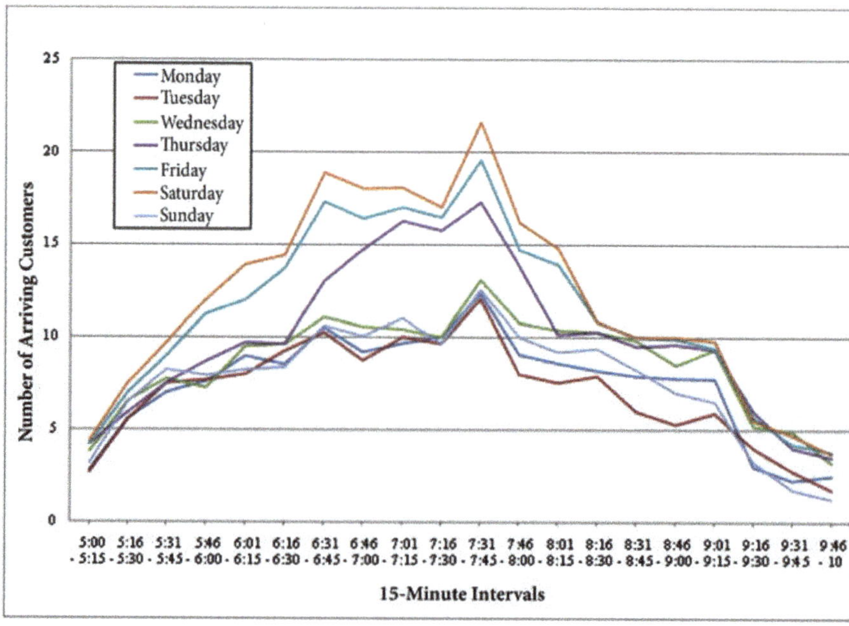

- Average dining duration, taken from the POS system and measuring the time from check-opened to check-closed, of 79 min.
- Throughput time for a table, from seat to ready for reseating, of 86 min.
- Revenue, averaged over 3 months, by day of week

Monday	$3,879
Tuesday	$3,686
Wednesday	$4,721
Thursday	$5,476
Friday	$6,641
Saturday	$7,463
Sunday	$4,077

Using all the tools possible from this chapter, what can you tell about the operations and performance of McArdees? What other information would you need to perform a baseline analysis?

INTERNET ACTIVITY

Go online and search for a table for a party of two at the most popular restaurant in your town for a busy Saturday at 7:00 p.m. Is a table available at the requested time? If not, were other times offered? Describe the RRM technique of demand smoothing and discuss if you think it is being used in this scenario.

Imagine that a table for two is only available at either 5:15 p.m. or 10:00 p.m. What are some ways this restaurant could entice you to make a reservation at one of these alternate times instead of choosing a competitor at 7 p.m.?

GLOSSARY

Bottleneck – The process within a system that limits the operation and output of the entire system.

Capacity – The supply of seats a restaurant has available to accommodate customers.

Dining duration – The amount of time a customer spends at a restaurant, measured from arrival to departure.

Suboptimal solution – An RRM solution that has a positive impact in one area but a negative impact on the overall service system.

Throughput rate – The number of customers that flow through a service system over a certain time.

Throughput time – The time a customer spends in a service system from enter to exit.

REFERENCES

American Society of Mechanical Engineers. (1947). *ASME Standard: Operation and Flow Process Charts, 1947*. New York.

Cross, R. G., Higbie, J. A., & Cross, D.Q. (2009). Revenue Management's Renaissance: A Rebirth of the art and Science of Profitable Revenue Generation. *Cornell Hospitality Quarterly, 50* (1), 56-81.

Fitzsimmons, J. A., & Fitzsimmons, M. J. (1999). *Service Management – Operations, Strategy, and Information Technology.* (2nd ed.) New York: Irwin/Mc Graw-Hill.

Gilbreth, F. B., & Gilbreth, L. M. (1921). *Process Charts.* Paper Presented at the Annual Meeting of the American Society of Mechanical Engineers, New York.

Ishikawa, K. (1968). *Guide to Quality Control.* Tokyo: JUSE.

Kimes, S. (1989). Yield Management: A Tool for Capacity-constrained Service Firms. *Journal of Operations Management, 8* (4), 348-363.

Kimes, S. (1999). Implementing Restaurant Revenue Management: A Five-step Approach. *Cornell Hotel and Restaurant Administration Quarterly, 40* (3), 16-21.

Kimes, S., & Chase, R. (1998). The Strategic Levers of Yield Management. *Journal of Service Research, 1*(2): 156-166.

Kimes, S., Barrash, D., & Alexander, J. (1999). Developing a Restaurant Revenue-management Strategy. *Cornell Hotel and Restaurant Administration Quarterly, 40* (5), 18-29.

Kimes, S., Chase, R., Choi, S., Lee, P., & Ngonzi, E. (1998). Restaurant Revenue Management: Applying Yield Management to the Restaurant Industry. *Cornell Hotel and Restaurant Administration Quarterly, 39* (3), 32-39.

McGuire, K. (2016). *Hotel Pricing in a Social World.* Hoboken, NJ: Wiley.

Noone, B., & McGuire, K. (2013b). Pricing in a Social World: The Influence of Non-price Information on Hotel Choice. *Journal of Revenue and Pricing Management, 12,* 385-401.

Rohlfs, K. (2009). *The Role of Space in Revenue Management* (Doctoral Dissertation). Cornell University, Ithaca, NY.

Sinclair, J. (2010, September 19). *Restaurant* Operators Ignoring *RevPASH are* Missing *a* Trick: *Real* Revenues. Retrieved May 22, 2011, from http:// www.foodservice.com.

CHAPTER 10

Restaurant Revenue Management: Advanced Demand Management Concepts

Kristin V. Rohlfs

OVERVIEW

The field of restaurant revenue management (RRM) combines elements of demand management with concepts of supply management to provide both a theoretical base and an operational plan to maximize the revenue a restaurant can make. The demand side of RRM includes issues related to pricing, how and when customers arrive at the restaurant, and ways to influence customer behavior and the customer experience.

LEARNING OBJECTIVES

After studying this chapter, you should be able to evaluate restaurant demand in the context of RRM. Specifically, you should be able to:

- Explain ways in which restaurant demand impacts restaurant revenue and discuss how managing demand fits into RRM
- Evaluate several demand management techniques for restaurants and identify the strategies to use in different operational situations
- Describe variable pricing and apply it to a restaurant. Assess variable pricing practices, such as price fences and couponing

- Examine basic ways to determine menu prices, focusing on data-based menu engineering
- Perform a basic analysis of restaurant arrivals and compare the ways in which arrivals can be measured
- Determine when waiting lines occur and describe the different methods for managing them

OUTLINE

Introduction

Demand Side of RM = Demand Management

Pricing

- Variable Pricing
- Variable Pricing Strategies
- Setting Prices

Arrivals

- Types
- Basic Arrivals Analysis
- Forecasting Demand

Waiting Lines

- Why They Happen
- Psychology of Waiting Lines
- Wait List Management

Summary
Discussion Questions
Applications

- Cayuga Resort
- Northman's

Team Activity
Internet Activity
Glossary
References

SO WHAT?

A goal of almost every food or beverage service operation is to be profitable. No restaurateur starts a business to have lagging revenues and elevated expenses. To help ensure that a restaurant is maximizing its revenue stream, many operators employ the theories and techniques of restaurant revenue management (RRM). Some well-known RRM tools frequently used to manage demand include an often costly multiple-platform reservations system and restaurant seating and POS systems.

In many restaurants, managing demand is the responsibility of the host function. However, this is often a low-paying position that does not require any business training or restaurant experience. Why would this be the case?

INTRODUCTION

Like most service industries, the restaurant industry faces an imbalance between supply and demand at different times. When demand is too low to fill available seats, restaurants must try to attract additional customers and find alternate ways to generate revenue. When demand is more than can be served by the seats or tables or kitchen, restaurants would like to serve as many of the most profitable customers as possible. Restaurant revenue management (RRM) is used to maximize the revenue per available seat hour (RevPASH) by stimulating demand when it is low and redistributing and serving demand in the most profitable way when it is high (Kimes et al., 1998).

The demand side of RRM is the focus of this chapter. Because all parts of a restaurant are directly exposed to demand fluctuations and demand behavior; understanding patterns and qualities of demand is integral to using RRM to its fullest. RRM aims to increase top-line revenues generated by an operation and has traditionally focused primarily on front-of-house (FOH) concerns.

DEMAND SIDE OF RM = DEMAND MANAGEMENT

Managing demand means making sure all the operating policies and procedures, prices, and sales and marketing programs are designed and functioning to attract and maintain the most profitable customer base. The set of demand management strategies being used must work collectively in the best interests of a business, with no secondary objective overshadowing the primary RM goal of optimizing revenue. The demand management side of RRM combines traditionally different operations management (e.g., forecasting) and marketing (e.g., pricing) methods and techniques to influence demand in a way that maximizes RevPASH.

Common demand management practices include:

1. Influencing the type of requests for service
2. Influencing the timing of requests for service
3. Shifting demand to periods that are less taxing on the operating system
4. Shifting demand to products that are more profitable

QUESTION TO CONSIDER

Services implement demand management practices in various ways. For instance, airlines influence the timing of requests for seats on flights by offering significant discounts for booking early. And hotels shift demand from peak to off-peak nights by having length-of-stay restrictions.

Food and beverage outlets frequently use the four types of demand management practices previously listed. To influence the types of requests for service, a restaurant may use atmosphere and table size to attract higher-revenue-per-person parties of two. A common strategy to influence the timing of service requests is to issue coupons for specific times only. To shift demand, many restaurants use early bird specials or happy hour discounts. And many restaurants train staff to shift demand to different products by upselling and suggestive selling.

Can you think of another strategy a restaurant could use for each of the four demand management practices?

Demand management tactics are usually used reactively when demand is greater than supply. The problem with reacting to demand is that if an operation changes course quickly, without proper planning and analysis, it could suffer declines in productivity, quality, and profit (Croxton et al., 2002). Using demand management tactics proactively when demand is less than supply gives operators more control over the how and when demand arrives and how and when the service system processes demand.

Pricing

Along with duration, pricing is considered one of the strategic levers of RM. These strategic levers are the demand-side elements that an operator could potentially control in an effort to satisfy as much demand as possible in the most revenue-enhancing way (Kimes & Chase, 1998). Pricing is used in RRM to entice demand to move to different time periods or products and/or to stimulate new demand.

Variable Pricing

In theory, every customer has a time-sensitive price he/she is willing to pay for any good or service. A restaurant would hypothetically be in a revenue-maximizing position if it were able to charge different prices to different customers in different circumstances. Varying prices for every transaction are unrealistic but a restaurant can apply variable pricing to a lesser, but still profitable, extent.

Consider the graphs in Figure 10.1. They are basic economic price-quantity graphs with the revenue determined by the amount sold and price charged. Figure 10.1a shows one month of revenue from the baked ziti entrée at a family-style Italian restaurant. When one price—$14 in this case—is charged for the baked ziti, 100 dishes are sold, bringing in revenue of $1,400. Figure 10.1b shows the potential revenue that could be made from baked ziti when three prices—$8, $14, and $20—are charged. At $8, 65 dinners are sold, 35 are sold at $14, and 25 are sold at $20, which totals $1,510. More of the potential revenue is captured when more prices are offered.

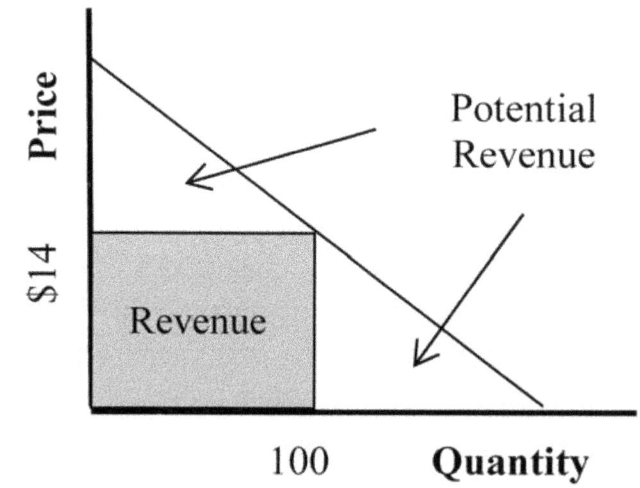

Figure 10.1a: Effect of Variable Pricing: Charging One Price

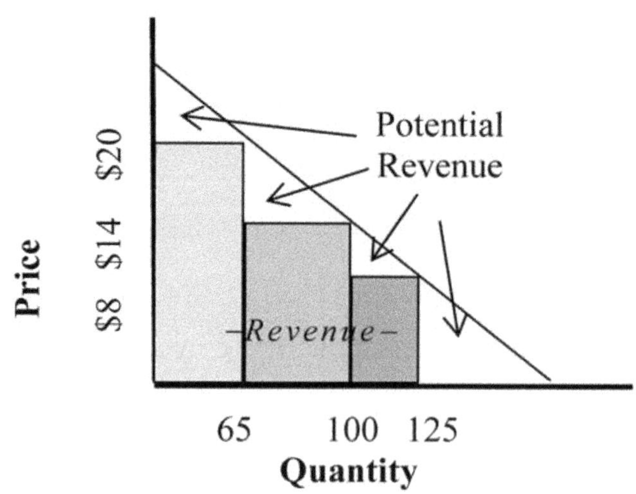

Figure 10.1b: Effect of Variable Pricing: Charging Multiple Prices

Research has shown, though, that customers only tolerate variable pricing under certain conditions, including

- customer value and company value are balanced (i.e., prices can be raised to maintain profits, but not to raise profits) and
- customers have been made to expect to be charged different prices at different times and for different products (i.e., as in the airline, hotel, and car rental industries) (Kimes & Wirtz, 2003; Simon & Dolan, 1999).

The use of variable pricing in restaurants can be more complex than in other service situations. To start with, the customer has a large amount of control over the duration of the service, making the determination of when/how/to what extent to vary prices almost impossible. In addition, a restaurant does not just sell food; it also sells the use of a seat at a table, along with the restaurant's atmosphere, for a period of time. That is, restaurants often sell a time-based experience.

THINK HISTORICALLY

In the early 1990s, when the application and success of yield management (now more commonly known as revenue management) in the airline industry was emerging, Robert Crandall, then the CEO of American Airlines, famously said "If I have 2,000 customers on a given route and 400 different prices, I'm obviously short 1,600 [prices]."

Now, over 20 years later, the use of variable pricing has not reached such an extreme level but customers undoubtedly have accepted that prices—especially on services—change without warning.

Because restaurants sell an experience, it would seem that variable pricing would be a fantastic idea, since every customer would have a different price in mind that she is willing to pay for her experience.

However, consider this theoretical scenario: Becky, Pat, and Lou have enjoyed a wonderful dinner at Ray's Lobster & Crab, which practices pure variable pricing. When the bill came, Becky told the waiter she had a discount code she got online, Pat commented that she thought the crab was worth less than it was priced on the menu, and Lou didn't think it was crowded enough to warrant the peak-hour surcharge.

This type of scenario would present operating and customer service problems and would likely cause dissatisfaction for all parties. Can you think of examples of what could go wrong in a restaurant that heavily uses variable pricing?

The extent to which variable pricing can be used in RRM has yet to be fully studied by researchers and tested by restaurant operators. Although prices now cannot be varied to an extreme extent, adding some element of variable pricing into the demand side of RRM is beneficial to maximizing the revenue a restaurant's supply can generate.

Variable Pricing Strategies

Three variable pricing strategies that can be used by a restaurant to optimize revenues are as follows:

1. The use of price fences (Kimes et al., 1998): Fences are restrictions or conditions put on some aspect of a service that effectively lets a restaurant charge different prices to different customers. A common price fence used in the restaurant industry is a mandatory gratuity for large parties. Some price fences are tangible; something physical is attached to the price, like a bottle of champagne or seating at the chef's table. Some price fences are intangible; the conditions put on the restaurant service cannot be seen, like a noncancellable reservation.

   Price fences can be based on characteristics of demand, such as party size or group affiliation, or characteristics of supply, such as table location, time of day, or added amenities. The set of price fences that will be successful in maximizing revenue differs based on a particular restaurant and its customer base. Research has shown that customers find some fences unfair, such as pricing based on table location (Kimes and Wirtz, 2003). Therefore, while some creativity can be used in determining appropriate price fences, customer response and satisfaction should always be considered and incorporated into this variable pricing strategy.

2. Issuing coupons with restrictions: Coupons with restrictions are not a new concept to the restaurant industry. When used appropriately, they can bring in demand during slow periods by offering pricing incentives. Restrictions attached to a coupon can also encourage discount-seeking customers to dine during an off-peak time, so that more price-insensitive customers can be efficiently served during peak hours. An example of a coupon with restriction would be a 50%-off coupon that can be used after 7:00 p.m. on the weekends for

Tyrel's Burger Stop, a fast casual restaurant located in the heart of the Wall Street financial district.

3. Adjusting service offerings: Changing what is available for customers to purchase at specific times is another variable pricing technique. Examples of adjusting a service offering include having different menus/prices for lunch and dinner and making a reduced-price pre-theater menu only available until 6:30 p.m. Limiting what is offered for sale can potentially defer demand from overcrowded, peak hours to shoulder or off-peak periods.

Whatever variable pricing strategies are used, research has shown that presenting price differences as discounts instead of premiums makes variable pricing seem more acceptable to customers (Kimes & Wirtz, 2003). This practice is called framing. For example, a restaurant that offers both a lower-priced lunch menu and a higher-priced dinner menu should frame the lunch menu as a discounted dinner menu instead of vice versa.

SEEING FURTHER

A popular variable pricing strategy is the online group coupon. Groupon and LivingSocial are examples of websites that sell huge discounts in the form of coupons. Many restaurants have been using these types of sites to stimulate demand.

However, Alex Failmezger, an RRM executive, has observed: "These coupons are really taking a toll on the industry because, in some cases, they overstimulate demand but from the wrong customers at the totally wrong price. Already-struggling restaurants hoping to boost short-term revenue need to make certain they can cover the costs to fulfill all of the coupon purchases. Plus, group coupons attract discount-seekers, who may not always be the best repeat business prospects."

Alex agrees that in the right situation, group coupons can be a good variable pricing strategy to use to attract demand or, with the right restrictions, smooth it from peak periods. She just warns restaurateurs, "If your demand is already strong, there is no need to issue a group coupon. Everyone already wants to go to your restaurant and giving them a discount just sets you up to never get to charge them full price!"

What are some situations where using a group coupon with restrictions would be beneficial to a restaurant? What are some restrictions that could be used to create a profitable, but still customer-friendly, coupon deal?

Another wide-reaching discount strategy that has gained popularity in the restaurant industry is social media marketing. Gracie Doren, an independent F&B consultant, commented that "giving discounts for checking in or following an establishment are certainly great ways to reach an expanded potential customer base. But a good social media strategy requires planning, analysis, flexibility, and attention, and doesn't always need to be about cost and coupons."

Can you think of any social media campaign in the F&B industry that positively or negatively impacted your perception of the business? Was there a discount associated with this campaign?

Setting Prices

Restaurants can determine their prices—no matter the extent to which they use variable pricing—in several different ways. A full discussion of menu pricing is outside the scope of this chapter, but a synopsis of several common pricing methods is provided below.

- Cost-plus: Each menu item's price is based on the cost to make it plus a predetermined markup. Costs include ingredients, condiments and garnishes, overhead, and may/may not include labor. Markups are generally chosen based on a variety of factors, including the atmosphere provided to customers, labor (if excluded from the cost portion), and investment goals.
- Competition-based: Under this market-based approach, menu item prices are set by benchmarking the prices of similar items from competing restaurants and tailoring them as needed. An extreme example of competition-based pricing is Wally's Clam Shack charging $12.99 for a bucket of fried clams simply because both Under-the-C Clam Stand and Von's Clam Truck charge that price.
- Demand-based: Prices are set based on what customers will support. If a series of menu items prepared tableside by a chef has enough

demand to sell out every night, the price set will be as high as possible until interest decreases, which signals that price should be decreased.

In recent times, the restaurant industry has greatly expanded its use of marketing and delivery systems that make the price of restaurant services more transparent than ever before. Restaurant websites and third-party reservation sites, such as OpenTable.com and Yelp.com, provide sample menus, oftentimes complete with prices and service charges. A consequence of these market changes is that restaurant pricing is heavily competition- and demand-based (Clifford, 2012).

Menu Engineering

For a restaurant that uses a traditional prepriced, preprinted menu, menu engineering can help optimize prices of individual items based on the popularity and profitability of all items. A popular analytic tool associated with menu engineering is the 2 × 2 Boston Consulting Group (BCG) matrix, shown in Figure 10.2. This matrix provides a clear visual of how a set of menu items perform in relation to each other. Menu sections, such as starters, entrees, and desserts, are usually analyzed separately.

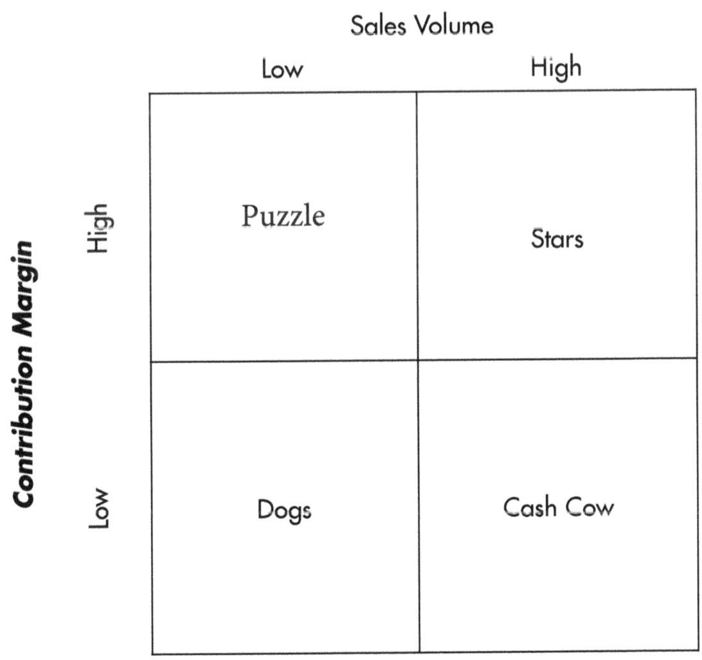

Figure 10.2: BCG Matrix to Categorize Entrees

Each menu item is categorized based on its level of sales and level of contribution margin.

Contribution margin = price – food cost

The four performance categories for menu items are

- Cash cows: Items are popular but either costly to make or priced low to encourage sales.
- Dogs: Items are neither popular nor profitable; they are items that have traditionally been on the menu.
- Puzzles: Items do not sell well, but make a good profit when they do.
- Stars: Items are the favorite items of both customers and operators because they are both popular and profitable.

A BCG matrix analysis requires sales, price, and food cost data for each item. The basic steps to constructing a BCG matrix for one menu category are illustrated using the following example:

The Cove is a small, upscale restaurant located at a winery in the Finger Lakes region of New York. Its signature menu item is a duck dish because the logo of the winery includes a duck. Data was collected for each menu item for the past 3 months:

Entrée	Number Sold	Price –	Cost =	Contribution Margin
Filet	1200	$42	$10	$32
Lamb	850	$38	$9	$29
Duck	650	$35	$8	$27
Sea Bass	1000	$38	$9	$29
Chicken	1050	$28	$6	$22

1. Calculate the averages for sales and contribution margin:

   Average number sold: (1200 + 850 + 650 + 1000 + 1050)/5 = 950

   Average contribution margin = ($32 + $29 + $27 + $29 + $22)/5 = $27.80

2. Compare the number sold and contribution margin (CM) of each menu item to the averages:

   Filet—number sold: 1200 > 950 CM: $32 > $27.80

   Lamb—number sold: 850 < 950 CM: $29 > $27.80

Duck—number sold: 650 < 950 CM: $27 < $27.80

Sea Bass—number sold: 1000 > 950 CM: $29 > $27.80

Chicken—number sold: 1050 > 950 CM: $22 < $27.80

3. Determine the category of each item based on if number sold is higher or lower than average and if CM is higher or lower than average :
   - Cash cow—high sales, low CM—chicken
   - Dog—low sales, low CM—lamb
   - Puzzle—low sales, high CM—duck
   - Star—high sales, high CM—filet and sea bass
4. Graph the results. The lines marking the four quadrants are the average Number Sold on the x-axis and the CM on the y-axis.

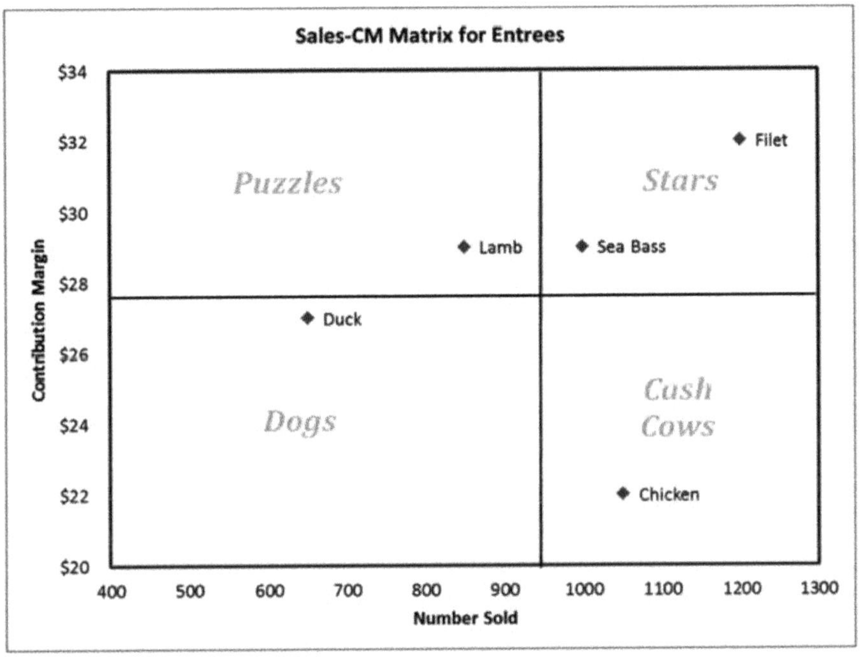

Different pricing strategies are associated with the different categories but the goal for each is to maximize the performance of the menu by essentially trying to make all menu items into stars. Some strategies for items within each category are

- Cash cows: Raise price, highlight on menu, modify item to decrease cost;
- Dogs: Raise price, remove from menu;

- Puzzles: Highlight/change menu position, lower price, modify item to decrease cost, remove;
- Stars: Highlight on menu, raise price.

Solutions are unique to the operations, demand-base, and competitive market of a restaurant. Periodically performing a menu engineering analysis using a BCG matrix not only helps fine-tune menu pricing but also helps ensure that production costs are regularly reviewed and demand trends are followed.

In the example of The Cove, the chicken is a Cash cow. Its sales volume is high and its cost is the lowest on the menu, so a marginal price increase could potentially increase CM without radically decreasing the number sold. The Duck entrée is a Dog but should not be removed from the menu since it is the restaurant's signature dish. Instead, management could consider raising its price to increase its CM and move it closer to the Star category. The Lamb is a Puzzle, as it is one of the higher-CM items on the menu but is not as popular as most of the other dishes. Highlighting the Lamb on the menu to drive sales could help make it a Star. The Sea Bass and the Filet are the Stars of the menu, as both high sales and high CMs. The Filet is by far the most popular and profitable entrée, and its pricing does not need any adjustment in this analysis. The Sea Bass is also a Star, performing well relative to most other menu items. Management could highlight it to grow sales, increase its price, or do nothing and choose to focus resources on the other categories at this time.

SPREADSHEET EXERCISE 10.1

Bello's, a casual, full-service restaurant in Buffalo, NY, has been a local favorite for the past 17 years. It was owned and operated by Sergey Yevgeny until a month ago, when he sold Bello's to Raul Pena, a relatively new chef. As part of his restaurant training, Raul took several business classes and learned that an analytical approach to menu planning could help his new restaurant be as successful as possible.

Raul wants to thoroughly analyze the current menu before making any changes, so he pulled sales, pricing, and cost data from Bello's POS system, provided in the Excel spreadsheet. A screenshot of the data is

	A	B	C	D	E
1	Item	Category	# Sold	Total Cost	Pric
2	Almond Cake	dessert	415	$2.75	$8.0
3	Apple Crostada	dessert	540	$3.00	$8.0
4	Arugula Salad	appetizer	535	$3.00	$9.0
5	Berry Tarte	dessert	564	$2.50	$8.0
6	Calamari	appetizer	745	$3.25	$14.0

To Do

1. Sort and separate data into menu categories and calculate the average sales for each category. Determine the CM for each menu item and calculate the average CM for each menu category.
2. Compare each item to the averages, using = IF statements as necessary. Determine the Stars, Cash cows, Puzzles, and Dogs for each menu category.
3. What changes would you suggest to the menu?

Arrivals

Arrivals refer to the number of parties or customers arriving to a restaurant in certain time periods. This is the demand for the restaurant and it generally follows patterns by day, time, season, or year. Obtaining precise information on arrivals can be complicated: Imagine how difficult it would be to track every customer walking in the door—no matter if he was seated, left the restaurant, or waited at the bar for an hour—for hours every day of the week for weeks.

If a restaurant uses wait-list/reservation management technology, considerable information on arrivals can be easily obtained. If a wait-list/reservation management system is not used, point-of-sale (POS) data can serve as a proxy for when a check is opened but it does not always reflect when the customer arrived to the restaurant, especially if there was a wait for a table. RRM analyses can use the time the check is opened in the POS plus an additional time measure to estimate arrivals. This additional time addresses the time-shift problem of using POS data by accounting for time before checks are opened and can be estimated via a time study.

PROS & CONS

12Q Bistro is a very popular restaurant in Portland, Oregon. 3Spark, the parent company of 12Q Bistro, plus six other F&B establishments, has just hired the JCM Restaurant Consulting Group to help build and integrate a Restaurant Revenue Management strategy for 3Spark.

The analysts at JCM contacted the GM of each 3Spark restaurant and asked for several specific data sets, including demand by hour for each day of the week. When Ann, the GM at 12Q Bistro, tried to pull together the data, she quickly realized that there are a number of possible times when demand could be recorded:

- At the time a party arrives
- When the table's check is opened
- When the party is seated
- When the table's check is closed

What are the pros and cons for each option of recording demand?

Suppose Ann also wants to provide the JCM consultants with data on Arrivals. Which of the options would you recommend Ann choose as a measure of arrival time?

Types

Customers physically arrive to a food and beverage (F&B) outlet in different ways, depending on the nature of the facility. For example, customers walk up to a boardwalk ice cream stand, drive up to a drive-in restaurant or drive-through window, or park/valet and walk into a sit-down restaurant.

In RRM, however, the concept of types of arrivals refers to how the customer first approached the dining experience at a restaurant—by making a reservation, simply walking in, or calling ahead to be put on a wait list.

Restaurants choose the type(s) of arrivals to use based on the type of restaurant and how the operators want business to be conducted.

Walk-ins

All quick-service restaurants and countless casual sit-down restaurants operate solely on a walk-in basis. An advantage of taking only walk-in customers is fairness, as customers are usually served on a first-come-first-served (FCFS) basis. In addition, many restaurant customers do not want to be bothered with making reservations, so walk-ins force flexibility into a service delivery process.

A disadvantage of walk-in demand is that it can be unpredictable and variable. And while restaurants can try to encourage demand to come in at different times, arrival time is ultimately under the walk-in customer's control. Plus, using walk-in demand practically guarantees that customers will have to wait at the restaurant during excess demand periods. However, a well-controlled waiting line is a way to inventory service demand and have it present and ready to be processed when a table becomes available.

Reservations

Finer dining restaurants rely heavily on reservations, and many moderate, sit-down eateries accept reservations for large parties. Taking reservations gives an operator control over the arrival of demand to a service system. However, it also assumes the risk of losing the opportunity to make money off a table if the party does not show up for the reservation. Restaurateurs have several ways for managing no-shows for reservations, including requiring a credit card guarantee and overbooking the restaurant in anticipation of no-shows.

Many restaurants take some reservations but leave the rest of the seats and tables open for walk-in business. Most restaurateurs and dining room managers use knowledge of their demand base and historical data to set the number of reservations to accept for different dates and different times. However, determining the optimal number of reservations to accept and the number of no-shows to anticipate is a mathematical problem that is outside the scope of this chapter.

Call-ahead Seating

Another form of arrival used by some sit-down restaurants is call-ahead seating. In call-ahead seating, customers call in advance of their desired arrival time to be put on the waiting list. The advantage of using call-ahead seating is that customers reduce the amount of time they must wait at the restaurant, which positively impacts customer satisfaction (Noone et al., 2007).

In addition, research has shown that accepting call-ahead seating slots for up to 50 percent of the total number of expected parties decreases the average wait for all customers—those using call-ahead seating and those simply walking in and waiting (McGuire & Rohlfs, 2005). However, call-ahead seating reduces the chance that waiting customers will spend money at a bar (if available). It also requires good communication with all customers, so parties waiting in-house do not perceive a violation in FCFS if a party that seemingly joins the wait later is seated first.

QUESTION TO CONSIDER

Imagine that you are the new owner of a 150-seat Louisiana-style sit-down restaurant and oyster bar. Business is good and waits at peak dinner hours on the weekends can sometimes exceed 45 min. During the week, waits are closer to 10–15 min at the busiest hours. What types of arrivals would you recommend the owner use and at what times?

Basic Arrivals Analysis

A basic analysis of arrivals begins with collecting data and cleaning it of outliers or other dirty data. Cleaned arrivals data is then sorted by hour and day of the week and the average number of arrivals for each hour and each day of week is calculated. Analyzing arrivals by hour and by day of week is a good place to start for most sit-down, full- service operations. Restaurants that are quick-service style or that have high levels of steady demand warrant a more detailed analysis, such as using 15-min increments.

Graphing Arrivals

The next step in a basic arrivals analysis is graphing arrivals to show patterns and trends in demand as it enters the restaurant system. Data patterns usually have a short- to medium-term time frame and can be seasonal or cyclical. Data trends usually refer to systematic ups and downs over longer periods of time. Graphs showing different trends are in Figure 10.3: Figure 10.3a shows no trend, as the data clusters around a horizontal line and Figure 10.3b shows an upward trend as data, consistently, is increasing.

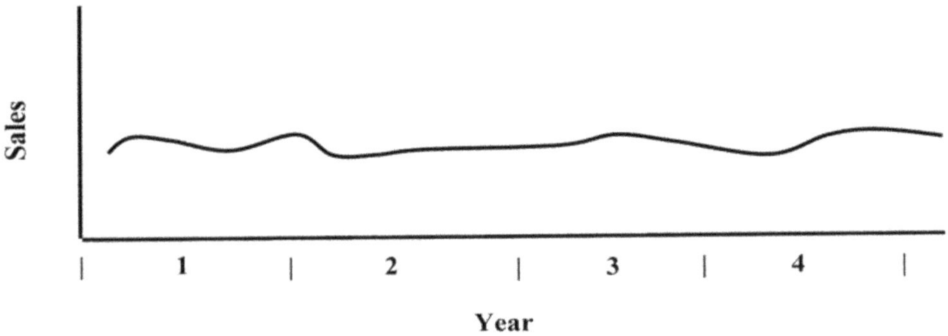

Figure 10.3a: No Trend in Data

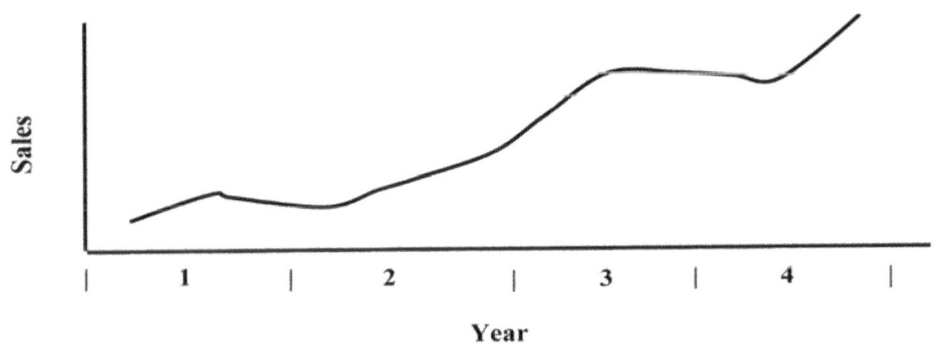

Figure 10.3b: Trend in Data

Patterns are sometimes harder to discern and can reflect short seasonal effects or more extended cycles in demand. Examples of different patterns are shown in Figure 10.4: Figure 10.4a shows seasonality, since the data has consistent peaks and valleys across time; Figure 10.4b shows cyclical data with gradual increase and decrease over more extended periods.

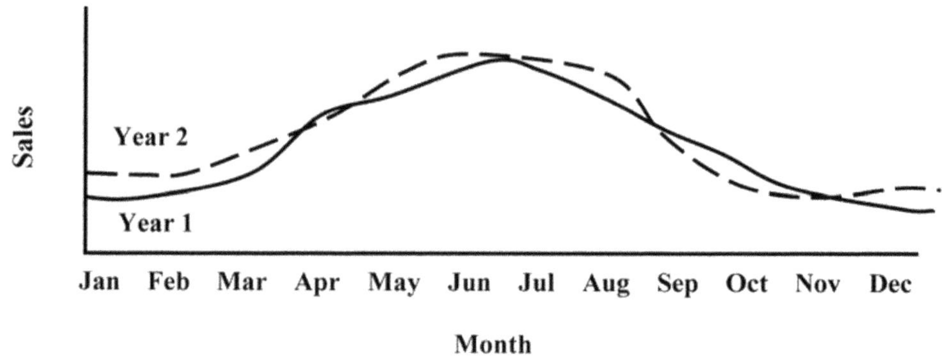

Figure 10.4a: Seasonal Pattern in Data

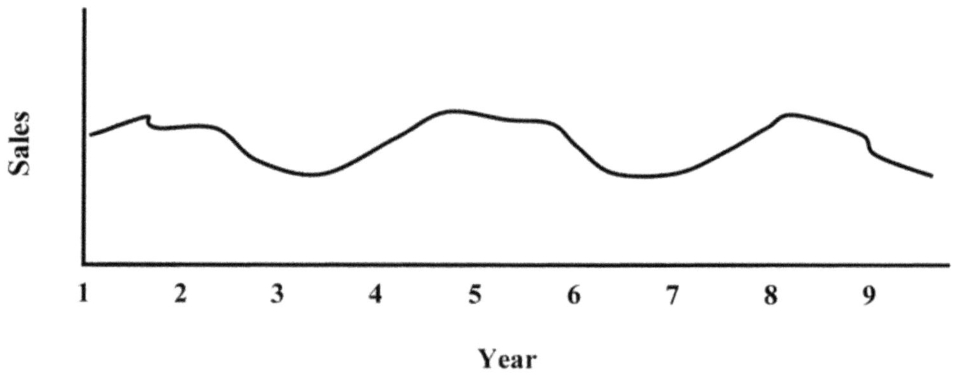

Figure 10.4b: Cyclical Pattern in Data

From a basic graph of arriving demand, the following periods are noticeable:

- Peak demand periods: Times when demand is consistently at its highest.
- Shoulder periods: Times of increasing demand before a peak period and decreasing demand after a peak period.
- Off-peak periods: Times when demand is consistently at its lowest.

REAL PEOPLE

Troy Copper is the new manager of the Old County Buffet, a buffet restaurant located in the Gables Senior Community in Boca Raton, Florida. Troy collected data for the past year from the POS system and averaged the number of customers that arrived within each 15-min time period by each day of the week. Because of the serve-yourself nature of the restaurant and the no-wait tolerance of the customer base, no additional time had to be added to account for waits or predining processes.

Troy was able to graph the true arrivals to the buffet. From the graph, it can be seen that the number of customers arriving to Old County starts off strong at open, peaks around 6:00 p.m. every night, and falls off quickly afterward. The shoulder time for most days is one-sided, from 5:45 p.m. to 7:00 p.m., when demand falls sharply on many days. Demand on Wednesday is particularly interesting, as it is consistently higher than any other day. It turns out that the buffet issues weekly Wednesday two-for-one coupons, which attracts a tremendous amount of demand.

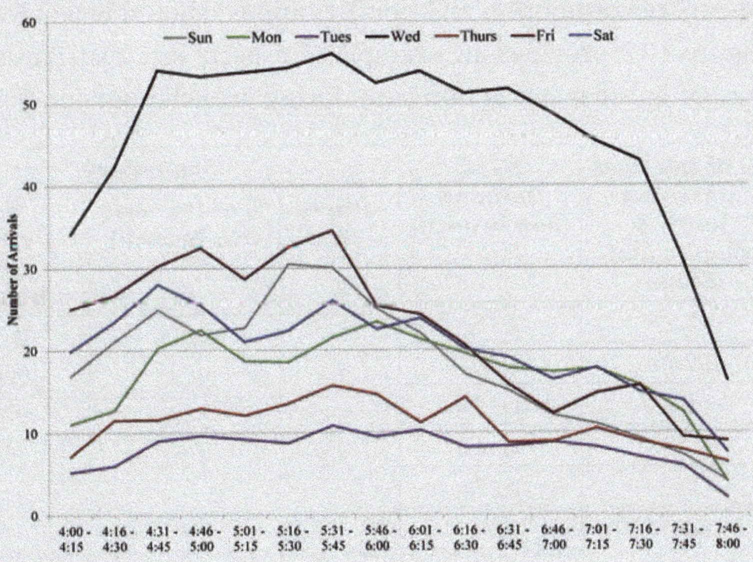

Analysis by day of week for Old County Buffet

How do you think Troy changed Old County Buffet's coupon strategy to smooth demand? Why is demand smoothing a good RRM strategy to use here?

Party Size Distribution

A considerable amount of demand to many restaurants comes in the form of parties of customers. The distribution, or percentage breakdown, of party sizes can be gathered from arrivals information as long as only an insignificant number of arriving parties leave before being seated. Understanding the party size distribution of a restaurant's demand is useful in many operating situations, including assigning servers to stations and determining the best table mix for the restaurant.

A count of the number of parties of each size can usually be garnered from wait-list/reservations and/or POS system data. It is simple to then calculate the party size distribution of demand. For example, a diner served 2400 parties over the past week and 1340 parties of those were parties of 4. Therefore, the

% of demand from parties of 4 = 1340/2400 = 70%.

For most RRM analyses, determining the overall average party size distribution is sufficient, although atypical or demand-stimulating events (e.g., a children-eat-free promotion or 2-for-1 coupons) should be analyzed separately. Figure 10.5 provides an example of a party size distribution for a Chinese restaurant that serves dim sum during brunch hours on Sundays.

Party Size	% of Demand (Mon-Sat lunch & dinner, Sun dinner)	% of Demand (Sun brunch)
1	11.2%	8.0%
2	52.9%	23.7%
3	16.2%	14.5%
4	12.2%	22.4%
5	3.9%	10.2%
6	2.0%	7.7%
7	1.0%	5.2%
8	0.7%	8.3%

Summary		
Party Size	% of Demand (No brunch)	% of Demand (Sun brunch)
1-2	64.1%	31.7%
3-4	28.4%	36.90/o
5-6	5.8%	17.90/o
7-8	1.7%	13.5%

Figure 10.5 Example of a Party Size Distribution Analysis

SPREADSHEET EXERCISE 10.2

Kollam is a full-service Indian restaurant that serves lunch and dinner Tuesday–Sunday. You have one month of covers data, included in the Excel spreadsheet (a screenshot is provided below). You would like to determine the party size distribution of demand at Kollam for both lunch and dinner meal periods.

	A	B	C	D	E	F	G	H	I	J	K	L	M	N
1	LUNCH CHECKS										DINNER CHECKS			
2		Party Size										Party Size		
3	Day	1	2	3	4	5	6	7	8+		Day	1	2	3
4	1	2	11	13	9	8	1	1			1	10	13	26
5	2	5	14	22	12	3	5		1		2	9	13	21
6	3	1	21	9	15	2		1	2		3	8	21	22
7	4		26	10	11	4	1	2			4	2	26	9
8	5	3	17	10	13	2	2	3			5	5	24	15
9	6	6	14	26	18	3	4	1	3		6	11	22	35

TO DO

1. For each meal period, calculate the percentage of total demand for party sizes 1–8+.
2. Does the mix of party sizes differ between lunch and dinner?

Forecasting Demand

Accurate demand forecasts are essential to effective demand management because if an operator cannot anticipate demand, she cannot properly plan for it. Forecasting demand is already done in restaurants as it serves as the basis for staffing decisions and raw ingredient purchases. Most restaurants already forecast demand in the form of covers or the number of dinners expected to be served per night. In an RRM analysis, this forecast is evaluated for accuracy and how it accounts for elements including: Time, demand characteristics, like party size or purpose of visit, and distribution channel differences.

Forecast Considerations

The time horizon of the forecast is a basic consideration in evaluating a forecast for RRM purposes. Common options are yearly, quarterly, monthly, weekly, and daily. In general, longer forecast horizons are associated with less accurate forecasts. So, forecasts made today for 10 years in advance will not be as reliable as forecasts made for next month. The appropriate forecast horizon depends on the restaurant situation but all forecasts should be updated as time progresses.

Another aspect of restaurant forecasts that should be noted relates to a technical element of forecasting. Specifically, forecasts use past arrivals data to predict future demand. One aspect of demand that most arrivals data does not include is the number of customers who intended to purchase service from the restaurant but left before they did. Actual demand plus this intended demand (often referred to as Additional Demand in the hotel world) unconstrained demand. Intended demand represents the demand that was not able to be processed by the restaurant.

Obtaining accurate unconstrained demand data is not a simple task. Consider a restaurant operating in a Food Court at a suburban U.S. shopping mall. Unconstrained demand for a restaurant for a Saturday lunch service would be the actual customers served plus possible customers—the number of customers who paused and read the menu board but ultimately did not order. Collecting this type of unconstrained data could be done by manual observation but this is time-consuming and still does not entirely precise.

Many restaurants have websites and/or participate in an online restaurant network like OpenTable. Often, interest in a restaurant can be gauged using "clicks," or the number of times a user looks at a restaurant's page or searches for a table. However, this can greatly overestimate demand, as many clicks come from information-gathering and were never serious demand inquiries.

Forecast Methods

Qualitative forecasting methods use intuition, judgment, and information to estimate future demand. Methods of qualitative forecasting include:

- Executive judgment: Relying on a manager's years of experience to forecast demand.
- Grass roots: Having those in closest contact with customers, such as servers and hosts, forecast demand.
- Market research: Using gathered information on competitors, area demographics, and local economic conditions to forecast demand

- Panel consensus: Having experts use market research information to agree on a forecast.

RRM is a data-driven field, so an RRM program would advocate using more data-driven forecasting methods, which generally result in more accurate forecasts. Quantitative forecasting methods can be classified as either time-series or causal.

- Time-series forecasts use past data and historical patterns to forecast future performance. Time-series forecasts use only past information from the same data series; for instance, restaurant demand for next week's forecast uses only demand from past weeks.
- Causal forecasts use past data plus additional external information to predict future demand. For example, demand is forecast using past data plus extra factors such as weather, local hotel occupancy, and area happenings.

If restaurant demand data shows no trend and no pattern, then a simple time series method called the simple moving average—where the forecast for the next period is simply the average of the data from the last several periods—can be used to forecast future demand. If restaurant demand data shows no trend but does have a pattern, time series methods that are more appropriate for forecasting include the weighted moving average and exponential smoothing. The forecast from either of these methods is a weighted average of past data, so more important periods have more weight in determining the forecast.

For restaurant demand data with a trend, more complicated causal methods are appropriate to use for forecasting. These include trend-adjusted exponential smoothing, simple linear regression, and multiple linear regression. All of these methods use historical data instead of averages or smoothed averages and use mathematical equations and models to forecast future performance. This advanced level of statistics is outside the scope of this chapter.

The forecast method a restaurant uses is often based on factors in addition to trends and patterns in data. Other considerations include the anticipated use of the forecast, data availability, and data reliability. Certainly, though, the best method to use is the one that produces the most accurate forecast.

Forecasts are checked for accuracy by measuring the error between what actually happened and what the forecast projected would happen. For instance, if the forecast for June sales at Sal's Hotdog Stand was $3,000 and Sal only sold $2,600 worth of dogs, the forecast error would be +$400. Many different measures can be determined from this simple error data, including the cumulative forecast error, bias, mean squared error, mean absolute deviation, and mean absolute percent error. All of these error measures help reveal the strengths and weaknesses of the different forecasting methods depending on a restaurant's particular demand and operating characteristics.

Waiting Lines

Queuing theory is the mathematical study of queues, also known as waiting lines. A waiting line is made up of arriving customers that cannot be served right away. The benefit to a service of having waiting lines is that customers are essentially inventoried demand waiting to be served by the system when it has the capacity. However, customers notoriously dislike waiting lines and often include the presence or absence of a line in purchase decisions.

Why They Happen

Even with excellent forecasting, all restaurants face some variability in their service systems. Waiting lines occur because of this variability and particularly the uncertainty in the

- size of demand and the timing of arrivals for a service,
- duration of a service,
- behavior of customers as they arrive and wait in line for the service.

To understand to what extent waiting lines will occur, it is helpful to compare the rate at which customers arrive at a service and the rate at which customers can be processed by the service. The Greek letters lambda (λ) and mu (μ) are always used to denote average arrival rate and average service rate in queuing theory:

λ = arrival rate = rate at which customers arrive

μ = service rate = rate at which customers are served

Compare the two rates. If

- λ and μ are almost equal, then systems will sometimes develop long waiting lines, will sometimes have no waiting lines, and will have average-size waiting lines most of the time,
- λ is much greater than μ, then the system will eventually collapse because more customers are arriving than can be processed,
- λ is much less than μ, then the system will not experience waits but will likely not be making a profit if not enough customers are arriving.

For example, customers arrive to Yuma Smoothie Shop at a rate of 15 per 30 min. Customers are served at a rate of 14 per 30 min. The arrival rate (per 30 min) is $\lambda = 15$. The service rate (per 30 min) is $\mu = 14$. λ and μ are almost equal with customers arriving a little faster than they can be served, so Yuma Smoothie Shop usually has a short line.

QUESTION TO CONSIDER

A small pub can serve, on average, 10 customers per hour. If its arrival rate is 6, would it have a waiting line?

A mall bistro has an arrival rate of 32 customers per hour during peak times. If its service rate is 22, does it have a waiting line? How could this situation be remedied?

Line Terms and Types

Lines are characterized by quantity (single or multiple lines) and server (single or multiple servers). Common types of lines are as follows:

- Single line, single server (e.g., single-register coffee shop)
- Single line, multiple servers (e.g., bank, post office)
- Multiple lines, multiple servers (e.g., toll booth, grocery store)

A hybrid line combines line types at different stages of the wait. An example of a hybrid line is the line for an airline check-in system—it includes a single-line, multiple-server component for coach passengers and a single-line, single-server component for first-class passengers.

Three terms—balk, renege, and jockey—are commonly used to talk about the behavior of customers with regards to waiting lines.

- Customers balk when they decide not to join a line, even though they had intended on purchasing the service at the end of the line.
- Customers renege when they leave a line after they have joined it but before they purchased the intended service.
- Customers jockey when they leave a line and join another, anticipating that the new line will be shorter than the old one.

Many larger F&B outlets face a choice between the single line, multiple servers and multiple lines, multiple servers types. The pros and cons for both are as follows:

Line Type	**Pros**	**Cons**
Single line, multiple server	- Fair since customers are served first come-first served - Lines appear to move fast - No jockeying occurs - Transactions are more private	- Line looks long - Takes a lot of space to accommodate
Multiple lines, multiple servers	- Can save space - Lines look shorter, so there is less balking	- Unfair since the first customers are not guaranteed to be the first served

Psychology of Waiting Lines

Along with the quantitative theories and calculations available to understand waiting lines, plenty of research has been conducted on how customers react and respond to waiting. In general, customers try to avoid waiting; it increases the investment a customer makes in a transaction, prevents the customer from using that time more productively, and can actually cause psychological pain (Schwartz, 1975).

Many researchers agree on the following eight propositions related to waiting lines (Dube-Rioux et al., 1989; Maister, 1985; McGuire et al., 2010):

1. Unoccupied time feels longer than occupied time: Businesses often use strategies to combat this; for instance, amusement parks use televisions mounted near lines for rides and spas occupy customers by having them wait in a serenity room with additional distractions.
2. Preprocess waits feel longer than in-process waits: It feels longer to wait for a bartender to take an order than for him/her to deliver the drink, regardless of whether the time to do both tasks was equal.
3. Anxiety makes waits seem longer: People perceive the wait at a doctor's office to be longer than the wait at a salon.
4. Uncertain waits feel longer than certain waits: Many call centers try to alleviate this by automatically telling a customer his estimated wait. Restaurants also use this strategy when hosts quote wait times to arriving parties.
5. Unexplained waits feel longer than explained waits: Often, businesses inform customers on operations and issues to increase wait-time tolerance. Think of how a pilot update passengers when the wait on the runway begins to feel too long.
6. Unfair waits feel longer than fair waits: Providing roped areas for lines helps customers monitor the fairness of the lines themselves. Also, training employees with standard operating procedures (such as not spending more than 30 s on a phone call if a customer is waiting in-person) is another strategy that addresses this.
7. The more valuable the service, the longer the customer will wait: Customers are more tolerant of waiting in line on December 26 to pay for items on sale than they were two days before when paying full price.
8. Solo waits feel longer than group waits.

Wait list Management

In a sit-down restaurant, when all tables are occupied, the next party to be seated starts a waiting line. At this point, many restaurants simply record a name and party size for customers(s) waiting for a table in the order of arrival, thus creating a wait list. Managing the wait list entails trying to match party and table sizes while maintaining the FCFS rule, quoting accurate and reliable wait times, communicating with customers, preserving customer satisfaction, and essentially ensuring that the inventoried demand is available to be processed when supply is unoccupied.

A number of different tactics can be used to manage a restaurant wait list. Many restaurants use buzzers to alert a party when its table is available; this technique helps mask any violations of the FCFS rule and can thus help the restaurant better match party—to table size. Another wait list management technique is to use a boarding pass system, which is a two-wait system; customers wait in one line to receive a boarding pass and then in another line—perhaps even at another time—to "board" the restaurant. The total wait is split up, making it seem shorter, and customer time is occupied, which also makes a wait seem shorter. Call-ahead seating allows for virtual waits, so customers can use their time waiting for a table in a more valuable manner, which should cultivate repeat business from customers.

SUMMARY

The demand side of RRM is concerned with the number, type, and profitability of customers that frequent a restaurant. Operators have less control over demand than they do capacity, so understanding and applying demand management tools and strategies can help a restaurateur operate more effectively and maximize profitability. Practices that influence the timing of demand and/or the services demanded must work in harmony with capacity management to avoid suboptimal RM solutions.

DISCUSSION QUESTIONS

1. Customers arrive to the drive-thru window at the Coffee Hut every 2 min. What is the arrival rate per hour? If the staff at the drive-thru can process a customer in 45 s, what is the service rate per hour at the Coffee Hut?

   What can you deduce about the line at the drive-thru window?

2. Taking reservations is one way a service business can try to reduce the uncertainty of arrivals. Predicting when a customer is going to walk in the door could help management precisely plan and manage an experience that delights a customer in the most efficient and cost-effective way.

   For a restaurant, however, taking a dinner reservation does not reduce arrival uncertainty as much as it does for a hotel that takes a room reservation. Explain some reasons for this.

3. Calculate the contribution margin for each entrée in the following table. Average the three contribution margins together and compare the average to each entrée. Which entree has above- average contribution margins? Which entrées have below-average margins?

entrée	**Price**	**Food Cost (%)**
Halibut	$25	38%
Pork chops	$16	32%
Petite filet	$34	40%

4. Demand at Curet, a restaurant in Los Angeles, can be categorized in a number of ways. Looking at demand by day of week yields different information to the dining room manager than does looking at demand by party size or by time-of-day. What are some other classifications of demand that may be helpful for an RRM analysis?

5. Sketch a visual of these two types of lines:
   - one line, three servers;
   - two-stage line with Stage 1: Three lines, three servers; Stage 2: One line, two servers.

APPLICATIONS

Cayuga Catering

Cayuga Quick Grub has one drive-through window to serve its customers. A study of the lunch hours found that cars arrive to the speaker at a rate of four cars every 30 min. Data on drive-through times has shown that the time it takes for people to place an order at the speaker, proceed to the window to pay for the order and collect the order at the window averages about 6 min per car. Determine the arrival rate and service rate for the drive-through window process and comment on the waiting line situation at the drive-through.

Northman's

Pete Abrams is the owner of a very successful middle-tier restaurant called Northman's in San Francisco. Pete and the dining room manager, Sandy, are hoping to develop an appropriate and effective wait list management plan for Northman's. Unfortunately, Pete and Sandy do not agree on the following two main issues:

- Whether or not to use call-ahead seating.
- How to seat parties—on an FCFS basis or on a match-party-size-to-table-size basis (right sizing)?

Sandy does not want to use call-ahead seating or right-sizing; she is adamant that customers will be very angry if a party that entered after them is seated first. Pete thinks both of these practices would be beneficial in decreasing wait times, preserving customer satisfaction, and fulfilling as much demand as possible in a timely manner.

Help Pete by providing support for the use of call-ahead seating and right-sizing. Answer questions such as: How would wait times likely be impacted under both strategies? How could the issue of potentially angry customers be handled?

TEAM ACTIVITY

This case should be completed in teams of two to three. Imagine that all the members of your team have been hired into Royale Casino's management program. Program members rotate working in different areas of the casino and you are assigned to manage the buffet restaurant while its general manager is on leave for the next 6 months.

After observing dinner operations for a few days, your team notices the following things:

- Demand is very strong from 5:30 p.m. to 7:00 p.m., and customers wait for what seems to be a long period of time. Customers do not look happy in line.
- During peak hours, tables are only unoccupied when waiting to be bussed and then waiting to be seated.
- Lots of customers balk and renege, especially after being quoted the wait time.
- Demand builds up slowly to 5:30 p.m. but falls off quickly after 7:00 p.m.

Customers arrive at the buffet and wait in line to pay one of two cashers. They then snake through a roped-off line in a large holding area. At the front of this line, each party chooses to join one of three very short lines, each headed up by a host. The floor manager finds an unoccupied table for the party and informs the host of the table assignment. The host then takes the party to its table.

On the basis of this information, recommend some demand management strategies for the restaurant. What additional information would you need to ensure that these strategies are appropriate for the situation? What additional information would you need to determine how to customize these strategies?

INTERNET ACTIVITY

Do an Internet search for "restaurant group coupons." Did you find any discounts that seemed too good to be true for you, the customer? Assume that the going rate for a restaurant to participate in a group coupon is 50 percent of the amount charged. For example, if a coupon allows a customer to purchase a $30 meal for $15, the restaurant pays the coupon site half of that, or $7.50. On the basis of this, did you find any "deals" that are likely to negatively impact the restaurant's bottom line?

GLOSSARY

Balk – When customers who had intended on joining a system do not do so once they see the line.

Contribution margin – The profitability of a menu item, measured by its price less its food cost.

Data patterns – Consistent ups and downs in data over the short to medium term.

Data trends – Consistent ups and downs in data over a long period of time.

Jockey – When customers leave one line to join an- other line.

Renege – When customers leave a line before being served.

Unconstrained demand – The total demand in a segment or overall in the absence of any constraints.

Variable pricing – The practice of charging different prices to different customers.

REFERENCES

Clifford, S. (2012, September 4). When it Comes to Reservations, Time is Money. *The New York Times*. Retrieved from http://www.nytimes.com.

Croxton, K., Lambert, D., García-Dastugue, S., & Rogers, D. (2002). The demand management process. *The International Journal of Logistics Management, 13* (2), 51–66.

Dube-Rioux, L., Schmitt, B., & Leclerc, F. L. (1989). Consumers' Reactions to Waiting: When Delays Affect the Perception of Service Quality. *Advances in Consumer Research, 16*, 59–63.

Kimes, S. (1989). Yield Management: A Tool for Capacity-constrained Service Firms. *Journal of Operations Management, 8* (4): 348–363.

Kimes, S., & Chase, R. (1998). The Strategic Levers of Yield Management. *Journal of Service Research, 1* (2), 156–166.

Kimes, S., Chase, R., Choi, S., Lee, P., & Ngonzi, E. (1998). Restaurant Revenue Management: Applying Yield Management to the Restaurant Industry. *Cornell Hotel and Restaurant Administration Quarterly, 39* (3), 32–39.

Kimes, S., & Wirtz, J. (2003). Has Revenue Management Become Acceptable? Findings from an International Study on the Perceived Fairness of Rate Fences. *Journal of Service Research*, 6 (2), 125–135.

Maister, D. (1985). *The Psychology of Waiting Lines* [White paper]. Retrieved June 16, 2001 from davidmaister.com/articles

McGuire, K., Kimes, S., Lynn, M., Pullman, M., & Lloyd, R. (2010). A Framework for Evaluating the Customer Wait Experience. *Journal of Service Management, 21* (3), 269–290.

McGuire, K., & Rohlfs, K. (2005). *Wait List Management: A Simulation Study.* Paper Presented at the HEC 80 Conference, Ithaca, NY.

Noone, B., Kimes, S., Mattila, A., & Wirtz, J. (2007). The Effect of meal pace on Customer Satisfaction. *Cornell Hotel and Restaurant Administration Quarterly, 48* (3), 231–244.

Schwartz, B. (1975). *Queuing and Waiting.* Chicago: University of Chicago Press.

Simon, H., & Dolan, R. (1999). Price Customization. *The Journal of Professional Pricing, 7* (3), 15–18.

CHAPTER 11

Restaurant Revenue Management: Advanced Supply Management Concepts

Kristin V. Rohlfs

OVERVIEW

The objective of Restaurant Revenue Management (RRM) is to ensure that the capacity offered by a restaurant serves the demand for a restaurant in the most profitable way. The capacity side of the RRM equation is usually under the control of the restaurant operator to a greater extent than the demand side. This chapter covers the aspects of RRM related to supply.

LEARNING OBJECTIVES

After studying this chapter, you should be able to evaluate restaurant supply in the context of RRM. Specifically, you should be able to:

- Relate capacity planning and capacity management to RRM
- Explain ways in which optimizing capacity usage leads to maximizing revenue
- Perform an analysis of both occupancy and dining duration
- Construct and perform a table mix analysis
- Name several RRM solutions to possible supply side issues

OUTLINE

Introduction

Supply = Capacity

- Capacity Planning
- Capacity Management

Capacity in Restaurant Revenue Management

- Utilization = Occupancy
- Dining Duration
- Differences in Supply Offered
- Supply Mix
- Layout of Supply

Summary

Discussion Questions

Applications

- Vail Ski Mountain Resort
- Arepas
- Tacky Fingers

Team Activity

Internet Activity

Glossary

References

SO WHAT?

Some RRM research looks at how differences in what ***seem-to-be*** identical **physical inventory** units contribute to the goal of maximizing revenue (Rohlfs, 2009). For example, hotel rooms with one king, one queen, or two double beds are all considered standard rooms. And all seats in a restaurant seem to be identical, but they really differ by table type (e.g., banquette, round), table size (e.g., four-top, eight-top), and the amount of space tables take up (e.g., 45 square feet, 108 square feet).

In the context of RRM, space is defined as the physical area that is needed to put a unit of inventory into use. Space is an important facet of the RRM problem since some physical inventory units (e.g., 8-tops) take up more space than other physical inventory units (e.g., 2-tops). So, a restaurant may be able to capture more revenue if it takes space into account when determining its capacity profile.

To understand better, imagine this scenario:

You are planning a restaurant and tell your designer to allot 15 square feet of space for each seat. A portion of the drawing she gives you is shown below. You are surprised at how tiny the two-tops look next to the six-tops. What do you think is the problem with the drawing?

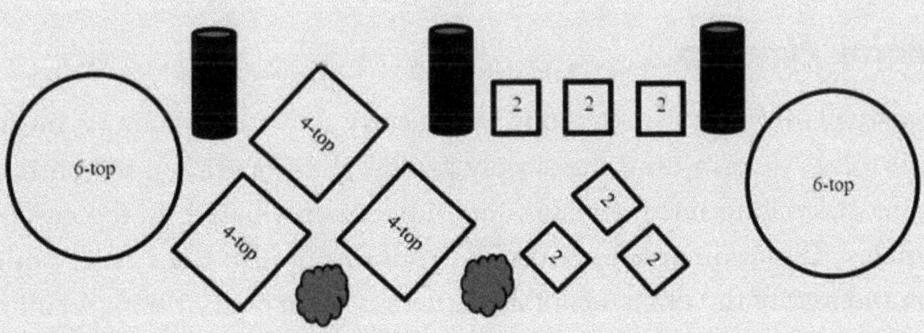

INTRODUCTION

RRM practices can optimize the revenue that a restaurant generates over a period of time. RRM combines elements of both demand and supply management in an effort to influence how and when demand occurs and how it is processed by the service system once it arrives. For the most part, operators have more control over what is supplied to customers demand from operators.

This chapter focuses on the supply side of RRM. Because RRM aims to increase top-line revenues generated by an operation, it has traditionally focused on front-of-house (FOH) concerns. Accordingly, supply in an RRM context generally does not mean the raw ingredients needed to provide food to customers. Instead, supply refers to the dining experience provided to customers—the food plus the time and effort spent doing actions in a restaurant, such as entering, ordering, receiving, consuming, paying, and exiting.

SUPPLY = CAPACITY

Supply—also known as **service capacity**—is the amount of output a service system can produce (Lovelock, 1984). The capacity of a service can be defined and measured in different ways, including the level at which full inputs are used, the point at which a bottleneck develops, or the maximum output that can be produced in a specified time period. For a restaurant, capacity could involve factors such as employees, seats, tables, and kitchen capabilities. In RRM, the capacity of a full-service/sit-down restaurant is usually measured by the total number of seats in its dining room available to be sold. Because restaurants have a time element, a sit-down restaurant could also measure capacity by seat hours.

Capacity Planning

Capacity planning is usually done in the early stages of opening a business and involves determining the supply profile of an operation which means making risky, long-term decisions and investments based on forecasts and estimates. The optimal supply profile would minimize the costs of operations and satisfy the demands of customers (Eppen et al., 1989). A full supply profile has many long- and short-term elements, including: location of facility, size and layout of facility, space allocation for production/customer use, type/amount/mix of physical inventory, service process design, flexibility in service system, and employee/staffing requirements.

Many aspects of a restaurant's long-term supply profile are determined by corporate standards, site location and availability, opportunity, competition, and estimation (Bradach, 1997). The aspects of capacity planning most relevant to day-to-day RRM are shorter-term decisions that pertain to FOH operations, such as: the amount of physical inventory (seats and tables) put into use and the space allocated (to the dining room). Determining the optimal, or "right," amount of physical inventory can be especially important for a service because there is no significant buffer between production and consumption.

Capacity Management

For a service system, capacity management follows capacity planning, as long-term decisions about the supply drive the real-time management of supply. The goal of capacity management is operate a system in a way that maximizes the amount of revenue the system can generate, without compromising quality and increasing costs.

Capacity management helps services use the four types of resources—equipment, employees, facilities, and information—as productively as possible. Using resources is expensive for a restaurant, as they generally account for most of the costs associated with operating a restaurant (taxes, insurance, and rent are excluded). Resource costs can be fixed (e.g., manager salaries) or variable (e.g., server wages, paper goods, and food costs). An additional cost of using resources is the opportunity cost of forfeited revenue if no resource is available to do its part in the service delivery system and fulfill demand.

Restaurant resources, or inventory, can be classified as either physical or nonphysical. **Nonphysical inventory**—employees and information—are needed to produce a service, but are not dedicated to one customer at a time. Examples of nonphysical resources are servers, cooks, and ambience. **Physical inventory**—equipment and facilities—is also needed to produce a service experience for customers. Physical resources can be shared, such as ovens and tables, or dedicated to one customer at a time, such as seats and silverware rolls.

Two traditional strategies for managing resources are the chase and the constant methods. The *chase method* calls for using flexible capacity so that a delivery system can respond quickly and easily to demand (Johnston, 1999; Sasser, 1976). Essentially, supply is supposed to "chase" demand. Trademark chase techniques include using shared equipment, scheduling short-term employees, and increasing customer participation in the service delivery process.

The *constant method* involves operating with a fixed amount of capacity. Supply is held at a constant level, and in manufacturing, all output not immediately sold is put into inventory (Crandall & Markland, 1996; Sasser, 1976). Constant method strategies include operating under a long-run outlook, and using skilled, permanent workers.

THINK HISTORICALLY

The nature of services—specifically, their immediacy and inherent lack of an inventory cushion—requires mixing aspects of the chase and the constant methods. Services that can effectively mix the strategies can keep costs down and support an agile service system that reacts well to variations in demand (Sasser, 1976). Traditional chase strategies that have long been used by restaurants include eliminating service bottle-necks and opening earlier/staying open later. A more contemporary strategy used to help supply react better to demand is opening a "next-door" add-on restaurant adjacent to a popular counterpart.

Traditional constant strategies utilized in restaurants include seating customers only at certain times, offering incentives to encourage customers to vacate tables as needed, and offering limited menus during the busiest times. A more contemporary constant strategy used by many restaurants is waitlist management, which focuses on making waits more expected, comfortable, and acceptable to customers.

A chase strategy frequently used in high-capacity restaurants is opening and closing dining room sections as needed. What are some other chase strategies used in restaurants today?

A constant strategy frequently used by all types of full-service restaurants is taking reservations. What are some other constant strategies used in restaurant today?

The footprint of a restaurant (the space allocated to the kitchen, dining room, restrooms, etc.) is not easily altered in a way that could considerably change the number of customers who can fit at any given time. Because of this, total restaurant capacity is substantially fixed and it would seem that restaurants should follow the constant strategy for capacity management. However, restaurants have a higher level of flexibility in their capacity than many other services. If necessary, a restaurant can add another table or seat to its inventory to fulfill demand without incurring a significant additional cost, which is a chase capacity management strategy.

The complexity of managing the capacity of service business varies. A reservations-only restaurant is an example of a less complex capacity management situation. Predictable demand and flexible resources are characteristics of generally straightforward capacity management. Ordering and scheduling of resources can be completed with much more accuracy if demand is known ahead of time.

More complex examples of capacity management situations include a full-service casino or an expansive theme park. Volatility in demand and fixed resources usually make managing capacity much more complicated. There are also usually many more resources to be managed, and planning around a variable demand pattern is not easy.

QUESTION TO CONSIDER

A factor that impacts the management of all capacity is customer involvement in the service process. In reality, customers often unknowingly manage capacity themselves. Think about this situation: you are planning a visit to a very popular theme park on the most crowded day of the year. One strategy you consider to avoid the largest crowds, and make your time at the park more enjoyable, is to visit the park later in the evening. This strategy also benefits the park because you are effectively moving your use of the park facilities to times that could better accommodate you.

What are some other strategies you could consider to make the most of your planned visit to the theme park? How do these strategies also help the park manage capacity?

CAPACITY IN RESTAURANT REVENUE MANAGEMENT

The supply side of RRM focuses on optimizing how and when restaurant capacity is used for the objective of maximizing revenue. Traditionally, RRM has been most useful when a service is operating at, or close to, capacity. As RM has evolved into a more strategic, customer-centric discipline, tools and techniques have expanded to include those that help in creating and managing demand when capacity is not being highly utilized (Cross et al., 2009).

As in all areas of RRM, evaluating supply requires collecting and analyzing pertinent data. The operating situations of a restaurant will dictate the level of detail required and the data available. Different RRM programs involve different amounts and types of data. In addition to information on the supply profile, supply side measures used in the analysis of the physical inventory of a restaurant include: table occupancy, seat occupancy, demand mix by party size, and dining duration by party size.

REAL PEOPLE

Isaac Cohen understands all too well that behind any restaurant that uses RRM is good data. Isaac is a sales director at a leading company that develops and provides technology and data systems to assemble and analyze information from a restaurant's point-of-sale (POS) system, making it a great platform to help get the data needed to perform an accurate and meaningful RRM analysis.

According to Isaac, "Sometimes, new customers express unease over the 'wall of numbers' that comes with RRM. Nowadays, getting the numbers is easier. Training owners and managers how to appropriately and accurately interpret them is now a focus."

Do you see RRM as an overwhelming "wall of numbers"? Or do you find exploring data to be interesting? If you were a restaurant owner and felt the first way, what qualifications would you look for if you hired someone to apply RRM to your establishment(s)?

Utilization = Occupancy

Utilization—known as occupancy - measures how efficiently physical capacity in a restaurant is being used. Two occupancy measures—*table occupancy* and *seat occupancy*—help track how well the physical inventory of the service is working. The two measurements are both important, because although seats are the smallest inventory unit in a restaurant system that can generate revenue, they are situated at tables, which are the actual units sold in most restaurants. The formulas for these occupancies are:

$$\text{Seat Occupancy per Time Period} = \frac{\text{Customers Served per Time Period}}{\text{\# of Seats}}$$

$$\text{Table Occupancy per Time Period} = \frac{\text{Parties Served per Time Period}}{\text{\# of Tables}}$$

Many restaurant operators are familiar with seat occupancy and calculate seat occupancy by:

- Summing the number of covers for a time range, with covers being defined as the number of people whose check was opened during that time range (e.g., a party of 4,seated at a six-top at 6:35 p.m. would translate to 4 covers in the time range of 6:00–6:59 p.m.)
- And then dividing this number by the total number of seats in the restaurant.

PROS & CONS

The Pizza Factory is located in a popular shopping mall in Dallas, TX. It is one of the most successful restaurants in the area, with table occupancy hovering around 95%. The wait for a table averages 60 min at lunchtime and 90 min during dinner hours.

Lemongrass Grill is located in the same mall as The Pizza Factory. It is not nearly as busy, with an overall table occupancy around 35%. Lemongrass Grill rarely has a wait, and often has a group of staff standing idle at the entrance.

What are the pros and cons of a 95% occupancy for: the wait staff, the kitchen, the customers, and the reputation of The Pizza Factory?

What are the pros and cons of a 35% occupancy for: the wait staff, the kitchen, the customers, and the reputation of Lemongrass Grill?

Occupancy is linked to a time period, and depending on how it is calculated, represents either a snapshot in time or a picture over a time range. For example, the occupancy at Em's Café *at* 5:00 p.m. is 60 percent because 39 of the 65 seats on the dining-room floor have customers in them. However, occupancy at Em's Café *from* 5:00 to 6:00 p.m. is only 27 percent. This is because 20 customers exited the restaurant between 5:00 and 5:14 p.m., 10 more left by 5:29 p.m., and an additional 6 were gone by 5:44 p.m. Averaging the occupancies for each of these 15-min snapshots gives the occupancy *from* 5:00 p.m. to 6:00 p.m., which is quite different from the occupancy *at* 5:00 p.m.

Occupancy at 5:00 = 39/65=60%
Occupancy at 5:15 = 19/65=29%
Occupancy at 5:30 = 9/65 =14%
Occupancy at 6:00 = 3/65 = 5%
Average = 27%

An example of calculating *at* occupancy is as follows: Paprika is a 276-seat restaurant that has 64 tables. Every day for 3 months, the host counts the number of seats and the number of tables occupied at 6:00, 7:00, 8:00, and 9:00 p.m. She averages the data by day-of-week and hour, which results in the following operating statistics for Saturday nights:

Hour	Seats occupied	Tables occupied	Seat occupancy*	Table occupancy*
6 p.m.	169	50	61%	78%
7 p.m.	200	64	72%	100%
8 p.m.	153	51	55%	80%
9 p.m.	104	27	38%	42%

*Overall occupancy at the beginning of the hour

Another way to determine occupancy *over* a time period is to collect check and cover data *at* a certain time and then adjust it to account for customers who began the service in one time period, but ended in the next. A measure of duration can be used as a proxy for this adjustment.

Regardless of the method used, occupancy calculations should always be clearly labeled by the time or time range they represent or else data could be misinterpreted. Additionally, a consecutive string of occupancy figures provides insight into trends in physical inventory utilization.

In most RRM programs, calculating occupancy by day-of-week and hour is sufficient. However, restaurants with short dining durations may benefit from understanding average occupancy by 15-min periods. Additionally, calculating restaurant occupancy by table type can yield useful information, especially when analyzed in conjunction with spend by table type.

When analyzing occupancy of the same dining room over time—such as month-to-month—an increase in seat occupancy means that capacity is being utilized more effectively, so more customers are moving through the restaurant system. A decrease in seat occupancy signals that fewer customers have been served over the time period, which could be the result of a breakdown in operations or changes in customer demand.

SPREADSHEET EXERCISE 11.1

Crow & Steel, a 980-seat, high-volume breakfast buffet in Las Vegas, NV has hired you to develop an RRM program. You are developing the baseline for your analysis and need to calculate and graph both table and seat occupancy. Cover and check data are included in the Excel spreadsheet. Screenshots of the Excel file are:

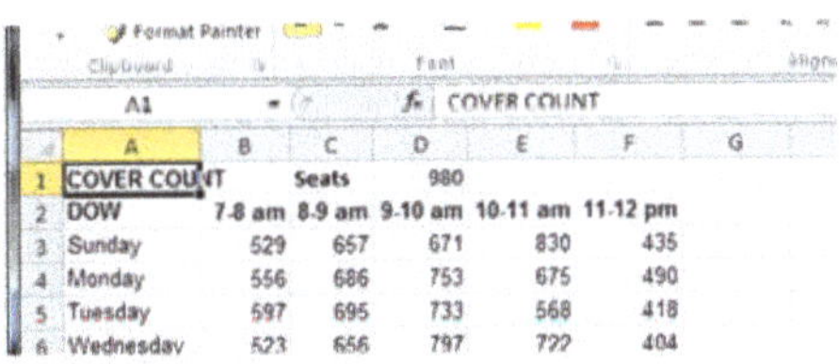

	A	B	C	D	E	F
1	COVER COUNT		Seats	980		
2	DOW	7-8 am	8-9 am	9-10 am	10-11 am	11-12 pm
3	Sunday	529	657	671	830	435
4	Monday	556	686	753	675	490
5	Tuesday	597	695	733	568	418
6	Wednesday	523	656	797	722	404

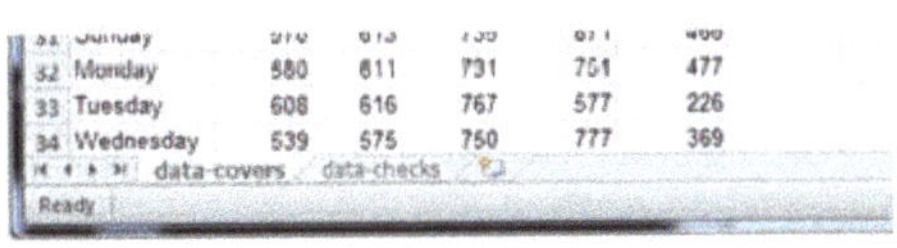

32	Monday	580	611	731	751	477
33	Tuesday	608	616	767	577	226
34	Wednesday	539	575	750	777	369

Crow & Steel has 300 tables, and the table mix is as follows:
150 two-tops; 120 four-tops; 20 six-tops, and 10 eight-tops

TO DO:

1. Average the Number of Checks by hour and day-of-week. Assume duration is 1 h/table. Calculate the overall table occupancy by hour and day-of-week.
2. Average the Number of Covers by hour and day-of-week. Assume duration is 1 h/table. Calculate the overall seat occupancy by hour and day-of-week.

Dining Duration

A party occupies a table at a restaurant for the duration of a meal; this means a table (and its corresponding number of seats) is taken out of the physical inventory available to serve other customers. Dining duration is significant in RRM because effectively, in addition to selling an actual meal, a restaurant is selling the use of one or more of its physical inventory units for a period of time (Kimes et al., 1998). So if an operator is able to control the time a customer occupies a seat at her restaurant, she can better manage RevPASH.

Duration of any restaurant service experience is unpredictable. Upon entering a restaurant, no customer could precisely answer the question: how long will you be sitting at your table? Most restaurateurs are able to provide a good estimate of how long any meal would take at their establishment. However, approaching the issue of dining duration from the angle of "how is physical inventory used" yields insight into how well a restaurant is operating and if it is making as much money as it could be.

Dining duration is a function of several factors, including:

Front-of-House	Back-of-House	Customers
Individual servers	Equipment	Expectations
Server responsibilities	Staffing	Preferences
Level of staffing	Menu	Party size

Measuring Duration

The data used to calculate dining duration are usually gathered from the POS system. If duration is not automatically computed by the POS, this simple formula can be used to determine for dining duration:

Dining duration = The Time a Check is Closed by Processing Payment – The Time a Check is Opened in the System

The mean and standard deviation of dining duration are the statistics of most interest in RRM. The mean simply reflects how long a table is occupied, on average, over many transactions. The standard deviation measures variability—to what extent the length of time a table is occupied—over many transactions.

Duration times calculated using POS data are not always completely accurate. Some activities keep a table occupied but are not captured by the POS data. These include the time it takes for a server to greet a table and open its check in the POS system and the time a party at a table lingers after its check has been closed. So measuring duration using POS data can understate the true amount of time a physical inventory unit is in use.

In addition, using POS data does not provide information about the steps in the dining process. Studying a process by breaking it into smaller elements is a technique that dates back to Frederick Taylor, the "father" of scientific management, in 1881. It is applicable here because understanding which activities within the dining process take the longest and/or vary the most can help isolate problems and identify areas that can be improved. Performing a manual time study provides the needed information.

The procedure for performing a time study is easy:

1. Determine the steps of the dining process to include.
2. Develop a worksheet for data collection that has spaces for each piece of information that should be noted about each observation.
3. At the restaurant, select several tables to observe and note the clock time at which each stage of the dining process begins for each table.

Duration is usually measured by day-of-week, meal part, and party size. As usual, a minimum of 30 observations for each day-of-week and each meal part under study should be collected for a statistically sound analysis. More observations result in more accurate analyses.

The steps to include in a time study depend on the individual restaurant. Some common steps include:

- Seating
- Taking drink orders
- Drink delivery
- Taking food orders
- Appetizer delivery
- Entrée delivery
- Offering dessert and coffee
- Taking dessert orders
- Dessert delivery
- Check presentation
- Check pickup
- Check return
- Departure
- Bussing table
- Resetting table

A sample of a portion of a completed time study is provided in Exhibit 1.

Table #	Party size	Time										
		Party seated	Drink order taken	Drink delivery	Food order taken	Appetizer delivery	Entrée delivery	Check dropped	Check picked up	Check returned	Party departure	Table bussed and reset
17	2	6:31:30	6:33:01	6:35:22	6:35:57	6:42:31	6:51:10	7:12:02	7:14:23	7:18:32	7:19:18	7:21:04
20	3	6:33:59	6:34:58	6:37:19	6:40:46		6:50:25	7:07:18	7:12:06		7:15:55	7:20:46
21	6	6:36:04	6:38:11	6:41:01	6:42:29	6:49:15	6:59:18	7:25:47	7:31:35	7:34:48	7:36:04	7:39:15
19	4	6:39:27	6:41:33	6:45:50	6:47:17	6:53:00	7:02:43	7:18:32	7:21:12		7:23:46	7:25:02
17	2	7:22:45	7:24:24	7:28:13	7:29:48		7:41:31	7:59:34	7:59:59	8:02:13	8:03:55	8:06:28

Exhibit 1: Example of a Time Study Worksheet

QUESTION TO CONSIDER

You extracted data from your restaurant's POS to calculate dining duration for each day of the week. You scrubbed the data for problems, and of the 1200 transactions you pulled, you found four outliers—observations that are noticeably unlike the rest of the data in some manner. The outliers are listed in the table.

Table identifier	Table size	Party size	Check opened	Check closed
Z2	4	4	8:16:08	11:58:49
X17	8	6	8:19:19	8:21:22
F1	4	9	8:25:30	9:29:00
Z9	2	1		

What is wrong with each of these data points? What should you do with them?

Analyzing Duration

A spreadsheet or other data-analysis program is used to calculate the desired metrics using the data collected from the POS and/or time study. There are three steps to a basic data analysis for a duration study:

1. Calculate the time spent on each activity for each observation.

   For example, the time from seat to greet = drink order taken−time seated and the total duration for each observation = departure−time seated.

2. Calculate the average and standard deviation for the overall dining process and for each activity. The mean, or average, reflects how long tables are generally occupied (and how long each activity takes) and the standard deviation measure show variable these average numbers are. Using the observations in Exhibit 1, Exhibit 2 gives examples of time measurements that may be of interest.

		Time Study Calculations						
Table#	**Party Size**	**Seat-to-Drink Order**	**Drink Order-to-Delivery**	**Food Order to-App. Delivery**	**Food Order-to-Eittree Delivery**	**Check Process**	**Total Time Customer Occupies Table**	**Bus Process**
17	2	0:01:31	0:02:21	0:06:34	0:15:13	0:06:30	0:47:48	0:01:46
20	3	0:00:59	0:02:21		0:09:39	0:04:48	0:41:56	0:04:51
21	6	0:02:07	0:02:50	0:06:46	0:16:49	0:09:01	1:00:00	0:03:11
19	4	0:02:06	0:04:17	0:05:43	0:15:26	0:02:40	0:44:19	0:01:16
17	2	0:01:39	0:03:49		0:11:43	0:02:39	0:41:10	0:02:33
Average		0:01:40	0:03:08	0:06:21	0:13:46	0:05:08	0:47:03	0:02:43
Standard Deviation		0:00:28	0:00:53	0:00:33	0:02:58	0:02:42	0:07:41	0:01:24

Exhibit 2: Example of a Time Study Spreadsheet Analysis

3. Determine average and standard deviation by other levels of detail desired, such as hour or party size. Exhibit 3 gives examples of ways to summarize the results of a dining duration analysis—by hour by party size and activities by party size.

	Dining Duration by Hour by Party Size									
	1	**2**	**3**	**4**	**5**	**6**	**7**	**8**	**9**	**10**
5PM	Avg: 58:39	Avg: 57:33	Avg: 55:38	Avg: 59:16	Avg: 59:38	Avg: 64:23	Avg: 74:01	Avg: 80:01	Avg: 86:36	Avg: 88:45
	SD: 5:16	SD: 8:01	SD:5:16	SD: 8:56	SD: 5:16	SD: 7:32	SD: 8:19	SD: 9:12	SD: 13:19	SD: 14:00
6PM	Avg:52:51	Avg: 52:33	Avg: 56:11	Avg: 59:01	Avg: 60:40	Avg: 63:54	Avg: 74.02	Avg: 75:26	Avg: 85:34	Avg: 89.23
	SD: 5:04	SD: 6:44	SD:5:15	SD: 7:31	SD: 8:08	SD: 8.23	SD: 8:19	SD: 10:19	SD: 12:59	SD: 15:46
7PM	Avg: 52:45	Avg: 63:09	Avg: 58:19	Avg: 60:52	Avg: 60:01	Avg: 65:13	Avg: 80:09	Avg: 89:06	Avg: 84:13	Avg: 90:15
	SD: 10:12	SD: 8:56	SD: 14:12	SD: 8:22	SD: 9.44	SD: 10.17	SD: 9:41	SD: 9:20	SD: 10:09	SD: 18:26

Exhibit 3a: Example of a Dining Duration Analysis

	Dining Duration by Steps in a Meal by Party Size					
	Seat-to-Greet		Order-to-Entrée Delivery		Check Delivery-to-Exit	
Party Size	Avg	Std Dev	Avg	Std Dev	Avg	Std Dev
1 -2	3:17	1:09	20:17	9:35	10:12	6:05
3-4	3:31	2:25	23:41	11:53	14:29	7:16
5-6	3:43	2:12	29:25	14:51	14:00	7:29
7 -8	4:00	2:38	36:26	15:40	16:26	8:07

Exhibit 3b: Example of a Dining Duration Analysis

Another useful metric in analyzing duration and its stages is Coefficient of Variation (CoV). The CoV scales the standard deviation for an activity by the size of its mean, so apples-to-apples comparisons of performance can be done across different processes.

As a rule of thumb, if the CoV is above 0.5, the process is likely a problem area and should be studied as soon as possible. If the CoV is below 0.5, the process is likely satisfactory.

The formula for CoV is:

Coefficient of Variation (CoV) = Standard Deviation/Average

An example of calculating the CoV is as follows: the check process at a restaurant takes 7 min, 45 sec on average and has a standard deviation of 5 min, 20 sec. The average duration of the seating process is 3 min, 20 sec, with a standard deviation of 1 min, 5 sec. The CoV calculation for each is:

CoV for the check process = 5:20/7:45 = 0.688

CoV for the seating process = 1:05/3:20 = 0.325

Notice that the CoV for the seating process is less than 0.5, while the CoV for the check process is greater than 0.5. The CoV rule of thumb would identify the check process as the problem area between these two processes.

CoV calculations are easily accomplished and only require two summary statistics for each process—average duration and standard deviation of duration. Recall the time study data from Exhibit 2, reprinted here:

		Time Study Calculations						
Table#	**Party Size**	**Seat-to-Drink Order**	**Drink Order-to-Delivery**	**Food Order to-App. Delivery**	**Food Order to-Elltree Delivery**	**Check Process**	**Total Time Customer Ocruples Table**	**Bus Process**
17	2	0:01:31	0:02:21	0:06:34	0:15:13	0:06:30	0:47:48	0:01:46
20	3	0:00:59	0:02:21		0:09:39	0:04:48	0:41:56	0:04:51
21	6	0:02:07	0:02:50	0:06:46	0:16:49	0:09:01	1:00:00	0:03:11
19	4	0:02:06	0:04:17	0:05:43	0:15:26	0:02:40	0:44:19	0:01:16
17	2	0:01:39	0:03:49		0:11:43	0:02:39	0:41:10	0:02:33
Average		0:01:40	0:03:08	0:06:21	0:13:46	0:05:08	0:47:03	0:02:43
Standard Deviation		0:00:28	0:00:53	0:00:33	0:02:58	0:02:42	0:07:41	0:01:24

Notice the average and standard deviation summary rows. A simple spreadsheet analysis of time study data provides the necessary data for the CoV calculation for each stage of the dining experience:

	Standard deviation	**/**	**Average duration**	**=**	CoV
Seat-to-drink order	0:00:28	/	0:01:40	=	0.28
Drink order-to-delivery	0:00:53	/	0:03:08	=	0.28
Food order-to-appetizer Delivery	0:00:33	/	0:06:21	=	0.09
food order-to-entrée Delivery	0:02:58	/	0:13:46	=	0.22
Check process	0:02:42	/	0:05:08	=	0.53
Bus process	0:01:24	/	0:02:43	=	0.52

A CoV >0.5 indicates that a process is too variable. Every process in a system will experience some variability, but a high CoV reflects excessive inconsistency in an area. In this example, this check and bus processes serve as good starting points to address and find potential opportunities to more effectively manage overall dining duration. For instance, in analyzing the check process in this example restaurant, it was found that the wait staff was not closing out checks immediately upon payment, which falsely increased the average of the process. In reality, the customer-centric portion of the check process was very efficient.

After pertinent duration metrics have been determined and calculated, they need to be understood and used to answer questions such as: *Why is that step in the process too long? Why is this process so variable? What is the bottle neck? Where should I put extra resources?*

SEEING FURTHER

Pam Artly, a new assistant manager at a well-established and popular restaurant, decided to take the initiative and use some RRM tools to examine issues the restaurant was having. After authorizing a lengthy time study, she analyzed dining duration and found a huge problem with the time between entrée and check delivery—the time that it was actually taking customers to eat. With a CoV of 0.867, the time to dine was extremely variable.

After using a fishbone diagram, Pam determined that the high CoV was caused by a combination of two things: including too many outliers in the analysis and the check-dropping process. In fact, Pam found so many outliers in her sample that she was compelled to take a closer look at the transactions.

Upon further investigation, Pam discovered that three servers had been providing free food to tables of friends and family, so nothing was entered in the "check delivery" field in the data for the duration study. A glitch in the spreadsheet analysis interpreted this as the closing time, so many durations for the entrée-to-check delivery time were grossly overstated.

Consequently, the CoV was not as alarming as it appeared at the beginning of the duration analysis and was able to benefit from refining the process for dropping checks and retraining servers accordingly. Of course, the three servers who were involved in the crimes Pam uncovered were terminated.

What other potential causes of the high CoV do you think were included on the fishbone diagram?

Why do you think anything above 0.5 is the threshold for an unacceptable CoV?

Controlling Duration

As previously mentioned, in addition to selling an actual meal, a restaurant is selling the use of one of its physical inventory units for a period of time

(Kimes et al., 1998). An interesting characteristic of restaurants is that customers largely determine the amount of time an inventory unit is used. The more control an operator can gain over the duration that seats are occupied, the better he can manage RevPASH.

Having control over duration means having a low standard deviation of dining duration and an average dining duration that is suitable for the type, size, location, and atmosphere of restaurant under study.

Controlling duration can be accomplished in different ways (Kimes et al., 1998):

- Reducing the time it takes to accomplish steps in the service process.
- Standardizing services so that the variation inactivity times is reduced or eliminated.
- Increasing forecast accuracy so that optimal staffing levels can be determined and accurate wait times can be quoted.

If an operator could regulate how long customers sit at seats in her restaurant, she could potentially serve more customers and perhaps even fit in another table turn, close earlier, or fine-tune employee schedules to save money. A few specific duration management strategies are as follows (Kimes et al., 1999; Kimes et al., 1998):

- Retool a menu to exclude items that cause customers to linger and items that take too long to prepare.
- Hire a dedicated host, food runner, or busser if it is found that any of these processes are significantly holding up the restaurant system.
- Use cues to let customers know it is time to move along in the meal process.

Another duration management strategy is to speed up the pace of meals during busy periods. This type of duration reduction technique is recommended only for casual and upscale casual restaurants, as customers at fine dining restaurants expect a leisurely pace. To preserve customer satisfaction, the best times to increase the pace of a meal are during the pre-dining and post-dining stages (Noone et al., 2007).

Note that controlling duration does not always equate to decreasing duration. Research has shown that the revenue increase from decreasing duration is marginal and not nearly proportional to the amount of the decrease (Thompson, 2009). Take, for example, the following case: The owner of Bistro 7, a small, upscale jazz fusion restaurant located in St. Louis, is considering adopting several RRM strategies to decrease average dining duration. If he can decrease the amount of time a customer spends at a table by 10 percent (from 62 min to 56 min), he should expect an increase in revenue of less than half of that, or less than 5 percent.

Differences in Supply Offered

As discussed earlier in this chapter, physical inventory units—restaurant seats—can really be very different even if they appear to be identical. The most recognizable difference in seats is to what table size is it assigned (e.g., two-top, four-top). Another difference in seats due to the table size at which a seat is situated is the amount of space that is taken up by the seats at a table (e.g., 45 square feet, 108 square feet). Recall that "space" in an RRM context refers to the physical area that is needed to put a unit of inventory into use.

Fences

Both physical and nonphysical restrictions—known as **fences**—can be placed on supply to segment it into specialized categories. This way, the same inventory—seats—can be used to create a larger variety of service products, such as a character breakfast at a theme park. Fences also create a situation where different prices could potentially be charged to different customers based on the location of a table or time-of-day specials (Kimes et al., 1998; Kimes & Wirtz, 2003).

Another fence that differentiates seats that seem to be identical is the **seating assignment rule**. This is the rule a restaurant uses to determine which party size can sit at which table size.

- A strict seating assignment rule dictates that party sizes are only seated at their closest matching table size. For instance, parties of 1–2 sit only at two-tops, parties of 3–4 sit only at four-tops, and parties of 5–6 sit only at six-tops. This is quite unrealistic in a real-world restaurant.

- The relaxed seating assignment rule is on the other end of the spectrum and allows for party sizes to be seated at any table size larger than the party. For instance, parties of 2 can be seated at two-tops, four-tops, six-tops, or eight-tops, but parties of 6 can only be accommodated by six-tops or eight-tops. This is also a bit unrealistic, as a party of 2 will seldom be seated at an eight-top.
- Right sizing is usually the seating assignment rule most restaurants use. This simply means trying to seat a party at the table size that fits it best, but using other reasonable table sizes to accommodate parties as needed.

Combining Tables

Whether or not tables can be combined is another characteristic that not all supply units may have. Restaurants frequently combine smaller tables (and the seats situated at them) to make a larger table. Not all tables are combinable; for instance, some are too large to move and some are anchored booths.

More importantly, though, is the question: Is it better to use tables that can be combined or to have the proper mix of tables, including dedicated ones that can only accommodate parties that are the same size or smaller than the table? The answer to this depends on the restaurant. In a study, it was found that:

- Smaller restaurants (e.g., 50 seats) that do not serve many large parties benefit from using combinable tables.
- Smaller restaurants that serve many large parties benefit from using dedicated tables.
- Larger restaurants (e.g., 200 seats) benefit from using dedicated tables (Thompson, 2002).

QUESTION TO CONSIDER

Combining tables can mean that one or more units have to be taken out of inventory and put on hold until all the tables needed are unoccupied and ready to be combined. Why is this not desirable?

Supply Mix

Another aspect on the supply side of RRM that impacts how much revenue can be generated is the mix of physical inventory units used. As with a duration analysis, the inventory under consideration in a supply mix analysis is tables. Research has shown that better matching the physical supply of tables to customer demand characteristics positively impacts revenue (Kimes & Thompson, 2004).

Supply mix at a restaurant is often determined subjectively. For example, the mix of tables used in many restaurants follows corporate standards, reflects what is offered by competitors, or is chosen to support the image and atmosphere desired for the facility (Katsigris & Thomas, 1999). There are several different quantitative, objective techniques and tools available to help determine the optimal table mix for a restaurant.

The Team Activity provided in this chapter sets up an example that demonstrates why having the right table mix is important. This example will be used throughout the rest of this section, so it is recommended that the Team Activity be completed at this point.

Percentage Match

The simplest method of determining an appropriate table mix matches the percentage of table sizes supplied to the percentage of table sizes demanded. Using the Shockwave example from the Team Activity, the mix of parties coming into Shockwave, based on the arrivals information the instructor announced, is:

Party Size	Demand Mix %*
1	16.67%
2	50.00%
3	22.22%
4	11.11%

*Note that this demand mix does not include the parties of five or more that could not be accommodated.

The percentage-match method for determining the best table mix for Shockwave is straightforward and has two steps:

1. Determine the demand percentages for each of the two table types supplied, remembering the seating rule that parties of 1–2 should be seated at two-tops when possible and parties of 3–4 should be seated at four-tops.

   Parties of 1 and 2 = 16.67% + 50.00% = 67% Parties of 3 and 4 = 22.22% + 11.11% = 33%

2. Estimate the number of tables by applying the party size percentages to the number of seats available:

   % Parties 1–2 × 36 seats = 0.67 × 36 = 24 seats

   Divided by 2, since there are 2 seats per two-top = 12 two-top tables

   Estimate the number of four-tops:

   % Parties 3–4 × 36 seats = 0.33 × 36 = 12 seats

   Divided by 4, since there are 4 seats per four-top = 3 four-top tables

Percentage-Duration Match

Adding more information into a table mix analysis will often produce more accurate results. For instance, adding duration to a table mix analysis accounts for how long different parties actually occupy tables. However, more information can quickly complicate the problem.

To illustrate, suppose duration information was collected for Shockwave, the restaurant from the Team Activity. The demand characteristics now known are as follows:

Party Size	Demand Mix %*	Duration
1	16.67%	45 min
2	50.00%	50 min
3	22.22%	55 min
4	11.11%	60 min
*Note that this demand mix does not include the parties of 5 or more that could not be accommodated.		

The percentage-duration match method determines its recommended table mix as follows (Kimes & Thompson, 2004):

1. Determine the total amount of time needed to accommodate the demand for seats that are situated at different table types:

For two-tops: [demand percent for parties of 1 × duration for parties of 1]

+ [demand percent for parties of 2 × duration for parties of 2]

= [0.1667 × 45] + [0.50 × 50] = 32.5

Multiplied by 2, since there are 2 seats per two-top = 65min

For four-tops: [demand percent for parties of 3 × duration for parties of 3]

+ [demand percent for parties of 3 × duration for parties of 3]

= [0.2222 × 55] + [0.1111 × 60] = 18.8889

Multiplied by 4, since there are 4 seats per four-top =75.56 min

Sum of both = 65 + 75.56 = 140.56 min

2. Calculate the percentage of this total time demanded for seats that is needed to satisfy customers at each of the table types.

   Two-tops: 65/140.56 = 46.25%   Four-tops:75.56/140.56 = 53.75%

3. Estimate the number of tables by applying the percentages to the number of seats available:

   Two-tops: 0.4625 × 36 seats = 16.6482 seats/2 = 8.3241 tables

   Four-tops: 0.5375 × 36 seats = 19.3518 seats/4 = 4.8379 tables

   The number of tables can only be an integer, so the table mix that best matches demand to supply, accounting for duration, is rounded to: 8 two-top tables and 5 four-top tables.

More Complex Methods

The two main problems with the percentage match and the percentage-duration match methods in determining the best table mix are as follows:

- *Recommended table mixes that cannot fit into the dining room space available.* These simple models allocate the existing number of seats to different tables without initially taking into account the actual space each table needs.
- *Table mixes may be based on the wrong number of seats.* The two simple models work by allocating the existing number of seats to different groups of demand. However, the number of seats in use may not be right for the operation and the space it has available.

Many complex table mix models have been developed and tested to either solve these problems or to include more demand and/or supply information and assess if better results can be achieved (Kimes & Thompson, 2004, 2005; Rohlfs, 2009; Thompson, 2011).

One common aspect most of these models share is the use of Integer Programming (IP), which is a mathematical model used to solve a problem with many parts. The purpose of using an IP is that table mixes are often unrealistic because the recommended number of tables is a fraction. Simple table mix methods simply round to the nearest whole number using conventional rounding rules, so the table mixes they produce are not "optimal" in that, while they capture a good amount of available revenue, they do not capture all of it.

Demand intensity and demand value can also influence the results of a supply mix model, but usually to a lesser extent than party size and duration. Additionally, table space measurements and table seating options could possibly impact supply mix models.

Space Allocation

Space allocation, the final model presented in this chapter, specifically addresses the two problems listed above. It takes space considerations into account and determines the mix *and* number of tables that maximize revenue potential. It does not include duration data, as testing of this model has indicated that it does not yield better results. Using an IP is outside the scope of this chapter, so conventional rounding methods to determine the final table mix recommendation are used.

The space allocation method begins by determining a few space measurements:

- The size of the **planning square** required for each table size. A planning square is the square foot age required to accommodate the following for each type of table (Rohlfs, 2009):
  - The physical size of a table top
  - The size and number of chairs at the table
  - The area needed for people to sit in the chairs when a table is occupied

- The area needed for staff to circulate around the table during dining service

- The total amount of useable FOH area. Useable dining space includes the area that can actively be used to put physical inventory. It does not include stairs, poles, and FOH requirements such as restrooms and coat-check areas. This should be carefully measured to find this total.

Returning to the Shockwave example, standard-size tables will be used, and the following square footage information is now known:

Table Size	Square footage requirements
2-top	31.5 square feet
4-top	43.75 square feet
Useable FOH space = 610 square feet	

1. Determine the total amount of space needed to accommodate the demand for seats that are situated at different table types:

   For two-tops: [demand percent for parties of 1 × space for parties of 1]

   + [demand percent for parties of 2 × space for parties of 2]

   = [0.1667 × 31.5] + [0.50 × 31.5] = 21.00

   Multipliedby2, sincethereare2seatspertwo-top=42.00squarefeet

   For four-tops: [demand percent for parties of 3 × space for parties of 3]

   + [demand percent for parties of 4 × space for parties of 4]

   = [0.2222 × 43.75] + [0.1111 × 43.75] = 14.58

   Multiplied by 4, since there are 4 seats per four-top = 58.33 square feet

   Sum of both = 42.00 + 58.33 = 100.33 square feet

2. Calculate the percentage of this total space demanded for seats that is needed to satisfy customers at each of the table types.

   Two-tops: 42.00/100.33 = 41.86%

   Four-tops: 58.33/100.33 = 58.14%

3. Estimate the number of tables by applying the percentages to square footage available to fit tables:

   Two-tops: 0.4186 × 610 square feet = 255.35 square feet

   = 255.35/31.5 square feet per table = 8.11tables, rounded to 8 two-top tables

   Four-tops: 0.5814 × 610 square feet = 354.65 square feet

   =354.64/43.75 square feet per table = 8.11tables, rounded to 8 four-top tables

4. Calculate the number of seats to be used in the restaurant:

   8 two-tops × 2=16 seats   8 four-tops × 4= 32 seats   16 + 32 = 48 seats

Once a table mix that better matches demand is adopted, seat occupancy would be expected to increase. If it does not, it is likely that the average seat occupancy is already quite high or that the demand information upon which the model is based is incorrect. These table mix models are perfectly sensitive to changes in a restaurant's demand mix, so even small changes in the distribution of party sizes could drastically impact the recommended number of tables.

SPREADSHEET EXERCISE 11.2

A restaurant is under construction and is ready to order tables and chairs. You are tasked with determining the physical inventory to purchase. You have the following information:

	Expected Demand Mix	Square Footage Requirements (includes space for chairs and movement)
Parties of 1 and 2 at 2-tops	30%	30 sf
Parties of 3 and 4 at 4-tops	50%	40 sf
Parties of 5 and 6 at 6-tops	10%	55 sf
Parties of 7 and 8 at 8-tops	10%	65 sf

TO DO

Use the Excel spreadsheet to determine how many 2-top, 4-top, 6-top, and 8-top tables to order.

Layout of Supply

The layout of a dining room, including seat types and table types and locations, is another aspect of restaurant operations that can be tied in to RRM. All of these characteristics further differentiate physical inventory not only in their looks and comfort, but also possibly in the amount of space they take up.

Seat types include chairs, stools, banquettes, and booths. Table types include freestanding, booths, cocktail tables, and communal tables. Table locations range from anchored to a wall or other obstruction, in the center of the room, in a corner, or with a view.

In addition, certain table types sometimes encourage customers to behave in a certain way; gaining more control over customer behavior is frequently used in RM and RRM (Katsigris & Thomas, 1999). For instance, dining duration at round tables has been shown to be longer than dining duration at square ones. This information about a supply side atmospheric characteristic of a restaurant would be helpful for both a restaurateur trying to decrease the amount of time customers spend at tables and a fine dining operator wondering how his customers would perceive a switch to square tables.

SUMMARY

The supply side of RRM is concerned with how well the physical capacity of a restaurant is being used to capture and generate revenue. As capacity is usually under the control of the restaurant operator to a much greater extent than demand, learning, and applying the capacity management tools associated with RRM provides restaurateurs with many opportunities to improve a business. While different capacity strategies are useful when demand is high compared to when demand is low, applying RRM techniques helps an operation use its available supply to effectively and efficiently serve its demand.

DISCUSSION QUESTIONS

1. In the simplest terms, the objective of RRM is to use the fundamental supply and demand conditions of a restaurant to maximize revenue. What elements of the supply are under the control of the restaurant? What elements of demand are under the control of the restaurant?

2. Flo's is a breakfast-only diner, open from 5 a.m. to 11 a.m., and very popular with the employees of a local package delivery warehouse. Flo recorded the "at" seat occupancy for each 15-min period from 8:00 to 10:00 a.m. over a few weeks; the averages are provided below. What is the "from" occupancy for each hour? Which method of recording occupancy do you think is more useful for Flo?

Time	Seat Occ	Time	Seat Occ	Time	Seat Occ	Time	Seat Occ
8:00a.m.	92%	8:30a.m.	94%	9:00a.m.	99%	9:30a.m.	96%
8:15a.m.	60%	8:45a.m.	55%	9:15a.m.	51%	9:45a.m.	66%

Party of 1	Party of 2	Party of 3	Party of 4	Party of 5	Party of 6	Party of 7	Party of 8	Party of 9	Party of 10
5%	25%	5%	25%	3%	5%	5%	15%	5%	7%

3. The current mix of tables at a restaurant with 102 seats is as follows: 4 two-tops, 18 four-tops, 2 six-tops, and 1 ten-top. The seating rule currently used at the restaurant is to seat the largest waiting party at tables as they come available. Demand at the restaurant is distributed as shown in the table below.

   What is your opinion of the current table mix?

4. Recall that fences are used in RRM to differentiate seats, so these identical physical inventory units can be sold as different products. Offering tables of different sizes is a type of fence; the seats situated at a 6-top are used to accommodate a party that would not be able to use the seats at a 2-top, as a larger party could not fit. Describe how a seating assignment rule can be used as a fence to differentiate identical inventory.

5. Conceptualize (but do not try to calculate) a table mix model using the percentage-duration method for a restaurant with the following characteristics.

Party Size	% of demand
1–2	5%
3–4	15%
5–6	25%
7–8	30%
9–10	25%

Table Size	Duration
Two-top	52 min
Four-top	57 min
Six-top	66 min
Eight-top	71 min
Ten-top	min

Use able FOH space for tables = 8000 square feet current number of seats=535.

Be sure to first define the seating rule the restaurant will follow.

6. Restaurants usually follow a hybrid of the constant or the chase methods for managing capacity. Because a restaurant has a fixed amount of space to serve customers, it has to use some constant strategies. However, restaurant capacity can be quite flexible and often can be changed at a low cost to better accommodate demand, which are characteristic chase strategies. What are some other constant and chase strategies that coexist in a restaurant operation?

APPLICATIONS

Vail Ski Mountain Restaurant

Vail Ski Resort Mountain Restaurant serves lunch from 11:00 a.m. to 3:00 p.m. every day. When the restaurant opens, guest slowly, but steadily, arrive until about 12:15 p.m. when groups of customers coming off the slopes show up. This influx of demand "clumps" lasts until about 1:30 p.m. What supply related RevPASH strategies would you suggest and for what times?

Arepas

The manager of Arepas, a Colombian-themed, quick casual restaurant, would like to perform an analysis of duration—how long it is and how much it varies.

You visit Arepas and write down your observations about the dining process:

- Customers wait for a long time at the hotel and when they first walk in.
- It takes a long time to navigate through the maze of tables when being seated.
- Servers bring fried plantains to the tables when greeting customers.
- The menu offers no appetizers.
- The dessert menu is limited, but the coffee and liqueur selection is impressive.

- Servers are trained to bring the check with the entrée.
- Cash and credit cards are accepted.

Design a time study data collection worksheet for the manager.

Tacky Fingers

A popular BBQ restaurant is opening a very large second location across town. You met the owners at a cocktail party and got to talking with them about RRM. They were especially interested in the table mix material and offered you lots of free BBQ if you would help them determine the best table mix. You agreed and collected the following information:

Party Size	Expected Percent of Demand	Table Size	Planning Square
1–2	25%	Two-Top	28 square feet
3–4	50%	Four-Top	44 square feet
5–6	25%	Six-Top	72 square feet

Useable FOH space for tables = 3220 square feet

TEAM ACTIVITY

This activity should be completed in conjunction with the Supply Mix section of this chapter.

You are challenged with helping your brother's beachside, surf-themed restaurant, Shockwave. In teams of two to three, determine the appropriate table mix for its 36 seats.

Your brother can get a good deal on new two-tops and four-tops, so these are the only two table types that he will use. Fire codes indicate that no more than two people can be seated at a two-top and no more than four people at a four-top. You are to assume that tables cannot be combined.

Decide how many of each table type you will have (remember that you only have 36 seats). Use the table sizes and restaurant footprint in the Appendix to sketch a layout for Shockwave.

The seating rules Shockwave will follow are:

- First Come, First Served.
- Attempt to seat each party at the table size that most closely matches its size (e.g., parties of one are seated at two-tops; parties of two are seated at two-tops, parties of three are seated at four-tops).
- If that match is not available, the party is then seated at the next largest available table size (e.g., parties of one or two are seated at four-tops if all two-tops are taken).

Now let's test how your table mix performs. As you go through the list of parties arriving to Shockwave (Arrivals), you should:

- Seat each arriving party at appropriate tables by marking an X for each customer on the table.
- Keep track of any parties that cannot be accommodated, recording them as lost demand.

Arrivals:

Party #	1	2	3	4	5	6	7	8	9	10	11	12	13	14	15	16	17	18	19	20
Party Size	2	4	2	5	3	1	3	2	4	2	2	6	3	2	2	1	2	2	1	3

After all parties have arrived, answer the following questions:

1. Your table occupancy should be 100 percent. Why? Is this realistic?
2. What is your restaurant's seat utilization?
3. How many customers were lost?
4. Which table mix performs the "best"?

INTERNET ACTIVITY

Go to http://www.bu.edu/revpash/, an online app that uses seat capacity and revenue to calculate and graph RevPASH. Use this RevPASH app and the information provided to calculate how well the 60 seats at Vi's Lakeside Diner are generating breakfast revenue.

The data you will enter into the hourly tab is:

Day 1	Revenue	Customers
Hour 1	$400	30
Hour 2	$600	40
Hour 3	$650	50
Hour 4	$375	30

Day 2	Revenue	Customers
Hour 1	$450	30
Hour 2	$700	50
Hour 3	$900	60
Hour 4	$550	40

Day 3	Revenue	Customers
Hour 1	$500	35
Hour 2	$700	50
Hour 3	$875	55
Hour 4	$500	40

- After you've entered Day 1, press the Flow Data button. Click on the Daily tab to see that the data have been summarized and transferred.
- Returning to the Hourly tab, click on the Clear Table button. Re-enter 60 available and enter Day 2 data. Press the Flow Data button and check the Daily tab that the data have been transferred.
- Again, clear the Hourly tab, enter Day 3 data, and flow the data to the Daily tab.

Look at the Charts tab. What day generates the most revenue per seat?

GLOSSARY

Duration – The amount of time a customer spends at a restaurant, measured from arrival to departure.

Fences – Differences in physical inventory units.

Nonphysical inventory – The intangible resources required to deliver a service.

Physical inventory – The tangible resources required to deliver a service.

Planning square – The square footage required to accommodate a table in a restaurant.

Seating assignment rule – A guideline used to regulate which party size can sit at which table size.

Service capacity – The amount of output a service system can produce.

REFERENCES

Bradach, J. (1997). Using the Plural for Min the Management of Restaurant Chains. Administrative Science Quarterly, 42 (2), 276–303.

Crandall, R., & Markland, R. (1996). Demand Management—Today's Challenge for Service Industries. Production and Operations Management, 5 (2), 106–120.

Cross, R. G., Higbie,J. A., & Cross, D. Q.(2009).Revenue Management's Renaissance: Are Birth of the Art and Science of Profitable Revenue Generation. Cornell Hospitality Quarterly, 50 (1), 56–81.

Eppen, G., Martin, R. K., & Schrage, L.(1989).A Scenario Approach to Capacity Planning. Operations Research, 37 (4), 517–527.

Johnston, R. (1999). Service Operations Management: Return to Roots. International Journal of Operations & Production Management, 19 (2), 104–124.

Katsigris, C., & Thomas, C. (1999). Design and Equipment for Restaurants and Food Service: A Management View. New York: Wiley.

Kimes, S. (1989). Yield Management: A Tool for Capacity-Constrained Service Firms. Journal of Operations Management, 8 (4), 348–363.

Kimes, S. (1999). Implementing Restaurant Revenue Management: A Five-Step Approach. Cornell Hotel and Restaurant Administration Quarterly, 40 (3), 16–21.

Kimes, S., Barrash, D., & Alexander, J. (1999). Developing a Restaurant Revenue-Management Strategy. Cornell Hotel and Restaurant Administration Quarterly, 40 (5), 18–29.

Kimes, S., Chase, R., Choi, S., Lee, P., & Ngonzi, E. (1998). Restaurant Revenue Management: Applying Yield Management to the Restaurant Industry. Cornell Hotel and Restaurant Administration Quarterly, 39 (3), 32–39.

Kimes, S., & Thompson, G. (2004). Restaurant Revenue Management at Chevys: Determining the Best Table Mix. Decision Sciences, 35 (3), 371–392.

Kimes, S., & Wirtz, J. (2003). Has Revenue Management Become Acceptable? Findings from an International Study on the Perceived Fairness of Rate Fences. Journal of Service Research, 6 (2), 125–135.

Lovelock, C. (1984). Strategies for Managing Demand in Capacity-Constrained Service Organizations. The Service Industries Journal, 4 (3), 12–30.

Noone, B., Kimes, S., Mattila, A., & Wirtz, J. (2007). The Effect of Meal Pace on Customer Satisfaction. Cornell Hotel and Restaurant Administration Quarterly, 48 (3), 231–244.

Pullman, M., & Thompson, G. (2003). Strategies for Integrating Capacity with Demand in Service Networks. Journal of Service Research, 5 (3), 169–183.

Rohlfs, K. (2009). The Role of Space in Revenue Management (Doctoral dissertation). Cornell University, Ithaca, NY.

Sasser, W. E. (1976, November- December). Match Supply and Demand in Service Industries. Harvard Business Review, 48, 133–140.

Thompson, G. (2002). Optimizing a Restaurant's Seating Capacity: Use Dedicated or Combinable Tables? Cornell Hotel and Restaurant Administration Quarterly, 43 (4), 48–58.

Thompson, G. (2009). (Mythical) Revenue Benefit of Reducing Dining Duration in Restaurants. Cornell Hospitality Quarterly, 50 (1), 96–112.

Thompson, G. (2011). Inaccuracy of the "Naïve Table Mix" Calculations. Cornell Hotel and Restaurant Administration Quarterly, 52 (3), 241–252.

APPENDIX: MATERIALS FOR TEAM ACTIVITY

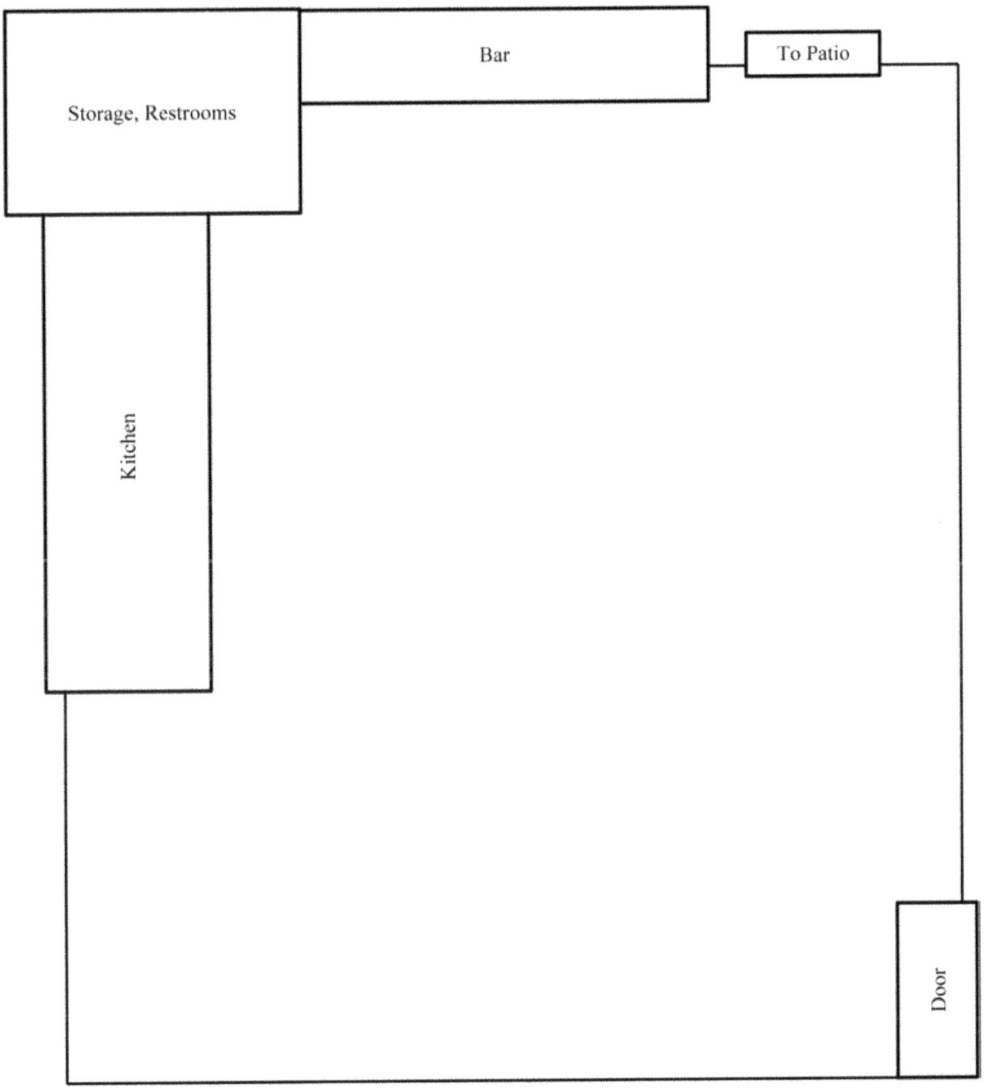

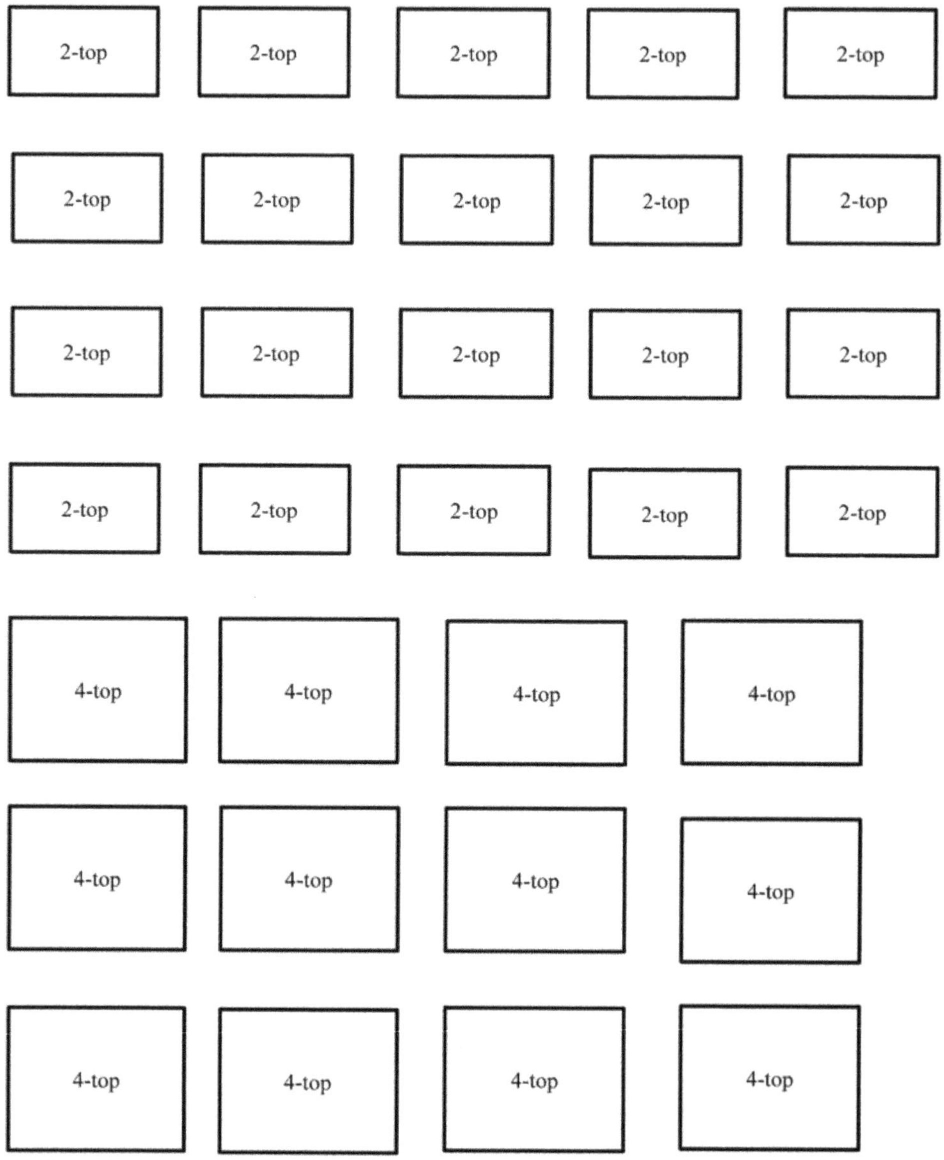
2-top
2-top
2-top
2-top
2-top
2-top
2-top
2-top
2-top
2-top
2-top
2-top
2-top
2-top
2-top
2-top
2-top
2-top
2-top
2-top
4-top
4-top
4-top
4-top
4-top
4-top
4-top
4-top
4-top
4-top
4-top
4-top

CHAPTER 12

Function Space Optimization

Marianna B. Accomando and Bob Chamberlin

OVERVIEW

Revenue management in the hospitality industry has traditionally been associated with the management of sleeping rooms. A strong database of information and multiple distribution channels allowed you to position your inventory to an eager public. In this chapter, however, we are going to examine a revenue stream that isn't as clear-cut as rooms: Function Space, and the multiple revenue streams associated with banquet/catering events.

Traditionally, function space was an afterthought. The "Group" segment which was coming to our property needed a place to meet and we provided "Function Space" to accommodate their needs focusing on filling high margin sleeping rooms to achieve bottom line results. The multiple revenue sources associated with events was complicated to track and understand so they were only partially considered or evaluated. Database management has finally caught up and now we can understand exactly what the guest requires and what it costs to deliver. As we mine our database, we begin to grasp the multiple revenue streams associated with events which can produce 30–40 percent of a property's entire revenue production. Technological advances have allowed us to understand that Function Space revenue is not an ancillary byproduct of filling sleeping rooms but a symbiotic and lucrative partner in the success of a property. Only by looking holistically at each piece of business that comes to your property can you determine the best fit to achieve your property's potential. In this module, we will focus on the use of a new set of criteria with which to evaluate the opportunities in front of sales managers, general managers, and ultimately asset managers and owners. With a diminishable inventory function space, optimization seeks to yield the inventory to its highest value and margin.

LEARNING OBJECTIVES

After studying this chapter, you should be able to:

- Describe the relationship between hotel rooms and function space
- Translate the concepts of function space optimization into a Yield Management Strategy
- Apply the Yield Management Strategy to increase bottom line profit
- Identify what we are selling and its relationships within Space Optimization theory
- Segment your customer base and sales force to position yourself for success
- Justify the importance of communication in keeping your team focused and aligned

OUTLINE

Introduction

- The Evolution of Function Space
- Think Historically

Closer Look: Function Space Optimization

- Similarities between Rooms and Function Space
- Unique Characteristics of Space
- Function Room Revenue Sources
- Flow Through Percentages
- Upselling Opportunities

Segmentation and the Negotiation Process

- The Group Segment

Communication and Communication Tools
Closing
Summary
Discussion Questions and Applications

INTRODUCTION

Another Busy Day!

Is there anyone who thinks the pace of business is slowing down or that the decisions we make daily are getting easier? Case in point: the decisions a Sales Manager faces daily. Typically, the first thing one would check is your **Request for Proposal (RFP)** inbox. You have 15 requests since 6 pm last night all looking for a response within 24 h with requests ranging from:

(1) A group looking to arrive October/November requiring 900 rooms with a peak room night of 250. They need general session space for 600 with breakouts, breakfast, lunch, and a dinner/reception upon arrival. They are looking for an answer by 2 pm.

(2) Another group has no date flexibility arriving in May for three nights, with peak rooms at 325 rooms, requiring all your function space with a food minimum of $250k.

(3) A catering request for your best ballroom on a Wednesday night in April, F&B minimum $90k.

(4) A group looking for 30 sleeping rooms with meeting space for 75 people requiring breakfast, breaks, lunch, and breakout space arriving in two weeks.

(5) A large group looking for your best rate and F&B prices to arrive over July 4. They require 90 percent of your room inventory, multi occupancy rooms taking all double doubles but only 50 percent of your function space with breakfast, lunch, and general session.

These are the types of decisions a property is faced with on a daily basis, competing against multiple properties, all with the knowledge that the first responder normally gets the business 70 percent of the time. While speed of response is a major factor, responses based on accurate fundamentals and training win the game.

SO WHAT?

In "Another Busy Day!" you get a sense of the pace and demands of a sales environment matched against the needs of the client. There are so many factors involved in deciding what piece of business is the best fit, but there is one overriding factor of all, time. Why is time so important? What makes it a leading factor in every decision and negotiation which takes place in a hospitality organization?

The Evolution of Function Space

Function space optimization is a relatively new concept, an emerging science (Kimes, 2011). The number one trend in business today is *analytics.* Analytics is about being able to gather, mine, and develop strategies based on solid empirical data. It is crucial to evaluate all the information available and act on it. Marketing has always been about understanding your customer but never before has so much information been available to identify likes, needs, and habits and tie them to the assets used to satisfy the guest. **Function space optimization** is an analytical process which is evolving quickly to meet the challenges of a highly competitive environment providing the foundation to develop a winning strategy.

THINK HISTORICALLY

Function space management 30 years ago consisted of manually logging your event into a function book called the "Bible." You hoped that while you were selling the space to your client another colleague wasn't selling the same space to theirs! Then the Direct Operating System (DOS) arrived, an operating system which actually allowed a sales person to view the "Bible" electronically at their desk and manage a properties function space in real time. As Sales and Catering databases evolved a team approach to selling became apparent, now you can track a sale from the initial "prospect" status of meeting the client, to generating a contract and sending it off, "tentative" status, to the actual signing and receipt of the contract, "definite" status.

You also began to realize efficiencies of production as menus were loaded into your system and detailed instructions were produced called Banquet Event Orders (BEOs). Operationally, properties were realizing great efficiencies in "function space management," while all along more and more data was being collected:

- Data on contract decision makers
- Where the business originated from and how often
- How much revenue was being generated and who were your best customers
- What types of requests were most prevalent and what did you need to have on hand to satisfy those requests

We now had concrete data to direct our strategic decision making.

Questions:

The evolution of "SPACE" has transitioned from a perspective of operations to sales: how does this change benefit your organization?

Databases were overflowing with information and while business realized the potential, there was still a divide between having the information and accessing it for analytical purposes. No longer is that a problem, we now have the tools; all that's left is to ensure the information being entered is accurate. We now have at our disposal a wealth of information collected and refined over decades from which Function Space Optimization has emerged.

CLOSER LOOK: FUNCTION SPACE OPTIMIZATION

Space optimization is about the management of an extremely perishable resource representing between 30 percent and 40 percent of total revenue generated by your property. It is referring to a resource that extends beyond just physical space and into food and beverage revenue and margin management. A common term when referring to the profitability of an item is **yield**. What is the maximum return one can expect from a product or resource? Initially used as a model from the airline industry, hotels use yield as a base for room's revenue and **flow through** management. From this base, yield has developed into a science or discipline called **yield management**.

Yield management is a variable pricing strategy, based on understanding, anticipating, and influencing consumer behavior in order to maximize revenue or profits from a fixed, perishable resource such as an airline seat or hotel room. As a specific, inventory-focused branch of revenue management, yield management involves strategic control of inventory to sell to the right customer at the right time for the right price. Applying the rules of supply and demand to identify patterns of seasonality by month, week, day, and time of day, you develop a variable or dynamic pricing strategy to maximize the return on your perishable product. Developing tiered pricing allows you to easily adapt to demand and time constraints, shifting your selling strategy to obtain the maximum return on your product without losing the sale. Space optimization is a natural extension of revenue management as we apply many of the same principles used from the yield management of sleeping rooms to function space (Kimes and McGuire, 2001).

Similarities between Rooms and Function Space

(1) It is the same life cycle of perishability, what you don't sell today you lose forever.

(2) It is subject to the same rules of constrained and unconstrained demand.

(3) A critical component is the identifiable patterns of seasonality by month, week, and day.

(4) Time is fundamentally important. Specifically how much time prior to the expiration date of the diminishable inventory do we have (Booking Window)?

Taken down to their essences, function space and sleeping rooms are the same, they are space. A physical structure located in a specific location/vicinity with offerings that attract visitors.

Unique Characteristics of Space

Distinct Meal Periods: in looking at the yielding of space we can determine that there are typically four separate periods of the day that allow for revenue generation:

- Morning: 6 am to noon
- Lunch: Noon to 2 pm

- Afternoon: 2 pm to 6 pm
- Dinner: After 6 pm

Four distinct opportunities to produce revenue in a 24-h period, which unlike the typical sale of a hotel room is a BIG PLUS! The notion of "time" similarly affects the sale of both rooms and space, but the opportunity to subdivide space into four revenue producing units is a unique characteristic of function/event space and these subdivisions into meal periods affords us an opportunity for variable pricing (Kimes and McGuire, 2001).

Pricing in relation to space is not the same as rooms. The **best available rate (BAR)** pricing of sleeping rooms allows you to quickly adjust to changes in demand but with function space the revenue streams are fixed. However, the option of adding food and beverage can give you flexibility. Food and Beverage (F&B) prices are typically set in advance, printed, and distributed in a menu format which is then given to clients limiting your ability to flex price. What you can do however is determine your seasons (high, medium, and low) for your geographic area, identify your most profitable space and then set revenue minimums which you will accept from those specific venues over that time period. There are a wide range of items from which revenue is produced when looking at Space Optimization. When evaluating a piece of business one must consider not just the season or demand period, but the flow through percentage of the item to maximize returns.

Function Room Revenue Sources

(1) Food and Beverage: The menu and its offerings provides opportunity for variable pricing techniques. The packaging of items with upgrade options allows a sales manager the unique opportunity to increase revenue while satisfying the needs of the client. We will delve deeper into this concept shortly

(2) Rental Fee: Rent is the opportunity for variable pricing when providing a quote to a client. Like average daily rate (ADR) in rooms, you are not constrained by the printed menu pricing set in F&B, but a sliding rent scale affords the opportunity to sell the space and flex as demand dictates.

(3) Administrative Fee: An almost 100 percent flow through item on the **Profit and Loss Statement (P&L)**. Think of this fee in the same manner as shipping and handling. It is a fee provided to the management of the facility producing the event. It is not a gratuity to the banquet staff but incremental top line revenue for management in exchange for servicing the event

(4) Resources: These are ancillary items which every event needs:

- Audio visual
- Linen and chair upgrades
- Chef, bartender, attendant, or coat check fees
- Staging and lighting upgrades
- Security personnel

Linked to each of these revenue sources is a flow through percentage. Flow through or revenue conversion, is what flows from the point of generation, through associated costs to produce the item or service sold, to the bottom line of the P&L and ultimately to the owners of the property (see also Kimes and Renagan, 2011, p. 24).

Flow Through Percentages

- Rent: flows at approximately 90 percent. The labor expense of the function room set up and fixed costs of energy are all that apply to decrease the margin of profit in this revenue stream. This revenue stream is the most flexible when negotiating a contract, however, it is often the first expense a client will try to contain. From the property perspective, this is a highly valuable and dynamic revenue stream. With a high flow through which can flex over high and low demand periods it is a key to high return in a space optimization strategy.
- Administrative Fee: 100 percent flow through, a beautiful thing. Administrative fees average 7–10 percent of F&B revenue based on the type of facility and location.
- Resources: varies;
    - Audio Visual could average 35–55 percent profit given the setup of the contract with an outsourced vendor or the internal cost of fixed assets which constantly need upgrading and labor to ser-

vice the need. Do you contract out or produce in-house? That is a critical business decision which affects margin to an overall P&L.

- Linen and Chair upgrades: upsell pricing can support a "markup" of handling this outsourced revenue stream
- Chef, Bartender, Security Fees: 80–90 percent flow through based on the labor demand/schedule.

- Food and Beverage: this items flow through can vary widely based on cost of goods sold for each geographic location factoring in transportation costs, production, and service labor expenses as well as the menu engineering. Competitive pricing and ultimately, the desired margin/flow through the owners expect are fundamental. The best way to analyze flow through is by meal type. While varying by geographic area, cost of goods sold and labor, some averages are:
  - Continental Breakfast: highest flow through due to the low cost of goods and lack of dedicated staff flexing to serve multiple events simultaneously, all set as buffets. Average flow through 50 percent.
  - Breakfast: similar to continental, average flow through 50 percent.
  - Lunch: varies based on the option for buffet or served meals and the volume of each for the property. Average flow through 45 percent.
  - Dinner: typically the lowest flow through due to the highest expense in labor for the culinary team and production of a specific plated meal. However the addition of alcoholic beverages at higher margins than food will improve this flow through. Average flow through 35 percent.
  - Reception: based on the purchase or on site preparation of the product, this can be a high margin event based solely on the cost per piece vs. retail pricing and the service style which replicates a buffet. Average flow through 55 percent.
  - Break: high margin item served in buffet style with minimal labor dedicated to the service. Like continental breakfasts, the ability to have multiple events at one time with limited staffing helps control costs. Average flow through 50 percent.

- Wedding: as a specific meal type, "bundling" pricing can be instrumental for margin impact here with guaranteed F&B service at a price per person driving a high margin. Average meal only flow through 30 percent.

Distinguishing meal periods is vital because of both the cost of goods sold by meal period and the labor cost to produce those meals. Looking at breakfast; eggs and coffee as a one or two course breakfast compared to a dinner which may be three to four courses requiring intricate preparation and production costs allows us to compare the margin for each meal period. Culinary and service teams brought in for an 8-h shift can prepare two to three meal periods in the morning (breakfast or continental, lunch, and a break) with lower cost products. Alternatively the team brought in from 3 pm to 11 pm to prepare a single reception/dinner menu has substantially increased costs. Products are more expensive and we have only one meal period over which to spread labor costs. Not only must we consider maximizing the space, we need to consider maximizing the efficiency of resources needed to produce the meals. When you can relate flow through of each item and meal type to the season, (month, day and time of day) you are operating in, then and only then can you communicate a solid Function Space Optimization strategy to deliver optimal results. The mix of meal types you sell to your client determines the profit which will be delivered to the owners.

Upselling Opportunities

Suggestive selling can also impact the flow through of a meal period to improve the margin of the meal. While not a consideration at the start of the booking process, designing a menu which increases the average check can significantly impact profitability. Let's look at beverage sales. If the sales team can improve the beverage margin by selling a "package beverage service" by the hour for each of the guaranteed guests in attendance, it will impact the flow through to the positive. Why? The preponderance for all guests to drink at the same level over a set time is unlikely, unless the demographic is the same. As a result, top line revenue improves with a guarantee of sales, flowing positively to the bottom line. This is relevant in both the actual meal period and when analyzing opportunity. Certain types of business have the ability to increase expectations and others are less likely to drive the opportunity for upsell. As another example, selecting additional items on a coffee break can substantially increase the average check for that meal period. Coffee breaks in general have low labor support and multiple breaks can happen at the same time with limited service dedicated to that meal period. The potential to drive revenue by adding additional menu items on high margin meal types will help the flow through. In evaluating business this should all be considered because events that are part of bookings laden with high margin meal periods become more attractive in the booking process, more revenue flows to the bottom-line.

PROS & CONS

With ***"Flow Through"*** in mind, list the Pros & Cons of Package Pricing vs Per Item Pricing

Flow Through Example

A single all day event for 100 people–

Labor Shift	Meal Period	Covers	Avg. Check	Flow Through percent	Net Rev.
6 am to 3 pm	Breakfast	100	$30	50%	$1,500
	Breaks	200	$20	50%	$2,000
	Lunch	100	$40	45%	$1,800
	Total	400	$18.25	48%	**$5,300**
3 pm to 12 am	Reception	100	$38	55%	$2,090
	Dinner	100	$75	35%	$2,625
	Total	200	$58	42%	$4,715
				Increased Profit	$585

Understanding the flow though of each meal period is the key to understanding the profitability of your facility and the optimization of your space. In this example the labor and cost of goods sold for the morning/lunch period vs evening period delivers a 6 percent increase in profit, an additional $585 to the bottom line.

Space Optimization is about fitting the right piece of business into the best function room on the proper date. Only by analyzing each **Request for Proposal (RFP)**, then breaking out the requested meal period and matching to available space and sleeping room patterns can you optimize your space to meet budgeted objectives.

How do you match the RFP request with the proper space? Data from your Sales and Catering database is the key. It contains everything you need to know in ranking your function space based on revenue production. All that is required is a measurement technique to turn the information in the database into usable standards for space valuation. The standard measurement of space is in square feet. A hotel or function facility is as much a piece of real estate as a warehouse or office complex measured and valued in revenue per square foot. Yes, the offerings of the function space add complexity through scenic views, room layouts and décor, but the basic measurement is revenue per square foot. Some identify the calculation as **Revenue per Available Space (RevPAS)** but the formula is the same.

Revenue/Sq. Ft.

Total revenue generated in the space for a specific time period/Square footage of the space:

Ballroom 1 is 15,000 sq. ft.

Revenue generated in the month $500,000.

$500,000/15,000 sq. ft. = $33.33 per sq. ft.

It is important to use this calculation to identify your highest revenue generating space, yet equally important to view the calculation in terms of time. Time is at the root of space optimization. Time identifies the perishability of the product. Time segments the selling period into four distinct meal/selling periods. At the start of this discussion we asked, why is time so important when considering a space optimization strategy? Time identifies your high, medium, and low season. Time communicates when to implement or change your selling strategy, when to drop or raise your price based on the booking window. Time is the essential component which defines and sets the parameters of your entire selling strategy.

Only when applying the Revenue per Sq. Ft. calculation on a daily, monthly, and meal period basis can you best understand and rank the value of your space. The *Function Room Occupancy Report* brings this all together. It relates the demand utilization of the space by month, day of week, and time of day producing an occupancy percentage for measurement, tracking, and comparison.

As in any business where you are called upon to identify your best employee, menu item, or car type it is imperative in the hospitality industry to comprehend which of your physical assets is the most valuable and why. With that data you set minimum revenue expectations driving both the top line and margin limits dictated by owners. Would we put a prom in a prime ballroom on a highly sellable night? To answer this, we analyze the occupancy report, identifying demand patterns and revenue per Sq. Ft. returns contrasted against the contribution dollars of the business we are considering. We need to keep in mind that each piece of business yields differently. Perhaps the prom, with a chicken dinner and no alcohol is “trading down” on our best space not optimizing the day/time patterns. If demand shows that we could place another dinner in this prime real estate with a higher contribution and additional revenue sources (such as alcohol, rented linens, and other resources) we would not want to under yield the room with the less contributing event. Equally we would not want to break a sellable group pattern with a social event in the middle of the week if we could sell to a weeklong group. The consideration of all these inputs constitutes a function space optimization strategy easily identifiable because of the Function Room Occupancy Report.

Function Room Occupancy Report

Dates: October
Status: Definite

	Sq Ft	1	2	3	4	5	6	7	8	9	10	11	12	13	14	15	16	17	18	19	20	21	22	23	24	25	26	27	28	29	30	31	Occ %	Revenue	Rev / Sq Ft
		We	Th	Fr	Sa	Su	Mo	Tu	We	Th	Fr	Sa	Su	Mo	Tu	We	Th	Fr	Sa	Su	Mo	Tu	We	Th	Fr	Sa	Su	Mo	Tu	We	Th	Fr			
October																																			
Ballroom 1	5,880	D	D		D	d	D	D	D	d	D	D		D	D	d	D			D	D	d	D	D		D	D	D	D	D	D		80.65%	208,949	$35.54
Morning			D			d	d	d	D	d	D	D		D	d		d			D	D	d	d	D				D	D		D		61.29%	10,602	$1.80
Lunch			D			d	d	d	D	d	D	D		D	d		d			D	D	d	d	D			D	D	D		D		64.52%	48,779	$8.30
Afternoon		D	d		D	d	D	D	D	d	D			D	D	d	d			D	D	d	D	D		D	D	D	D	D	D		77.42%	20,203	$3.44
Evening		D	d		D	d	D	D	D		D				D		D			D			D			D	D	D		D	D		54.84%	129,366	$22.00
Ballroom 2	7,524	D	d		D	D		d	D	D	D	D	D	D	D	D	d	d	D		d	D	D	D	D	D	d	D	D	D	d		87.10%	391,439	$52.03
Morning		D			D	D			D	D	D		D	D	D	d	d	d	D		d	D	D		D		d	D	D	D	d		70.97%	28,505	$3.79

Lunch		D	d		D	D		d	D	D	D		D	D	D	d	d	d	D		d	D	D	D	D		d	D	D	D	d		80.65%	15,305	$2.03
Afternoon		D	d		D			d	D	D	D	D	D	D	D	d	d	d	D		d	D	D	D	D	D	d	D	D	D	d		83.87%	57,705	$7.67
Evening		D	d		D			d	D	D	D	D	D	D	D	D	d	d	D		d	D		D		D	d	D	D	D	d		77.42%	289,924	$38.53
Ballroom 3	6,115	d	d	d	D	D		d	D	D	d	D	D	D	d		d		D		d	D	D	d		D	D			d	d		74.19%	66,663	$10.90
Morning			d	d				d	D	D		D		D								D	D	d		D	D			d	d		45.16%	25,420	$4.16
Lunch		d	d	d				d		d	d	D									d	D	D	d		D	d			d	d		48.39%	21,282	$3.48
Afternoon		d	d	d	D	D		d		D		D	D		d		d		D		d	D	D	d		D	d			d	d		64.52%	10,842	$1.77
Evening		d			D	D			d	D		d	D		d		d		D		d	D	d			D					d		48.39%	9,120	$1.49

Capital D = Complete Ballroom in Use Small d = Divisable ballroom only a portion in use

Figure 12.1: Function Room Occupancy Report

Pulling directly from the Sales and Catering database the Function Room Occupancy Report highlights by function room, how the space is being utilized. Which meal period is generating the highest return in which month and day of week. Linked to a specific function room you derive expected minimums to define your yield strategy. This report highlights the status of business, for example Definite, Tentative, and Prospective, identifying if a ballroom is subdividing by using lower case and capital letters (see sample *definite* report above). Ballroom 1 subdivides into three parts providing greater flexibility when determining its best use, the report highlights this. Only when you view your data in this manner can you truly understand and yield your product effectively. Looking historically at the data you can set anticipated revenue minimums based on identifiable patterns. From a future perspective you can develop a sales strategy to optimize the utilization of the space and yield the anticipated returns based on; business on the books, what status they're in, how long have they been in that status and how much time is left for selling, the "booking window." Everything you need to know is condensed into an easily accessible format.

QUESTION TO CONSIDER

Looking at the Function Room Occupancy Report above Ballroom 3 is producing $10.90 sq. ft. for the month. This is far below the other ballrooms: what factors could be influencing this and what can be done?

The Revenue per Sq. Ft. is not only used to identify selling patterns or value space, when viewed over time it can indicate trends. It starts the investigation as to why is the space generating this value? Has the value changed and why? Is it a result of a physical change, selling strategy, guest's perspective? Reports and metrics identify possibilities how you use them is summed up through your Optimization Strategy.

In a hotel environment, space optimization focuses on yielding space when sleeping rooms are needed. The success of the property mandates that you consider the relationship between function space and sleeping rooms. Sleeping rooms provide the greatest flow thorough which translates to the highest ADR and RevPAR. So in order to maximize both you want just enough function space to fill the group segment, or do we? Every Yield strategy focuses on finding balance between the segments.

Full service hotels may divide room segments into the three main categories:

(1) **Transient:** Individual travelers who are staying for business or leisure

(2) **Group:** Organizations or corporations who gather for a shared purpose.

(3) **Crew:** Airline employees or longer term stays who by their nature are transitory and need temporary housing.

The demand of your market will dictate the probable mix with the Group segment laying a base which requires function space. To understand this symbiotic relationship between rooms and space consider the:

ROOMS TO SPACE RATIO

#Sleeping Rooms/Sq. Ft. Function Space

Evaluate two properties:

500 room property with 200,000 sq. ft. of space

1000 room property with 60,000 square feet of function space:

The Ratio

500 rooms/200,000 sq. ft. = .0025

1000 rooms/60,000 sq. ft. = .016

When the ratio is low you have too few rooms to fill the space and a high ratio indicates your space may not be sufficient to ensure all the rooms can be filled. Remember we are looking for the balance of both to employ in our Yield Management Strategy.

PROS & CONS

Every market is different but on average a ratio of .016 is utilized.

Which "Rooms to Space Ratio," .0025 or .016, is better and why?

Understanding this relationship is the foundation of a comprehensive revenue strategy. It signals just how many sleeping rooms are required by a "Group" to lay a base and yield the property. Every revenue management strategy has a focus on Revenue per Available Room (RevPAR) but RevPAR excludes banquet revenue from its calculation. A comprehensive strategy optimizes all revenue streams. The food and beverage contribution from sleeping rooms is best summarized in the:

GROUP BANQUET REVENUE CONTRIBUTION =

Banquet Revenue/Group Rooms Consumed

Example: $100,000/575 rooms = $173.91 Group Banquet Revenue Contribution

What this is telling you is that for each room night associated with the group segment $173.91 of banquet revenue is being generated. Group Banquet Revenue Contribution tracked by year and month provides the historical baselines to evaluate all future business presented in the group segment over this particular date range or season.

A Group piece of business, or the total mix of business, can only be properly evaluated when you understand these ratios. Rooms to Space sets the boundaries of what is possible. In a complete yield management strategy, Transient, Group, and Crew rooms are balanced within the demand needs of your location. In the quest to maximize RevPAR each segment plays a part in maximizing profit. The Group and Crew segments lay the base for sleeping rooms with higher Transient ADR filling the gaps maximizing return. To understand and maximize the return of Group ADR and F&B

revenue the **Group Banquet Revenue Contribution** ties the Rooms and Banquet revenues together to give an accurate depiction of the business or mix you are considering. When you look at, and understand the amount of banquet revenue generated in relation to each group room night consumed, tie that revenue to the function space utilized, and measure it against historical parameters, can you accurately evaluate a piece of "Group" business and find the optimal mix of Transient, Group, and Crew.

Let's demonstrate: If Transient gives us the greatest flow through we must want to allocate the most rooms to this segment, right?

Consider this

Total Rooms	500
Occupancy %	80.00%
Cont. Margin	$171.00
REVPAR	**$241.68**

Segment Mix		**Picked up Rooms**	**ADR**	**Bqt Rev**	**Ttl Rev**
Transient	70.00%	280	$329		$92,120
Group	20.00%	80	$259	$13,680	$34,400
Crew	10.00%	40	$200		$8,000
Total	100.00%	**400**	**$302.10**		**$134,520**

High ADR $302.10 and REVPAR $241.68 generates $134,520 Nice Return
Alternative View focusing not on ADR & RevPAR but on *Total Return*

Total Rooms	500
Occupancy %	80.00%
Banquet Cont.	$171.00
REVPAR	**$213.68**

Segment Mix		**Picked up Rooms**	**ADR**	**Bqt Rev**	**Ttl Rev**
Transient	20.00%	80	$329		$26,320
Group	70.00%	280	$259	$47,880	$120,400
Crew	10.00%	40	$200		$8,000
Total	100.00%	**400**	**$267.10**		**$154,720**

As you can plainly see, only when you consider all the revenue streams can you achieve optimal revenue generation. Focusing on a high REVPAR never factored in the banquet revenue revealed in the above analysis, and when considered, the shift in segment mix between Transient and Group delivered an additional $20,200.

SPREADSHEET EXERCISE 12.1

To Do:

You have a 200 room property with 10,000 sq. ft. of meeting space which breaks out as follows;

• 5000 sq. ft. Ballroom	Average Checks	
• 2500 sq. ft. Ballroom	Cont. Breakfast - $30	Breakfast - $34
• 1000 sq. ft. Conference Room	Lunch - $54	Break - $17
• 3/500 sq. ft. Meeting Rooms	Dinner - $75	Reception - $60

Focusing on Event Type, Flow Through, Covers and Group Banquet Revenue Contribution evaluate 2 pieces of business to choose the better fit arriving in May for 2 days with an ADR of $329 per night.

Sleeping Rooms per night 1st Day Events 2nd Day Events

1) 100/20 Dinner 100/Reception 100 2 Breaks 100 ea./Breakfast 100 Lunch 100
2) 75/75 Cont. breakfast 125 /Lunch 125/Break 125 Cont. Breakfast 125/Lunch 125

1. Would you change your segmentation strategy and how would that effect your distribution strategy?

Speed to market and accuracy mandate that this process of calculating revenues and flow through, especially for a sales manager on the clock whose time is far more valuable connecting with clients, be automated. To that end, the Revenue Maximization sheet (REVMAX Sheet) was created. This sheet automates the process, providing insight and learning as well as speed to market. The REVMAX sheet is both an analysis/sales tool and method of communication allowing sales managers speak to their business at hand.

The sheet details the following criteria which are all instrumental in consideration for contracting business, not only with rooms and associated banquet revenue, but all business generating revenue for your property.

1. Room pattern being requested, number of sleeping rooms Blocked and Rm Rate Offered and if Commissionable to a third party. It also denotes the existing business on the Definite line and how this will impact the pattern for the time period.
2. Minimum Available Rate (MAR): A rate determined by the Director of Revenue based on history and forecast
3. Meal Type, Covers and Revenue projected to be generated by the group
4. Function Rooms to be used and number of Days required
5. Revenue produced by each Meal Type
6. Anticipated Profit by each revenue stream; F&B Profit, R-O (Rent/Other) Profit, Rm Profit, Total Profit.
7. Group Banquet Revenue Contribution generated
8. Total Profit Margin
9. Comments to inform the management team of pertinent information on Group History, Competition, is the group flexible or is this the only or preferred date. Any information relevant to help us arrive at an optimal decision.
10. Group Banquet Revenue Contribution, Rooms Only: This section breaks the final decision into 3 categories based on all the information entered, comparing input to history providing 3 alternatives for Banquet Revenue and Group Banquet Revenue Contribution:
    a. Way To Go = Exceeding historical levels
    b. Bring to REVMAX =Close to historical averages but allows the Sales Manager to argue why this piece of business should be taken, even at the lower margins i.e. (Valued Client, Booking Window Closing, Other Meetings in the Pipeline, Pattern compliments other groups to optimize revenues)
    c. Time To Talk: business should be turned down not meeting minimum potential.

11. Rooms Only: Is based on a properties size designating the importance of F&B contribution to the success of a property. If a group is going to use rooms only and no function space, then the pattern requested needs to be a need date or else should be turned down in favor of business with Rooms and F&B producing high Group Banquet Revenue Contribution.

Obviously the best scenario is to have a group whose banquet revenue and Group Banquet Revenue Contribution both display "Way To Go." In the case they do not: look at other factors such as profit margin (profit margin = profit/revenue) or items highlighted in the comments section to help sway the decision process. The multitude of factors affecting the outcome is what makes function space optimization so challenging. The best use of this form is to provide direction and team discussions. Objectively the best decisions are arrived at collectively, with each stake holder presenting their unique position. The REVMAX Sheet puts in front of everyone the unique characteristics of a piece of business highlighting key points. Only when you can present the information in a concise, usable and consistent format such as this can a proper decision be determined.

A critical component to success today is speed to market. 70 percent of first responders to an RFP get the business. However speed without accuracy is a recipe for disaster. The REVMAX Sheet, like any computer generated revenue management tool, helps base decisions on empirical data. It brings together all the individual parts of the group piece of business, presenting a comprehensive view. It also goes to the next step and looks at profit margins to help guide the Sales Manager in negotiations. The piece of information not automated is the detailed knowledge/intelligence of the sales manager who produces it. That qualifying process is important because it determines from the customer any flexibility in dates or needs as well as any historical references that will help us determine the highest yield/conversion, hence the comment section. A good Sales Manager given the proper tools can steer a client to a date that is best for all.

REVMAX Sheet

Grp, Name -

Sales Mgr. -

Arrival Date - **08/25/2018** Wedding/Catering Date -

										Labor Day
Day	Sat	Sun	Mon	Tue	Wed	Thu	Fri	Sat	Sun	Mon
Date	25-Aug	26-Aug	27-Aug	28-Aug	29-Aug	30-Aug	31-Aug	01-Sep	02-Sep	03-Sep
Definites	187	64	5	55	155	151	67			
Block	**5**	**50**	**90**	**90**	**90**	**90**	**5**			
MAR	$287.00	$260.00	$305.00	$305.00	$305.00	$305.00	$260.00			

Group Rooms

Meal Type	Covers	Revenue	Meal Type	Covers	Revenue
Cont. Bfst,		$0	Dinner	95	$7,125
Breakfast	400	$13,600	Reception	95	$5,700
Lunch	400	$21,600	Break	800	$13,600
			Wedding		$0

Total F&B	Rent/Other	Rm Rev	Total Rev
$61,625	$5,000	$113,022	$179,647
F&B Profit	R-O Profit	Rm Profit	Total Profit
$28,778	$4,600	$80,246	$113,623

Rm Rate Offered	$299.00
Comm. %	10.00%

Single	$299.00
Double	$299.00

Tot. Rev Par: $427.73

Cont. Margin: $158.63

PROFIT MARGIN: 63.25%

Function Rooms	Days
PLZ	
SPT	5
FLG	4
LIB	4
CON	4
LTH	5
HBV	
CTV	
SKY	
AMP	
CNG	
WTF	
HAI	
BKB	
FED	

Banquet Rev.	Time To Talk
Cont. Margin	Way To Go!
Rooms Only	

Comments

Figure 12.2: REVMAX Sheet

Source: Flow throughs used in this example are illustrative of this particular property's profit calculations. Please refer to the student supplement for additional explanation.

In this example the mix of meal types generates $61,625 flowing at 47 percent to the bottom generating $28,778. The high level of breaks flowing at 50 percent makes this a highly desirable piece of business, however the amount of space required to hold this event and the revenue generation opportunities of the space indicate this is not a good piece of business, "Time To Talk." The $5000 in rent flowing at 90 percent helps, but is still not enough giving the Sales Manager the opportunity to flex the rent up to make it more attractive. If the rent went to $25,000, $5000 per day the total Banquet revenue generated would bring this in line from a purely F&B banquet perspective. From a rooms perspective the $113,022 flowing at 71 percent, $80,246 with 10 percent commission is great. What makes the rooms perspective even better is that it takes only 420 total rooms to generate $66,625 in total banquet revenue sending Group Banquet Revenue Contribution up to $158.63 a "Way To Go."

So is this a good piece of business? Looking at Banquet Revenue only, no, but adding Rooms, the mix of meal types and rental, with the knowledge we are heading into Labor Day, a slow period, this is a GREAT piece of business which will generate a profit of 63.25 percent!

As you can see there are a multitude of factors here but the REVMAX Sheet condenses them down to an easily understandable format that takes only minutes to complete providing answers based on empirical data.

SEGMENTATION AND THE NEGOTIATION PROCESS

REAL PEOPLE

*Emily Smith the Director of Sales at a large convention property adjacent to the city's convention center has been seeing an erosion of group profitability. An analysis revealed Rental Revenue was down 40 percent, City-wide sleeping rooms up 25 percent, Commission percentage up 10 percent and a large shift in covers from Breakfast/Breaks to Dinner/Reception. She has hired you to help return her Groups Sales operation to historic profitability levels. What recommendations can you offer?

*Name has been concealed.

We touched earlier on the importance of segmenting your business to achieve maximum return, now let's look a little deeper into the importance each segment plays in segmenting of your sales force. Like any product a business sells, the seller must identify a need in the community, develop a product to satisfy the need and find a way to distribute it at a price the community is willing to pay. It is vital to understand what you have to offer and who you are offering it to. To understand your customer's needs one common rule is to identify like characteristics and segment them into groupings to discover viable options which will appeal to them.

Taking the characteristics of each segment into account hotels develop a yield management strategy and balance the mix to achieve the optimal return. When looking at this segmentation, "Group" is the only one which will require function space. Now that we have identified the "Group" segment as the one with a need for function space, we need to subdivide it further to focus our selling efforts. When we speak about "Group" who are we referencing?

The characteristics of the "Group" segment refer to the reasons they gather. Are they a corporation gathering to review a new selling strategy, train or reward employees? Is it an organization gathering to show new products, bring together experts from their fields of expertise to teach and inform? Whatever the reason, they gather with a shared purpose and characteristics which we can identify and use in our strategy of Space Optimization.

THE GROUP SEGMENT

- Group (Large): Typically defined as over 75 rooms on peak night
    - o Citywide: 4–10-year booking window. Will fill a city with peak night rooms exceeding 2000 total rooms nights (typically using a convention center /complex and contributing high F&B to the center or the surrounding hotels; including opening receptions or dinners of 2000–10,000 guests.
    - o Trade Show: 2–5-year booking window requiring large exhibit space for booth displays, and product demonstrations. Could use 100,000 to 1,000,000 sq. ft. facilities.

  - Self-Contained: 1–5-year booking window. The most profitable business as all sleeping rooms and F&B can be contained within your facility. This provides the highest contribution margin for the property.

The "Group" team traditionally lays a base of business for the property. Because of the volume they provide in both rooms nights and function space /food and beverage revenue, they are afforded the best (lowest) pricing. Typically, this business, due to the longer booking window has the best availability for their needs. The Group segment provides the foundation for the property establishing an inherent demand for the remaining inventory. With this base, the remaining inventory can now be sold for future groups at higher/dynamic prices.

- Small Group Meetings: Typically defined as less than 75 room night's peak and 50–100 guests for meetings. By their very nature they are the most profitable segment. They book short term 3 to 90 days out which when viewed through the prism of supply and demand indicates they will pay the highest rates. (Yield Management share an unwritten rule: *Always be the last to fill!* In times of unconstrained demand the property which fills last can demand the highest price) The small meetings team/catering and events sales team, is critical in any yield management strategy as they not only get the highest prices but fill around a "Large Group" base so all the space is used and none perishes once the consume day is completed. Communication of need dates and time periods to this team is critical as this is the most effective conversion segment with the guest on the phone live. Therefore this team needs to be aware on a daily basis of where opportunity lies and must clearly understand the value of each function room as well as the flow through percentages we reviewed earlier. Short term sellers, this agile and fast paced team can often sway the financial results for the property in a given month.
- Social Catering: 80 percent of this business books in the year of the event. The booking window can be very short which by its very nature means you can place it where you need it. Often it desires week nights as well as weekends and holidays for Birthdays, Anniversaries, Mitzvahs, Corporate Events and Nonprofit Fund Raisers.

This business segment can fill the gaps left from groups not utilizing evenings where the space would otherwise sit empty and continue to optimize the inventory. This segment is important because it often establishes the "reputation" in the business community for the property. The events this segment produces often speak to the creativity of the property, community engagement and ability for the property to create a name for itself in the local business and social scene.

- Weddings: 6 month to 1.5-year booking window. A highly profitable subset of Social Catering separated only because of the booking window and specific need for weekend/holiday demand dates. The potential here is not only for high revenue opportunities (especially with the opportunity to bundle beverage and other services). As well, weddings have a high emotional bonding value for the property. The repeat potential for business from this segment is extremely high. Having been the venue for such a personal and memorable lifetime experiences, the preponderance for the venue, especially a hotel, to be the purchaser's destination of choice and the property garnering a customer for life is very high. This creates a specific, however not totally quantifiable value for the decision making process. Lastly, weddings are almost recession proof. This is where dynamic pricing and contribution are effective.

Segmentation by market naturally points to a strategic division of your Sales force. When you understand the characteristics of your customer you can focus your sales team's efforts to produce the optimal result. You build your pricing and yield strategy by layering Large Groups in as a base business component. Short term business fills in with higher contribution while Social Catering/Weddings balances out the week. Weekly pattern management recognizes that each day contributes uniquely to your Function Space Optimization Strategy. Once you understand the booking window and the segments' characteristics, you can implement a selling strategy founded in yield management principles while taking advantage of seasonality and the strength of your product. Having a sales force responsible for different market segments offers a safety net of overlapping opportunities. When one team doesn't produce as expected another team can compensate according to the time horizon or booking window.

This is where negotiating comes in. Once selling teams are educated in the science of space optimization, and they are utilizing the REVMAX sheet to present business opportunities to management and their coworkers daily, they can begin to negotiate for the optimal result. Should the rate be higher? Lower? How effective is the weekly booking pattern? What is the Group Banquet Revenue Contribution? All these questions must be considered. However the time to have that negotiating process is not just with the customer, it is with the internal management team to first determine the highest and best use of the available rooms and space based on the time left to sell the diminishable inventory remaining. Then the negotiating conversation happens with the customer!

Accurate forecasts are the communication vehicle which allows Sales Teams to react to changing conditions. Identifying new bookings which then create more demand or conversely communication of cancellations to create a sense of urgency to fill is essential for success. Communication is the key to keeping your Yield Management strategies on track. Not only communication to upper management but throughout the entire organization. We all need to be pulling in the same direction to achieve desired results. Set in place a schedule of meetings and insure that all the stake holders are present and prepared. Publish reports to inform the staff of current and anticipated conditions.

COMMUNICATION AND COMMUNICATION TOOLS

1. REVMAX Meeting: Held daily to review complex pieces of business that require a team perspective. With all members of the sales force present providing their insights you not only arrive at a consensus but a better educated Sales force. The team sees business from all angles and better understands the needs of the property.
2. Merchandise Meeting: Held monthly bring Operations and Sales together to review how the business which has been sold is coming together. Are minimums going to be met or exceed? Is the space which was sold going to be adequate or is there a possibility to release space for sale by the short term bookers. Have we yielded the property appropriately, is there any short term change to consolidate expenses and drive margin? Many pieces of business were sold years

ago and only this interaction between Sales and Operations can optimize the results as they are today.

3. Forecasts: Weekly for operations to schedule and plan, monthly to review the business for the next 90 days to focus Sales, Marketing and Operational initiatives.
4. Pace Reports: An analytical perspective of Rooms and Banquets to see how we are "Pacing" to Budget, Forecast, and history. The Pace Report is a good indicator of anticipated pickup from this point in time compared to what's on the books. Will we make budget and if not is there time to put a strategy in place to overcome the short fall.

SPREADSHEET EXERCISE 12.2

To Do:

Build a Pace Report to answer this question:

As we enter Q4 will we make budget at year end? (Use history to predict/forecast the future)

YTD (Year To Date)
Information

	Status	October	November	December
Definlte = $13,691,785	Definite	$1,901,090	$1,401,994	$1,617,619
Budget = $14,390,678	Tentative	$ 122,919	$ 29,513	$ 258,686
	Prospect	$ 84,102	$ 93,962	$ 336,991
Last Year = $14,064,563	Last Year	$2,469,901	$2,113,707	$2,640,181
STLY = $14,064,563	STLY	$1,830,285	$1,518,402	$2,000,086
(Same Time Last Year)				

SUMMARY

Function space optimization is a holistic approach to the analysis of business opportunities. A logical extension of Revenue Management is applying Yield strategies to an equally perishable product, function space. It focuses on understanding your assets and your place in the market. Establishing base line measurements to monitor and evaluate performance against history and competitors, segmenting the market and sales force to identify trends and capitalize on opportunities as never before. With an educated sales force focusing on the principles of meal period flow through, product life cycle and asset valuation, viewed through the prism of revenue per sq. ft. and rooms to space ratios, it provides a greater understanding of what we are selling and to whom we are selling it to, ultimately leading to optimization of all assets.

Enhanced analytical capabilities in data mining are shining lights on hidden opportunities as never before. The detail found in a Function Room Occupancy report not only shapes a selling strategy but allows you to react quickly to an ever changing, competitive environment on a timely basis. Managing booking windows and selling patterns against available space and revenue minimums sets a framework for enhanced returns. Establishing a communication system founded upon solid data, keeps the entire team pulling in the same direction. Function space optimization focuses on revenue generation which when combined with operational efficiencies of the past makes a perfect marriage and recipe for long term success.

SEEING FURTHER

Continued advancements in technology and the use of algorithms will lead to the development of tools which will advance the calculation of time in the equation. These tools will suggest alternative dates, times and function rooms moving ever further toward a holistic view of business encompassing; Rooms, Space and F&B factoring in booking windows. Function Space Optimization has and will continue to be a difficult calculation taking into consideration all the factors we have discussed thus far, but we are inching ever closer to a Revenue Management System that takes all aspects of revenue generation into account to produce optimal results for a property.

The owner of a downtown property with a mix of business 70 percent Transient/30 percent Group is ecstatic that his STR report shows him leading in his Comp Set RevPAR. How can Function Space Optimization help him?

DISCUSSION QUESTIONS

Question 1: Is there ever a bad piece of business? What factors should be considered when relating your properties needs to the piece of business before you?

Question 2: The Group requires 20 breakout spaces with no F&B but will generate $75,000 from a dinner and reception while only using 50 sleeping rooms: is this a good piece of business?

Question 3: Catering has a $50,000 dinner for a Wednesday in October 5 months away; should we take it?

APPLICATIONS

The Excelsior Hotel—Case Scenarios

Property Description: The Excelsior is a downtown property in a tier 1 city with 428 rooms and 162,000 Sq. Ft. of meeting space. High demand months are April–June, September–October and December. High demand days of the week are Tuesday–Thursday and Saturday. The property space breaks out as:

1. Property Function Rooms: Purple denotes highest revenue producers based on Revenue per Sq.Ft.

   PLZ—7524 sq ft sub-divides into 3 rooms
   SPT—3680 sq. ft. sub-divides into 3 rooms
   FLAG—1868 sq. ft.
   LBT—902 sq. ft.
   CONST—1254 sq. ft.
   LTHS—6115 sq. ft. sub-divides into 2 rooms
   HBV—5880 sq. ft. sub-divides into 3 rooms
   CTV—5415 sq. ft. sub-divides into 3 rooms
   AMP—400 seat Amphitheater
   CNG—782 sq. ft.
   WTF -5546 sq. ft. sub-divides into 3
   HALL—115,000 sq. ft. Exhibition Hall
   BKB—1100 sq. ft.
   FED—850 sq. ft.

Businesses to be Evaluated

Below are two **REVMAX** sheets which lay out the piece of business which we must accept or turn down. All pertinent information is contained within each sheet. The challenge is for you to determine whether this business should be bid on or turned down and why? *The Banquet Revenue, Group Banquet Revenue Contribution and Rooms Only sections have been removed as to not give the answer:*

1) Business A: Orthopedic Summit: This is a "Group" piece of business effectively selling out your property of both sleeping rooms and function space as it layers over an existing piece of business. The booking window is long so there is plenty of time. Is this best choice at this point of time?
2) Business B: Spin Council—Is a "Catering" piece of business using your largest space. Space is wide open in October and your booking window is 6 months. No sleeping rooms are required and looking at your Definite line on the REVMAX sheet sleeping rooms are available.

Grp, Name - **Orthopedic Summit**

Sales Mgr. -

Arrival Date - Event Start Date -

Day	Wed	Thu	Fri	Sat	Sun	Mon	Tue	Wed	Thu	Fri
Date	16-May	17-May	18-May	19-May	20-May	21-May	22-May	23-May	24-May	25-May
Definites	198	157	143	4						
Block	**165**	**170**	**170**	**85**						
MAR	$299.00	$299.00	$299.00	$299.00						
Group Rooms	High	High								

Meal Period	Total Covers	Revenue	Meal Period	Total Covers	Revenue
Cont. Bfst.	630	$18,900	Dinner	300	$22,500
Breakfast		$0	Reception	600	$36,000
Lunch	900	$48,600	Break	900	$15,300
			Wedding		$0

Total F&B	Rent/Other	Rm Rev	Total Rev
$141,300		$158,769	$300,069
F&B Profit	**R-O Profit**	**Rm Profit**	**Total Profit**
$66,510	$0	$112,726	$179,236

Rm Rate Offered	$299.00
Comm. %	10.00%

Single	$299.00
Double	

Tot. Rev Par
$508.59
Cont. Margin
$239.49

PROFIT MARGIN	59.73%

Space Required	# of Days		
PLZ	4	Banquet Rev.	[redacted]
SPT	4		
FLG	4		
LIB	4	Cont. Margin	
CON	4		
LTH			
HBV			
CTV		Rooms Only	
SKY			
AMP			
CNG			
WTF			
HAL			
BKB			
FED			

Comments

This Group is only looking at our city and will require the majority of the remaining space at our facility for all 4 days and sleeping rooms. Majority of attendance is local but will require sleeping rooms for some attendees that is commissionable at 10% and and this group has history to support the proposed Group rate and F&B minimum.
Some space on the property is already filled with another group and this group requires the remaining space but will not pay RENTAL.

Grp, Name - **Spin Council**

Sales Mgr. -

Arrival Date - Wedding/Catering Date -

	Columbus		Yom Kippur							
Day	Mon	Tue	Wed	Thu	Fri	Sat	Sun	Mon	Tue	Wed
Date	10-Oct	11-Oct	12-Oct	13-Oct	14-Oct	15-Oct	16-Oct	17-Oct	18-Oct	19-Oct
Definites	93	14	40	44						
Block	0	0	0	0						
MAR	$341.00	$341.00	$341.00	$341.00						

Group Rooms

	Covers	Revenue		Covers	Revenue
Cont. Bfst,		$0	Dinner		$0
Breakfast		$0	Reception	700	$42,000
Lunch		$0	Break		$0
			Wedding		$0

Total F&B	Rent/Other	Rm Rev	Total Rev
$42,000	$10,000	$0	$52,000
F&B Profit	R-O Profit	Rm Profit	Total Profit
$21,840	$9,200	$0	$31,040

Rm Rate Offered	$0.00
Comm. %	

Tot. Rev Par	$0.00
Cont. Margin	$0.00

Single	$0.00
Double	

PROFIT MARGIN	59.69%

Space Required	Days
PLZ	
SPT	
FLG	
UB	
CON	
LTH	
HBV	
CTV	
SKY	
AMP	
CNG	
WTF	
HAL	1
BKB	
FED	

Banquet Rev.	[redacted]
Cont. Margin	
Rooms Only	

Comments

Local Social account which will not require sleeping rooms using only the exhibit hall with all day setup for the evenung event.
All property space is currently on hold as we look for a large group to provide a base of business.

TEAM ACTIVITY

Let's evaluate a piece of business. In this activity, divide the class into the representative roles of a Sales organization.

Break the class into the following roles:

1. Group Sales Managers
2. Catering Sales Managers
3. Small Meetings Sales Managers (Select one member of this team to present the business)
4. Wedding Managers
5. Director of Sales
6. Director of Revenue

As you review the business to decide to accept or not, ask each team to provide their unique perspective of the business, and then as a team, make the decision to accept or decline and why. The Director of Sales and Director of Revenue are the ultimate decision makers taking all the voiced perspectives into account The ultimate goal of this team activity is to learn the perspective of the other team members and the business opportunities they represent. Ultimately, there is room for each sub segment in any Hotel. The key to the puzzle is balancing business, finding the integrated day which supports multiple sub segments maximizing the day's opportunity and margin. The lead roles of Director of Sales and Director of Revenue are to facilitate the conversation. They look to build consensus from the team, with respect for each piece of business, and are ultimately final decision makers of what is the optimum fit.

Business To Be Presented:

Engineering Alliance: This Lead came into the property in February for May of the same year arrival, with minimal sleeping rooms required. All pertinent information is contained in the REVMAX Sheet including the comments section.

Team Perspectives

1. Group Sales Managers: Your responsibility is to book large volumes of business for the current year as well as any future years. You are responsible for generating both rooms and associated food and beverage revealed through the Group Banquet Revenue Contribution. You are always interested in multiple night patterns with open space to layer in a base of business.
2. Catering Sales Managers: Your responsibility is to fill the gaps left by the Group and Small Meetings Sales Managers. Your main opportunity periods are evening and weekends. Your focus is food and beverage top line revenue.
3. Small Meetings Sales Managers: Your goal is to fill gaps left by the Group Team who lays the base. You are looking for the best fit with overall, high contribution. As in any yield strategy the short-term bookings are usually the highest rated contributors providing the best REVPAR and Group Banquet Revenue Contribution.

(Remember the rule of thumb: Be the last to fill its always the highest rated business) To this end, you always want to save some rooms and space for the short-term meetings team.

4. Wedding Sales Managers: While not a role in every hotel the focus of this specialist team is weekends and holiday periods driving room nights, F&B revenue and ultimately profit.
5. Director of Sales: Your role is to balance the selling initiatives to achieve the strategic sales strategy. You have to think "big picture" always and keep the customers need in check with ownership objectives while motivating the entire selling team to achieve top line revenues.
6. Director of Revenue: Your role is optimization of the opportunity presented while balancing the "big picture" perspective. Often a counter role to the Director of Sales in that this role focuses on net operating profit as opposed to top line revenue. This role does not manage employees but manages the business principles of the organization.

INTERNET ACTIVITY

- Research your local Convention and Visitors Bureau website to identify the role they play in both selling the city as a destination and their role in the lead distribution to hotels and facilities in their community.

GLOSSARY

Banquet event order (BEO) – Form generated by your Sales and Catering system delivering detailed instructions to all operational teams in your organization.

Profit and loss statement (P&L) – This financial statement details the revenue, expenses, and profit (loss) generated during a fixed period of time.

Revenue per available space or revenue per square foot **(RevPAS)** – The revenue generated on a square foot basis for a specific period of time.

Request for proposal (RFP) – A detailed requisition a client sends to properties to begin a dialog. It details the needs of the client (dates and size constraints) and allows the property to match its facilities to those needs.

Constrained/unconstrained demand – Economic terms to describe the level of demand irrespective of supply. Unconstrained demand dictates that demand exceeds supply and a property finds itself in the driver's seat for Rate and Function Space Minimums. Constrained indicates supply exceeds demand and you are in a buyer's market.

Group Banquet Revenue Contribution – the banquet revenue generated from each Group room night consumed.

Contribution margin ratio – Banquet revenue/group rooms consumed – a performance metric that ties sleeping rooms to banquet revenue for a comprehensive view of business.

Flow through – The revenue that flows to the bottom line after all expenses have been deducted.

Function space optimization – The application of yield management principles to function space to optimize the return on an extremely perishable resource.

Pace reports – An analytical report on how current business performance is relative to budget, forecast, and history.

Retail rate/best available rate (BAR) – The rate a customer pays "off the shelf," often referred to as "best available."

Revenue per available room (RevPAR) – Total rooms-related revenue per the number of available rooms in the hotel over a period of time: [Rooms Revenue/(Rooms Available * Number of Days)].

Rooms to space ratio – Sleeping Rooms/Sq. Ft Function space: A metric which allows you to define the structure of your property enabling you to see the symbiotic relationship of rooms and space.

Yield management – A variable pricing strategy, based on understanding, anticipating and influencing consumer behavior in order to maximize revenue or profits from a fixed, perishable resource.

Yield – The return or profitability of an asset.

REFERENCES

Kimes, S. E. (2011). The future of hotel revenue management. *Journal of Revenue and Pricing Management, 10*(1), 66-72.

Kimes, S. E., & McGuire, K. A. (2001). Function-space revenue management: a case study from Singapore. *Cornell Hotel and Restaurant Administration Quarterly, 42* (6), 33-46.

Kimes, S. E. & Renagan, L. M. (2011). The role of space in revenue management. In *Revenue Management: A Practical Pricing Perspective*; Yeoman, I., McMahon-Beattie, U., Eds.; Palgrave and Macmillan: Basingstoke, pp 17–28.

CHAPTER 13

Cruise Line Revenue Management

Adam Snitzer

OVERVIEW

At its core, cruise line revenue management is similar to hotel revenue management. Like his or her hotel revenue management counterpart, the cruise line revenue manager's job is to fill ships to capacity at the highest prices available in the market. But consumers buy cruises very differently than they buy hotel room nights; and commercial terms and practices vary significantly between these two sectors of the hospitality industry. Cruise line revenue managers are tasked with achieving exceedingly high capacity utilization and have a vast array of tools at their disposal for meeting that challenging objective.

LEARNING OBJECTIVES

After studying this chapter, you should be able to:

- Describe the cruise industry's evolution from a narrow market niche for wealthy travelers to a rapidly growing vacation alternative that appeals to tens of millions of guests around the world
- Differentiate between hotel revenue management and cruise line revenue
- Explain the roles that those differences play in allowing cruise line revenue managers to achieve full capacity utilization
- Understand the key tools available for managing prices
- Detail the types of strategic cruise line prices
- Explain how cruise line revenue managers use discounted prices to stimulate demand
- Be familiar with cruise line revenue management systems

OUTLINE

Cruise Industry Evolution

- Brief History
- Capacity Growth
- Ship Size/Amenities
- Internationalization of Passengers
- Worldwide Deployment

Difference between Cruise Line revenue management and hotel revenue management

- Discretionary, Leisure Travelers
- Fixed Embarkation and Debarkation Dates
- Long Booking Window
- Option Periods, Deposits, Final Payments and Cancellation Fees
- Per-Person Pricing
- Captive Audience for Ancillary Revenues
- Year-Round Ship Deployments versus Seasonal Ship Deployments
- Wave Season

Implications for Cruise Line Occupancy

Tools for Managing Cruise Line Prices

- Worldwide Guest Sourcing
- Customer Databases
- Ship Configuration

Cruise Line Pricing

- Strategic Cruise Pricing
- Tactical Cruise Pricing
- Pricing Constraints

Cruise Line Management Systems

Conclusion

SO WHAT?

While cruise revenue managers and hotel revenue managers face similar challenges, cruise line revenue managers operate in a very different environment. Which aspects of the cruise line operating environment are most different from the hotel operating environment? Why do you think those differences are so important?

CRUISE INDUSTRY EVOLUTION

Brief History

Ships have been transporting passengers across oceans for thousands of years. But the idea of modeling a ship after a hotel is a relatively recent innovation. The Prinzessin Victoria Luise, built for the Germany-based Hamburg America Line in 1900, is credited with being the world's first cruise ship. The ship boasted 120 luxuriously appointed staterooms as well as all the trappings of a private yacht.

Around the same time, steamship lines also began to compete by trying to outdo each other, and by laying claim to being ever more spacious, luxurious, faster, and safer than any ship that had sailed before. Sadly, we have all heard the tragic story of the doomed Titanic, which in 1912 with capacity for 2200 guests and crew was the ill-fated wonder of ship building engineering.

As new laws slowed the flow of immigrants and as commercial flights overtook sea voyages as the most popular way to cross the oceans, the old steamship lines tried to reinvent themselves by attracting leisure travelers to warm and culturally interesting destinations. But for the most part, the steamboat companies stayed married to their age-old maritime traditions and cruising remained a narrow niche for wealthy and older travelers.

In time, however, the epicenter of passenger shipping moved from New York and the Atlantic Ocean to Miami and the Caribbean Sea. A group of entrepreneurs repurposed some old ships, installed a new technology called air conditioning, and went on to establish Norwegian Cruise Line Holding, Royal Caribbean Cruises Ltd., and Carnival Cruise Line.

Today, those three companies make up more than 75 percent of the worldwide cruise market. They operate more than 200 ships, all of which dwarf the Titanic in terms of size and onboard amenities

Capacity Growth, Ship Size, and Onboard Amenities

Since 1998, the world's cruise ship capacity has increased 181 percent from 185K guest berths to 521K berths in 2018. Passenger growth has been even more dramatic. In 1998, the Cruise Line Industry Association reported that 5.9 million people took a cruise. By 2017, that number had increased by 337 percent to 25.8 million. And as of 2018, there were 106 new cruise ships on order, representing another 261,812 **cruise berths.**

Three factors are responsible for the cruise industry's growth:

1. The construction of ever larger ships.
2. The spread of cruising's appeal to international consumer markets.
3. The deployment of cruise ships to far-flung destinations around the world.

During this period of rapid cruise industry growth, cruise ships themselves have undergone tremendous change. They have gotten much bigger, and with the increased guest capacity has come a host of new onboard venues and amenities.

For example, Royal Caribbean's Quantum of the Seas carries 4,180 guests who can "fly" 300 feet above the sea level in a giant mechanical arm, go skydiving at sea, crash into each other in bumper cars, fly on a trapeze at circus school, or jog around a giant track. To say nothing of an enormous fitness center, outdoor, poolside movie screen, a casino, show lounge, music hall, basketball courts, and more than 20 distinct dining venues.

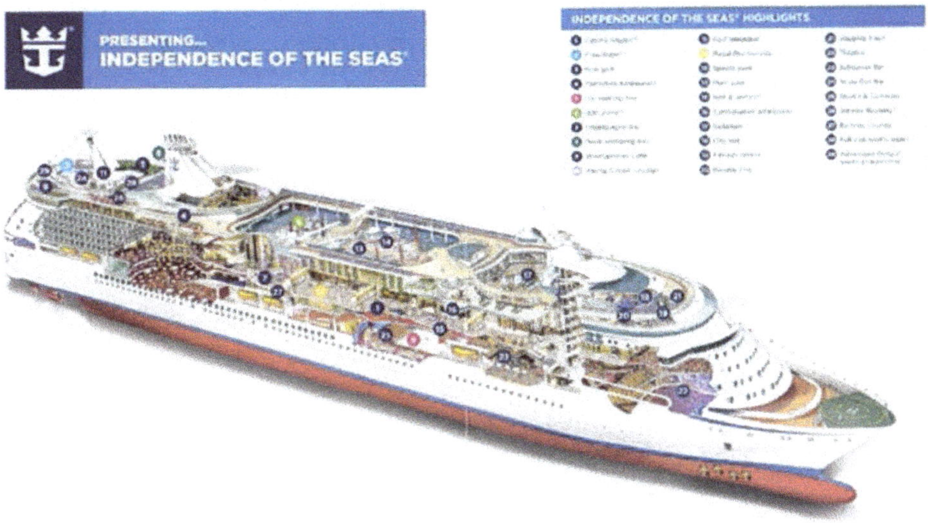

Source: Royal Caribbean International company brochure.

Internationalization of Passengers

In the early days, cruising appealed to a narrow market segment. Most guests were older, retired North Americans and Brits. Today, cruising attracts guests from virtually every major demographic including its traditional base of older retirees, but also families with children, baby boomers, time-pressing young professionals, spring breakers, and honeymooners. And cruising has expanded its reach far beyond North America and the U.K. The appeal of cruising has spread throughout the European continent. The number of Europeans cruising has increased 155 percent from 2.7 million in 2003 to 6.9 million in 2017. Today, guests from emerging markets in Asia represent the fasting growth segment of cruisers. In fact, some industry forecasters predict that China will soon become the world's second largest cruise market.

Worldwide Deployment

As cruise lines' fleets have expanded to include more ships and as their guest sourcing has spread to more international markets, ship deployment has expanded as well. In cruising's early days, most ships were deployed in the Caribbean calling on ports in the Bahamas, San Juan, Jamaica, Mexico, and the U.S. and British Virgin Islands. But cruising soon expanded to summer deployments in Alaska and the Mediterranean with port calls in cities like

Barcelona, Marseilles, Rome, Venice, Istanbul, and Athens. As more ships came online, deployment spread to far-flung destinations around the globe.

The Most Popular Cruise Regions by Percentage of Capacity.

Rank	Cruising Region	Percent of Cruise Capacity (%)
1	The Caribbean	35.4
2	The Mediterranean	15.8
3	Europe (without Med)	11.3
4	Asia	6.0
5	Australia/South Pacific	6.0
6	Alaska	4.3
7	South America	2.1
8	All Other	13.8

Source: CLIA, 2017 Annual Report

SPREADSHEET EXERCISE 13.1

1. Given the Net Ticket Revenue Yield assumptions below, build an MS Excel spreadsheet to evaluate the revenue potential from keeping a ship on a year-round Caribbean itinerary versus putting the ship on a seasonal itinerary split between the Caribbean and the Mediterranean. Assume that the ship's capacity is 3000 and that the spring and fall repositioning cruises are both 14 nights long. In this exercise, assume that operating costs and onboard revenues are the same in both year-round Caribbean deployment as in a seasonal split between Caribbean and Mediterranean itineraries.

	Operating Days	Caribbean Yield	Mediterranean Yield	Positioning Yield
Jan	31	$130		
Feb	28	$135		
Mar	31	$138		
Apr	30	$140		$90
May	31	$145	$167	
Jun	30	$148	$170	
Jul	31	$155	$185	
Aug	31	$165	$185	
Sep	30	$125	$180	
Oct	31	$128		$90
Nov	30	$128		
Dec	31	$160		

Based on all of this expansion and growth, it is clear that with more than $40 billion in annual ticket and onboard revenue, the worldwide cruise industry offers ample challenges for revenue management professionals.

THINK HISTORICALLY

In the mid-1900s, the passenger shipping industry was virtually wiped out by two things: (1) Changes to immigration laws that dramatically curtailed the flow of people from Europe to the United States and (2) the advent of commercial flights across the Atlantic Ocean, which were dramatically faster and cheaper than crossings by ship. What threats do you see, if any, to the modern day cruise industry? What steps should cruise lines be taking to mitigate these threats?

Hotel and Cruise Line Revenue Management Compared

There are many differences between hotel and cruise line revenue management, which will be explained in detail below. But fundamentally, the revenue management principles are the same.

RevPAR is the main measure of hotel revenue management success. RevPAR combines a hotel's average daily rate (ADR) with its occupancy. RevPAR can be calculated as ADR × Occupancy. Or, it can be calculated as total guest room revenue per night divided by the number of total available room nights.

The corresponding metric in the cruise industry is **Yield**. In fact, revenue management in the cruise industry is sometimes also referred to as yield management. Yield combines a cruise line's average daily rate, which is referred to as average per diem (APD) or as net per day (NPD) with its occupancy. APD is calculated by subtracting travel agent commission from the amount a guest pays for their cruise and then dividing that result by the cruise length. Yield is then calculated by multiplying APD and the occupancy percentage. Alternatively, Yield can be calculated as total net ticket revenue divided by the available capacity nights.

Occupancy = 105%

APD = $140.00

Yield = $147.00

Like RevPAR in hotels, a cruise lines' Yield statistic is used to evaluate revenue performance across multiple types of ships, varying cruise lengths, different itineraries, different times of year, etc.

Question to Consider #1

A cruise line revenue manager is considering two different promotions. Calculate which has the higher APD. The first promotion is a cruise only fare of $999 per person for a 7-day cruise. The second promotion has a fare of $1599 and includes free air from Chicago for a 10-day cruise. The airfare costs $350 roundtrip. Both fares are subject to a 15 percent travel agent commission.

Differences Between Cruise Line Revenue Management and Hotel Revenue Management

Cruise ships are sometimes characterized as floating hotels; and in many regards—with their casinos, pool decks, sweeping lobbies, ornate dining rooms—some cruise ships do resemble Las Vegas style resorts. But while cruise line revenue management challenges are similar to resort hotels, they are different from city-based hotels in several important ways.

Discretionary, Leisure Travelers

While the meeting and incentive market is an important subset of cruise lines' group business, on average it accounts for a very small percentage of cruise passengers. For all practical purposes, all cruise guests are leisure travelers. Unlike business travelers, for whom a hotel stay is a company-paid means to achieve a business objective, cruise guests are paying their own way to enjoy a personal vacation.

Furthermore, even among personal travelers, a hotel stay is typically a means to another, compelling objective such as visiting family, attending a special event such as a wedding or school reunion, or sightseeing in an interesting city. The motivations of cruise guests are purely discretionary. They rarely "need" to go on a cruise and are often flexible in their dates and destinations.

As a result, cruise pricing typically goes down close to a voyage's **departure date**. While that's not necessarily the case for the most popular destinations and during the busiest seasons, in general, cruise prices fall as the departure date nears.

Fixed Embarkation and Debarkation Dates

Cruise durations are fixed, so cruise line revenue managers do not have to cope with uncertain arrival and departure dates and significantly varying demand between weekdays and weekend days.

Cruises vary in length from 3-day weekend vacations that depart on Friday and return on Monday to 120-day around the world cruises that leave in January and return in April. The most common cruise length is 7 days, which fits well with most people's vacation plans, although 10-, 11- and 14-day cruises are also common.

While cruise lengths vary, any given cruise has a fixed duration with a discrete start and end. All guests arrive on the same day to **embark** the ship and they all leave the ship on the same **debarkation day**. From an operational perspective, embarkation and debarkation days are known as "turnaround" days. In the morning, guests leave from the cruise that is just ending. In the afternoon, new guests embark a sparkling clean ship that has just been prepared by the housekeeping staff for a new cruise. Cruise ships remain in-service at all times, other than during mandatory maintenance periods every other year.

Long Booking Window

A cruise is typically opened for sale in a cruise line's reservations system a year-and-a-half before the departure date. Especially long cruises, or voyages to exotic destinations, are opened even further in advance. One cruise line, Crystal Cruises of Miami, Florida, has found success by opening their world cruises for sale as early as 3 years prior to departure.

Cruises to the same, or similar, destinations are typically opened together as a new season. Cruise line revenue managers present the new season to the marketplace as an event with specially crafted pricing aimed at the groups market and at past guests, two segments which book far in advance. The early reaction to a new season is often an important harbinger of how future demand will develop during the rest of the booking window. These early booking patterns help cruise line revenue managers establish pricing strategies and action plans for implementation as the cruise's departure date approaches.

Once a new season is launched, a cruise line's revenue management system measures each individual cruise against expected booking patterns. These expectations vary by type of cruise, season, customer segment, distribution channel, and point-in-time in the booking horizon. Booking patterns, and variances to expectations, inform cruise line revenue managers about which pricing and inventory settings will lead to optimal revenues for each cruise.

Option Periods, Deposits, Final Payments, and Cancellation Fees

Cruise line booking terms vary significantly from hotels. Cruise line booking processes typically follows these steps:

Guests make a reservation and are allowed to hold it for up to 48–72 hours without a **deposit**. This is called an **option period.**

At the end of the option period, guests are required to pay a deposit. In most cases, the deposit is fully refundable in the event of cancellation long before the cruise departure date. Some cruise lines, however, assess an administration fee in the event of cancellation. Once guests make a financial commitment to their reservation, the cancellation rate is low, typically less than 10 or 12 percent.

As the departure date approaches, **full payment** becomes due. Due dates for full payment vary by cruise length, with longer cruises requiring full payment earlier than shorter cruises. For a 7-night cruise, final payments are typically due 60–75 days prior to departure.

Cancellations made after final payment are subject to an escalating schedule of **cancellation penalties**. Guests who cancel at 45 days, for example, are often subject to a penalty of 50 percent of the cost of cruise. Guests who cancel at 30 days typically pay a penalty of 75 percent. Guests who cancel within 14 days are likely to lose the entire cost of their cruise.

As such, close-in cancellations and no-shows are rare in the cruise industry. This gives cruise line revenue managers a clear sense of how much inventory remains and it greatly reduces the industry's overbooking risks.

Norwegian Cruise Line (NCL) Payment Terms and Cancellation Policy					
Cabin Deposit	Final Payment	Cancellation Penalties by Days Prior to Departure			
Per Person	Due Date	75–56	55–30	29–15	14 days or less
$250	75 days prior	Deposit	50% of cruise fare	75% of cruise fare	100% of cruise fare

Source: NCL Company Brochure.

Per Person Pricing

A hotel's capacity constraint is its number of rooms, which can be purchased for one or more nights. Therefore, hotel pricing is expressed on a per room, per night basis.

A cruise ship's capacity constraint is its number of **lifeboat seats**. A portion of a ship's lifeboat seats are, of course, reserved for the crew. The remaining lifeboat seats establish the upper boundary of how many guests a ship can carry.

Therefore, cruise ship capacity management works as follows: The number of cabins on a ship times two establishes the **double occupancy capacity** of a ship. If a ship has 1500 cabins, it has a double occupancy capacity of 3000. (Note: Some cruise ships have cabins specifically designed for a **solo traveler**. The number of these cabins is multiplied by one, not by two.)

The difference between 3000 and the number of lifeboat seats establishes the capacity for **third and fourth guests** in a cabin. On most ships, the number of lifeboat seats above the double occupancy capacity is 400 to 600, or even more. These third and fourth guests in a cabin are accommodated in sofa beds or in bunk beds that pull down from the ceiling.

In this way, a cruise will often sail with more guests than the ship's double occupancy capacity. So, by industry convention, a cruise line's occupancy rate can be more than 100 percent. If a ship with a double occupancy capacity of 3000 is carrying 3150 guests due to family and friends traveling in third and fourth berths, the occupancy for the cruise is 105 percent, which is calculated as 3150 total guests divided by the ship's 3000-person double occupancy capacity. Furthermore, when one person is in a cabin, it is counted at 50 percent occupancy, which somewhat offsets the impact of thirds and fourths.

For these reasons, cruise pricing is expressed on a per person basis, not on a per cabin basis. Also, since cruises are sold in their entirety, not per night, cruise pricing is expressed on a per person per cruise basis. (Note: While some people in other industries may well question cruise line occupancy calculations, what's reflected in this textbook chapter is consistent with industry practices, including SEC filings among the public companies, including Carnival, Royal Caribbean, and NCL).

Captive Audience for Ancillary Revenues

A strong cruise itinerary includes plenty of time for guests to experience interesting destinations. But it also includes a lot of time onboard the ship where guests can partake in a myriad of spending opportunities. Cruise ships boast large casinos, numerous bars and lounges, expansive retail shops, specialty restaurants, as well as other onboard revenue venues.

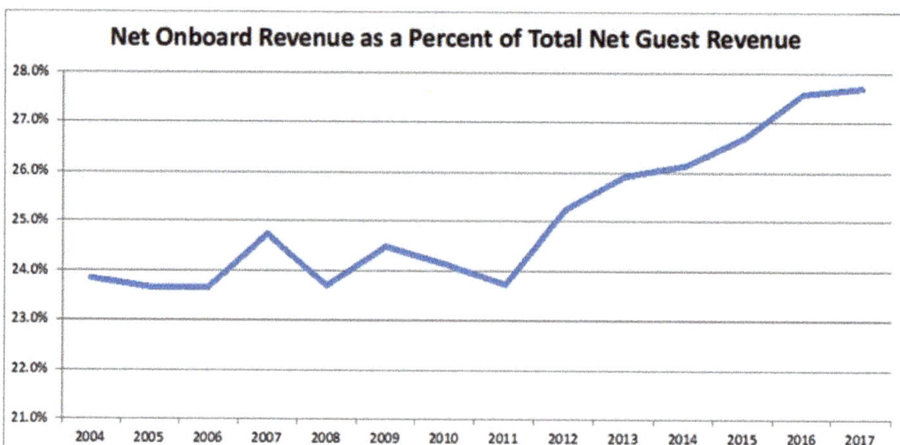

Source: Public financial documents from Carnival Corporation, Royal Caribbean Cruises Ltd., and Norwegian Cruise Line Holdings.

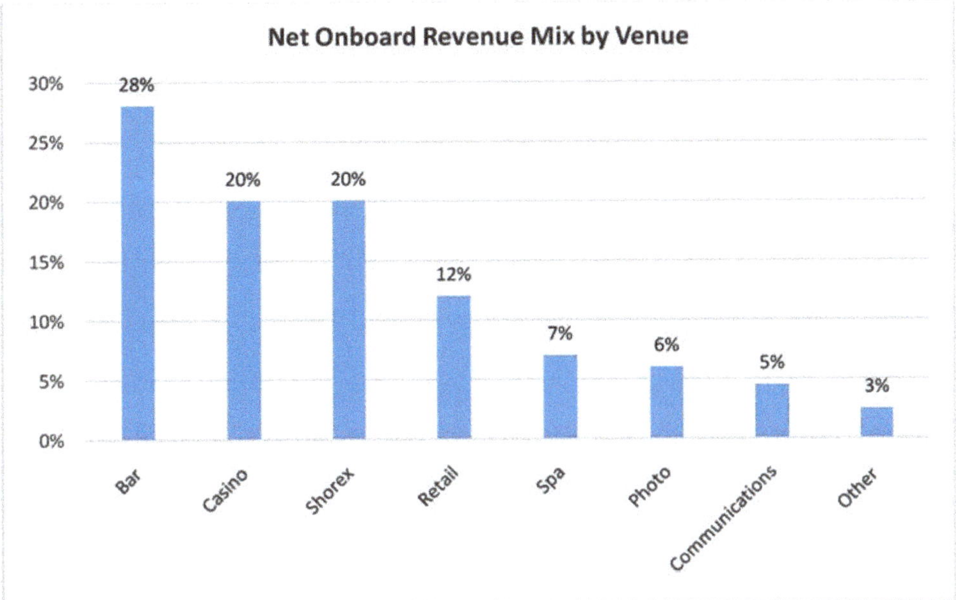

Source: Estimations based on author's industry experience.

These ancillary onboard revenues account for 25 percent or more of a cruise line's total revenue and is one of the most important reasons the cruise industry is so strongly biased towards sailing without any empty cabins. Today, onboard revenue assumptions play a key role in the recommendations generated by cruise line **revenue optimization models**, which are programmed to use the contribution of onboard revenue in their algorithms.

Year-round Ship Deployments versus Seasonal Ship Deployments

Hotels are fixed in a certain spot and are forever tied to the seasonal demand patterns of their location. Cruise ships, on the other hand, are able to move. So they tend to follow the good weather, which minimizes their days spent operating in an off-season during which pricing and/or occupancy would otherwise be particularly low.

Some ships are deployed on **year-round itineraries** in the Caribbean, which enjoys good weather and relatively strong consumer demand at all times. Other ships are deployed on a **seasonal itinerary** in which it might spend November through March in the warm, sunny Caribbean and then April through October in the warm, sunny, and culturally fascinating Mediterranean. The revenue benefits of such a seasonal deployment would be somewhat offset by the relatively low revenue opportunity of two repositioning cruises across the Atlantic Ocean, one in the Spring and another in the Fall.

The balance between year-round and seasonal deployments, and the number of days spent repositioning is an important factor in cruise line revenue management.

Wave Season

The two-and-a-half month booking period from early January through late March is known in the cruise industry as the annual "Wave" season. During these 10 weeks, cruise lines book close to 40 percent of their reservations for the coming year. From a promotional standpoint, Wave season for cruise lines is like retailers' Black Friday, Cyber-Monday, and holiday shopping season all rolled into one.

In the months leading into the Wave season, cruise line revenue managers are able to clearly read the demand characteristics of each departure for the coming calendar year. Cruise pricing and inventory control settings are fine-tuned accordingly. But more importantly, strong promotional offers are launched into the general marketplace, supported by millions of dollars of advertising spend and significant support from the sales department and its distribution channels.

Wave promotions work at two levels. Strategically, they are designed to promote cruises in general with special offers that are widely available across hundreds of cruises. Tactically, cruise line revenue managers aim the most compelling offers at sailings that need the greatest demand stimulation.

Wave season is so important to demand patterns that the timing of its impact is carefully calibrated into all cruise line demand forecasting models.

By the end of March, when the Wave season is over, cruise lines have typically booked 85 percent or more of their revenue goals for the current calendar year. As such, when Wave season is over, cruise line revenue management departments begin to turn most of their attention to the following calendar year.

Implications for Cruise Line Occupancy

Let's recap the factors listed above:

Cruises have a fixed start date and end date. Cruise guests must book an entire cruise. So there are no broken room nights caused by a mismatch of arrivals and departures.

The sales cycle for cruises begins a year-and-a-half or more from the departure date. So there is a long time for cruise line revenue managers to adjust pricing and inventory settings in response to demand characteristics and to sell all available capacity.

Capacity is constrained by the number of lifeboat seats, which are greater than the double occupancy capacity of the ship, allowing cruise line revenue managers to aim for occupancies of more than 100 percent.

Onboard revenues are a significant portion of a cruise line's total revenues. Therefore, the opportunity cost of an empty cabin is comprised of both the lost ticket revenue and also the lost onboard revenue. As such, cruise line revenue managers are highly motivated to fill every cabin, even if it means significantly reducing ticket prices in discrete, covert markets.

Ships are deployed in a way that maximizes demand throughout the year and repositioning cruises are kept to a minimum. So there is never a time at which full occupancy is not possible.

Wave Season brings a surge in cruise bookings when demand characteristics are clear and allows cruise line revenue managers to optimize prices. Cruises with strong demand can be managed to maximize prices. Cruises with weak demand can be priced to stimulate sufficient demand to achieve occupancy targets.

For all of these reasons, cruise line revenue managers are able to achieve occupancies unlike any other sector of the travel industry. One measure of excellence among cruise line revenue managers is a propensity to sail without a single empty cabin. In fact, the most successful cruise line revenue managers have a credo: "Zero tolerance for empty cabins."

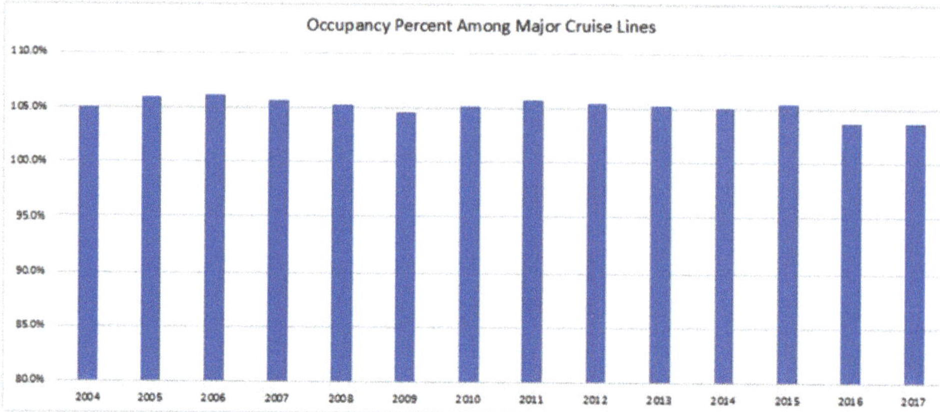

Source: Annual reports for Carnival Corporation, Royal Caribbean Cruises Ltd., and Norwegian Cruise Holdings.

SPREADSHEET EXERCISE 13.2

Build an MS Excel spreadsheet to decide how to approach the following cruise line revenue management problem:

There are 200 unsold beds in inside cabins on a departure 60 days out. The forecast for the main strategic market estimates there is demand for 150 beds at the current price of $799 per person, leaving 50 beds empty. Based on observed price elasticity, every $5 reduction in price increases demand by 2 percent. In other words, lowering the price from $799 to $794 will increase demand from 150 guests to 153 guests. Additionally, based on previous experience, a covert tactical promotion to a select market is likely to generate 50 guests at a price of $599 per person.

Which is a better revenue management decision and why? Reducing prices in the main strategic market to fill the 50 beds? Or, leaving the price as is in the strategic market and implementing the covert tactical promotion?

Does your decision change if the covert tactical price required to generate 50 beds is $399?

Tools for Managing Cruise Line Prices

In order to support their **full ship mentality**, cruise lines have built significant **passenger sourcing infrastructure** and they have also configured their ships with revenue optimization in mind. Both factors are key tools used by revenue managers.

Worldwide Guest Sourcing

Cruise lines have saleforces that establish deep and broad relationships with individual travel agencies and travel agency consortia around the world. The major cruise lines have a significant sales presence in all of the important global cruise markets. Even small cruise lines typically maintain salesforces in their main domestic market as well as one or two additional international markets.

The diversity of international guest sourcing is used by cruise line revenue managers in three key ways:

1. Willingness-to-Pay: Guests' willingness-to-pay varies geographically. A French guest, for example, thinks of the Caribbean as a far-away and exotic destination, particularly in February when France is dark and cold. But a February cruise to the Caribbean is a quick, easy getaway for someone who lives in Miami. In this case, the French guest is likely to be willing-to-pay more than the Miami guest for a February Caribbean cruise. On the other hand, the Mediterranean is a far-away and exotic destination for a Miami guest, who is likely to be willing-to-pay more to sail out of Marseille in June than a French guest. A cruise line revenue manager will set prices according to these varying geographic preferences.
2. Disguising Differential Pricing: For reasons that will be discussed later in this chapter, a cruise line revenue manager tries to mask the fact that cruise guests pay different prices. International guest sourcing helps in this regard for two reasons. First, international currencies and exchange rates can help to make direct price comparisons difficult. Second, commercial terms in international markets often vary. Taxes, for example, are typically assessed in addition to cruise fares in the U.S. market. In Europe, on the other hand, they are bundled into the price, which further obscures direct comparisons across international prices.
3. Close-in Discounting: In some cases, in order to fill every cabin, it becomes necessary for a cruise line revenue manager to offer close-in

discounts to stimulate demand. But if the distressed inventory is on Mediterranean sailings, it is harder to stimulate demand among North American guests because they still have to buy an expensive long-haul flight across the Atlantic. It is much easier to stimulate demand among French and Italian guests who can drive to the cruise port. In these cases, international passenger sourcing capabilities are a key resource for cruise line revenue managers.

Customer Databases

In addition, cruise lines maintain large computerized customer relationship management (CRM) systems. These customer databases contain details about the lines' **past guests** and **prospects**. Past guests are people who have already sailed with the cruise line one or more times. Prospects are people who have visited the line's website and requested additional information but have not yet sailed with the company. Both past guests and prospects are marketed to constantly. It is not unusual for cruise lines, both large and small, to send promotional emails on a daily basis to certain segments of their customer database.

The ability to "mine" the customer database is used by cruise line revenue managers in three key ways:

1. Stimulate demand: Working together with the marketing department, cruise line revenue managers are able to address demand shortfalls by using promotional offers to stimulate demand among large numbers of potential guests.
2. Control **dilution**: A risk of lowering prices is that people who are already booked at higher prices may demand a refund. Cruise line CRM systems typically track which guests are booked on future cruises. These guests can be suppressed from promotional communications.
3. Test price points: Response to email offers is almost immediate. So cruise line revenue managers can test the effectiveness of various price points and offers before committing to a large scale promotion.

Ship Configuration

Cruise ship cabin configurations are designed to maximize the total units of demand while at the same time capturing maximum value from different cruise customers' willingness to pay. A cruise ship can have up to 30 different **cabin categories** ranging from small, windowless rooms on low decks to expansive, multi-level suites on upper decks. Prices for a 7-day cruise could easily vary across these cabins categories by 785 percent, from a low of $949 per person to a high of $8399 per person, with many price points in between. In this way, cruise line revenue managers are able to use a single cruise ship to appeal to a wide array of guest demographics, from value-oriented vacationers on a relatively tight budget, to luxury and high-end amenity seeking guests at the opposite end of the willingness-to-pay spectrum. A revenue-maximizing cruise ship is broken down into six major cabin categories, each aimed at a distinct willingness-to-pay guest segment:

Cabin Type	**Cabin Characteristics**
Inside	Standard size cabins, no window. Usually on low decks, close to the waterline, which by cruise industry convention are less desirable than upper decks.
Outside	Standard size cabins, with a fixed window.
Balcony	Standard size cabins, with a sliding glass door that opens onto a private balcony overlooking the ocean. Most cabins on modern cruise ships fall into this category.
Premium Balcony	Same as standard balcony cabins, but with upgraded amenities such privileged access to the Spa or concierge services.
Suite	Larger cabins, typically one-and-a-half to two-times the size of standard cabins. Also have upgraded amenities such as priority lines for embarkation and debarkation, access to premium seating in the show lounges and exclusive dining rooms, concierge services and upgraded in-room amenities such as large screen TVs and larger bathrooms.
Super Suite	Very large cabins, sometimes as much as 1500 square feet or more. Include all of the features of standard suits plus butler service, in-room dining rooms, multiple bedrooms and bathrooms, huge wraparound balconies and state-of-the-art entertainment systems.

Royal Caribbean Oasis of the Seas, sample pricing by cabin category.

7-Night Caribbean Sailing.

Cabin Category	Description	Sq Ft	Price per Person
RS	Royal Suite	1284	$8,399
SL	Sky Loft Suite	722	$7,769
L1	Crown Loft Suite	545	$4,099
L2	Crown Loft Suite	545	$3,749
OS	Owner's Suite	569	$3,549
GS	Grand Suite	371	$2,899
JS	Junior Suite	287	$2,099
B1	Boardwalk View Balcony	182	$1,269
B2	Boardwalk View Balcony	182	$1,249
C1	Central Park View w/Balcony	182	$1,219
C2	Central Park View w/Balcony	182	$1,199
D1	Superior Ocean View w/Lg Balcony	182	$1,559
D2	Superior Ocean View w/Balcony	182	$1,509
D3	Superior Ocean View w/Balcony	182	$1,479
D4	Superior Ocean View w/Balcony	182	$1,449
D5	Superior Ocean View w/Balcony	182	$1,389
D6	Superior Ocean View w/Balcony	182	$1,359
D7	Superior Ocean View w/Balcony	182	$1,329
D8	Superior Ocean View w/Balcony	182	$1,299
BV	Boardwalk View	187	$1,089
CV	Central Park View	194	$1,049
F	Ocean View Stateroom	178	$1,089
H	Ocean View Stateroom	178	$1,069
I	Ocean View Stateroom	178	$1,049
PR	Promenade Stateroom	193	$1,129
L	Large Interior Stateroom	178	$1,039
M	Large Interior Stateroom	178	$999
N	Large Interior Stateroom	178	$979
Q	Interior Stateroom	150	$949
Weighted Average Price			$1,379

Source: Royal Caribbean International website.

Question to Consider #2

A cruise line revenue manager is considering making a change to which of the company's ships is deployed in Alaska. The ship configurations and predicted selling prices per cabin type are contained in the table below. Which ship would you send to Alaska and why?

	Ship 1		Ship 2	
	Number of Cabins	**Per Person Price**	**Number of Cabins**	**Per Person Price**
Suites	50	$1,499	150	$1,349
Balconies	500	$1,199	500	$1,199
Window	100	$999	50	$1,049
No Window	100	$899	50	$949

In addition to providing built-in willingness-to-pay filters, cruise ship cabin configurations also provide useful inventory management functionality. When necessary, cruise line revenue managers are able to use excess demand from lower priced cabin categories to supplement weak demand in higher priced cabin categories. When faced with this demand scenario, cruise line revenue managers oversell lower cabin categories and upgrade those guests into higher cabin categories where demand is insufficient to fill the available space. This is especially convenient and revenue maximizing for the following reasons:

1. Lower price dilution: The price difference between an inside cabin and an outside cabin, or between an outside cabin and a balcony cabin could be as little as $25 or $50 per person. If the demand shortfall in lower cabin categories is not significant, planned upgrades can be a cost-effective solution.

2. Easier than implementing a promotion: While cruise lines launch promotions all the time, there are many steps involved: such as setting up the price program in the reservations system and coordinating with the marketing department. Setting the inventory control parameters to oversell a cabin category and then upgrading guests into a higher category is administratively easier. Some cruise line reservations systems can do this automatically, on the basis of business rules entered into the reservation system by the revenue management department.

3. Less disruptive to guests who are already booked: Promotions can sometimes be disruptive to guests who are already booked and may have already paid a higher fare. Free upgrades, on the other hand, are typically considered simply the luck of the draw as cabins are assigned.

Cruise Line Pricing

There are two basic types of cruise line pricing: strategic and tactical. Strategic cruise pricing refers to the prices that are set-up when a cruise is opened for sale in the reservations system, typically 18-months prior to departure. Tactical pricing refers to price adjustments and promotional offers that are implemented in response to actual booking patterns.

Strategic Cruise Pricing

When establishing strategic prices, cruise line revenue managers perform a detailed analysis of how current and historical prices have performed for the same or similar cruise itineraries. In cases where historical prices have often been increased, cruise line revenue managers may decide to increase strategic prices for the new season. If historical prices have often been decreased, or if an unexpectedly high number of promotions have been needed to fill capacity, cruise line revenue managers may decide to set strategic prices lower for the new season.

In addition to analyzing historical price performance, cruise line revenue managers will also consider anticipated changes in the operating environment. If the line is introducing a new ship onto an itinerary, cruise line revenue managers will often decide to increase prices on the expectation that the new ship will attract more customer demand. If, on the other hand, competitors have announced a new entry or a capacity increase on an itinerary, cruise line revenue managers may reduce prices in anticipation of price pressure due to more competitive capacity.

When cruises are opened for sale, cruise line revenue managers publish a comprehensive set of prices for all cabin categories. That set of prices typically includes the following:

Strategic Price Program Type	Description
Brochure	Cruise line brochure rates are like the MSRP of a car. No one pays this price, but it is used to establish a reference price against which discounts are positioned. Not all cruise lines use brochure rates.
Early Booking	This is a special price, typically positioned as a percentage off the brochure rate, to encourage guests to book early. These prices are often positioned as having set expiration periods and as being subject to increase as the sailing date approaches. The actual change in these prices is dependent on the demand characteristics for a sailing.
Past Guest	Past guests can make-up as much as 40% of a cruise line's guests. To insure loyalty, past guests are often given an additional discount off the Early Booking rates.
Group – Promotional	Groups comprise an important part of a cruise line's total guest mix. In many cases, travel agents will organize a group promotion which typically includes a special price and/or onboard amenity as well as an opportunity for the travel agent to earn extra commission.
Group – Meeting & Incentive	Meeting and Incentive groups are also an important part of a cruise line's total guest mix. Because these groups tend to be bigger than promotional groups and because they tend to have different requirements for onboard services, these groups are priced separately.
International	Most, if not all, of a cruise line's prices are converted from a base currency into other international currencies. These conversions include any variances in commercial terms from market to market and any decisions to favor one market over another based on a cruise line's international priorities and strategies.
Net, non-commissionable	Cruises are often included in tour operator programs, where the cruise is part of a larger vacation package. In these cases, cruise lines provide a tour operator with a net, non-commissionable price, which is typically fixed throughout the booking window, regardless of how market prices may change.
Charter	Small cruise ships with fewer than 750 beds are often chartered for meeting and incentive programs. For these ships, its typical for cruise line revenue managers to provide the sales force with rates for full ship charters.

PROS & CONS

When crafting strategic pricing, some cruise line revenue managers prefer to start with prices on the high side and then discount later to fill in the gaps. Other cruise line revenue managers prefer to start with prices on the low side then increase prices as ships fill. Which approach makes more sense to you and why?

Tactical Cruise Pricing

Once a cruise season has been opened for sale and the strategic pricing has been launched, cruise line revenue managers begin to track the pace of bookings relative to expected booking patterns. These booking patterns are tracked in a detailed manner and are discretely measured across cabin categories on the ship, across customer segments in the market place and across geographic sectors of the distribution channel. As the actual booking pace begins to vary from expectations, cruise line revenue managers begin to adjust prices accordingly.

Stronger than expected demand scenarios put cruise line revenue managers in the catbird seat. With 100 percent occupancy assured, they can shift the guest mix away from lower priced segments and increase rates in core markets. In this case, cruise line revenue managers raise prices in order to guard against **spilling** demand which would otherwise exceed supply.

Weaker than expected demand scenarios are an entirely different matter. When demand is weak, mitigating the risk of **spoilage** is a serious challenge. Organizationally, responsibility for addressing these challenges typically falls to the revenue management team, which is expected to reduce rates by the minimum amount required to sufficiently stimulate enough demand to fill the at risk cabins. In this role, the revenue management team is expected to provide leadership and direction that will steer the sales and marketing teams toward activities to address the problem sailings. Solving a weak demand scenario requires well-crafted promotions that are properly communicated to the distribution channel and to the customer database.

The components of a well-crafted cruise promotion are:

1. Aimed at the right part of the ship: Cruise line revenue managers pay careful attention to which cabin categories need promotional support. If the suites are on pace to sell-out, for example, any promotions should exclude suite categories.
2. Targeted to an underperforming customer segment: When possible, it is better to stimulate demand among weak performing customer segments. If that approach fails, a cruise line revenue manager may have no choice but to further stimulate demand among customer segments that are already performing as expected.
3. Targeted to an underperforming sector of the distribution channel: Sometimes a particular travel agency consortium is underperforming. In these cases, it may make sense to offer special sales incentives to steal share from other cruise line alternatives.
4. Discounted enough to stimulate sufficient demand without giving away more than necessary: Cruise line revenue managers rely on price elasticity models and assumptions about price/demand relationships to determine the level of discounting necessary to stimulate just the right about of additional demand.
5. Compelling and easy to communicate: In order to successfully stimulate demand, cruise line promotions must be easy to understand and offer a compelling reason to book. Many cruise lines accomplish this by using high brochure prices to offer a Two-for-One deal, which is a very effective promotional tool. In other cases, cruise lines offer additional amenities for free, such as free airfare, free hotel nights before or after the cruise, or free drinks onboard.

To achieve their promotional objectives, cruise line revenue managers turn to two types of promotional offers:

1. Percent Off/Dollars Off: Traditionally, cruise line revenue managers have stimulated demand by simply lowering cruise fares. The classic technique is the use of the brochure rate as a reference price and offer a large discount (up to 50% or more) with a very compelling lead rate, such as $499 for a 7-night Caribbean cruise. Alternatively, cruise lines often express their discounts as dollars-off the standard cruise fare. Such dollar-off discounts can be as high as $500 to $1000 off per person, or even higher for ultra-luxury cruise lines.

2. Value added: Recently, cruise line revenue managers have developed a preference for using value-added promotions to stimulate demand. The list of free value-added amenities used by cruise line revenue managers includes: drinks packages, onboard spending credits, free WiFi, shore excursions, specialty dining, cabin upgrades, third and fourth berths, and gratuities; plus air credits and even reduced deposits. Cruise line revenue managers like these promotions because their cost to the cruise lines is dramatically lower than customers' perceived value. A $100 drinks package, for example, costs less than $15. A $50 shore excursion credit costs only $25. Free third and fourth berths cost very little outside of summer and school holidays. And reduced deposits are only a minor cash flow issue. In this way, cruise lines are able to preserve a lot of net ticket revenue while sacrificing very little net onboard revenue.

Pricing Constraints

It is a reality that in the dynamic pricing environment of a revenue management system, customers frequently pay different prices for essentially the same product. But, over the relatively short duration of most flights, airline passengers do not speak to their seatmates about how much they paid for their tickets. Similarly, individual hotel guests do not speak to the people across the hall about how much they are paying per night.

But the social milieu on a cruise ship is quite different. Strangers meet over dinner, at the card tables in the casino, in the bars and during a variety of group activities around the pool or during shore excursions. It is not unusual for people to talk about how much they paid for their cruise.

So one unique challenge for a cruise line revenue manager is to craft a tactical pricing strategy that does not leave certain guests feeling ripped off and angry with the cruise line or with their travel agent. Most people are comfortable with the concept of "book early as save." So if a guest paid more than another guest who booked earlier, that is viewed as fair. A problem can arise, however, when a guest who booked early paid more than a guest who booked later.

In these cases, revenue managers try to disguise their discounts by bundling the deal into a value added promotion, or offering the special price for limited customer groups such as residents of certain states or senior citizens. Sometimes cruise line revenue managers will use restrictive fares that offer less flexibility and choice. With these fares, guests are not able to choose a specific cabin or may not be permitted to hold a cabin without an immediate deposit.

REAL PEOPLE 1

During the worldwide financial crisis of 2008, the bottom fell out of the ultra-luxury cruise market. Demand fell off sharply just as significant new capacity was coming online. Some of the ultra-luxury brands resorted to deep discounts to spur demand and keep ships sailing full. One cruise line executive, Frank Del Rio, took a different path. Instead of lowering prices for the Regent brand, he added value by making the product truly all inclusive. He even took the then unprecedented step of including shore excursions in the cruise fare.

1. What are the pros and cons of Del Rio's approach?
2. What do you believe were the strongest aspects of his strategy?

If you were a cruise line revenue manager, would you have adopted the same approach?

Avoiding Close-in Discounting

The best cruise line revenue managers address weak demand scenarios early, as soon as booking patterns begin to vary from expectations. Otherwise, they may be left with too much space to sell too close to departure, when cruise lines and other travel companies dump their space in a panic. Because cruises are typically sold to leisure travelers who make their vacation plans far from departure, there is relatively little natural demand for cruises within 30 days of departure. At that point, any unsold cabins are considered at risk of sailing empty, with the corresponding lost ticket and onboard revenues. Therefore, cruise lines that are caught with too much space close to departure offer highly distressed prices in order to assure 100 percent occupancy, even at very low APDs. The problem has become so bad that senior management at one cruise line issued an outright ban on discounting within 30-days of departure.

REAL PEOPLE 2

Royal Caribbean Cruises, Ltd., Chairman and CEO Richard Fain was fed-up with close-in discounting. Even though close in sales made up just a small percentage of the company's overall bookings, Fain and his senior advisors felt that such discounts were highly disruptive; denigrated the brand's image, and encouraged people and travel agents to wait until the last minute for a better price. In April 2015, Fain put a new hurdle in front of his company's revenue management department. He banned last minute cruise discounts.

1. What are the pros and cons of Fain's approach?
2. What do you believe were the strongest aspects of his strategy?

If you were a cruise line revenue manager, would you have adopted the same approach?

Cruise Line Revenue Management Systems

In the early days of the cruising, there were no computerized systems. Customer service agents on roller skates would manually update customer reservations in berthing books. Years later, when cruise line revenue management practices first started to take hold, revenue managers would go from meeting to meeting carrying reams of paper reports and use rulers to keep track of rows and columns of numbers that spanned the full width of legal-sized paper.

There are still vestiges of those old paper-based reports, but most large cruise lines have installed computerized revenue management systems that use high-level mathematics to forecast demand, gauge consumers' price elasticity, and recommend optimal prices and upgrade limits.

At some cruise lines, the revenue management system's recommendations are first presented to cruise line revenue managers for evaluation and approval prior to implementation. At other cruise lines, recommendations that fall within carefully defined parameters are automatically sent directly to the reservations system.

Computerized revenue management systems for cruise lines are expensive and take a long time to implement. Therefore, they have not yet been adopted by smaller cruise lines where the scale of the business is such that the revenue management team can be successful with well-defined processes and a combination of MS Excel and paper-based reports.

CONCLUSION

It is true that the airline, car rental, and hotel industries are much bigger than the cruise industry and offer many more potential jobs for travel industry revenue management professionals. But with its unique characteristics and drive for 100 percent occupancy, the cruise industry offers an exciting opportunity for revenue management professionals looking to be challenged and willing to assume important leadership roles within their companies.

SEEING FURTHER

The sophistication of cruise line revenue management has increased as the business has grown. Today, all major cruise lines use predictive demand modeling and revenue optimization models to support decision making about price and inventory settings. But cruise line revenue management continues to be used primarily as a tactical method to manage the physical inventory of cabins and determines things such as the number of cabins to sell at a given price and when to open and close prices.

Some revenue management departments in other hospitality sectors are taking a more customer-centric approach and are using strategies and promotions to maximize the lifetime value of a customer and are blending both ticket revenues and onboard revenues.

What are some of the ways that you think cruise line revenue managers could leverage the data in their CRM systems to increase cruise line profitability?

DISCUSSION QUESTIONS

1) With the cruise industry continuing to grow, more and more cruise lines are diving into the hot market of Asia, more specifically China. The Chinese government is predicting that by the year 2020, the cruise traffic in China will amount to 4.5 million passengers (Forbes). What do you think makes cruising so popular in Asia? How does cruising in Asia compare to cruising in others parts of the world, such as Europe, the Caribbean, and Alaska?
2) In order to stay afloat in the competitive cruising industry, Norwegian Cruise Line plans to spend $400 million to build new ships and improve older ones (Skift). With the introduction of the Norwegian Edge program, ships from the company's extensive fleet are going to be modernized and improved upon. What areas do you think the company should focus allocating that money when improving their ships? Which will be the most profitable and set the cruise line apart from others?
3) Which types of cruises are the most expensive for customers yet still generate the highest demand?

APPLICATIONS

Application 1

Silvio Pascual is deciding between a free air promotion or a residents special at $899 per person to help solve a demand shortage problem of 100 guests on a 7-night Caribbean cruise departing in 6 months. Silvio has decided to focus his analysis and recommendations on the states of Ohio and Arizona and is evaluating the following facts:

	Ohio	Arizona
Current Cruise Price	$1299	$1299
Current Air Price	$499	$599
Air Cost	$350	$475
Commission Rate	15%	15%

What additional information is required in order to make the best possible decision? Would you recommend a reduced air promotion or a residents' special promotion? Why? What additional information would assist in making the best possible decision?

In your analysis, you should assume that all the promotional options will generate the incremental 100 guests required to fill the sailing. Be sure to consider air costs and commissions on both cruise fares and air add-ons.

Application 2

Isabel Alonzo has been asked by the owner of a small-ship cruise line to help decide whether the line should build a new ship. The owner has asked Isabel to consider the following questions:

1. Where should the ship be deployed?
2. How many suites and super-suites should the ship carry?
3. What pricing can the company expect?
4. How would the pricing of other ships already in the fleet be impacted?
5. What types of investments would the company have to make in marketing and sales infrastructure to fill the additional, new capacity?

Your first step is to perform an analysis of the company's historical performance. What information is required regarding:

Yields by itinerary?
Prices by cabin category?
Premium pricing that can be achieved on new ships versus older ships?
Size of the company's past passenger database?
Potential to grow the company's traditionally strong guest sourcing markets? Opportunities to expand into new guest sourcing markets?

For this exercise, formulate how you would approach such an analysis and discuss how the findings would influence your recommendations.

TEAM ACTIVITY

The sales and marketing departments have come to the revenue management department for approval to implement a "Kids Sail Free" promotion in third and fourth berths. In order to generate as many bookings as possible, they'd like to make the promotion available on all future departures. Using the internet, research if and how this sort of promotion is currently used by major mass market cruise lines. What are the booking terms, conditions and restrictions? Would you approve this promotion? Why or why not? If not, what would you propose as an alternative and why?

INTERNET ACTIVITY

Using the Internet, study the types of promotions that are in use at three or four cruise companies. Separate the promotions into two categories: Value Add and Dollars/Percent discount.

What is similar between the two examples? What are the significant differences? Which do you believe would work better and why?

In your evaluations, assume that the profit margin on beverage packages is 75 percent, on Spa services the profit margin is 55 percent and on shore excursions, the profit margin is 45 percent.

GLOSSARY

ALBDs – Abbreviation for available lower berth days, which is the measure of cruise capacity. Some cruise lines refer to PGCDs, which means potential guest cruise days.

APD – Abbreviation for average per diem, which is the net ticket revenue divided by the number of days in the cruise. Some cruise lines refer to NPD, net per diem, which is the same statistic.

Cabin categories – Cruise ship cabins have different physical attributes and/or different locations on a ship. Similar cabin types are grouped into the same cabin category and sold at the same price.

Cancellation penalties – Fees assessed in the event that a cruise is canceled after the full payment due date.

Crew – The cruise ship staff is referred to as crew. This includes hotel operations staff who serve the guests and marine and technical staff who operate and maintain the ship.

Cruise berths - Beds on a cruise ship are referred to as berths. The first two beds in a cabin are referred to as lower berths. The third and fourth beds are referred to as upper berths.

Cruise length – The number of days in a cruise.

Debarkation day – The date the cruise arrives at its final port of call and passengers leave the ship.

Departure date – The date the cruise departs from its first port. Also referred to as embarkation date.

Deposit – The payment required to hold a reservation. Can range from $500 to $1,000 dollars or more.

Dilution – The amount of a refund given to a guest who converts to a tactical promotion after having already booked at a higher fare.

Double occupancy capacity – By cruise industry convention, each cabin has a capacity of two guests (a small percentage of cabins are designed for single guests) and a double occupancy capacity of 2. If that cabin carries a third guest, its occupancy is 150% (3 divided by 2.) If that cabin carries four guests, its occupancy is 200% (4 divided 2.) In this way, cruise ship occupancy typically exceeds 100%.

Embark – To board a ship.

Full payment date – The date the full payment for the cruise is due, typically 30 days or more before the start of the cruise.

Full ship mentality – Cruise line revenue managers are expected to sell every cabin on a ship prior to the departure date. This is a cultural imperative at the most successful cruise lines.

Itineraries – The cruise region and the ports of call during the cruise.

Leisure travelers – People traveling as part of a personal vacation without a business purpose. Leisure travelers tend to be more price sensitive than business travelers and tend to book further in advance.

Lifeboat seats – By law, a cruise ship must carry lifeboats with enough seats for every person onboard the ship, including both guests and crew members.

Net onboard revenue – Onboard revenue after deducting the cost of goods sold.

Net ticket revenue -- Ticket revenue after deducting travel agent commission or other direct sales costs (such as airfare for air-inclusive tickets.)

No-shows - Guests holding a fully paid reservation who do not cancel in advance and who do not show up at the ship on the departure date. Typically, very few people are no-shows.

(NPD) – Net per day - See APD

Occupancy – The percentage of available capacity that is occupied or sold. Calculated as the guest cruise days divided by the ALBDs.

Onboard revenue – Revenue derived from onboard sales in venues such as bars, casinos, shore excursions, gift shops, spas, etc.

Option period – The number of days between the time of reservation and the time the reservation will automatically cancel if a deposit is not received. Can range from 1 day to 1 week.

Passenger sourcing infrastructure – In order to fill all capacity for all departures, cruise lines build customer relationship management systems to facilitate frequent direct marketing to past guests and prospects. They also deployment sales teams around the world to build and maintain relationships with the travel agency distribution system.

Revenue optimization models – Large cruise lines use mathematically sophisticated models to forecast demand at various price points and in various markets and recommend prices that will result in the highest profit contribution.

Seasonal itinerary – Some cruise ships are deployed on various itineraries throughout the year. For example, a ship might sail in the Caribbean in the winter and reposition to Alaska for the summer, returning the Caribbean in the Fall.

Solo traveler – A cruise passenger traveling alone in a cabin.

Spill – When there is more demand than supply, the demand that can't be accommodated is "spilled."

Spoilage – When there is less demand than supply, any cabins that sail empty are "spoiled."

Third and fourth guests – Cruise ship cabins are designed to accommodate three or four guests, and sometimes more. Most often, these guests are children sharing the same cabin as their parents.

Ticket revenue – Revenue derived from cruise fares and does not include any ancillary revenues from onboard or other sales.

Travel agent commission – Roughly 65% of cruises are sold through travel agents who earn commissions ranging from 10% to 20% of Ticket Revenue.

Two-for-One – The most effective cruise line promotion is offering two for the price of one. Some cruise lines purposely set their brochure rates high enough so they are willing to accept that fare for the first guest and no fare at all for the second guest.

Year-round itineraries – Some cruise ships are deployed on the same itinerary year round, often in the Caribbean.

Yield – The most important revenue management statistic in the cruise industry. Yield can be calculated two ways: 1) Average per diem times occupancy percentage, and 2) net ticket revenue divided by ALBDs. But equations give the same result.

REFERENCES

Anonymous, PR Newswire. (2010). CLIA's 35th Anniversary Puts Spotlight on Remarkable Story of Growth & Evolution of Cruise Industry: History of Industry's Leading Trade Association Parallels Dramatic Transformation of Cruising, Cruise Ships, Consumer Expectations. *Proquest.* Fort Lauderdale.

Biehn, N. (2006). A Cruise Ship Is Not a Floating Hotel. *Journal of Revenue and Pricing Management, 5*(2), 135-142.

Cruise Lines International Association: Press Releases. (2005). Strong 3rd Quarter Passenger Growth Extends 2005 Trend for CLIA-Member Cruise Lines. *Cruise Lines International Association.* New York.

Cruise Lines International Association: Press Releases. (2006). Cruise Industry Reports Double-Digit Growth in Second Quarter 2006. *Cruise Lines International Association.* New York.

Cruise Lines International Association: Press Releases. (2009). The State of the Cruise Industry in 2009: Well-Positioned for Challenging Times. *Cruise Lines International Association.* Fort Lauderdale.

Cullen, K. (2015). *The evolving dynamics of revenue management. A Comprehensive Revenue Optimization Road Map for Hotel Owners, Operators and Practitioners.* HSMAI Foundation.

Garin, K. A. (2006). *Devils on the Deep Blue Sea. The Dreams, Schemes and Showdowns That Built America's Cruise-Ship Empires.* New York, NY: Penguin.

Green, M. (2015). CLIA Reports on Cruise Trends for 2015. *Travel Age West.* Northstar Travel Media Group.

Lieberman, W. (2012). Pricing in the Cruise Line Industry. In Ö. Özer & R. Phillips (Eds.), *The Oxford Handbook of Pricing Management*; ; Oxford, UK: Oxford University Press, 199-216.

Maddah, B., Moussawi-Haidar, L., El-Taha, M., & Rida, H. (2010). Dynamic Cruise Ship Revenue Management. *European Journal of Operational Research, 207,* 445–455.

Mathisen, O. (2012). State of the Industry Report. *Cruise Industry News.* New York.

More, R. (2015). Why Holiday cruises are more expensive. *Examiner.com.*

Royal Caribbean International Company Brochure. (2008). *Independence of the Seas.*

Sampson, H. (2016, January 22). To Get an Edge on Competition Norwegian Cruise Plans to Spend $400 Million. *Skift.com.*

Scott, L. & Ramdeen C. (2013). Cruise Ship Itineraries and Occupancy Rates. *Tourism Management, 34,* 236–237.

Selby, D. (2013) Revenue Management in the Cruising Industry. In P. Legohérel, E. Poutier, E. & A. Fyall, A. (Eds.), *Revenue Management for Hospitality and Tourism*; ; Woodeaton, Oxford: Goodfellow Publishers Limited, pp. 157–168.

Shao, H. (2014). Fast Sailing: China's Cruise Market to Become World's Second Largest by 2017. *Forbes Asia.*

Sun, X.; Jiao, Y., & Tian, P. (2011) Marketing Research and Revenue Optimization for the Cruise Industry: A Concise Review. *International Journal of Hospitality Management, 30,* 746-755.

Toh, R., Rivers M., & Ling T. (2005). Room Occupancies: Cruise Lines Out-Do the Hotels. *International Journal of Hospitality Management, 24,* 121-135.

CHAPTER 14

Total Revenue Management

Gabor Fenyves

OVERVIEW

Over the last decade, the hospitality industry realized that revenue managers cannot solely focus on room pricing and inventory management. Long gone are the days when guests were assigned a monetary value solely based on a room rate. A more holistic approach needs to be taken and all revenue streams per guest should be considered to truly drive total hotel profit instead of just room's revenue. Improvements in technology are enabling revenue managers to measure the overall guest spend and guide the sales and marketing team to attract these high-value segments to the hotel. This new revenue management branch is called total revenue management (TRM).

LEARNING OBJECTIVES

After studying this chapter, you should be able to:

- Explain the key foundations of TRM
- Identify the different RM time-based metricize used to measure auxiliary revenue performance
- Describe and implement a revenue management strategy to a nonroom outlet
- Perform calculations to evaluate which business is most profitable based on TRM
- Combine all outlet revenue management strategies into a holistic TRM approach
- Apply a framework to implement a successful TRM strategy
- Discuss the opportunities and future of TRM

OUTLINE

Introduction

What is Total Revenue Management?
Total Revenue Management Framework

- Non-Room Level Optimization
- Know the Existing Theory and Metrics
- Spas
- Spa Characteristics
- Spa Optimization
- Golf Courses
- Golf Characteristics

Demand Forecasting
Price Optimization

- Casinos
- Customer Segmentation
- Demand Forecasting
- Pricing
- Groups
- Pricing Strategy

Displacement Analysis

- Catering

Creative RM Strategy
Future Opportunities for TRM
Discussion Questions and Applications

INTRODUCTION

In the past, revenue management (RM) was solely focused on room's revenue being the most important factor in maximizing profit. Most methods that were used in order to optimize business mix looked only at room revenue and occasionally food and beverage in the decision-making process. Customers who were willing to pay a higher room rate were considered the hotel's "best" guests. This meant that the optimization of other revenue streams was overlooked or little focus was placed on sources such as restaurants, spas, or golf courses in the optimization decision. Only in the last couple of years has total revenue management come to the forefront of incorporating all guest spend at non-room outlets into a comprehensive strategy. Even though more hotels are adopting such a comprehensive RM model the industry is slow to keep up with such changes due to the availability or cleanliness of data. There is also not a clear unified measurement to compare a hotel's performance against its competitive set.

SO WHAT?

Due to the success of revenue management being applied to hotel rooms, expanding the horizon into other revenue-generating areas is the next opportunity. How do you think competitive analysis and benchmarking tools need to evolve in order to keep up with such trends?

WHAT IS TOTAL REVENUE MANAGEMENT?

TRM is the holy grail of RM. It shines a light on what is possible when a hotel focuses on optimizing revenue on all levels instead of just the room's department. When implemented efficiently, TRM takes into account all possible guest revenue-generating streams and enables revenue managers to drive the highest overall hotel profit.

There are five basic characteristics that need to be demonstrated in order for revenue management to be successfully implemented (Kimes, 1989).

1. Relatively fixed capacity
2. Time perishable inventory
3. Time-variable demand
4. Segmentable market
5. High fixed and low variable costs

If an outlet demonstrates the above-mentioned criteria then implementing a revenue management strategy can be successful. Hotel rooms are the traditional example where RM is most prevalent as it typically is the most profitable. However, other revenue centers, such as spas, golf courses, casinos, or even meeting space, are prime examples where revenue management strategies can be further applied. Applying RM tactics to improve profits generated from these revenue streams is one part of TRM. TRM then combines these decisions from all revenue streams on a customer level to generate the optimal mix. It focuses on not just maximizing individual revenues per customer at the outlet level but the combination of all transactions within the hotel.

TRM strategy relies heavily on the mix of business that the hotel is receiving and making sure that the correct segments are being attracted. TRM decisions need to involve the sales and marketing teams so that they are targeting the most profitable segments. A revenue management culture needs to be instilled in all the outlets of the hotel so that every employee is dedicated on the profitability of the entire operation. This is critical for implementing a successful TRM strategy. This chapter will focus on how RM tactics can be implemented at various non-room outlets. It will then look at combining the outlets' RM strategies into a holistic TRM framework and what is required to be successful in the long run. Finally, it will look at the future of TRM and where the boundaries can be pushed to generate higher profits.

TOTAL REVENUE MANAGEMENT FRAMEWORK

In order to implement a total revenue approach, there needs to be a comprehensive framework that allows hotels to find untapped opportunities and deploy strategies based on total guest spend. There has been research and strategies developed for various aspects of auxiliary revenue management, such as golf and spa. However, very few have combined these individual outlets' revenue strategies with a TRM framework. It is no longer enough to simply approach local revenue optimization on an outlet level to make granular decisions. On a customer level, a more holistic method is necessary to better understand the impact of total guest spending on the hotel's overall profit.

There are four key pieces for implementing a successful strategic TRM framework.

1. Outlet Level Optimization
2. Guest level revenue management
3. Profit focus
4. Total revenue management ICEing

The first step is to make sure that optimizing has been implemented on an outlet level. Optimization on the outlet level allows the hotel to generate incremental revenue that was previously untapped. The second step goes hand-in-hand with the third step which is optimization on the customer level whilst making sure profit is the focus. These two steps allow the hotel to attract the right mix of business that is most profitable for the entire operation instead of just one outlet. The final step, which is the "icing" on the framework, is to make sure that TRM practices are incentivised, communicated, and employees are educated (ICEing). Using the combination of these four levels the hotel can deploy a successful TRM strategy. Below, each level will be discussed in detail.

OUTLET LEVEL OPTIMIZATION

In general, hotels already have a robust room's revenue management strategy in place. However, most hotels are lagging or struggling in identifying other potential incremental revenue-generating opportunities.

Here are the steps adapted from McGuire (2016) that can assist in implementing revenue management strategy for any untapped outlet.

1. Know the existing theory and metrics
2. Roadmap for new outlets
3. Recognize "immediate wins"

4. Break down intraorganizational silos
5. RM celebrations

Each stage is very unique and has its own objective with a focus on an outlet TRM revenue framework. Working through each of these steps will help hotels implement a revenue management strategy and drive incremental revenue. Once implemented, it can then be integrated with a customer level optimization for a holistic TRM strategy.

Know the Existing Theory and Metrics

The following will outline some of the key theories, best practices, and metrics for implementing a revenue management strategy for most common hotel outlets. These are ready to go RM tactics that can immediately be implemented on an outlet level.

Spas

Many hotels and resorts have spas that are considered a key auxiliary revenue generator. However, it is very rare that spa revenue management techniques are implemented. This is mainly due to the fact of how spas currently measure their performance and view their sales. Reconfiguring some of these metricize allows spas to implement a successful RM framework that can then be incorporated into a TRM strategy. A TRM strategy not just enables the spa to maximize its own outlet revenues but makes sure that customers that are visiting the spa are the most profitable for the hotel.

Spa Characteristics

Spas are very similar to hotels and have all five characteristics for a successful revenue management strategy to be implemented (Kimes, 2009). The number of spa treatment rooms and therapists are considered a fixed capacity. The building's physical limitations cause a natural constrain and all rooms might not be available due to a specialized therapist not being on duty. Demand is highly variable by time, causing some periods to be busier than others. Urban spas can be significantly busier over Saturdays whilst midweek could be much quieter. Customers can also be segmented easily. For example, a segment could be a leisure day user living nearby the spa. Such a customer would be available to visit the spa any time of the day, in contrast to a corporate guest who has limited time allocated during the day for a spa visit. Most spas demonstrate high fixed costs and low variable costs. Facilities and in some cases salaried therapists are also considered fixed costs. In most cases spas usually would need to make enough revenue to cover their variable costs and at least a portion of their fixed costs.

Spa operators, in general, look at cost and revenue for any given month but ignore the time factor in the equation. Kimes suggests that a spa inventory should be considered only the actual time the treatment rooms are available for treatment (both room and therapist) instead of just the physical rooms or therapists. If the capacity of the spa is not fully occupied at any given moment it is lost forever. The best way to measure spa effectiveness is to look at the **revenue or contribution per available treatment hour (RevPATH)**. This measurement not just focuses on volume of sales (average customer expenditure) but also incorporates a time-related revenue factor (occupancy). RevPATH can be calculated by multiplying the treatment room occupancy by the average treatment-related expenditure per person. It can also be calculated by dividing revenue for a specific time period by the number of treatment hours available to the same time frame (Kimes, 2009).

QUESTION TO CONSIDER

A spa has five treatment rooms that on Tuesday between the hours of 1:00 p.m. and 4:00 p.m. make $755 in revenue. Calculate their RevPATH for the spa over the given time frame. What would you say to the owners when asked how the spa is performing in the market if you know that other spas have a RevPATH of $73?

Spa Optimization

By analyzing RevPATH and looking at low and peak demand periods a spa revenue management strategy can be developed. The two revenue management levers that can be implemented are time management and price management (Kimes, 2009).

Time management is the first lever that has to do with controlling the customers' time at the spa. Spas sell a fixed time slot for each treatment with a defined duration. The easiest way for spas to manage time is to vary the treatment lengths being offered from the standard 1-h treatment to treatments ranging from 30 to 90 min. However, guests are actually buying an "experience" and not just a time slot. Hence there needs to be a fine-line in managing the duration of the guests' stay without inhibiting their experience. Even though this can be sometimes difficult, the primary driver to controlling the time slot is making sure that the treatment can be completed in the allocated time frame. By training therapists and setting up various cues for the guests, such as chiming of a bell or offering a beverage to indicate that the service is over, helps in managing the allocated treatment time. Also, looking at ways to reduce the changeover between treatments can allow spas to schedule more appointments resulting in increased revenue.

Managing the uncertainty of arrivals is also vital in controlling time and maximizing RevPATH. Making sure that reservations are being taken over peak periods can significantly reduce uncertainty. Collecting advanced deposits or credit card guarantee bookings helps spas forecast their arrivals better and manage inventory. Yet, it still does not guarantee full capacity over peak periods. There could still be a reliance on last-minute walk-in traffic or guests not honoring their reservations. By collecting no show, cancelations, and walk-in data, spas can look at setting up an overbooking policy that should help minimize potential arrival risk.

During low demand periods, spas need to focus on attracting more customers. This can be done by offering special priced treatments to attract customers that are available to fill the gaps.

Price management is the second lever that has to do with offering differential pricing based on the level of demand at the spa. Typical hotels and airlines offer differential pricing to their guests based on the demand levels and are often fenced. Spas on the other hand, in general, tend to offer the same price regardless of customer demand or segment without any real rate fences. There might be a peak and off-peak pricing structure at some spas but it is not fully integrated into a maximizing RevPATH strategy. Implementing rate fences, such as room location, view, time of day/week, or length of treatment, can help build a strong revenue management strategy to help drive the highest margin business at peak times. At the same time, steps also need to be taken to entice demand to be generated over slow periods. This is usually done with discounting such as a two for one offer, reduced premium services, or added value items such as complimentary retail products. By having these fences and pricing strategies spas are able to drive RevPATH.

SPREADSHEET EXERCISE 14.1

Super Beauty Spa

The owner of Super Beauty Spa has appointed you the new manager for their 20 room day spa. You are tasked to identify peak periods to see if there is a way to drive additional revenues. At the same time, you also want to note soft periods to see if there is a way to attract more business to the spa. The owner has never heard of RevPATH before and has only been tracking number of treatment rooms occupied and the total revenue per hour.

1. Calculate the spas occupancy per hour
2. Calculate what is the average spend per guest per hour (assume that one treatment room is occupied by one guest)
3. Calculate RevPATH and graph the results in a line graph
4. Where are the hot periods and what would you implement to help drive more revenue?
5. Where are the cold periods and how can you attract more business to the spa?

Golf Courses

As revenue management becomes widespread outside of the hospitality and airline industry, golf courses are an ideal candidate to follow suite. Applying some key revenue management levers to optimize utilization can play an important component in improving golf course profitability. Combining revenue generated from golf with room's revenue can help to establish the overall most profitable guest which is a key in TRM.

Golf Characteristics

Golf courses possess the key characteristics to implement a successful revenue management strategy. They have perishable inventory, predictable demand, limited capacity, varying customer price sensitivity, and high fixed and low variable costs (Kimes & Schruben, 2002). Tee times are perishable inventory and cannot be resold or kept for another day; if they are unsold they disappear. There are only a limited number of tee times that a golf course can accommodate on a given day. Due to the flow of the game tee times need to be spaced out so that players do not impede other players ahead or behind them. Capacity restrictions are due to the size of the golf course, numbers of holes, and the hours of operation. Golf courses vary highly in size and can range anywhere from 9 to 36 holes. Most typical golf courses are around 18 holes. Customer price sensitivity can be based on various demand periods due to seasonality, day of the week, and even time of the day. Less price-sensitive players are willing to pay premium rates to play during high demand periods (for example early in the morning on the weekends), whereas more price-sensitive players might wait for later in the day and potentially mid-week or leverage potential discounted offered. Golf courses also have a high fixed cost due to turf and clubhouse maintenance but a low variable cost as the impact of selling one additional tee time is relatively minimal.

A performance baseline needs to be established in order to measure the success of revenue management techniques implemented to golf courses. We are all familiar with the standard RM indicator used for hotels and airlines. For golf courses, this metric is **revenue per available tee time (RevPATT)** (Pekgun et al., 2014). To make sure that RevPATT is being fully optimized we need to take a look at demand forecasting and price optimization for tee times and relate it back to the overall revenue management goal.

Demand Forecasting

One of the challenges golf courses face is to accurately forecast demand since customers make tee time reservations through different channels, whether online or in-person and for different size parties. There is a maximum of 4 players per tee time and golf courses need to find the best way to combine 2 and 2 players or 3 and 1 players to fill the entire spot. If players prefer to claim the entire tee time over peak periods and are less than 4, then the golf course should charge a higher price to account for the potential displacement from that time slot. The following is a list of items that need to be considered when forecasting demand for a golf course:

- Day of the week, weekday/weekend
- Time of the day

- Weather
- Size of party (1–4)
- Booking lead time
- Season
- Player skill level
- Member versus visitor

A combination of these elements can assist in creating a comprehensive microlevel forecast. Which then allows golf courses to identify patterns and trends to determine when is it appropriate to apply revenue management strategies to optimize revenues.

Price Optimization

As with all other revenue management areas the key is to determine what is the best price to charge customers during peak and off-peak times to maximize revenue. Since we have determined when customers are booking and their patterns, a systematic pricing structure needs to be implemented based on the demand periods and the price elasticity of demand. One method that is suggested which simplifies pricing structures is to offer a base rate and adjust it with addition or multiplication offsets depending on the selected variable options (Pekung et al, 2013). For example, multiply the base rate for a single player by a demand period multiplier and by the number of players within the party (base rate × 1.2 peak period multiplier × 2 players = 2 player pricing over peak period). This sort of pricing would mainly be used for visitor pricing as member pricing is usually fixed. Member demand also needs to be taken into consideration as it has an impact on capacity. Pricing also needs to be in conjunction with continuous monitoring of competitor pricing to remain market centric. As within the hospitality industry customers are savvier and are easily able to benchmark your pricing vs the competition using the Internet.

One pitfall that needs to be addressed is the fact that the duration of a game of golf is highly unpredictable (Kimes, 2000). Within the hotel or airline world guests clearly purchase a defined time frame of utilization. Guests stay for a set number of nights or use the seat for a predefined time until they arrive at their destination. Whereas, golfers book a round of golf with no time restriction and can play as long as they wish until the round is completed. This puts some uncertainty into booking tee time frequency and causes delays. Therefore, even though theoretically it might make sense to schedule more tee times to generate more revenue due to slow play, all scheduled players might not be accommodated (Kimes & Schruben, 2002).

QUESTION TO CONSIDER

Your golf course has a RevPATT of $89. The neighboring golf course down the street has a RevPATT of $103. Calculate your RevPATT index. What does it mean if you had a -4 percent index change year over year? What if the change was 3 percent?

Casinos

Casinos are a perfect example of where TRM can be effectively used. Large casinos such as the ones in Las Vegas have a variety of revenue streams such as restaurants, bars, and night clubs as well as the main source of income the casino itself. Most guests that gamble are part of a casino loyalty program that allows casinos to collect highly valuable customer data. Casinos need to make sure that they use this data to establish three key pillars: customer segmentation, demand forecasting, and strategic pricing. With these pillars combined the value of a guest can be calculated and TRM can be implemented.

Customer Segmentation

Customer segmentation can get a little more complicated in casinos than in the traditional hotels. This is mainly due to accurately assessing the contribution of hotel guests from the casino floor. One way to do so is to use a tiered based system that analyzes guest valuation based on gambling behavior (Kuyumcu, 2002). Data could be taken from the hotel's loyalty system that tracks basic information, such as demographics, betting frequency, amount per hand, favorite games, and winnings. This information can then be used to create guest valuation segments. Below are some examples that casinos use to establish different levels of customers based on their value:

Level	Customer Valuation Summary
1	• Customer value is based on the total amount of money wagered per visit • Customer value is not discounted by how much the customer wins
2	• Customer value is based on the total amount of money wagered per visit • Customer is tracked by type of game—machine or table game • Customer value is not discounted by how much the customer wins
3	• Customer is tracked by the customer's betting frequency, dollar level per bet, favorite slot machines, and gaming tables • Customer's winning profiles are monitored and customer value is discounted by how much the customer wins • The probability of winning at each gaming machine or table is taken into account to compute the customer's expected worth to the resort

Adapted from Kuyumcu (2002).

The above measurements create a net worth per customer based on their level of spend. In the first level, only the basic information is collected and the value of the customer is not reduced by their win. This level is for recreational gamblers that frequent casinos occasionally and bet small amounts. The second level is for customers that are more frequent to casinos and wager a fair amount of money per visit. Their favorite machine/table game is tracked but their value is not discounted by their winnings. The final level is for high rollers, often referred to as "whales" in the casino industry. These players spend a lot of money in and wager large hands. These customers are one of the most profitable segments for casinos so more information is collected. Furthermore, due to the amount of money that whales gamble, the value of their winnings is discounted from their profile. Since the casino can lose significant amount of money from these payouts, the probability of each guest winning is also monitored.

All of these segments are linked by one metric which is the theoretical win or "**theo**." The theo is calculated by multiplying the coin-in amount by the hold percentage. The coin-in amount is the total money spent by a customer on a given occasion. The hold percentage is the probability that the casino will win a specific play. For example, if the coin-in from a customer is $10 and the slot machine is programed to return $7 to the customer on average then the hold percentage is 30 percent. The average theo of all games played by the customer over a given period is called the **average daily the-**

oretical (ADT). This value can also be supplemented with a more holistic spend that incorporates all revenue streams of the casino and not just floor spend. Basically, the higher the ADT of a customer the more valuable they are to the casino as they spend more.

There are two potential pitfalls in trying to truly provide an accurate total value of a customer. First, data can easily be collected from most electronic games, such as slot machines, but table games like blackjack pose a higher challenge. Not all transactions are digitally monitored and amount per hand or betting frequency becomes harder to attribute to an individual guest. Second, there is a new trend evolving where guests visiting casino resorts such as Las Vegas are not only going there for the gambling. They are visiting to dine, drink, and have fun using various resort amenities. Yet, casinos still tend to places a large amount of value on just casino spending and undermine other revenue streams. This could be because customer spending is much harder to monitor and attribute to an individual due to the frequency of cash transactions. However, by understanding all revenues associated with a customer a more comprehensive segmentation can be created and better TRM decisions can be made.

THINK HISTORICALLY

Harrah's Entertainment is currently one of the leaders in casino loyalty program or so-called "slot club." Even though these loyalty programs have grown popular over the last 30 years they were met with some resistance when casinos tried to pioneer such programs in the 80's. Casino managers claimed that these programs were creating barriers between casinos and their guest's individual needs. Fred Kiser, Vice President of Marketing for Becker Gaming's Arizona Charlie's brand, at the time remarked, "They don't keep coming back to us for slot clubs, we don't have one. They like the personal attention ... We don't have to put them in a computer and turn them down for a complimentary show or restaurant because they missed the number of points needed for that day. This happens in other places" (Pledger, 1994).

Why do you think not adopting a "slot club "would have been a critical mistake as it relates to casino TRM?

Demand Forecasting

It is imperative to have a clear understanding of demand patterns in casinos and to forecast accordingly. As with most forecasting methods, historical data is the prime information used to understand unconstrained demand. The forecast can then be used to make strategic revenue management decisions on what RM levers need to be adjusted to maximize revenue.

This forecast should be done on a granular level where each customer segment's unconstrained demand is calculated. By understanding the behavior of each segment casinos can better prepare their strategies accordingly. For example, due to continued last-minute booking pattern of high valued players, it might be necessary to hold back some rooms to accommodate such guests. Also, understanding same day or walk-in reservations and no shows will have an impact on your demand forecasting or overbooking levels.

Pricing

In the traditional hotel environment, the objective of revenue management is to drive RevPAR ideally through rate as it has the greatest impact on bottom-line profitability. This might not always be the case for casinos. Studies have shown that profitability is higher for casinos when they are able to run at a higher occupancy and lower ADR (Norman and Mayer, 1997). This is due to the potential auxiliary-spend of guests through other revenue centers once at the casino. This forces revenue managers to apply a unique pricing strategy to casinos and plays an important factor in TRM.

Opportunity costs should be taken into consideration as guests are frequently given a complimentary room which could be counterintuitive if the objective is to maximize room revenue and not total revenue. There is a revenue optimization calculation often used in the casino industry to determine when to provide a complimentary room (reinvestment amount) or a guest-centric room offer. The **reinvestment amount** basically is the monetary value corresponding to the services and products given away to the customer (Hendler & Hendler, 2004).

We can use ADT and the reinvestment amount to determine the optimal room rate offer for a guest or if the guest should be offered a complimentary room night. The casino must first determine what its optimal reinvestment amount usually calculated as a percentage of ADT. There is no industry standard for what the reinvestment amount should be but it ranges anywhere from 12 percent up to 30 percent depending on how much competition there is in the market. Once a reinvestment amount is established, we can then subtract it from the best available rate for the desired stay period. Whatever the remaining value is should be the optimal rate offered to the guest. If the reinvestment amount is equal to or greater than the daily room rate the guest should be offered a complimentary room as their theoretical daily spend would offset the room revenue loss. Using the ADT and reinvestment amount, casinos can optimize total revenue based on individual customer value (Hendler & Hendler, 2004).

QUESTION TO CONSIDER

Assume that a specific customer has an ADT of $500. The casino has determined that they have a 30 percent reinvestment policy based on the ADT value of the guests. The hotel is currently selling at BAR rate of $250. Based on this information what rate should the casino should offer to the customer?

Groups

Groups have always been looked at as a way to support hotel operations and as a good base to fill the hotel with rooms that could not be sold to transient business (Cullen & Helsel, 2010). However, there is a huge potential in breaking down groups into their own revenue-generating discipline and incorporating it as a part of a TRM strategy. With a proper plan in place for groups, hotels can make sure that all revenue potential can be maximized.

Pricing Strategy

It is important to establish a strong group pricing strategy that is in line with the hotel's transient pricing strategy. Establish what the need and peak periods are and use that to create a pricing guideline. Equip the sales team with this pricing guideline so they understand how the future outlooks are able to sell the product effectively. By providing a pricing tool to the sales team, it empowers them to be involved in educated and immediate pricing discussion with potential clients. Not having to continually check-in with the revenue director for a rate whilst on the road.

However, it is imperative that it is understood that the rates provided to the sales team should only serve as a guideline. Various other elements can have an impact on the rate offered to a group, which require the rate to be fluid and dynamic. Arrival pattern, F&B revenue, other group prospects or even a displacement analysis should be used once the sales manager is able to get a better understanding of the group's needs before a final rate is offered.

Based on Cullen and Helsel (2010), the following chart outlines some of the elements to consider when creating a group pricing strategy:

Pricing element	Purpose
SWOT	Similar to the transient segment, the hotel must understand its attributes, strengths, and weaknesses as it relates to its competitive set. This must be conducted from a group perspective and how the hotel attempts to satisfies the group's needs.
Market position	An analysis must be conducted to see how the hotel should be positioned in the market compared with its competitors. This will play a key role in determining group pricing.
Seasonal demand	Rates must be flexible and based on demand/season in the marketplace.
Walk away rate	Establish the lowest rate the hotel is willing to accept during each season. This will serve as a guide to knowing when to walk away from a piece of business.
Group segmentation	Identify specific group segments that the hotel is targeting and create specific price points.
Special need periods	Pinpoint any high need periods such as holiday, special events or low demand periods in the market. Create a forward-looking action plan to target these periods and deploy a group strategy in advance.
Rooms types	Understand the various group types that are being contracted to groups and their associated price points.
Room costs	Knowing the direct and indirect cost associated with rooms helps focus the pricing strategy on driving profit.

Displacement Analysis

It is very important to make sure that the full impact of taking a certain piece of group business is understood. Due to the constraints imposed by the hotels, physical capacity not all sources of business can be taken over a given day. This means that the hotel will potentially have to turn away some business if demand exceeds capacity. In most cases, such a displacement, it relates to group as it usually takes up a large percentage of rooms in the hotel. A group displacement analysis should be conducted in order to understand what brings the most value to the hotel. This type of analysis allows the hotel to compare the total value of group business against the total value of transient business. Based on the loss or gain in revenue or profitability the business is accepted or rejected. The total value of group business should include F&B spending, meeting room rental, and any other outlet revenue stream minus the appropriate costs. The following is a basic example of a displacement analysis:

	Transient	**Group**
Number of rooms	20	20
ADR	$200	$150
Room's revenue total	$4,000	$3,000
Ancillary revenues	$1,500	$5,000
Rooms costs	–$900	–$900
Catering costs	–$0	–$1,500
Total	$4,600	$5,600

In this displacement analysis, we are comparing 20 group rooms to 20 transient rooms on a certain day. Just by looking purely at room's revenue it would make more sense to take the transient piece of business as it produces $1,000 more in revenue. However, when we look at it from a TRM perspective we need to look at all sources of revenue and cost to establish the most profitable piece of business.

The group brings in an additional $3,000 in F&B revenue, $1,000 in AV rental and $1,000 meeting room rental. This is a total of $5,000 in auxiliary revenues. The costs should then be factored out from each segment. Cleaning of $900 is the same for both transient and group as it is based on the number of rooms. Group has a catering cost of $1,500 due to additional labor and meeting room setup. This displacement analysis shows that when all revenues and costs are factored in the group is actually a better piece if business as it generates $1,000 more in total revenue for the hotel.

This sort of analysis can be done with a lot more detail to even provide a greater in-depth understanding of any potential displacement. Other factors such as cost of walk, cost of acquisition, or even length of stay can be used to create a comprehensive analysis. It can also be used to see what rates are needed to break even between two segments or should there be a need to increase rates.

SPREADSHEET EXERCISE 14.2

Holloway Suites

You are the brand new revenue manager for the Holloway Suites and have been approached by your sales team on a potential group business for this year in May. The new group is looking for 75 rooms per night at a rate of $160. The arrival pattern would be Monday to Thursday and they would have breakfast and lunch every day with two coffee breaks for a total catering contribution of $85 per room per night. The exact arrival dates for the group are currently not fixed but the sales team is eager to sign the deal and are drafting up the contract. Knowing that your peak occupancy nights are Tuesday and Wednesday you suggest to the sales team that you will do a quick displacement analysis to see if this is the right piece of business for the hotel.

You pull the historical day by day revenue and occupied rooms for last years from your property PMS. Historically in the month of May, the hotel had 40 percent of the rooms occupied Monday through Wednesday by group which made up 35 percent of the revenue for those days.

The hotel's catering cost is $30 per room per night. Transient guests have an average auxiliary spend of $35 per room per night. Assume that any sort of displacement the hotel is going to have is from the transient segment and that forecasted occupancies and business mix are going to be exactly the same this year as they were last year.

1. Using the data provided, fill in the segmentation mix day by day for group and transient.
2. Fill in the average historical occupancies based on the day of the week.
3. Based on the arrival pattern for the group, calculate the displacement value for the new group for each day.
4. Should this group business be accepted based on historical averages for the month of May? If so, why?
5. Would your recommendation change if the group were to specifically ask for arrival the 3rd Monday of the month?

Catering

There are typically two types of catering events, one that involves hotel room nights and one that is catering only. They both have an impact on TRM and can help drive revenue contribution. Catering contribution per group room is one measurement that can be used to assess the value of a piece of catering business. However, this metric is only useful if the catering business has group rooms attached to it. An overarching measurement that includes both types of catering source is **revenue per available square foot (RevPAS)**. The following items are examples that can contribute to RevPAS (Cullen & Helsel, 2010).

- Catering menu
- Audiovisual/Internet
- Parking
- Valet
- Meeting and function space rental

Looking at the contribution margin of each item based on profitability helps revenue managers make sound decisions to assist the TRM strategy. The price of items should be adjusted based on-peak and off-peak periods. This will overall assist in driving total contribution.

PROS & CONS

Group contribution is mostly evaluated based on a one time piece of business. List the pros and cons of such a decision.

Creative RM Strategy

Implementing a creative revenue management strategy means your need to think beyond the rooms' only revenue source. Many hotels have some sort of retail area, sell various forms of packages, or offer resort credits to drive additional revenue from guests. These are all considered to be a part of a creative revenue management strategy and should be included in the TRM goal.

Hotel packages, such as ones that include massages can be used in order to drive incremental business into the spa. Spas can then place their high sale volume items strategically on shelves in order to capitalize on impulse purchases. Resort credit can also be used to help entice guests to increase their spend at various outlets. Offering a $25 dinner credit to a couple, when the hotels know its average check is $45 per person, can help drive that additional spending that would not have naturally occurred. Hotels should think even further outside the box and look at unconventional revenue streams such as ATMs. Most hotels have an ATM in their lobby so that customers have access to quick cash. Hotels make money on the transaction fee that is being charged to the guest once they take out money. Looking at fluctuating transaction fees based on time of day and demand can be a very avant-garde way to drive additional revenue and be part of a TRM strategy. Another strategy that is becoming more common is the implementation of a resort or city-center fee for various services or amenities. This additional fee is added on top of the room rate and ideally incurs no cost for the hotel. This allows the incremental profits gained to flow directly to the bottom line. Las Vegas resorts have been using resort fees for years but recently it has started to pop-up in city centers such as New York hotels.

There is not one guideline as to where revenue management can be implemented. Each hotel must evaluate its own unique opportunities to identify what can be done to drive additional guest spend. It does not matter how small the revenue sources are it must be tracked on a customer level and incorporated into a TRM decision. By using all the data from the customer spend revenue managers can make the best decisions about most profitable guest mix.

REAL PEOPLE

Lisa Mathews* is the Director of Revenue Management at a luxury hotel in downtown Toronto. She has been trying to implement a TRM culture one step at a time by focusing on two areas, the restaurant, and spa. However, instilling a revenue management mindset with the staff continues to be a challenge. She is faced with pushback due to frontline staff being scared of guest's reaction to some of her new TRM initiatives. Restaurant servers and massage therapists are concerned that they will lose customers and their tips along the way.

How would you educate and convince employees in these outlets that a comprehensive TRM strategy can help drive profits into their respective departments?

*name changed

Roadmap for a New Outlet

This road-map shows hotels how to implement a RM strategy to a new outlet and adjust the existing theory in the previous section to fit the optimization problem at hand. In order to develop a revenue management process in a new outlet, there needs to be a very comprehensive understanding of the operations. Adapted from Kimes (1998) and McGuire (2016) there is a five-step process for implementing revenue management in a new outlet.

Establish a Baseline

Detailed information must be collected from the outlet and then analyzed thoroughly to understand the current state of the outlet. The information collected should focus on the key revenue management levers: price, duration, and space and how they relate to the current performance. Some examples of data collected should be pricing strategies, demand patterns, and inventory utilization. A revenue per available time-based inventory unit (RevPATI) to measure performance needs to be clearly established. Data can be collected from various sources including but not limited to the PMS, POS, reservations systems, and methodical observation.

Understand performance drivers:

Analyze the baseline performance and see if customers can be segmented based on their needs, demand patterns, price sensitivity. Try to pinpoint what is causing low and high demand periods and utilization patterns or anything that is impacting the outlets' RevPATI. Using tools, such as fish-bone diagram and service blueprints, to identify if staffing levels, technology, or job function is causing underperformance.

Develop an RM strategy

Once the performance drivers are understood, areas, where the revenue management levers can be applied, needs to be identified. Example of some questions that should be answered are:

- How can the outlets be optimized?
- Can demand be stimulated or restricted by altering prices?
- Will technology or staffing levels improve utilization?

- Are there ways to implement duration management?
- Are overbooking procedures effective or in place?
- Is there policies that are impeding revenue generation?

Implement the strategy

In order for the implementation of the strategy to be successful, it is essential that everyone within the outlet is engaged and understands the revenue management objective. Every employee needs to be trained on how the RM strategy benefits the outlet and themselves and there is a unanimous buy-in. The incentive plans also need to be realigned to reward for the desired outcome.

Monitor the outcome

It is not purely enough to identify, develop, and implement a RM strategy in a new outlet. Monitoring the outcome is as important not only to celebrate success but to further identify opportunities. The new results should be compared with the baseline performance and the outlet manager should be involved in further enhancing the strategy. A system also needs to be developed so that the RM practices implemented are continued even with staff turnover.

Recognize "Immediate Wins"

Once you have understood the theory and are working to implement the revenue management roadmap as outlined above, do not forget that small changes can have "immediate wins." Do not try to recreate the wheel by redeveloping processes and procedures but look for the small changes that can have a big impact on revenue. Try to answer the question "What can we do immediately that will generate more revenue for us?" Even though there are multiple new software solutions out on the market that can help almost optimize anything, small operation changes should not be overlooked. There are multiple examples identified in the theory above, such as credit card guarantees to decrease now shows (Kimes, 2009), golf marshals to speed up the game (Kimes and Schruben, 2002) or cross-training spa therapists (Kimes, 2009) that can be used as the groundwork for these changes.

Break Down Intraorganizational Silos

Once there is a revenue management program in place make sure that everyone is involved in its success. This means that all levels of the outlet, from front line staff to management are on board and understand their role and how it relates to the revenue management targets. However, that is not always enough and as many times the success of one department is linked to the performance of another. How successful would a front office initiative be without understanding how housekeeping impacts the outcome? This goes the same for many departments. Therefore, silos within the organization need to be broken down and links understood. All departments need to understand the others' revenue management objectives and can align their performance accordingly. This is one of the most important steps that is often overlooked in developing a TRM strategy.

RM Celebration

Make sure that the success of the program is publicized whenever possible. Using success stories and sharing them with all staff can be very helpful in instilling a RM mindset. The wins can also generate a hype about the initiatives and inspire the team on all levels to perform even better. These celebrations also help break down the silos between departments as mentioned in the previous step and create unity with a TRM focus.

The above framework should provide a solid foundation for implementing a related revenue management strategy. Once such a plan is implemented, it should then be incorporated into the overall TRM strategy where a more holistic approach is taken and revenue is optimized not just at the outlet level but the hotel level.

GUEST LEVEL REVENUE MANAGEMENT

We have until now looked at how to optimize on an outlet level. The second step of the TRM framework is to optimize on the guest level. Traditional segments are no longer enough to clearly identify the behavior of a guest. Business travelers are no longer just booking through the GDS and staying midweek. Business trips are merging with personal travel and corporate clients are booking directly on the hotel websites or using OTAs. As these market segments change, hotels need to start applying a more granular level segmentation where guests are grouped based on their spending power instead of traditional segmentation. A guest value revenue strategy needs to be implemented as a fundamental element of TRM. There are two potential ways to look at assigning a monetary value to a guest.

Value Per Stay

A value per stay method looks at the guest's total spend during their last stay and assigns a total spend value based on the past. This method is best implemented in the casino industry. As mentioned earlier in the chapter, a casino creates an ADT for each guest. By encouraging players to join their robust player loyalty program, guest's bets, and purchases can easily be tracked. A few resorts have started to use this approach in order to better track guest spending. Hyatt and Fairmont are looking in the near future to incorporate a proprietary in their RM practices a loyalty program scoring system based on historical spend. When total spend on a guest level is incorporated into the revenue management decision it tends to favor guests that have a higher value per stay.

Customer Lifetime Value

Customer lifetime value (CLV) is the second method that sums all profits from a given customer over their lifetime relationship with the hotel. The simplest way to calculate CLV is to assess guest profitability, forecast future spending, adjusting for probability of guest retention, discount this back to present value, and then sum up all transactions (McGuire, 2016). In this method, the revenue is accounted for the entire life horizon of the guest instead of just focusing on the short term potential.

In either method, the integration of marketing plays a vital role. Revenue managers are responsible for determining which customers are most profitable and group them based on value. Marketers are then responsible for attracting these high-value guests to the hotel. By having this close relationship with marketing and the data to support tactical decisions, a customized marketing campaign can be created to attract high-value segments. As this type of mindset progresses in the future the two disciplines, revenue management and marketing will start to blur.

An important piece that hinders the development of guest level TRM is the collection of clean data on a customer level. Most hotels currently do not have the capabilities to integrate all transactions from various points of sale unless guest's charge items to their room. Until this becomes feasible, there is no method that can give a 100 percent accurate value on an individual guest level. Furthermore, guest values change over time due to the fluctuation in the willingness to pay. Therefore, the TRM goal should always be to look at ways to grow the guest value over time. It is not enough to just simply establish what the anticipated guest value is and project it into the future. Long term growth opportunities need to be also incorporated into such calculation and impact TRM decisions.

PROFIT FOCUS

The third part of the TRM framework is directing the focus from revenues to profits. Once more revenue streams are integrated into the overall guest contribution profile the better hotels can identify their most valuable customers. For a TRM strategy to be successful in the long run a profit-focused revenue management philosophy needs to be shared equally by all departments. This is important as there will be occasions where one revenue stream might be sacrificed for the overall benefit of driving another more profitable revenue source. With the rising cost of distribution impact all channels it will not be enough to just optimize based on revenues without taking costs into the decision.

Measurements, such as total revenue per available room (TrevPAR) and gross operating profit per available room (GOPPAR) have made a step in the right direction to allow revenue managers not to just look at top line but include other revenues sources and costs. However, very few hotels are actually optimizing their mix based on these measurements. Furthermore, these metrics also have shortfalls. TrevPAR does not take into consideration the cost factor and GOPPAR does not accurately reflect topline room's revenue performance. These two measurements also look at the hotel's performance on a per room level versus on a per guest level.

A new metrics need to be developed that incorporates costs and per guest level measurement. Such a metric then needs to be unanimously adopted in order for TRM to be successful industry-wide. Similarly, to what casinos have done, hotels should also embark on establishing a theoretical contribution value per guest. Lifetime value per available customer or newly created **total contribution per available customer (TocPAC)** are metrics that try to put a value on customer contribution. TocPAC does not just take into consideration the associated costs with the room but also looks at the total value of the guest spend within the hotel. Below is the calculation for total guest contribution:

TocPAC = (Room's revenue + auxiliary revenue – variable cost)/number of guests

Revenue managers can look at TocPAC on a hotel, segment, or even individual guest level and find highest value guest. It can also be used to see the TRM strategy implemented is effective. Optimizing revenues to maximize TocPAC is not yet a common practice. However, in the future, this would allow hotels to take the right mix of business and make sure that rooms are always available to their most profitable customers. Forecasting, for each outlet, will also need to evolve encompassing a total contribution mindset. It will no longer be enough to just do a traditional operational forecast to help with better management of labor. A more granular approach will need to be taken where the focus will be on the profit by customer segment.

TOTAL REVENUE MANAGEMENT ICEING

The final part of implementing a successful TRM framework is the ICEing. It is like baking a cake. Once the cake is complete, the baker wants to make sure that there is something that holds the foundation together. The icing provides to extra flavor and decoration ensuring the cake is appealing and going to be eaten. This is very similar to what the objective of TRM ICEing is.

Incentives cannot solely be rewarded on department level achievements and must incorporate the profit goals for the entire organization. These goals need to be clearly communicated. Everyone must know who the organizations most valuable customers are and how each department and employee impacts the TRM strategy. Success needs to be communicated and celebrated so employees feel engaged and connected with TRM objectives. This also needs to be backed up by a solid education program. Employees need to know the basic TRM concepts and understand how small changes can have big impact on their own and the hotel's profits. Education will help break down silos between departments and provide an understanding of how to attract, nurture, and maintain the hotels' most profitable guests.

SEEING FURTHER

Technology has changed significantly over the past decade. More and more systems are now integrated making the abundance of guest data a reality. This trend will continue into the foreseeable future allowing for transactional data to be collected on an individual level no matter where at the hotel the purchase takes place. To have a successful TRM culture silos between departments need to be broken down and all outlets need to function as one unit.

Which department(s) other than revenue management do you think holds the key to success and why?

What sort of information do you think would help the hotels' goal of TRM?

FUTURE OPPORTUNITIES FOR TRM

TRM is still a new topic and there continue to be many developments. As technology and big data trends evolve, the application of TRM will be made much easier. Nonetheless, research by Noone et al. (2017) have identified some key areas that need to be further developed for TRM to be easily adopted by the hospitality industry.

A distribution strategy for s inventory needs to be created. Guest room distribution is still the main focus for hotels but a more holistic approach should be to be considered. Hotels need to identify ways to capture additional s revenue in advance. Whether, that is done through the booking engine, a mobile app, or via a third-party reseller. Furthermore, distribution costs should also be considered when developing such a strategy.

There needs to be an easy and accessible way of capturing more customer-level data. Profit contribution needs to reorganized in order to account for all costs on a guest level when making pricing decisions. It is not enough to just look at the traditional cost hitting the P&L statement but other indirect acquisition costs also need to be accounted for (e.g. merchant-model pricing). Furthermore, a more comprehensive process needs to be developed to account for the total spend of a guest. Enticing guests to join loyalty programs is scratching the surface but is nowhere near able to offer an all-encompassing picture of the true guests spend.

As the hotels move into the direction of looking at contribution per customer there needs to be a unifying element of total hotel profit. Revenue managers should no longer just be looking at driving top-line revenue but looking at ways to maximize total hotel profitability through all revenue streams. Once guests are on the property then revenue management strategies deployed in various outlets of the hotel should take over in assisting with TRM optimization. Each revenue-generating outlet of the hotel needs to be analyzed to see if there is an opportunity that creates incremental revenue.

Total hotel revenue management at its core is applying a revenue management mindset to all departments and attracting the optimal mix of business that delivers the highest levels of total hotel profit.

DISCUSSION QUESTIONS

Question 1: What are the necessary characteristics that need to be present in order for revenue management to be successfully implemented? Give an example of why each characteristic is important?

Question 2: Why is it best to use a RevPATI metric to establish a baseline and track performance?

Question 3: If you were to implement a RM strategy to a nonroom revenue-generating outlet, what sort of data would you ask the team to collect to establish a baseline?

Question 4: Why do you think it is taking so long for total revenue management to be implemented?

Question 5: Do you think there is an industry-wide definition of TRM? What are some areas that the definitions could vary?

Question 6: What do you think the future of TRM is? Where do hotels need to focus and what challenges do you expect they will encounter?

APPLICATIONS

1. Which of the two customer segments below would you accept to stay at your hotel purely based on TRM?
   - An individual corporate client arriving on Monday night for three nights with and ADR of $559. The guest has three breakfast at the hotel that costs $25 per breakfast. Hosts a client dinner one evening for a total of $275. Uses the limo service for $150 per trip to and from the airport and prints/faxes items at the business center for $40.
   - A leisure couple arriving Thursday for four nights with and ADR of $259. The guests have breakfast each morning for a total of $20 per person. They eat dinner twice in the restaurant for a total of $150 per dinner. The wife gets a spa treatment on Saturday for a total of $400 whilst the husband plays a round of golf for $300. They valet parked their vehicle for the duration of their stay for $55 a night.

Cost per occupied room is $60 per night. F&B cost margin is 30 percent. All other outlets have a cost margin of 10 percent.

2. You are the Revenue Manager of Historical Hamilton Hotel which has 150 rooms. The sales team has approached you with a new piece of business that they are looking at taking. It is over a highly compressed period so you suggest that a displacement analysis be done in order to make sure that taking the business makes the most total revenue sense. The group pattern is for arrival Monday and departure on Thursday for 80 rooms a night. The sales manager has indicated that the group has an ADR budget of $190 per room per night. The 150 attendees will have breakfast daily and one dinner at the property. They will also have a meeting room rental fee of $1,500 and AV for $900 per day.

You know that typically you are busy over the specific stay pattern with transient guests with an ADR of $299. Therefore, by taking this group the hotel going to walk 10 guests to another hotel for at an ADR of $280 per night. On average, transient guests have breakfast every day of their stay and one dinner at the property. You also know that 50 percent of guest use overnight parking which cost $25 per night and 70 percent pay to use the Internet at a daily rate of $9. Transient reservations have the following distribution source, 40 percent direct at property, 20percent GDS, 10 percent chain website and 30 percent OTA. Group reservations are 40 percent call in and 60 percent on the website.

The breakfast is $21 and a three-course dinner is $54 per person. Cost per occupied room is $50 per night. F&B and catering cost margin is 30 percent. All other outlets have a cost margin of 10 percent. Channel costs are $2 for direct, $7 for GDS, $5 for chain website, and $28 for OTAs. There is also a $2, 100 additional labor cost associated with the group. Assume that there is one guest per occupied transient room and all rooms have a three-night length of stay.

Calculate the displacement for the above scenario and decide on which piece of business is best suited for the hotel based on TRM principles?

What is the lowest ADR rounded to the nearest dollar that would you change your decision and the switch profitability from one segment to the other?

TEAM ACTIVITY

Hotels have a wide range of guests and it is sometimes difficult to narrow down the correct target segment that the hotel should focus on in order to have the highest total revenue. Luxury hotels, as well as resorts, have many different nonroom outlets including food and beverage, spa, and golf courses. Below you will find five typical guests with their spending habits who are most likely to stay at your property.

Guest 1: Basic massage, tee time on Thursday at 3:00 p.m., F&B $75, standard king room (three nights, Tuesday–Friday). Corporate traveler for a conference and leisure, before flying home.

Guest 2: Basic massage, basic manicure, and pedicure, deluxe suite (three nights, Thursday–Sunday), F&B $230. Leisure couple flying in from a major city for a romantic weekend.

Guest 3: Tee time on Saturday at 8:00 a.m., one-bedroom suite (one night, Saturday). Leisure couple driving in for a weekend getaway

Guest 4: Presidential Suite (one night, Tuesday), F&B $375. Corporate CEO for overnight business meeting

Guest 5: Tee time on Friday at 5:00 p.m., tee time on Sunday 2:00 p.m., standard double room (three nights, Friday–Monday), F&B $125. Leisure couple coming for a golf weekend

Assignment:

- Pick a resort in the US that has a golf course, spa, and restaurant.
- Choose a specific week and use real-time pricing information by browsing their website site (calling the hotel if you need more information) to determine how much revenue each of the five guests' stays generate at the resort (if couple, assume that both guests will play golf and/or have the same spa treatments).
- Identifying which guest profile generates the most revenue, then as a team, create five different marketing techniques you could use to attract a similar target guest.

INTERNET ACTIVITY

Casinos are very popular across America and not just for gambling. Many have multiple nonroom revenue outlets and operate as fully as a resort.

Choose a casino in Las Vegas, Nevada and explore their website. Identify a nonroom revenue-generating outlet (besides, golf, spa, or restaurant)

Go through each of the five steps (establish a baseline, understand performance drivers, develop an RM strategy, implement the strategy, monitor the outcome) of the roadmap to a new outlet.

For your chosen new outlet, write down what data you would need? What could be impacting the performance? What strategies you would implement? How would you go about implementing the strategy? How you would monitor the success?

GLOSSARY

(ADT) Average daily theoretical – The daily average "theo" of all games played by the customer over a given period.

(CLV) Customer lifetime value – The sum of all profits from a given customer over their lifetime relationship with the company.

Reinvestment amount – The monetary value corresponding to the services and products given away to a customer often expressed in terms of a percentage.

RevPAS – Revenue per available space, or revenue per square foot the revenue generated on a square foot basis for a specific period of time.

RevPATH – Revenue per available treatment hours.

RevPATI – Revenue per available time-based inventory unit.

RevPATT – Revenue per available tee time.

(Theo) Theoretical win – The "theo" is calculated by multiplying the coin-in amount by the hold percentage. The coin-in amount is the total money spent by a customer on a given occasion. The hold percentage is the probability that the casino will win a specific play.

(TocPAC) Total contribution per available customer – (Room's revenue + auxiliary revenue – variable cost) / number of guests

(TRM) Total revenue management – Decision process based on the sum of all revenue streams from both room and outlets on a customer level.

REFERENCES

Cullen, K., & Helsel, C. (2010). *The Evolving Dynamics of Revenue Management: A Comprehensive Revenue Optimization Road Map for Hotel Owners, Operators, and Practitioners.* HSMAI 109-120

Hendler, R., & Hendler, F. (2004). Revenue Management in Fabulous Las Vegas: Combining Customer Relationship Management and Revenue Management to Maximize Profitability. *Journal of Revenue and Pricing Management, 3* (1), 73-79.

Kimes, S. E. (1989). The Basics of Yield Management. *Cornell Hotel and Restaurant Administration Quarterly, 30* (3), 1419.

Kimes, S. E., & Schruben, L.W. (2002) Golf Course Revenue Management: A Study of Tee Time Intervals. *Journal of Revenue and Pricing Management, 1* (2), 111-120.

Kuyumcu, A. (2002). Gaming Twist in Hotel Revenue Management. *Journal of. Revenue and Pricing Management, 1* (2), 161-167.

McGuire, K. A. (2016). *Hotel Pricing in a Social World Driving Value in the Digital Economy*; Hoboken, NJ: Wiley.

Nair, H. S. (2013). *Big Data and Marketing Analytics in Gaming: Combining Empirical Models and Field.* Rochester, NY: Simon Graduate School of Business, Univ of Rochester: Rochester, NY, 2013.

Noone, B. M., Enz C. A., & Glassmire, J. (2017). Total Hotel Revenue Management: A Strategic Profit Perspective. *Cornell Hospitality Report, 17* (8).

Noone, B. M., Enz, C. A., & Glassmire, J. (2017). Total Hotel Revenue Management: A Strategic Profit Perspective. *Cornell Hospitality Report, 17* (8), 3-15.

Norman, E. D., & Mayer, K. J. (1997). Yield Management in Las Vegas Casino Hotels. *Cornell Hospitality Quarterly, 38* (5), 28-38.

Pekgün, P., Menich, R. P., Acharya, S., Finch, F. G., Deschamps, F., Mallery, K., van Sistine J., Christianson, K., & Fuller, J. (2013). Carlson Rezidor Hotel Group Maximizes Revenue Through Improved Demand Management and Price Optimization. *INFORMS Journal on Applied Analytics, 43* (1), 21-36.

Pekgün, P., & Garner B., & Uyar, E., (2014). Applying Pricing and Revenue Management in the Golf Industry: Key Challenges. *Journal of Revenue & Pricing Management, 13,* 470-482.

Pledger, M. (1994). Slot Clubs Making a Splash Throughout Vegas Casinos. *Las Vegas Review Journal,* p. E17.

CHAPTER 15

Revenue Management: A Hotel Owner's Perspective

Jonathan Jaeger and Lambis Pahiyiannakis

OVERVIEW

Hotel Revenue Management has become increasing vital to the success of a hotel; owners and asset managers must understand the underlying concepts in order to analyze and improve the performance of a hotel. A hotel owner's involvement in revenue management can vary dramatically based on ownership type and objectives. Important decisions regarding the pricing of hotel units are typically made by the revenue manager alongside other members of the executive committee and operations team. The owner and/or asset manager of a hotel may not be involved in everyday pricing decisions, but will typically maintain a level of oversight.

LEARNING OBJECTIVES

After studying this chapter, you should be able to:

- Explain the unique perspective hotel owners have towards revenue management and how it differs for institutional versus individual owners
- Analyze long-term revenue management goals as a hotel owner and demonstrate how to measure success
- Demonstrate why consistent revenue management is critical for owners with regard to both profitability and responsibilities to a hotel's lender
- Discuss the relationship between hotel owner and hotel operator and how it relates to revenue management
- Apply operational revenue management skills in order to identify the future potential of a hotel
- Describe ways for hotel management to maximize the value of a property through revenue management strategy improvement

OUTLINE

Introduction

- The Evolution of Revenue Management
- Hotel Ownership Types
- The Relationship Between Owner and Revenue Manager
- Ownership versus Revenue Management Objectives
- Macroeconomic Trends in Revenue Management
- Metrics to Measure Revenue Management Success
- Participating on Revenue Management Ownership Calls
- Cost per Guest Acquisition and its Importance to Profitability
- Price Elasticity of Demand
- The Focus on Profitability

Discussion Questions and Applications

SO WHAT?

Typical hotel ownership groups are **return on investment (ROI)** focused. While some hotel properties can appreciate as a result of external economic forces, the true value enhancement opportunity of a hotel investment can be expanded by sophisticated revenue management strategies. What factors within revenue management lead to either increasing or decreasing the value of a hotel?

INTRODUCTION

The concept of revenue management in hotels has evolved over the past decade. First utilized by the airline industry, revenue management has become one of the most important and complex facets of hotel management. Similar to airline or restaurant seats, hotel rooms are perishable, meaning rooms left vacant cannot be resold for that particular day. With the advent of new online booking companies and third-party travel agencies, the revenue manager is now responsible for repricing rooms on a minute-by-minute and on a channel-by-channel basis. Revenue Management initiatives can and do have an enormous impact on the value of a hotel.

Hotel owners must acknowledge that principles previously derived from **yield management** remain fundamental components of revenue management today. The following four conditions apply to Hotel Revenue Management:

- A fixed amount of resources is available for sale at any given time.
- Resources are **perishable** (after a given point in time, resources are not sellable).
- Different customers are willing to pay a different price for the same resources.
- There is some ability to predict future demand for resources.

Source: Stuart-Hill, 2016, pp. 1–5.

While all hotel owners have different agendas and programs for managing or asset managing a hotel, revenue management is now at the forefront of every decision being made regarding the revenue producing aspect of hotel management. The four factors listed above are true for all hotel assets. The last factor, regarding ability to predict future demand, has expanded in recent years given the creation of sophisticated forecasting tools such as Hotelligence, TAP Reports, and the products offered by Kalibri Labs.

Prior to the late 1990's and early 2000's, most hotels did not have a revenue manager; today the revenue manager is often one of the highest ranking members of the hotel executive team. While general managers were previously recruited, and hired primarily based on experience in the rooms, sales, and food and beverage departments, savvy hotel owners are now looking for operations executives who truly understand and have experience in revenue management.

Institutional hotel owners typically hire a third-party management company to manage the day-to-day operation of a hotel and do not typically focus on the minutia of a Hotel's Revenue Management strategies. This chapter will not focus on the different strategies and tools available for revenue managers, but will concentrate on how owners interface with the revenue management function of a hotel. Hotel owners with a propensity to understand the historical performance and future marketing strategies of a property must have a working knowledge of the subject. Many owners reserve the right to make higher level decisions regarding future pricing strategies. This chapter will explore how different hotel owners approach revenue management directly or indirectly through their management teams/operators.

The Evolution of Revenue Management

The advent of new technologies within the lodging industry has led to the increasing importance of revenue management. According to several hotel owners, the 2008/2009 downturn in the hotel industry was another catalyst for the revenue management concentration, for reasons which will be explored within this section.

New online travel agencies and their respective technologies have been defined as disrupters within the industry. Several of the more well-known online travel companies are as follows:

1. Priceline (Booking Holdings)
2. Booking.com (Booking Holdings)
3. Orbitz (Expedia, Inc.)
4. Expedia (Expedia, Inc.)
5. Travelocity (Expedia, Inc.)
6. Hotels.com (Expedia, Inc.)
7. Trivago (majority owned by Expedia, Inc.)
8. Hotel Tonight (Airbnb)
9. RoomsTonite

Within the list of online travel companies presented above, there has been a significant consolidation in the industry over the past several years. As a result, many of the agencies presented are now owned by the same parent company. Something all of these companies/websites have in common: they did not exist prior to the 1990's. All of the aforementioned sites offer a variety of products and services to different customers, but for the most part they represent additional booking options for the same perishable hotel room night. In other words, they have created an intermediary between the hotel product and the end user (customer). Without the proliferation of online booking agencies competing with direct sales methods by hotel owners, the revenue management field would not be as complex as it is today. Prior to the ease of booking a room online, consumers had few options when making travel plans. Many guests either called the hotel directly or went through a traditional "brick and mortar" travel agent. Now, hotel guests have seemingly endless options for booking the same hotel room, and many can be accessed directly from a smart phone. The entire process of booking a hotel room can now be completed within seconds.

THINK HISTORICALLY

Before the Internet technology boom in the late 1990s and early 2000s, many of thc aforementioned online travel agencies did not exist. According to CNN, during the mid-1990s there was a peak of 34,000 travel agents; today there are less than 13,000 retail travel agents in the United States. The following newspaper advertisements date back to the year 1900.

FOR CAPE NOME
Empire Line
OHIO
N. A. T. & T. CO.
S.S. ROANOKE
Cape Nome and St. Michael
ALASKA
CAPE NOME
SENATOR
FOR CAPE NOME
TACOMA
CITY OF SEATTLE
SKAGWAY
Cape Nome
Cape Nome — Pioneer Line
8 DAYS NOME
SanBlas
MAY 24
CAPE NOME
S.S. OREGON
FOR CAPE NOME
S. S. GARONNE
PASSENGERS AND FREIGHT
PACIFIC STEAM WHALING CO.
CAPE NOME
S. S. CENTENNIAL
VICTORIA
DIRECT FOR CAPE NOME
MAY 31
S. S. "BERTHA."
The White Pass & Yukon Route

Source: The Seattle Post Intelligencer, May 20, 1900, Page 35, Image 35.

The newspaper excerpt presented above includes advertisements for various cruise lines and trips throughout the Pacific Northwest. In order to reach potential consumers, cruise lines posted the above advertisements in newspapers as well as local gathering places such as general store and/or saloon.

In today's society, it is much easier and less expensive to reach a larger target market compared to the early 1900s prior to the advent of television and the Internet. However, what are some of the new challenges revenue managers face as it relates to the proliferation of new options available to consumers?

QUESTION TO CONSIDER

Hotel revenue managers must be cognizant of the different booking engines while developing pricing models. If a hotel room is priced at $99 on two different websites, what will drive the consumer to book directly on the hotel website versus a third-party travel agent?

PROS & CONS

The Buchin family from Indianapolis, Indiana is planning a trip to Boston for July 4th weekend. The Buchins are traveling with their two children, Michael and Jessica. While many hotel options are available, the Buchins prefer to stay in Kenmore Square in order to be near Boston University and Fenway Park and have thus selected the Hotel Commonwealth. List the Pros and Cons for the hotel owner if the Buchins buy an inclusive air and hotel package from Expedia or book direct through the hotel's website. Which booking channel is more profitable for the hotel owner?

The global economic recession had a major impact on the hotel industry beginning in 2008. According to STR Global (formerly Smith Travel Research), Revenue per Available Room (RevPAR) in the United States declined by 1.8 percent in 2008 followed by 16.7 percent in 2009. In 2009, the decline in United States performance metrics (occupancy and average daily rate) was devastating, forcing hotel owners to find creative ways to compensate for the changing conditions.

In addition to numerous cost cutting measures undertaken during the recession, owners were also keenly focused on revenue management and customer relationships. While the average decline in RevPAR during 2009 was 16.7 percent, many hotels did not experience such a dramatic impact. Hotel owners who initiated sophisticated revenue management strategies during the downtown were able to mitigate potential losses and obtain a larger market share against its competitive set.

For example, many hotels placed an emphasis on deploying strategies such as **variable and dynamic pricing** models during the downtown. The difference between variable and dynamic pricing has evolved over time. Variable pricing involves setting multiple price points for distinct market segments, whereas dynamic pricing involves changing prices over time in response to demand uncertainty (Sturman, Corgel, and Verma, 2011, 195–196). With sophisticated revenue management programs, operators can now set complex algorithms for pricing. For example, different rate fences can be set such as: minimum length of stay, rates quoted by place of origin, nonrefundable reservation fees, and cancellation fees. As revenue management continues to evolve, operators must become increasingly savvy when enforcing rate fences in order to better protect the integrity of a hotel room reservation. Room cancellations can have a dramatic impact on a hotel's performance, and hotel ownership groups are now focused on protecting reservations with strict cancellation policies, specifically at resort properties. However, many branded hotels are required to follow the cancellation policies of the parent company, thus leaving ownership with less control as it relates to cancellations.

HOTEL OWNERSHIP TYPES

The complex nature of hotel ownership is not known to many outside of the hotel investment community. Many believe a hotel branded as a "Marriott," for example, is owned by the parent company, however, for most branded properties that is not the case. Since the 1980s, many large hotel brand and management companies have moved towards as "asset light" strategy meaning they typically do not own and do not want to own the actual real estate. Most of the major brand companies (such as Marriott, Hilton, and Hyatt) today are primarily franchise and/or management companies and own only a limited number of (usually legacy) hotels. The business model of the brands is largely predicated on the generation of fees and income through real estate investments, although sometimes in order to expand in certain markets/locations they do participate by way of a real estate investment. This strategy was more common in the 1990s and early 2000s, but is no longer a widely accepted practice (The Economist, 2010, 1–2). The following list comprises the different types of hotel owners:

1. Private Equity
    - Examples include: Apollo Global Management, The Blackstone Group, Five Mile Capital Partners, Wheelock Street Capital
2. Real Estate Investment Trusts (REITs)
    - Examples include: HOST Hotels and Resorts, Pebblebrook Hotel Trust, Ashford Hospitality Trust
3. Insurance/Life Companies
    - Examples include: Prudential, MetLife, MassMutual
4. Individuals/Family Offices
    - Examples include: Cascade Investments, Ohana Real Estate Investors, MSD Capital
5. Sovereign Wealth Funds

- Examples include: ADIA, GIC, Anbang Insurance

While there are also other types of hotel ownership groups, most fit into one of the previous five categories. Different types of ownership groups can be more active depending on the current state of the economic cycle. For example, during the 2010–2012 recovery period following the economic recession, hotel REITs were the most active buyers due to their low cost of capital. However, after dramatic declines in the stock price and enterprise value of hotel REITs during 2015, most have become net sellers. Another investor group, international buyers, have become increasing active over the past several years, especially in gateway markets such as New York City and San Francisco.

Each type of ownership group has different objectives and procedures, especially in regard to revenue management. Individual owners typically have longer hold periods, meaning they own properties for a longer period of time and enjoy income based returns compared to Private Equity owners.

Private Equity companies are primarily driven by appreciation returns, thus a typical hold period is between 5 and 7 years. Ownership objectives as it relates to hotel performance and management can be drastically different if the owner is planning to hold the property for 5 years versus 50. Sovereign Wealth Funds do not always have an immediate exit strategy, as they often plan to hold the asset in their portfolio for generations.

QUESTION TO CONSIDER

Private Equity investors are often focused on the short term as opposed to the long term. For example, if a Private Equity owner had the option to patch a leak in the roof for a cost of $25,000 versus replacing the entire roof for $250,000; which option do you think the Private Equity owner would choose and why?

As it relates to revenue management, short-term owners may be focused on driving revenue and income in the near term and not on long-term client relationships. In most cases, Private Equity owners are much more hands on as it relates to asset management. Private Equity owners often retain a third-party management company (such as Aimbridge Hospitality, Pyramid Hotel Group, and Crescent Hotels & Resorts) to operate their properties in exchange for a fee. Many third-party management companies also hold a sliver piece of equity in the overall investment. This arrangement aligns the objectives of both owner and operator to maximize profit and returns. Each management company and/or asset manager has different levels of oversight on revenue managers. However, ownership groups such as sovereign wealth funds and high net worth individuals or families are primarily focused on retaining a hotel property's name or brand equity, with cash flows being merely a benefit during the term of the investment. The aforementioned ownership groups typically invest in real estate assets (like hotels) in order to protect their money from turbulence in other more volatile markets such as commodities or stocks.

One of the major differences between a corporate owned hotel asset versus an individual or family owned asset is the type of management/oversight. For example, a large management company with multiple assets in a certain market may have a team of revenue managers overseeing several properties, whereas an individual or family owned property typically has a revenue manager on site focusing solely on that specific asset. It is very important for a revenue manager to understand the objectives of ownership prior to accepting a position, as those objectives can vary dramatically.

The Relationship Between Owner and Revenue Manager

The relationship between a hotel owner and revenue manager varies depending on the ownership type. In an owner operated franchised hotel such as a Holiday Inn Express, the owner may handle the duties of revenue management personally. However, in a Four Seasons hotel owned by MSD Capital, there may not be any relationship between the ownership group and the revenue manager due to all of the parties in between. In the specific case of Four Seasons and other luxury brands, owners also tend to be restricted from operational level decisions, including revenue management.

All hotel owners have different management strategies, but the more open communication between owner and revenue manager typically results in stronger performance. By way of example, some management companies have a "heads in beds" strategy in which they would rather fill rooms at a lower rate, potentially in an effort to maximize ancillary revenues, versus other companies who focus on a higher average rate and are willing to forego rate for a lower occupancy. The revenue management strategy must fit within the overall strategy of ownership in order to meet budgetary goals.

In any hotel operation, it is important to define who is responsible and who has the final say in setting rates. In traditional hotels, the Director of Sales typically has the final say over what rate to offer a large group inquiring for a room block. However, more commonly now with sophisticated revenue management software, revenue managers are better able to predict future demand levels and quantify if the group should be accommodated or if the hotel is better off waiting for higher rated transient business. In many hotels today, revenue managers have the final say over a quoted group rate. Each owner and/or asset manager must establish a relationship with the revenue manager who works for them and their overall objectives.

REAL PEOPLE

Written by:

Barry A.N. Bloom, Ph.D.
President and Chief Operating Officer
Xenia Hotels & Resorts, Inc.

As bottom-line driven asset managers, one of the things we frequently try to understand is whether concierge floors are, in fact, additive to a hotel's ability to yield both revenue (and, thereby profit) or whether they are simply a marketing tool used by the brands to appeal to, and enhance the experience of, their loyal and frequent guests at the expense of ownership. In a recent example, we worked with one of our luxury hotel operators to analyze this topic.

The subject property is located in a large, but not primary U.S. market, with the hotel experiencing typical occupancy in the mid-60% range with a market mix of approximately 50% of its demand in the group segment. At these levels, it was unclear whether or not a concierge floor/lounge was accretive to the hotel or not, particularly given the relative few nights when the hotel was compressed and could yield guests onto the concierge floor at a premium price.

We initially considered a strategy which would close the concierge floor saving nearly $400,000 in annual operating expenses including five employee FTE's, cost of food and beverage, reducing rooms expenses due to higher housekeeping room credits, and reducing size and cost of guestroom amenities. We also calculated that by closing the concierge floor, revenue would decrease by approximately $150,000 in reduced rooms and honor bar revenue. Thus, we determined that the concierge floor was resulting in a loss of approximately $250,000 per year.

In conjunction with property management, as opposed to shutting down the operation completely, we also analyzed the opportunity to more actively promote the concierge floor while simultaneously revisiting the cost structure of the lounge. By working with revenue management and actively promoting the concierge floor through online and voice reservation channels, significant, trackable improvements were made in concierge floor revenue. Specifically, the premium for these rooms was allowed to float at various best available rate (BAR) levels rather than the previously fixed upgrade cost of $50 per night.

This dynamic pricing ranged from as low as $30 per night during low occupancy periods to as much as $100 per night during peak demand periods. In addition to the online and voice channel offerings, a rejuvenated effort was also made to upsell the concierge floor at the front desk through specific individual and team incentives designed to motivate the front desk agents to promote the concierge floor.

In the first 12 months following implementation, the hotel recorded approximately $300,000 in trackable revenue enhancement through upgrades and compression while simultaneously lowering expenses by $150,000. As a result of these efforts, the hotel is now earning approximately $50,000 in profit as compared to the prior loss of $250,000."

Questions:

1. Name several positive and negative factors that ownership may have considered when studying whether or not to abandon the concierge floor operation.
2. Do you think ownership ultimately made the right decision regarding the concierge floor?

Ownership Versus Revenue Management Objectives

The misalignment between hotel ownership and a revenue manager can be devastating to a hotel property's ability to maximize income, and therefore asset value. These situations typically occur within institutional owned assets where there are several degrees of separation between owner and revenue manager.

QUESTION TO CONSIDER

The subject property is a five-diamond resort located in the Caribbean and owned by a REIT. The hotel is currently operated by the brand with oversight from a third-party asset manager (such as LW Hospitality Advisors) that has been retained by ownership. Who does the revenue manager report to? What types of conflicts may arise between the asset manager and the revenue manager?

In situations as previously described, the revenue manager would be an employee of the Management Company and reports directly to the general manager. Depending on the relationship between the asset management (who represents ownership) and the Management Company, he/she may or may not have access to speak directly with the revenue manager without other members present.

Often times, asset managers and property level management including revenue managers have a difference of opinion regarding various strategies. When negotiating a management contract, owners should require control over important operational decisions relating to revenue management. In cases of disagreement, the management company and/or brand is ultimately an agent of ownership. Thus, in most cases, ownership has final approval rights in order to reach their specific objectives.

Macroeconomic Trends in Revenue Management

Macroeconomic trends can have a material impact on revenue management decisions. In many instances, hotel operators focus on microeconomic factors affecting the everyday operation of a hotel, such as controlling costs or capital expenditures pertaining to renovations. Their role is to manage the daily operation of the property, while the role of the asset manager and/or owner is to focus on the overall master plan. Asset managers may elect to introduce broader macroeconomic information to the revenue manager in order to better assist with pricing models.

In order to illustrate this point, let's analyze an energy related market such as Midland, Texas, which is located within the Permian Basin. The Permian Basin is a sedimentary basin largely contained in the western part of the State of Texas and the southeastern part of New Mexico. The basin area reaches from south of Lubbock, to south of Midland and Odessa, extending westward into the southeastern part of New Mexico. Throughout the Permian Basin, hotels are largely dependent on the energy industry, and more specifically, the level of exploration and drilling occurring in the area for demand.

There are several examples of macroeconomic data that could be helpful to a revenue manager in an energy related market. For starters, ownership may introduce data such as the overall price of oil. The price of crude oil began its decent in July 2014 and continued throughout 2015, with the largest percentage decrease occurring in December 2014 following OPEC's decision not to reduce production at its meeting in Vienna (November 2014). As presented on the following chart, the price per barrel of crude oil fell from \$105.79 in June of 2014 to a \$42.91 in November of 2015.

Crude Oil Prices Per Barrel (Monthly)											
Month/ Year	Price Per Barrel	% Chg	Month/ Year	Price Per Barrel	% Chg	Month/ Year	Price Per Barrel	% Chg	Month/Year	Price Per Barrel	% Chg
Nov-15	$42.91	-7%	Dec-13	$97.63	4%	Dec-11	$98.56	1%	Dec-09	$74.47	-5%
Oct-15	$46.22	2%	Nov-13	$93.86	-7%	Nov-11	$97.16	13%	Nov-09	$77.99	3%
Sep-15	$45.48	6%	Oc t-13	$100.54	-5%	Oct-11	$86.32	1%	Oct-09	$75.72	9%
Aug-15	$42.87	-16%	Sep-13	$106.29	0%	Sep-11	$85.52	-1%	Sep-09	$69.41	-2%
Jul-15	$50.90	-15%	Aug-13	$106.57	2%	Aug-11	$86.33	-11%	Aug-09	$71.05	11%
Jun-15	$59.82	1%	Jul-13	$104.67	9%	Jul-11	$97.30	1%	Jul-09	$64.15	-8%
May-15	$59.27	9%	Jun-13	$95.77	1%	Jun-11	$96.26	-5%	Jun-09	$69.64	18%
Apr-15	$54.45	14%	May-13	$94.51	3%	May-11	$100.90	-8%	May-09	$59.03	19%
Mar-15	$47.82	-5%	Apr-13	$92.02	-1%	Apr-11	$109.53	6%	Apr-09	$49.65	4%
Feb-15	$50.58	7%	Mar-13	$92.94	-2%	Mar-11	$102.86	16%	Mar-09	$47.94	23%
Jan-15	$47.22	-20%	Feb-13	$95.31	1%	Feb-11	$88.58	-1%	Feb-09	$39.09	-6%
Dec-14	$59.29	-22%	Jan-13	$94.76	8%	Jan-11	$89.17	0%	Jan-09	$41.71	1%
Nov-14	$75.79	-10%	Dec -12	$87.86	2%	Dec -10	$89.15	6%	Dec-08	$41.12	-28%
Oct-14	$84.40	-9%	Nov-12	$86.53	-3%	Nov-10	$84.25	3%	Nov-08	$57.31	-25%
Sep-14	$93.21	-3%	Oct-12	$89.49	-5%	Oct-10	$81.89	9%	Oct-08	$76.61	-26%
Aug-14	$96.54	-7%	Sep-12	$94.51	0%	Sep-10	$75.24	-2%	Sep-08	$104.11	-11%
Jul-14	$103.59	-2%	Aug-12	$94.13	7%	Aug-10	$76.60	0%	Aug-08	$116.67	-13%
Jun-14	$105.79	4%	Jun-12	$87.90	7%	Jul-10	$76.32	1%	Jul-08	$133.37	0%
May-14	$102.18	0%	Jun-12	$82.30	-13%	Jun-10	$75.34	2%	Jun-08	$133.88	7%
Apr-14	$102.07	1%	May-12	$94.66	-8%	May-10	$73.74	-13%	May-08	$125.40	11%
Mar-14	$100.80	0%	Apr-12	$103.32	-3%	Apr-10	$84.29	4%	Apr-08	$112.58	7%
Feb-14	$100.82	7%	Mar-12	$106.16	4%	Mar-10	$81.20	6%	Mar-08	$105.45	11%
Jan-14	$94.62		Feb-12	$102.20	2%	Feb-10	$76.39	-2%	Feb-08	$95.39	3%
			Jan-12	$100.27		Jan-10	$78.33		Jan-08	$92.97	
Fisc al Year Chg Dec - Nov 14/15 -28%				12/13	7%		10/11	9%		08/09	90%
Fisc al Year Chg Dec - Nov 13/14 -22%				11/12	-12%		09/10	13%			

Source: U.S. Energy Information Administration; Compiled by LW Hospitality Advisors®

QUESTION TO CONSIDER

How can a revenue manager use the information presented above regarding the constantly changing price of oil when making pricing decisions for a specific hotel property?

The dramatic decline in the price of crude oil is having a vast effect on hotel properties located throughout Texas, and specifically within the Permian Basin. Hotel revenue managers must utilize this information when making pricing decisions. Throughout conversations with large energy companies such as Exxon Mobile, Chevron, etc., it is apparent they are in the midst of reducing travel spending given the downturn in the market.

There are many other creative ways for revenue managers to utilize macro and microeconomic data in order to assist with pricing decisions. Within the Permian Basin, each county releases a monthly report containing the number of drilling permits that were issued. In order to better understand the activity of oil/gas companies in the area, revenue managers can track this information and remain informed on where companies are still actively drilling. During downturn periods, owner's typically place more emphasis on both Sales and Revenue Management strategies in order to protect their asset. Properties with attentive owners and revenue managers are able to outperform competitive properties during difficult times, such as the current situation in the Permian Basin and other energy dependent lodging markets throughout the country.

SPREADSHEET EXERCISE 15.1

Limited service hotel properties located in the Permian Basin are typically valued and appraised based on two metrics. The first is a Rooms Revenue Multiplier (RRM), and the second is a Capitalization Rate (cap rate). Based on the information presented in the attached excel spreadsheet for the West Texas Inn, please calculate the potential fluctuations in the value of the hotel based on changes to the property's RevPAR. There is one additional question as part of this exercise also included within the spreadsheet.

Metrics to Measure Revenue Management Success

A Revenue Management strategy is executed and measured based on predefined goals and objectives. Hotel managers must show results in order to prove they are effective managers assisting ownership in achieving overall investment goals. Results are measured by using certain benchmarks and metrics such as: occupancy, average daily rate (ADR), and RevPAR. Although these metrics are widely accepted as the most important tools for measuring success, their scope is confined to the top line (revenue only), while hotel owners are more focused on the bottom line, also known as profitability. As hotel guests continue to utilize online booking intermediaries when making reservations, the cost of guest acquisition (further discussed later in this section) has been increasing at a disproportional rate. Therefore, using RevPAR as the sole metric to benchmark a hotel against its competitive set seems to be an outdated methodology. Hotel owners want to establish that not only RevPAR has been maximized, but also that it has been strategically maximized by using the lowest cost channels and booking methods.

Entrepreneurial revenue managers have already created several new metrics that go beyond the traditional top line benchmarks. One of these new methods calculates RevPAR based on a net ADR (ADR less guest acquisition costs) as a metric that allows owners and managers to understand how efficient the booking channels selected were in securing guest business. Another method being put forward by revenue managers is measuring Total Revenue per Available Room which adds incremental spend into the RevPAR equation providing for overall revenue contribution or "guest value" by segment or channel. This becomes especially crucial at resort properties where the channel from which a guest books directly impacts the amount of ancillary dollars they spend in other parts of the resort (such as Food & Beverage or Spa). Finally, a metric currently on the rise in popularity is known as **Gross Operating Profit per Available Room (GOPPAR)** which factors in all operating costs (Parker, 2016, 1–3). Each of these newly introduced metrics suggests that hotel owners are becoming more sophisticated and are looking for ways to track overall profitability in addition to top line revenue. With revenue management tools continuing to become more advanced and with technological improvements of software that can track guests back to their origin, hotel owners are beginning to measure their managers' performance with an enhanced toolbox of metrics. As the measurement of success for a revenue manager continues to evolve, owners are also beginning to base executive incentive pay and bonuses on these new metrics.

SEEING FURTHER

The metric known as GOPPAR is an important indicator of hotel performance. GOPPAR is calculated as follows:

GOPPAR = GOP (Gross Operating Profit) / # of Available Rooms

When analyzing the GOPPAR of a hotel property, the results can differ dramatically based on many different factors. While results can differ, the GOPPAR metric is widely used throughout the industry to measure hotel performance. The GOPPAR provides ownership with a better indication of profitability when compared to RevPAR. As the industry continues to evolve, what other of metrics would be useful in assessing the performance of a hotel?

Participating on Revenue Management Ownership Calls

Revenue management is directly linked to a hotel's profitability, which in return is directly linked to ownership's top priority: retention and growth of real estate values. Asset managers understand how important revenue management is to a hotel's success, and therefore take an active role in collaborating with a property's senior management and revenue management teams. During these interactions, it is the asset manager's responsibility to ask investigatory questions and test the revenue management team, inquiring about how the long-term revenue management strategy is being implemented and how short-term strategies contribute to the owner's long-term goals.

An example of a long-term strategy from an owner's perspective is a strategy which optimizes profitability for the hotel overall and not just the rooms department which revenue management impacts directly. Another characteristic of a long-term revenue management strategy is one which focuses on long-term profitability, not just short-term profitability which is usually what a hotel management's team is incentivized on. A clear long-term strategy also forces a hotel management team to focus on ADR integrity. ADR integrity (also known as rate integrity) is a concept that guests value significantly. Guests and consumers in general want to know when they purchase a good or service, they are receiving the value they feel appropriate. Continuously fluctuating rates at a hotel to achieve maximum short-term occupancy confuses guests who may be used to paying a certain rate. While guests may or may not understand the dynamic pricing model, it is important not to employ extreme pricing fluctuations for repeat guests. Retaining rate integrity is critical to long-term ADR sustainability and growth of a hotel. From an asset manager's perspective, decisions such as rate parity in the short term should support the long-term revenue management strategy put in place for the entire investment horizon.

For example, a revenue management/sales team may be presented with the opportunity to secure a corporate account for a hotel which would lock in ADR with inflationary growth over the next 2 years. Although corporate accounts are critical for a hotel's revenue management success, an asset manager must inquire about the timing of these contracts and whether the hotel should be more willing to take on short-term risk. If ADR is forecasted to increase substantially over the near term, it may be beneficial for the hotel not to lock into a guaranteed contract and wait for other individual transient business. However, in softer market conditions, the hotel may create an advantage by securing base business at a certain rate thus reducing the sellable inventory when excess demand is limited. These are the types of discussions and decisions that take place in meetings or on calls between ownership and management.

Cost Per Guest Acquisition and Its Importance to Profitability

Selling the right room to the right customer requires revenue managers to be able to accurately segment their demand and control room inventory and pricing for each segment. Each segment of demand has different characteristics, including sensitivity to pricing (**price elasticity**), timing of booking, and brand sensitivity to name a few. One of the most important characteristics to hotel owners is the path each segment choses to book reservations, especially transient segments. The type of channel a booking comes through may directly impact the cost of guest acquisition. The cost of guest acquisition is defined as the cost a hotel owner incurs to procure a new guest to stay at their hotel. It is crucial to maintain a low cost of guest acquisition in order to maximize the profitability of each guest's stay at a property.

The booking channels that typically generate the most booking volume for hotels are the direct channels (e.g., website and direct phone line) and indirect channels which are primarily online travel agents (OTAs). OTAs are online services hotels utilize to sell hotel inventory that is targeted to price sensitive consumers who are brand agnostic and are looking for the best value available to accommodate their staying needs. Examples of the major OTAs are Expedia, Priceline, and Travelocity to name a few.

All reservations are not created equally. For a hotel owner who is primarily focused on a hotel's profitability (and value by relation), the customer's booking channel is of critical importance due to the cost associated with guest acquisition. Whether a hotel is supported by a major brand (Marriott, Hilton, Hyatt, etc.) or whether it is an independent hotel, it continuously invests in its marketing efforts which aim to publicize the hotel to guests seeking accommodations. Branded hotel owners market their hotels by investing in franchise fees, national marketing fees, and by operating in-house marketing departments. Franchise fees (also known as royalties) are fees branded hotel owners pay to the major brands such as Marriott, Hilton, and Hyatt in order to have the right to use those names and central reservations systems (CRS). National marketing fees are monetary contributions all branded hotels make that go towards advertising the brand as a whole. A good example of such advertising is watching the "Courtyard by Marriott" ads on TV during a sporting event. The purpose is to advertise the Courtyard by Marriott brand as a whole and increase brand familiarity of the specific brand of Marriott hotels, not promote a single Courtyard hotel. In-house marketing departments are staffed marketing teams whose sole focus is to promote the subject hotel and to secure group business and corporate negotiated business. Independent hotels do not pay the brand related fees and instead funnel their marketing efforts and expenditure into their on-property marketing teams. The size of the marketing team varies across hotels, with large hotels and resorts requiring a much larger staff and budget compared to smaller select service hotels requiring a lesser in-house marketing effort (especially if affiliated with a national brand).

An owner's choice to open a hotels inventory to OTAs is essentially a decision to outsource room bookings, which as discussed results in higher acquisition costs. OTAs are known to charge up to 20–30 percent of the rate advertised to a guest through their website, an expense which understandably can have a major impact on the profitability of such a guest, especially when it is layered on to the existing marketing costs described above. As a result, hotel owners drive their managers to generate bookings for their hotels through direct channels, which they have more control over and have already paid for through their fixed cost associated with operating the in-house marketing departments.

There are other downsides to using OTAs beyond increasing the cost of guest acquisition. Guests who book hotel stays through OTA tend to be hotel agnostic and the likelihood of converting them to a repeat guest decreases versus a guest who may not always place pricing at the top of their booking criteria. Additionally, the fact guests booking through OTAs are price sensitive usually means they tend to not generate revenue at **ancillary departments** in the hotel such as restaurants, room service, or even spas and golf at resort hotels.

OTAs do also benefit hotels. Revenue management is all about selling the right room to the right guest at the right time. OTAs can be very effective as a marketing expense targeted towards price sensitive guests, a group of guests who are hard to reach through direct channels. OTAs can be very successful at maximizing potential revenues if they are used carefully and strategically. The challenge for hotel owners and their managers is to control the amount of inventory outsourced to OTAs and the timing of opening such channels. Additionally, studies have shown a hotel's exposure through OTAs increases the hotels revenues through other online channels, including the hotel's website which is a direct booking channel preferred by owners (due to the lowest cost of acquisition).

Price Elasticity of Demand

Price elasticity of demand studies how sensitive consumer demand is to fluctuations in price. Put simply, when a good or service is defined as price elastic, it is considered to be a product very sensitive to small price changes. When a good or service is defined as price inelastic, it is considered to be a product not very sensitive to small price changes. In the hotel space, a hotel's product may vary from elastic to inelastic depending on the demand periods. During peak demand periods (such as conventions, Super Bowl weekend, etc.) price is highly inelastic and as demand peaks prices rise quickly. Alternatively, on a typical Sunday night (the least traveled day of the week) hotel rooms tend to be extremely price elastic, where a small change in price may affect the consumer's decision to choose one hotel over another.

Revenue management aims to target a variety of demand segments and price them according to their unique characteristics, including their propensity to be price elastic or inelastic to hotel pricing. This section of the chapter aims to discuss how price elasticity of demand for hotel rooms varies across economic cycles. Economic cycles are a focal point of hotel owners who are motivated to retain value through income during peaks and troughs of an economic cycle. Revenue management must therefore be fluid and understand what the macroeconomic trends are in order to accurately prioritize occupancy versus ADR and target each segment according to their continuously changing price sensitivity.

Not all goods and services are sensitive to changes in macroeconomic shifts. Basic necessities like food, housing, and fuel are the first to be expended on through a household's income. Things like travel and hotel rooms for the most part are discretionary needs that are consumed when households have enough disposable income to afford them. The same principle applies for corporations. Basic needs to continue operations are expended first, travel and especially incentive travel are considered luxuries. As a result, most guests whether travelling on their own or their company's expense tend to be more price elastic during recessions and more price inelastic during recoveries and expansions.

During economic downturns, there is typically downward pressure on ADR. While at the same time, a hotel owner's expenses typically continue to rise at an inflationary pace. This dynamic causes an exponential downward pressure on the hotel's bottom line. It is imperative for revenue managers to recognize which segments have become more elastic to price changes and decrease rates for those segments while maintaining rate integrity for segments that demonstration price elasticity resistance. Revenue managers must be careful however not to heavily discount hotel rates. Once a guest has grown accustomed to paying a lower rate for a hotel, they may be turned away during a recovery when ownership is seeking to aggressively increase rates.

During economic recoveries and expansions, owners should motivate revenue managers to drive ADR and take more risk during shoulder and off-peak seasons, asking them to keep discounted channels at a lower volume and influence guests to book through direct channels at higher rates. Increases in ADR are more typically profitable than increases in occupancy and revenue managers know at what level of occupancy they can reduce the need for discounted channels and go after higher rated business. During macroeconomic expansions, owners should ask revenue managers to move their focus off RevPAR and towards GOPPAR.

This phenomenon is something revenue managers need to be aware of and experienced in. A revenue manager cannot only identify what the macroeconomic state is at the present time but can also understand the changing market fundamentals and how to properly adjust occupancy and ADR over the next 12 or 24 months.

The Focus on Profitability

As portrayed within the chapter, revenue management initiatives are not only in place to maximize RevPAR, but also GOPPAR. In other words, a revenue manager should not only try to maximize revenue but also maximize the source of bookings that generate the most profit for the hotel. Typically, this means accepting higher rated business, even if that results in a lower occupancy.

Why is profitability so important for a hotel? The answer is to some extent intrinsic: as with all economic units, hotels drive to maximize profits. The basic principles of microeconomic theory posit that the ultimate goal of every business is to maximize profits. Non-institutional hotel owners are usually "one-dimensional" and focus solely on short-term profitability. However, institutional hotel owners are in some ways unique, and seeking profitability extends further than just what a hotel's bottom line reads.

First and foremost, profitability is the main criteria for valuation of a hotel asset. The higher the net income of a hotel asset, the higher its value will be. Equally as important is the consistency of profitability. Assets that can demonstrate consistent income generation through various stages of an economic cycle tend to be sought after by the hotel investment community and therefore benefit from a higher valuation. Consistent and high valuation of an asset is extremely important for institutional hotel investors who continuously track the value of their assets and base their decision making on how their existing portfolio is performing. Fluctuations in value create uncertainty for said investors and could significantly impact their investment decisions. Hotel investors, as any other investors, are primarily focused on retaining and growing the value of the investment.

Secondly, most institutional hotel owners typically place debt in the form of a commercial mortgage on their assets in order to leverage income returns and overall internal rate of return on the investment. Commercial mortgages are utilized by institutional investors to reduce the amount of equity needed for a property and replace it with funds (typically from a bank) that carries an interest rate below what their equity expects to earn. For example, if an investor acquires a hotel property for $100M that generates $10M of income, the equity would earn a 10 percent income return in the first year. If the investor can secure $60M of debt from a lender at an interest only rate of 5 percent, the investor would owe the lender annual interest (also called debt service) of $3M. With the debt in place, the investor would earn an annual income after debt service of $7M ($10M of income less $3M of interest) over an equity position of $40M ($100M acquisition price less $60M of debt), equates to a return of 17.5 percent. This simple example demonstrates how debt can be extremely accretive to an investor's income return. The hotel property is called the collateral of the loan and in the case of a default (e.g., the income of the property drops below the interest owed, in this case $3M), the lender may foreclose on the property and essentially take over equity ownership of the hotel.

SPREADSHEET EXERCISE 15.2

Based on the information presented in the attached excel spreadsheet for the Main Street Boutique Hotel, please calculate the following metrics: NOI, Cap Rate/Unleveraged Cash Yield, loan-to-value (LTV), Debt Service, Debt Service Coverage Ratio, Debt Yield, Leveraged Equity Position, and Leveraged Cash Yield. There are two additional questions as part of this exercise also included within the excel spreadsheet.

Using a hotel as collateral for a commercial mortgage is a complicated process that many recognized financial institutions would not consider. Hotels are generally known as one of the riskier asset classes when compared to other forms of real estate. Even financial institutions with a better understanding of the hotel industry are typically very cautious of placing debt on hotels and frequently establish protection mechanisms that provide them additional security when financing hotel assets. These tools are in place to protect the lender from fluctuations in the hotel industry which unlike other asset classes (office, retail, residential, etc.) are realized immediately due to the daily turn of inventory. Two common tools utilized by hotel lenders as protection mechanisms from such volatility are loan-to-value (LTV) tests, debt service coverage ratios, and cash sweeps (also known as Cash Traps).

When a lender issues a mortgage on any type of real estate asset, one of the most important metrics is the LTV ratio, which examines the amount of debt provided compared to the collateral's value. For example, if a hotel worth $100M received a senior mortgage of $60M, the loan is said to be a 60 percent LTV loan. Lenders decide on the outset of the loan what amount of LTV they are comfortable with and do not typically allow the LTV of the loan to far exceed that initial level. As a result, in the above example they may stipulate the $60M loan placed on the $100M asset may not at any time during the course of the loan become a 65 percent LTV loan. This would occur if the value of the hotel fluctuates downward. If the hotel, for example, decreased in value and was worth $95M, the loan would be deemed a 63 percent LTV loan, which would not yet trigger the LTV test provided by the lender. However, if the value of the hotel declined to $90M, the loan would be deemed a 67 percent LTV loan, an LTV level that would trigger the LTV test and would cause significant issues for the borrower. According to loan standards, the borrower would be in default on the loan.

Another very important metric lenders focus on during the outset of a loan process is the Debt Service Coverage Ratio (DSCR). The DSCR examines how much cash flow the collateral hotel generates in order to cover debt service, which is the annual interest and principal payment the hotel is liable for in order to service its loan. Let us use the same hotel from the example previously presented. If the subject hotel generates $10M of net operating income (NOI) and the $60M loan has an annual debt service of $3M, the debt service coverage ratio would be $10M/$3M, so 3.33×. In other words, the hotel can generate enough cash flow to cover its debt service plus an additional 233 percent. Lenders in the hotel industry typically seek to have a minimum of a 1.2×–1.5× DSCR at the outset of a loan. Inability to achieve the pre-agreed upon minimum DSCR may also lead to a loan default. The above loan example is represented in the exhibit below:

	Investment Without Debt	**Debt Terms**	**Investment With Debt**
Equity Investment	$100,000,000		$40,000,000
Commercial Mortgage		$60,000,000	
Loan-To-Value		60.0%	
Interest Rate		5.0%	
Annual Interest Owed		$3,000,000	
Annual Income/Return to Equity	$10,000,000		$7,000,000
Debt Service Coverage Ratio		3.3x	
Income Return	10.0%		17.5%

The commercial mortgage example presented above assumes an interest only mortgage with annual non-compounded payments.

QUESTIONS TO CONSIDER

When a prospective lender is underwriting a hotel loan, what are the most important factors that must be considered? How can lenders assure that loans are safe and income levels will remain above the desired debt service coverage ratios?

A loan default is without question a catastrophic result for an investment which may lead to repercussions from the lender in the form of Cash Sweeps or even worse, foreclosure. Cash Sweep is the process by which if the DSCR drops below a certain level, any net cash flow generated by the collateral goes directly into an account controlled by the lender. The cash is trapped in this account until either the DSCR rises above the lender's desired level or until the loan is paid off. Triggering a Cash Sweep puts hotel owners in a difficult situation, as they become completely unable to generate any cash flow for themselves or their co-investors in the asset. All the cash is controlled by the lender and releasing it generally requires legal involvement. Foreclosure is a legal process in which a lender attempts to recover the balance of a loan from a borrower, who has stopped making payments to the lender, by forcing the sale of the asset used as the collateral for the loan. A lender may also attempt to take over the equity position, thus assuming ownership control of the asset and forcing the borrower out of the investment, leading to a complete loss of the investor's equity.

Finally, generating free cash flow is extremely important for hotel owners because it allows them to continue reinvesting in their assets. Because hotel rooms are sold on a daily basis, they are subject to significant "wear and tear" that forces owners to continuously reinvest in the asset in the form of capital expenditures. This holds especially true for owners of branded hotels that have to comply with brand standards and are forced by the brands to renovate even if the hotel product has not reached the end of its useful life. Profitability of a hotel asset affords institutional hotel owners with the cash flow to spend on future renovations. In addition, cash flow provides owners with the confidence that any renovation expense made on the asset is a good investment that will continue to provide a return.

As illustrated, there are many reasons why hotel owners must motivate the executive team and revenue managers to strive for maximum and consistent profitability to ensure a stable hotel valuation, a credible standing with their lenders, and to ensure capital availability when the hotel is due for renovation. The strength of a hotel's bottom line is directly tied to the health of a hotel's ability to generate revenue. Therefore, revenue managers must be continuously challenged to drive performance and strive to flex their revenue management strategies and execute them with accuracy. Although the above concepts are of crucial importance to most hotel investors, high net worth investors or sovereign wealth investors may focus primarily on prestige or brand equity to retain and grow value. A good example of this would be the Langham Hotel in London. Its value stems primarily from its status as one of the oldest and most prestigious hotels in London and secondarily from its income performance. It also has tremendous value for Langham as a flagship property for the brand.

DISCUSSION QUESTIONS

Question 1: From an owner's perspective, what are several potential challenges of a brand managed hotel as it relates to revenue management and pricing decisions?

Question 2: How would an owner's decision-making process on a potential group booking change depending on the investment horizon/hold period?

Question 3: Why would a revenue manager ask about the owner's short- and long-term objectives prior to accepting a job at the hotel?

APPLICATIONS

Case 1:

John and Anna Bentley own a Holiday Inn in the suburbs of Houston, Texas. The hotel was developed by their father and they have been involved with the hotel, primarily on the revenue management side of the operation for several years. The hotel is a full-service operation with 250 rooms and 10,000 SF of meeting space which is utilized by local oil drilling and refining companies to host quarterly meetings and to house their corporate employees when they visit from out of town. Recently, the price of oil has dropped from \$80 to \$100 per barrel to approximately \$40, forcing some of the local oil industry firms to cut back not only on their travel but also on their quarterly meeting expenditures.

John and Anna have been tracking this sharp decline in the price of oil and understand this will impact their hotel. However, there is disagreement surrounding which revenue management strategy to implement. John believes the oil price shock will have a long-term impact on local corporate business, so he is inclined to renegotiate local negotiated rates at lower levels quickly to ensure loyal corporate demand continues to stay at the hotel. He also believes all specific marketing efforts should be implemented to secure the group business that delivers a fixed amount of rooms quarterly and guarantees the usage of the hotel's meeting space. Anna has a different opinion. According to her, the oil price shock will be short lived and local oil industry companies will not be significantly impacted. She believes they should hold a hard line with their corporate accounts and keep their negotiated rates in place. Based on her research, Anna says there are other demand sources in the market that will allow them to backfill corporate demand rooms (should they decrease) with OTA generated rooms. She also believes they have a competitive advantage with their meeting space compared to other competitive hotels in the market.

What do you think the correct revenue management strategy is for this hotel? How is John's strategy going to impact top and bottom line? How is his strategy impacting long-term performance of the hotel? How is Anna's strategy going to impact top and bottom line? What are the differences of corporate negotiated rate business and OTA business and which would you prefer to have at a time of rate uncertainty? Does John's strategy for increasing sales efforts of their meeting space make sense if Anna is right about their existing competitive advantage?

Case 2:

Philip Motely is the Director of Acquisitions for a small private equity real estate investment firm based in Boston, MA. Philip has identified what he believes is an interesting hotel acquisition located in Burlington, a prominent and growing submarket of Boston. He believes he could acquire the hotel and significantly improve revenue management initiatives by replacing current management with a local experienced management company. The following chart depicts the existing room night segmentation compared to the projections post acquisition:

Rooms	150			150		
Annual Room nights	54,750			54,750		
		Existing			**Projected**	
Transient	**Rooms**	**ADR**	**Revenue**	**Rooms**	**ADR**	**Revenue**
Rack	3,833	100.00	383,250	8,213	110.00	903,375
Corporate	2,738	80.00	219,000	3,833	85.00	325,763
OTA	6,570	90.00	591,300	5,475	90.00	492,750
Government	2,738	75.00	205,313	2,738	75.00	205,313
Other	1,643	80.00	131,400	1,643	80.00	131,400
Group						
Business	5,475	85.00	465,375	6,023	87.00	523,958
SMERF	9,855	75.00	739,125	9,855	80.00	788,400
Contract						
Airline	4,380	65.00	284,700	1,643	65.00	106,76
Total	37,230	81.10	3,019,463	39,420	88.22	3,477,720
Occupancy	68.0%			72.0%		

Philip is planning on obtaining debt for the acquisition, but understands he has to convince a lender of the value he is planning to add through revenue management. Given the remix presented above, what are the segments most impacted by the new budget? Which segments are increasing or decreasing in room night production and ADR? Do you think Philip's plan is realistic? How must Philip present his business plan to a lender to convince them of his strategy? What can be said of the profitability of this hotel with the projected segmentation mix? How is that important for a lender to understand?

TEAM ACTIVITY

In teams of three to four students, designate a project manager. Each student should choose an ownership company from the list of groups presented on page eight. Each member of the team should choose a company from a different group. The objective of this assignment is for each team member to conduct an interview (over the phone or in person) with a representative of the ownership company (preferable an asset manager). The following questions should be asked:

1. How do you approach revenue management from an owner's perspective?
2. Do you participate in monthly meetings with the revenue manager?
3. Does hotel management staff have the ability to make future pricing decisions, or do you require approval before any shifts in strategy?

Following the interviews, the team should prepare a PowerPoint presentation highlighting the similarities and differences between the different ownership groups/types. Which ownership group has the most involved approach to revenue management?

INTERNET ACTIVITY

There are many well-known hotel management companies in the U.S. Complete a Google search to find at least three companies. Do any of the companies mention revenue management on their websites? In comparison, also run a search for third-party hotel asset management firms and look for references to revenue management on their websites. Identify which company type (hotel management or hotel asset management) more frequently references revenue management.

GLOSSARY

Ancillary Departments – Providing necessary support to the primary activities or operation of an organization, institution, industry, or system (e.g., in a hotel the spa, fitness center, etc. would be considered ancillary)

Dynamic Pricing – Practice of pricing items at a level determined by a particular customer's perceived ability to pay.

Gross Operating Profit per Available Room (GOPPAR) – A company's revenue from sales in a given period of time less its cost of goods sold divided by the total number of rooms available for sale.

Macroeconomics – Branch of the economics field that studies how the aggregate economy behaves.

Perishable – An item or good likely to decay or go bad quickly (e.g., a hotel room is perishable and cannot be sold once the night has passed)

Price Elasticity – A consumer's willingness to purchase a product depending on the level of price.

Return on Investment (ROI) – Excess cash flow (profit) received over the initial investment. ROI is typically expressed as a percentage

Variable Pricing – A pricing strategy where a business offers varying price points at different locations or points-of-sale. This is a common approach used by retailers when the costs of offering certain goods and services and the level of market demand justify it.

Yield Management – Variable pricing strategy, based on understanding, anticipating, and influencing consumer behavior in order to maximize revenue or profits from a fixed, perishable resource (such as airline seats or hotel room reservations).

REFERENCES

Educational Institute of the American Hotels & Lodging Association. (2006). *Uniform system of accounts for the lodging industry* (10th ed.). Lansing, MI: Author.

Hales, J. A. (2011). *Accounting and Financial Analysis in the Hospitality Industry.* Upper Saddle River, NJ: Pearson Prentice Hall.

Hayes, D. K., & Miller, A. A. (2011). *Revenue Management for the Hospitality Industry.* Hoboken, NJ: John Wiley & Sons.

Parker, J. (2016). *GOPPAR (Gross Operating Profit Per Available Room) – Best Measurement of Success.* Retrieved from http://hotelexecutive.com/business_review/1920/goppar-gross-operating-profit-per-available-room-best-measurement-of-success%20).

Stuart-Hill, T. (2016). *Revenue Management: An Overview on Past, Present, and Future.* Retrieved from http://hotelexecutive.com/business_review/3194/revenue-management-an-overview-on-past-present-and-future.

Sturman, M.; Corgel, J., &Verma, R. (2011). *The Cornell School of Hospitality Administration on Hospitality.* Hoboken, NJ: John Wiley & Sons.

The Economist. (2010). *Asset-Light or Asset-Right?* Retrieved from http://www.economist.com/node/17463399.

Glossary of Terms and Abbreviations

A

AAA – American Automobile Association.

Ancillary Departments – Providing necessary support to the primary activities or operation of an organization, institution, industry, or system (example: in a hotel the spa, fitness center, etc. would be considered ancillary).

ADR – Average Daily Rate—Rooms revenue divided by rooms sold, displayed as the average rental rate for a single room.

ADT – The daily average 'theo' of all games played by the customer over a given period.

ALBDs (Cruise) – Abbreviation for available lower berth days, which is the measure of cruise capacity. Some cruise lines refer to PGCDs, which means potential guest cruise days.

APD (Cruise) – Abbreviation for average per diem, which is the net ticket revenue divided by the number of days in the cruise. Some cruise lines refer to NPD, net per diem, which is the same statistic.

ARI – Availability, Rates, and Inventory—referred to by connectivity systems.

ARI – Average Rate Index.

Arrivals – Amount of rooms set to arrive.

B

Balk – When customers who had intended on joining a system do not do so once they see the line.

Banquet Revenue/Group Rooms Consumed – A performance metric that ties sleeping rooms to banquet revenue for a comprehensive view of business.

BAR – Best Available Rate. (see Retail Rate)

BEO – Banquet Event Order (Space Optimization)—form generated by your Sales and Catering system delivering detailed instructions to all operational teams in your organization.

Billboard Effect – In the Cornell study (see Chapter 4), the billboard effect is the marketing and advertising benefits experienced by hotels when they're listed on online travel agent websites.

Bottleneck – The process within a system that limits the operation and output of the entire system.

Brand.com – The main reservation booking website for the hotel or chain.

BRG – Best Rate Guarantee.

BT – Business Transient.

Bundled Travel – Reservations where multiple travel services are combined such as flight and hotel.

Bundling – Inclusion of additional services to a room offering.

C

Cabin Categories – Cruise ship cabins have different physical attributes and/or different locations on a ship. Similar cabin types are grouped into the same cabin category and sold at the same price.

Cancellation Penalties (Cruise) – Fees assessed in the event that a cruise is canceled after the full payment due date.

Capacity (Restaurant)–The supply of seats a restaurant has available to accommodate customers.

Channel/Source – Platform or engine responsible for delivering a booking transaction. This could range from the hotel/brand call center, the hotel website, an online travel agency (OTA), a global distribution service (GDS), or the internal hotel sales team.

Channel Management – Where the sources of reservations are controlled for purposes of revenue and profit enhancement.

Channel Manager – A connectivity third-party system that pushes a hotel's ARI to a distribution channel.

Citywide – Event in the market that results in lodging demand adequate to fill the vast majority of all hotels.

Click – When a consumer clicks on a link.

CLV – Customer lifetime value—The sum of all profits from a given customer over their lifetime relationship with the company.

Clustering – Where a homogenous consumer market is divided into homogenous groups based upon.

Competitive Benchmarking – Conducting an analysis to understand the position of a hotel against that of its competitors.

Competitive Grid Analysis – A tactical tool that evaluate the product and service offering for the subject hotel and its competitors.

Competitive Set (comp set) – A group of similar and directly competing lodging properties to which an individual hotel's operating performance is comparable and compete for the same business.

Commission – Cost associated with booking a room where a percentage of revenue is due to the OTA or travel agent.

Constrained / Unconstrained Demand (Space Optimization) – Economic terms to describe the level of demand irrespective of supply. Unconstrained demand dictates that demand exceeds supply and a property finds itself in the driver's seat for Rate and Function Space Minimums. Constrained indicates supply exceeds demand and you are in a byers market.

Contribution Margin (Restaurant) – The profitability of a menu item, measured by its price less its food cost.

CTA – Closed to Arrival.

CTR – Click Through Rate—Percentage of clicks on a link or advertisement out of the amount of times the link or advertisement was shown.

Conversion – When a consumer has completed the payment in an online session.

Conversion Rate – Percentage of visits that resulted in bookings.

Cost of Acquisition – Fees, commissions, and expenses attributed to each booking from third party distributors or internal payroll including

GDS commissions, OTA commissions, direct marketing expenses and all customer acquisition payroll.

CoV – Coefficient of Variation.

CPOR – Cost per Occupied Room—This cost represents the expenses associated with occupying and servicing a room for one night. It includes costs such as labor (front office and housekeeping), cleaning supplies, linen and utilities.

Crew – The cruise ship staff is referred to as crew. This includes hotel operations staff who serve the guests and marine and technical staff who operate and maintain the ship.

CRS – Central Reservation System—A computerized backend system of a hotel's booking engine.

Cruise Berths – Beds on a cruise ship are referred to as berths. The first two beds in a cabin are referred to as lower berths. The third and fourth beds are referred to as upper berths.

Cruise Length – The number of days in a cruise.

Custom Tags – Are user-defined JSP language elements that encapsulate recurring tasks. Custom tags are distributed in a tag library, which defines a set of related custom tags and contains the objects that implement the tags.

D

Daily (Pickup) Pace – Net bookings and cancellations committed within a set booking period (i.e. last seven days) for a given stay date as compared to the same net bookings and cancellations that occurred over the same booking dates (by day of week) prior year.

Data Patterns – Consistent ups and downs in data over the short to medium term.

Data Trends– Consistent ups and downs in data over a long period of time.

Debarkation Day – The date the cruise arrives at its final port of call and passengers leave the ship.

Demand Generator – Any event, sports area, hospital, military base or business that creates lodging demand for a market.

Departure Date (Cruise) – The date the cruise departs from its first port. Also referred to as embarkation date.

Departures – Amount of rooms that will or have checked out.

Deposit (Cruise) – The payment required to hold a reservation. Can range from $500 to $1,000 or more.

Dilution (Cruise) – The amount of a refund given to a guest who converts to a tactical promotion after having already booked at a higher fare.

Dining Duration – The amount of time a customer spends at a restaurant, measured from arrival to departure.

Displacement Cost – The value of the business that will be turned away because the inventory has been committed to another segment (group, contract, etc.)

Distribution Channel – The chain of businesses or intermediaries through which a good or service passes until it reaches the end consumer; in the hotel industry distribution channels are business or intermediaries through which a customer can purchase a hotel room.

DORM – Director of Revenue Management.

Double Occupancy Capacity (Cruise) – By cruise industry convention, each cabin has a capacity of two guests (a small percentage of cabins are designed for single guests) and a double occupancy capacity of 2. If that cabin carries a third guest, its occupancy is 150% (3 divided by 2) If that cabin carries four guests, its occupancy is 200% (4 divided 2) In this way, cruise ship occupancy typically exceeds 100%.

Duration—See dining duration.

Dynamic Pricing – Practice of pricing items at a level determined by a particular customer's perceived ability to pay.

E

Early Departures – Rooms that are scheduled to depart on a later date but have checked out earlier than expected.

Extranet – Connectivity system website where hotel's upload their rates and availability to display on the associated third party website.

F

Fair Share – The proportional share of business assuming an even distribution of supply, revenue, and demand among all properties included within a competitive set.

Fences – (Restaurant Revenue Management)—Differences in physical inventory units.

Fencing/Segmentation Hedges – Methods of control used by Revenue Managers to manage which reservations they are willing to accept based upon the price being paid.

FIT – Frequent Independent Traveler or Foreign Independent Tour - prepaid packaged tours for individual travel.

Fixed Costs – Costs maintained even if the hotel was empty.

Flow Through (Space Optimization) – The revenue that flows to the bottom line after all expenses have been deducted.

Frame of Reference – Describes alternative choices in the market today to set a baseline of existing expectations and further support the Point of Difference.

Full Payment Date (Cruise) – The date the full payment for the cruise is due, typically 30 days or more before the start of the cruise.

Full Ship Mentality – Cruise line revenue managers are expected to sell every cabin on a ship prior to the departure date. This is a cultural imperative and the most successful cruise lines.

Function Space Optimization – The application of yield management principles to function space to optimize the return on an extremely perishable resource.

G

GDS – Global Distribution System—A worldwide computerized reservation network that provides transactions to travel agents, online reservation sites, and large corporations.

GM – General Manager.

GOPPAR – Gross Operating Profit per Available Room—A company's revenue from sales in a given period of time less its cost of goods sold divided by the total number of rooms available for sale.

GRI – Global Review Index.

Group Banquet Revenue Contribution (Space Optimization) - The Banquet Revenue generated from each Group night consumed.

H

HRM – Hotel Revenue Management.

HRP – Hotel Rooms Pricing.

I

Impressions – The amount of times an ad or link has been shown.

Index (Occupancy, ADR, RevPAR) – Property performance divided by competitive set performance multiplied by 100. Internationally, indexes are also referred to as MPI—Market Penetration Index (Occupancy Index), ARI—Average Rate Index (ADR Index), and RGI—Revenue/RevPAR Generation Index (RevPAR Index).

Inverse SWOT Analysis – Conducting a SWOT analysis through the lens of a competitor.

Itineraries – The cruise region and the ports of call during the cruise.

J

Jockey – When customers leave one line to join an other line.

K

KPI – Key Performance Indicator.

L

Leisure Travelers (Cruise) – People traveling as part of a personal vacation without a business purpose. Leisure travelers tend to be more price sensitive than business travelers and tend to book further in advance.

Lifeboat Seats – By law, a cruise ship must carry lifeboats with enough seats for every person onboard the ship, including both guests and crew members.

LOS – Length of Stay – Duration of a guest's stay beginning with arrival date. Revenue managers must manage revenue by adjusting strategies by arrival pattern as this is the control point.

LRA – Last Room Availability – a condition granted to Special Corporate accounts where their negotiated rate is automatically available if the hotel is selling standard inventory.

M

Macroeconomics – Branch of the economics field that studies how the aggregate economy behaves

MAPE – Mean Absolute Percentage Error.

MAR – Minimum Available Rate– The lowest rate the property management team sets for any day of the week to be quoted to consumers.

Market Segment – A subset of a customer group that can be easily identifiable by one or more common characteristics such as demographics, purpose of travel, and buying behavior.

Meta Search Engine – Travel website that uses multiple search engine's (OTAs and brand.com) data to produce a compiled result.

Micro-Segments – Segments that can be further broken out in order to more precisely group together those that share a similar level of interest in a set of features.

Mix of Sales – see Market Segmentation.

MLOS – Minimum Length of Stay.

Monthly Pace – Net bookings and cancellations committed currently for a given stay month as compared to the net bookings and cancellations committed same day (by numbered date) prior year.

Monthly Pickup Pace – Net bookings and cancellations committed within a set booking period (i.e. last seven days) for a given stay month as compared to the same net bookings and cancellations that occurred over the same booking dates (by day of week) prior year.

MPI – Market Penetration Index.

MXLOS – Maximum Length of Stay

N

Net Onboard Revenue (Cruise) – Onboard revenue after deducting the cost of goods sold.

Net Ticket Revenue (Cruise) – Ticket revenue after deducting travel agent commission or other direct sales costs (such as airfare for air-inclusive tickets.)

NOI – Net Operating Income

Nonphysical Inventory—The intangible resources required to deliver a service.

No-Shows – Rooms that are scheduled to arrive but do not before a new date arrives.

No-Shows (Cruise) – Guests holding a fully paid reservation who do not cancel in advance and who do not show up at the ship on the departure date. Typically, very few people are no-shows.

O

Occupancy (Cruise) – The percentage of available capacity that is occupied or sold. Calculated as the guest cruise days divided by the ALBDs.

Onboard Revenue(Cruise) – Revenue derived from onboard sales in venues such as bars, casinos, shore excursions, gift shops, spas, etc.

Opaque – Where a guest books and is unaware of which hotel they are booking until the non-refundable reservation is made.

Operations Forecast – Forecast utilized by operations leaders to appropriately staff the hotel.

Option Period (Cruise) – The number of days between the time of reservation and the time the reservation will automatically cancel if a deposit is not received. Can range from 1 day to 1 week.

OTA – Online Travel Agent (OTA) – Travel website allowing customers to plan and book travel.

Overbook – Selling hotel rooms beyond the hotel's capacity.

P

Pace – Tracking performance versus a previous period, mostly done to compare to the same moment in time as last year. For example, how many rooms were sold at this point last year for the upcoming month versus how many are sold today for the upcoming month?

Pace Reports – An analytical report on how current business performance is relative to budget, forecast, and history.

Passenger Sourcing Infrastructure – In order to fill all capacity for all departures, cruise lines build customer relationship management systems to facilitate frequent direct marketing to past guests and prospects. They also deployment sales teams around the world to build and maintain relationships with the travel agency distribution system.

PAX – Passengers on the Ground.

PED – see Price Elasticity of Demand.

Percent Change (% Chg) – Amount of growth—up, down, or flat—this period versus same period last year (day, week, running 28 days, running month-to-date). Calculated as ((TY-LY)/LY)*100.

Perishable – An item or good likely to decay or go bad quickly (example: a hotel room is perishable and cannot be sold once the night has passed)

P & L – Profit and Loss Statement—This financial statement details the revenue, expenses, and profit (loss) generated during a fixed period of time.

Physical Inventory – The tangible resources required to deliver a service.

Planning Square – The square footage required to accommodate a table in a restaurant.

PMS – Property Management System.

Point of Difference – What qualities separate the brand from its competitors. This trait must be imitable.

Positioning Statement – Statement of the hotel's product and service offering that address the target market it is trying to fulfil with a point of differentiation compared to existing substitutes and includes a reason why this organization is able to deliver the promise made.

PPC – Pay per Click—Ads that are placed on websites that cost a certain amount per each click on the ad itself.

Price Discrimination – Offering various prices to various consumers.

Price Elasticity – A consumer's willingness to purchase a product depending on the level of price. Price elasticity of demand shows the relationship between price and quantity demanded and provides a precise calculation of the effect of a change in price on quantity demanded. The following equation enables PED to be calculated.

$$\frac{\text{\% change in quantity demanded}}{\text{\% change in price}}$$

Price Inelastic – Where a customer is less sensitive to a change in price.

Product Differentiation – How marketers modify or add supply in order to better adapt to demand.

Product Type – Defined narrowly as the room type, package element or booking policy attached to the reservation or more broadly as the length of stay or lead time dimension. This meaning, that a product can be defined both by the physical attributes such a premium room type or package element just as much as it can be considered an accommodation available for purchase at the very last minute in a compressed market.

Profit – Total revenue minus costs.

Profit Margin – Percentage of profit out of total revenue.

Purchasing Behavior – Common purchasing patterns found within a given group of bookers including price sensitivity, responsiveness to various types of advertisement, propensity to cancel, and customer loyalty.

Q

Qualified Discount – Any discount that a consumer must be qualified for such as Senior Discount, AAA discount, Student Discount, etc.

Qualified Segment – A segment that requires some type of membership identification in order to qualify to receive the discount.

R

Rank (Occupancy, ADR, RevPAR, % Chg) – Property performance ranked versus hotels in the competitive set (e.g. a "3 of 6" ADR ranking means the subject hotel's absolute ADR is third highest of the six competitors).

Rate fences or Segmentation Hedges – Restrictions put in place to change the price point offered to a guest. Fences consist of 5 basic forms: physical form, controlled availability, customer characteristics, transactions characteristics, or product line.

Rate parity –Identical retail rate is quoted across all channels.

Reason to Believe – Provides the context of how the business is able to deliver on its positioning statement.

Reinvestment Amount – The monetary value corresponding to the services and products given away to a customer often expressed in terms of a percentage.

Remaining Demand – Number of rooms the hotel can expect to sell with unlimited physical capacity.

Remaining Supply – Number of rooms available for sale.

Renege – When customers leave a line before being served.

Retail Rate / Best Available Rate (BAR) – The rate a customer pays "off the shelf", often referred to as "best available"

Revenue Cycle –The ability of a hotel to drive and optimize demand while maintaining guest satisfaction.

Revenue Manager – The individual or team responsible for maximizing revenue within the constraints of available capacity and unconstrained demand through effective yield management.

Revenue Optimization Models (Cruise) – Large cruise lines use mathematically sophisticated models for forecast demand at various price points and in various markets and recommend prices that will result in the highest profit contribution.

RevPAR – Revenue Per Available Room – Total rooms-related revenue per the number of available rooms in the hotel over a period of time: [Rooms Revenue / (Rooms Available * Number of Days)].

RevPAS – Revenue per Available Space, or Revenue per Square Foot the revenue generated on a square foot basis for a specific period of time.

RevPASH – Revenue per Available Seat Hour.

RevPATH – Revenue per Available Treatment Hours.

REVPATI – Revenue per Available Time Inventory Unit.

RevPATT – Revenue per Available Tee Time.

RFP – Request for Proposal—A detailed requisition a client sends to properties to begin a dialog. It details the needs of the client (dates and size constraints) and allows the property to match its facilities to those needs.

RGI – Revenue Generation Index.

RM – see Revenue Manager

ROI – Return on Investment – Excess cash flow (profit) received over the initial investment. ROI is typically expressed as a percentage

Rooms to Space Ratio – Sleeping Rooms/ Sq. Ft Function space. A metric which allows you to define the structure of your property enabling you to see the symbiotic relationship of rooms and space.

Rooms Revenue – What a hotel receives for the sale of its rooms.

RRM – Restaurant Revenue Management.

S

Sales Strategy Meeting – Revenue management strategy meeting consisting of all members of the revenue management committee.

Seasonal Itinerary – Some cruise ships are deployed on various itineraries throughout the year. For example, a ship might sail in the Caribbean in the winter and reposition to Alaska for the summer, returning the Caribbean in the Fall.

Seating Assignment Rule – A guideline used to regulate which party size can sit at which table size.

Segmentation/Mix of Sales – How revenue managers and marketers classify and target customers in specific groups based upon their characteristics, behaviors, and preferences. The most common customer segmentation is transient, group and contract.

Segmented Data – Rooms sold and revenue data broken down by source of business (transient, group, contract) and source of revenue (room, food and beverage, other).

Service Capacity – The amount of output a service system can produce.

Shoulder Dates – Dates that fall on the sides of peak demand dates.

Shoulder Night – A night where total hotel demand is not strong enough to reach capacity.

SMERF – Groups booked that fit into the following classifications: Social, Military, Education, Religious, and Fraternal.

Smith Travel Research (STR) – Global provider of competitive benchmarking, information services and research to the hotel industry with performance data from over 63,000 hotels in 180 countries.

Solo Traveler – A cruise passenger traveling alone.

Spill (Cruise) – When there is more demand than supply, the demand that can't be accommodated is "spilled."

Spoilage – Each unsold room at the end of a period.

Spoilage (Cruise) – When there is less demand than supply, any cabins that sail empty are "spoiled."

Stayovers – Rooms that occupy the room overnight and for subsequent nights.

STLY – Same Time Last Year.

STR – Smith Travel Research.

Suboptimal Solution—An RRM solution that has a positive impact in one area, but a negative impact on the overall service system.

SWOT Analysis – A four quadrant analysis to examine the subjects Strengths, Weaknesses, Opportunities and Threats.

T

Target Market – Segment of customers the business it trying to reach.

Ticket Revenue – Revenue derived from cruise fares and does not include any ancillary revenues from onboard or other sales.

Theo – Theoretical win. The 'theo' is calculated by multiplying the coin-in amount by the hold percentage. The coin-in amount is the total money spent by a customer on a given occasion. The hold percentage is the probability that the casino will win a specific play.

Third and Fourth guests – Cruise ship cabins are designed to accommodate three or four guests, and sometimes more. Most often, these guests are children sharing the same cabin as their parents.

Throughput Time – The time a customer spends in a service system from enter to exit.

Throughput Rate – The number of customers that flow through a service system over a certain time.

TocPAC – Total contribution per available customer—(Rooms Revenue + Auxiliary Revenue—Variable Cost) / Number of Guests.

Travel Agent Commission (Cruise) – Roughly 65% of cruises are sold through travel agents who earn commissions ranging from 10% to 20% of Ticket Revenue.

TrevPAR – Total Revenue per Available Room—Total revenue that a hotel accumulates coming from rooms, F&B, and all other outlets per each available room in the hotel.

TrevPOR – Total Revenue per Occupied Room—Total revenue that a hotel accumulates coming from all outlets per the occupied rooms in the hotel.

TRM – Total Revenue Management—Decision process based on the sum of all revenue streams from both room and outlets on a customer level.

Two-for-One – The most effective cruise line promotion is offering two for the price of one. Some cruise lines purposely set their brochure rates high enough so they are willing to accept that fare for the first guest and no fare at all for the second guest.

U

Unconstrained demand – Total demand in a segment or overall in the absence of any constraints. (See also constrained/unconstrained demand.)

V

Variable Costs – Expenses from labor and supplies to service the room after use, the expense of the utilities associated with the guest's occupancy and a designated cash reserve towards a capital budget for replacing furniture, generally every 3–7 years, as part of a regularly scheduled refurbishment.

Variable Pricing – A pricing strategy where a business offers varying price points at different locations or points-of-sale. This is a common approach used by retailers when the costs of offering certain goods and services and the level of market demand justify it.

Variable Pricing (Restaurant) –The practice of charging different prices to different customers.

Visit – A visit is when a consumer accesses and has an interaction with a website.

Y

Year-Round Itineraries – Some cruise ships are deployed on the same itinerary year round, often in the Caribbean.

Yield – The return or profitability of an asset.

Yield (Cruise) – The most important revenue management statistic in the cruise industry. Yield can be calculated two ways: 1) Average per diem times occupancy percentage, and 2) net ticket revenue divided by ALBDs. But equations give the same result.

Yield Management – A variable pricing strategy, based on understanding, anticipating and influencing consumer behavior in order to maximize revenue or profits from a fixed, perishable resource (such as airline seats or hotel room reservations).

YOY – Year-over-Year.

Index

S

For Product Safety Concerns and Information please contact our EU
representative GPSR@taylorandfrancis.com
Taylor & Francis Verlag GmbH, Kaufingerstraße 24, 80331 München, Germany

www.ingramcontent.com/pod-product-compliance
Ingram Content Group UK Ltd.
Pitfield, Milton Keynes, MK11 3LW, UK
UKHW052215190926
475702UK00006B/1029
* 9 7 8 1 7 7 1 8 8 8 8 8 2 *